Raffaello Baldini

Small Talk

Translated by Adria Bernardi

Introduction by Adria Bernardi

Raffaello Baldini

Small Talk

Introduction and Translation
by
Adria Bernardi

❖ Gradiva Publications ❖

ISBN 1-892021-36-6

Typesetting: Donna Severino
Cover Design: Stephen Yeung
Cover Illustration: *La solitudine del venditore di palloni* (1968)
by Giulio Turci
Photo of Raffaello Baldini by Andrea Angeucci

Gradiva Publications is pleased to acknowledge the
generous support of the Sonia Raiziss Giop
Charitable Foundation.

TABLE OF CONTENTS

SNOW / LA NÀIVA

OUTSIDER / FURISTÍR

INTRODUCTION

The Poetry of Raffaello Baldini

When I first heard Raffaello Baldini read from his poems I heard something that I had not previously heard, and I realized I had slowed the pace of the poems too much. When I had a second opportunity to hear him read, I heard this same whispered urgency. Phrases and images accumulated with no respite; there was seemingly no pause for breath, which gave certain poems both incredible headlong movement and nearly unbearable weight. In 'E' *malàn*, (Noise) the element in the poem which accumulates is noise. This accumulation of sounds is a barrage and an overwhelming din that becomes transformed at the end of the poem. Baldini's language mimics spoken conversation; it is a language with edges and gnarls and spikes, and you arrive at the end of a poem out of breath.

All of his poetry, six collections, and his three theatrical monologues, are written in the dialect of his town of birth, Santarcangelo, which is located east of Bologna, near the Adriatic coast. All of his poems are situated in Santarcangelo. This is Baldini's poetic landscape. The geographical landmarks, the names, the place names, the nicknames, the gestures, are of this place. Baldini, born in 1924, lived his childhood and adolescence in this small town during the era of Fascist ascendancy, grip-hold, and war. His family owned the Caffè Trieste in the Piazza delle Erbe. Although he left Santarcangelo as an adolescent for the wider world to attend school in Rimini, and then studied philosophy in Bologna, and lived and worked in Milan from 1955 until the time of his death in 2004, for many years as an editor of the newsweekly *Panorama*, it was to the "small" language, as he called it, of the town that he returned for his poetry. When asked why, he replied that it was the only language in which these poems could have been written.

Along with Tonino Guerra (1920) and Nino Pedretti (1923), Baldini is one of a "trio" of poets who share origins in Santarcangelo and write in the romagnole dialect. As in other dialects, one-syllable words occur with more frequency than they do in standard Italian; there is also a preponderance of words that end in a consonant, rather than a vowel sound, as they do in standard Italian. This makes for rhythms that are clipped and broken, for sounds that are jagged and abrupt. The title itself, *"È malan"* suggests some of these differences between the Italian and Baldini's dialect: *è malan* has a swallowed, guttural, rushed sound, whereas the sounds in *il rumore*, in the Italian, are softer, more elongated. *Malan* ends with a stressed consonant sound; *rumore* ends with an open vowel sound.

Like the language of the poetry written in other regional dialects, including that of Pier Paolo Pasolini, Franco Loi, and Andrea Zanzotto, the source of these dialect poems is fundamentally oral language, a language spoken in a particular geographical place that is extremely confined. As the narrator of "The Bridge" (È pòunt) says, "from over on the other side you felt like an outsider / . . . they talked different over there." It is the language of the home, the village and the countryside, of shopkeepers, card players, housewives and children before they begin to attend school, and to step out of these spaces, for elementary school or the university, for financial or commercial ventures, into the worlds of regional or national politics, into science, technology, and aesthetic articulations, meant that one must leave off from this language. The closedness of a dialect stands in contrast to standard Italian, which was born out of deep intellectual and ideological needs for a language that extended beyond provincial and communal boundaries to redress cultural, political, intellectual, spiritual and psychological fragmentation. I speak here of Dante and of the Risorgimento.

Just as there is no liberation gained for these narrators by stepping outside the town line, no gesture of breath of clean air, no starting over, the words themselves are contained and constrained by forces that are beyond their control. These poems, and the words that make them, are controlled by limits, which are forces that act upon them. In the final editing of this manuscript, the one word that kept repeating inside my head was the Italian word, *chiusura*, or "enclosure." For an outsider to understand the significance of the dialect for these writers, it must be understood against, and from inside, the context of Fascism. For Baldini and children born into the era of fascism, and into institutions already controlled and dominated by the monolith, or the fear of the monolith, this debate between the whole and the parts, unification or assertion of the part, is ongoing, and it remains at the root of Italian cultural identity. And this debate between the whole, and the validation of the valid parts, the parts that are whole, the continual struggle between whole and part, is being replayed again and again in the political arena in the ongoing debate over national identity versus regional identity.

It is in this aspect of *chiusura* that the American reader, with our positivistic inheritances of Anglo-Protestant traditions, that we may find it difficult to enter Baldini's world, mistaking it for provincialism or narrow mindedness, and may find it useful look to other traditions to try to better understand these poems. They are of the body, they are, in Flannery O'Connor's term, incarnational, which puts them at odds with traditions that separate the mind and body. The gesture of the Baldini poem is not one that moves to liberate, nor to rebel, but neither does it submit, or lead. It may convey the sense of heavy endurance, yet not as victim, yet accept the press of the form it may well reject. Perhaps it is to the Russians that we should look, or closer to home, to our southern literary inheritances, and to other "outsiders," bound to place, or displaced, for help in putting Baldini in context, for example, to Faulkner's "Barn Burning" or "A Rose for Miss Emily," or to Zora Neale Hurston's *Mule Bone*, or Katherine Anne Porter's *Noon Wine*, or Eudora Welty's "A Worn Path" and "Where is This Voice Coming From," works in which the external pressures within the story act upon the agents, both internally and externally, pushing them, and at the same, the work itself, in its language and its structure, to the maximum point, thus yielding its form. It is the language itself that gives form, or gives it up, concedes it, reveals it.

In the introduction to Baldini's collection, *Ad nòta*, (Nighttime), the Italian literary critic Pier Vincenzo Mengaldo wrote "were it not for the lazy prejudices still alive that relegate a poet writing in dialect as 'minor,' even when he's major, Raffaello Baldini would be considered. . . one of the three or four most important poets in Italy." Baldini's *Furistír* (Outsider) was awarded the 1988 Viareggio Prize, the first time this distinguished prize for poetry was awarded to a work written in the dialect. In May 2004, Baldini was awarded the Dino Campana Award for his final collection, *Intercity*.

Mengaldo's assessment of Baldini's place among contemporary Italian poets again raises what tends to be the first question about the poet's work – why dialect. "It's probably an inevitable question," Baldini conceded in an interview. "To which there can be more than one answer, including, 'I don't know.' Which seems like a non-response, but it isn't.'"

To make a choice of dialect for one's poetic language means that there can be no illusion that language itself is anything other than fragmented. There can be no illusion, other than to begin with the premise that there exists a divide between self and other, between parts of self, and between the world outside and the world inside. To step across the Bridge is to know you risk, and to accept, not being understood. Baldini's poems grapple with marginality, and it is in the space of these poems that Baldini uses a very limited language, that language of a very small world, to open up a universe.

In poem after poem, what is explored through the speaker's small talk, is the relationship of the individual within an enclosed, poetically imagined, community, whose limits are as much linguistic as they are geographic. In the poem, "Solitaire," (*È solitèri*) the speaker has withdrawn from the others in a collective space by choice. In "The Bypass," this speaker describes an existence of having been marginalized by the experience of aging and the passage of time, as she sits in her niece's condominium. "What commotion down there, what things, what noise. / I sit completely still, my hands clutching the railing / and I see the world passing by." In "The Shop," the speaker who continues to putter around in the shop long after he's gone out of business, is considered an eccentric: "now they're saying I'm nuts / before they were saying I was a lazy bum. . ."

The second book of the collection, *Outsider,* explores the various meanings of isolation and marginalization – the relationship between individual and community, isolation within communities in flux, the changes that come with stage of life changes, including mid-life and the end-stages of life, the space between self and other, and the spaces between the parts of the self that speak or do not speak to each other. In the title poem, "Outsider," the speaker walks through his town, criticizing everything that's new, describing a place he no longer recognizes. Often, the speakers are individuals who give every appearance of being part of the community, but their private small talk reveals that he or she is living in an intensely and painful isolation. In "Night," a speaker who's tormented by insomnia keeps hearing someone knocking at the door: "I must have gone down six or seven times, / it seemed absolutely like they were knocking."

Many of Baldini's speakers or characters are marginalized by their sheer *antipatia*; they are difficult and unpleasant and sometimes nasty, what might be called in the American parlance, a royal pain. "*Ciacri*" is one striking example of this. The speaker nags her husband, gossips, and buttonholes every unwilling listener she can find as she goes through town doing her morning errands. Through the use of words and implied gesture, Baldini conveys the sense of a listener who is physically recoiling, as he or she tries to disengage from the conversation:

oh there's Dolores, wait
Dolores, I've got one thing to ask you,
are you in a hurry, it'll take just a second. . .

What the reader may witness and experience by the end of the poem is the excruciating isolation of a woman whose continual barrage of words have erected and reinforced barriers.

Many of Baldini's poems are given over to speakers who are unable to navigate a conundrum or free him or herself from an obsession, complete a task or dispel a great fear. The frustration, obsession or fear accumulates, expands and becomes distorted into what approaches the surreal. In "Yarn," it has fallen to the narrator to untangle a great mass of yarn. In "Bats," the speaker struggles against bats that have entered his room at night. In "Thieves," the speaker cannot shake off the way his world has been upended and violated after his house is broken into, even though nothing has been taken. He considers, at last, making an appeal to thieves, putting up flyers around town.

Critic Franco Brevini describes how the internal world of these voices folds into the external world and vice versa:

> "In Baldini, there is no split between the "I" and the world. The "I" constantly interweaves its connections with reality, discovers the impossibility of finding an order in them, or a reference point, or some instrument of orientation, and he ends up losing himself inside it. "

The myriad of voices that speak from within an enclosed community creates an overall effect of chorality – of things both spoken and unspoken in town – that resonates with the constraints of a place that is defined by itself and the world outside as parochial. These characteristics often lead to a comparison with Edgar Lee Master's *Spoon River Anthology*. This, in turn, has led other critics to respond that the comparison unnecessarily limits an understanding of Baldini's work, which represents, they argue, a more complex, layered and nuanced exploration. Dante Isella has written that Baldini's poems achieve "a spokenness that barely floats above the continuum of the prose, a monologal voice in which what is at stake is no longer the "I" of the writer but of each and every component of his own community."

Dialect, Baldini has said, is an "oral creature." The language of his poems and theatrical works mimics spoken language, and one of the major forms of address they use is dramatic monologue. Some of these are addressed to an unnamed other or to an other who speaks very little, or not at all. In many of his poems, it is as if an intense interior monologue has been made visible and the reader has been granted entry and placed inside, hearing the rumblings of an anxious soul. In these internal monologues, there is the suggestion of a spoken conversation in which there is no pause, no break, which accounts for much of the work's momentum. Mengaldo has referred to these as "monologues you lose your breath with."

The poems and the theatrical pieces employ a wide array of strategies to mimic spoken conversation, including the use of qualifications and adjustments. "Who knows, " he says in the poem, "Noise," as he attempts to explain where the noise would be located. "But getting closer, if you could. . . " "I'm saying, there's got to be a crashing. " Frequently, as in "Solitaire," the speaker's language mimics an extended self-argument, where he or she sets up a hypothesis, projects it to someone else, only to then rebut it.

It's not clear at the onset whom the speaker of the "Permit" (*Il permesso*) is addressing as he describes the woes of trying to get a permit to do renovations on his house. As the poem moves to the end, however, it becomes clear he's imploring a childhood classmate, who works as an administrator, for help; "I know you've got to go, but just one minute."

There is a plasticity and malleability present in the dialect that is not present in standard Italian, Baldini said in an interview with Daniele Benati. One aspect of the dialect's plasticity is an insistence upon the right to reiterate: "Whoever speaks in dialect doesn't feel bothered by a word that is repeated several times and then loops back again. Italian on the other hand is hypersensitive about it; it will not tolerate it." In Baldini's work, thoughts start up, stop, pick up where they left off several exchanges earlier. Subjects appear, disappear, and reappear much later. The train of thought is broken. Certain poems are a series of non sequiturs, shifts of subject, false starts and abrupt interruptions. There are, in addition to use of qualifications, other rhetorical techniques and elements of grammar that contribute to and intensify this sense of spokenness, including repetition, digression, exclamations, and interrogatives.

One strategy to which Mengaldo calls attention is a particular sentence pattern, where a sentence determined by a noun is immediately followed by one determined by a verb, and then back again. There are frequently quick changes in the subject of the sentence, as in the poem, "Noise": "the words she said that you couldn't understand, / Teresa, in the hospital before she died, / her people all around her, / with those hands and veins in her neck, / her breathing slowing down."

Another rhetorical device found in these poems is accumulation, a device by which words, sounds, images, and concepts, are repeated and added to each other, in a layering, or heaping, effect, intensifying a particular meaning or effect. As noted earlier, "Noise," is made up entirely of the speaker's description of sounds:

> the music of the carousel with its signal
> just before it starts to turn
> the bus at Borghi
> wheezing under the Arch like a human being,
> all that discoursing in the piazza,
> the spitting, the yawning, the cursing,
> Calèccia's hogs when they're being slaughtered

Brevini argues that in other poems, such as "The Cockaigne Tree," (*La cuccagna*), "Signature," (*La firma*), "Love" (*L'amour*), and "Snow," (*La nàiva*), this listing characteristic, "(l') *elencazione caro a Baldini*," (this listing so close to Baldini's heart) has shifted from a listing into an expansion, whereby the images

E' curtèl

Mo cs'èll che ta m'é pórt? s'u n tàia gnént.
E nu stam da guardè, vamn a tó un èlt.
Ta l'é tróv? dam aquè, dài, ch'e' vén nòta.
Ch'u t vénga un azidént, l'è pézz ch' nè préima,
quèst l'è ènca ruznéid. Dài, ch'a vagh mè.
Tén aquè, ta n si bón? t'é al mèni 'd mérda?
ciàpal par agli urècci e ténal férum
ch'e' squézza e' sangh in zéir e e' spórca tótt.

Il coltello. Ma che cosa m'hai portato? se non taglia niente. / E non starmi a
guardare, vammene a prendere un altro. / L'hai trovato? dammi qui, dai, che
viene notte. / Ti pigli un accidente, è peggio di prima, / questo è anche
arrugginito. Dai, che vado io. / Tieni qui, non sei capace? hai le mani di
merda? / prendilo per le orecchie e tienilo fermo /che schizza il sangue in
giro e sporca tutto.

Solitaire

You never stop learning.
I shouldn't have played the five of spades,
now I'll never get
the three of clubs,
it would have been better to stick with the king of diamonds,
the king and the jack, the jack of spades,
which were all right there,
so I could have had
two or three cards guaranteed, even more.
Just look how I've boxed myself in.
And if I go back?
No. Not possible. I've already played
the five of hearts, there's nothing to do about it,
in solitaire, in playing the cards,
it's the last one played, the biggest mistake
is getting greedy,
no, nothing here, in card games, your first task is to assess the
[situation, then
lay them down, one right after the other,
and even in laying them down
you have to be careful to pay attention
and not lay down too many
otherwise you screw yourself up,

E' solitèri

U n s finéss mai d'imparè.
E' zéinch ad spèdi a n l'éva da mètt sò,
andès e' tre 'd bastòun
a n'e' tir fura piò,
l'era mèi andè drétt se rè 'd denèri,
rè, e' su cavàl, e' fènt ad spèdi, e' sèt,
che i era tótt alè,
in módi ch'a zcruvéva
dò tre chèrti ad sichéur, magari piò.
Mo vèrda cm'è ch' l'è 'ndè a inciudès aquè.
E s'a turnéss indrí? no, u n s pò, ò zà mèss
e' zéinch ad còppi, u n gn'è piò gnént da fè.
L'è che te solitèri mètt sò al chèrti
l'è l'éultma, e' piò gran sbai
l'è fès inguluséi,
no, gnént, al chèrti e' prim lavòur l'è schvérzli,
pu fè al cadéini,
e ènca sal cadéini
bsògna stè 'ténti a no inzipèli trop,
parchè se no ta t fraigh,
ta n li pò lavurè, ta n li rigéir,

Il solitario. Non si finisce mai d'imparare. / Il cinque di spade non dovevo
metterlo su, / adesso il tre di bastoni / non lo tiro fuori piú, / era meglio
andar dritto col re di danari, / re, il suo cavallo, il fante di spade, il sette, /
che erano tutti lí, / in modo che scoprivo / due tre carte di sicuro, magari
piú. / Ma guarda com'è andato a inchiodarsi qui. / E se tornassi indietro? no,
no si può, ho già messo / il cinque di coppe, non c'è piú niente da fare. / È
che nel solitario mettere su le carte / è l'ultima, il piú grande sbaglio / è farsi
ingolosire, / no, niente, le carte il primo lavoro è scoprirle, / poi fare le
catene, / e anche con le catene / bisogna stare attenti a non inzepparle
troppo, / perché se no ti freghi, / non le puoi lavorare, non le rigiri, /

27

you can't work them anymore, you can't play them over,
which, after all, is the beauty of it,
you have to rule the cards,
it's there
where you test your ability,
without rushing, remaining still
for a long time,
studying the moves, and it's then
you realize
that you never know enough,
that you make mistakes
you never should make.

But this is all talk that doesn't mean a thing.
For me, this is the kind of solitaire
I've passed the afternoons playing
for more than ten years,
always this particular game. And it's not because I don't
know other versions
of solitaire, I know a ton, but I don't feel like changing,
you have to stick with the same game,
you choose the game you like, whichever fits you best,
then you can't change it, it's like going to war,
which then, when you get down to it, it's not always the same
                                                          [one,
so to speak,
it's always changing,
the cards are drunk,
they're spiteful and ignorant,
and you can't do a thing about it, they rule,
it's a great big comedy,
the game you seem to be winning you don't,

ch' l'è pu tótt e' su bèl,
al chèrti al va gvarnèdi,
l'è 'lè ch'u s vaid tótta l'abellità,
senza préssia, stè férum de gran témp
par studié al mòsi, e alòura ta t'incórz
che ta n nu n sé mai sà,
che t fé di sbai che ta n gn'é mai da fè.

Mo pu l'è tótt dizchéurs ch'i n vó dí gnént.
Mè quèst l'è un solitèri
ch'a i pas e' dopmezdè da piò 'd dis an,
sémpra quèll, e u n'è méggh' parchè a n nu n cnòssa,
a n so un straséin, mo a n gn'ò góst a cambiè,
e' solitèri l'à da ès éun sno,
u s capa quèll ch'e' pis, quèll ch'e' va mèi,
pu u n s cambia piò, l'è cumè 'ndè a la guèra,
e' cambia sémpra,
al chèrti agli è imbarièghi,
dispetòusi, ignurènti,
e ta n'i pò fè gnént, al cmànda lòu,
e l'è una gran cumédia,
e' solitèri ch' l'à da vnéi u n vén,

che è poi tutto il suo bello, / le carte vanno governate, / è lí che si vede tutta l'abilità, / senza prescia, star fermi del gran tempo / per studiare le mosse, e allora t'accorgi / che non ne sai mai abbastanza, / che fai degli sbagli che non li devi mai fare. // Ma poi sono tutti discorsi che non vogliono dir niente. / Io questo è un solitario / che ci passo il pomeriggio da piú di dieci anni, / sempre quello, e non è mica perché non ne conosca, / ne so una caterva, ma non ci ho gusto a cambiare, / il solitario ha da essere uno solo, / si scelgie quello che piace, quello che va meglio, / poi non si cambia piú, è come andare alla guerra, / che poi, in fondo, sempre quello, si fa per dire, / cambia sempre, / le carte sono ubriache, / dispettose, ignoranti, / e non ci puoi far niente, comandano loro, / ed è una gran commedia, / il solitario che deve venire non viene, /

right when you think it's looking good, you're stuck,
you can't move one single card, not even if it makes you start
[to weep,
and the game you don't seem to be winning,
the one where you're just flipping card after card,
all of a sudden starts to move, just try to figure the cards,
it organizes, makes things better, they become real.

At the table in the back
they play briscola,
I never envy them,
the game is this: you and the cards,
without sending signals.
But those guys in the back, now, they are truly unpleasant,
they grumble that I never buy,
they give me decks of cards
where it's a day's work just to shuffle them, they're worn out,
[they stick,
they're ready to be thrown out with yesterday's newspaper,
I've tried spitting on them, it doesn't help,
I pull them out with two fingers, pinch the card tight,
otherwise, they stick together,
sometimes
they're even from different decks,
decks patched together, they do whatever they want

u s férma te piò bèl,
u n s móv piò gnént gnénca s' ta t mètt a pianz,
e quèll ch'u n'à d'avnéi,
che t sté par amucé,
tótt t'un bot u s'armóv, va a capí 'l chèrti,
u s'acònda, u s'arbléss, e' vén reèl.

Me tavuléin in fònd
i zuga a bréscla, i n mu n fa mégga invéidia,
e' zugh l'è quèst, tè e 'l chèrti, e senza sgnè,
mo quéi che dlà, fighéurt, i è piò sgustéus,
i sbròuntla ch'a n cunsómm,
i m dà di maz ad chèrti ch' l'è fadéiga
ènca dèi dréinta, vèci, intacunèdi,
bóni da mètt tla pgnata par fè e' bród,
mè a próv da spudacé, mo u n s'i fa gnént,
a li chin tiré sò
sa do dàidi pr'e' lòngh, se no a n li spécch,
dal vólti agli è parfína scumpagnèdi,
l'è di maz rimidiéd, i fa cm'i pò,

si ferma sul piú bello, / non si muove piú niente nemmeno se ti metti a
piangere, / e quello che non deve venire, / che stai per ammucchiare, / tutto
in un botto si muove, vai a capire le carte, / s'accomoda, rimbellisce, viene
reale. // Al tavolo in fondo / giocano a briscola, non mi fanno mica invidia,
/ il gioco è questo, tu e le carte, e senza segnare, ma quelli di là, figurati, sono
cosí antipatici, / brontolano che non consumo, / mi danno dei mazzi di carte
che è fatica / anche mescolarle, vecchie, appiccicose, / buone da mettere
nella pignatta per fare il brodo, / io provo a sputacchiare, ma non ci si fa
niente, / devo tirarle su / con due dita per il lungo, se no non le spiccico,
/ delle volte sono persino scompagnate, / sono mazzi rimediati, fanno come
gli pare, /

and I don't say a word. I have to put up with it,
and, then, if I complain, they shout.
It's been a long time playing this game
that I've never won, and how could I ever win
when they keep giving me a deck with the six of clubs missing.

e mè a stagh zétt, u m tòcca tolerè,
e pu s'a m'alamént, i ragna lòu,
l'è da mò che mu mè sté solitèri
u n mu n vén mai, e avrébb avdài ch' l'avnéss,
i m dà un maz ch'u i amènca e' si 'd bastòun.

e io sto zitto, mi tocca tollerare, / e poi se mi lamento, gridano loro, / è da
non so quanto che a me questo solitario / non mi viene mai, e vorrei vedere
che venisse, / mi danno un mazzo che ci manca il sei di bastoni.

1938

Sometimes in the afternoon,
the schoolteacher from Sant'Ermete
closes herself up in her bedroom and lights up a Giubek.
She doesn't smoke.
Stretched out on the bed
she watches it burn.
She likes the odor.
     Sometimes
     she feels like crying.

1938

La mèstra ad Sant'Armàid
dal vólti, e' dopmezdè,
la s céud tla cambra e la zènd una Giubek.
La n fómma.
Stuglèda sòura e' lèt
la guèrda ch' la s cumsómma.
U i pis l'udòur.
Dal vólti u i vén da pianz.

1938. La maestra di Sant'Ermete / delle volte, il pomeriggio, / si chiude in
camera e accende un Giubek. / Non fuma. / Sdraiata sul letto / la guarda
consumarsi. / Le piace l'odore. / Delle volte le viene da piangere.

Hide-and-Seek

For hide-and-seek you've got to have good eyes, be smart.
I know all the best places, all the nooks only I know about.
This time I'm hiding between boards
at Bigudòun's lumber yard.
I can hear them talking, hear that they're calling out,
I peek through the cracks, I can see them running around,
that they're pointing to where they should go look.
I'm waiting right here,
not moving an inch,
I'm holding my breath.
Now it seems like they're a little bit farther away,
I'm still hiding, it's been an hour now,
I work myself into a tighter spot, like this,
between two stacks, I want to drive them crazy.
Where are they? I don't hear them anymore,
they don't know a thing, they're just wandering around willy-nilly.
I must have been here two hours by now,
since afternoon, it's night, and they,
poor dumb kids, are still looking, but they're not finding me,
I can't wait to see their faces when they find me in this spot.

Cut

A zughé a cut bsògna avài òc, ès féurb.
Mè a cnòss di póst, di béus ch'a i so sno mè.
Stavólta a m so masè tramèza agli asi
de magazéin de lègn ad Bigudòun.
A i sint ch'i zcòrr, ch'i cèma.
a sbarlòc dal fiséuri, a i vèggh ch'i zéira,
ch'i inségna se daid dò ch'i à d'andé.
Mè aspétt aquè, a n mu n móv, a téngh e' fiè.
Adès u m pèr ch'i s séa un pó sluntanè,
mè a stagh sémpra masèd, l'è bèla un'òura,
a m'inféil t'un budèl piò strètt, acsè,
fra do cadasi, a i ví fè dvantè mat.
Mo dò ch'i è? a n'i sint piò,
i n capéss mégga gnént, i va purséa.
E' sarà piò 'd do òuri ch'a so què,
l'è da òz dopmezdè, u s fa nòta, e lòu,
puràz, i zirca sémpra, mo i n mu n tróva,
e a i ví vdai a truvèm dréinta sté béus.

Nascondino.   Per giocare a nascondino bisogna avere occhio, essere furbi. /
Io conosco dei posti, dei buchi, che so solo io. / Stavolta mi sono nascosto
fra le assi / del magazzino del legno di Bigudòun. / Li sento che parlano, che
chiamano, / sbircio dalle fessure, li vedo che girano, / che si indicano col
dito dove devono andare. / Io aspetto qui, non mi muovo, trattengo il fiato.
/ Adesso mi pare che si siano un po' allontanati, / io sto sempre nascosto,
è ormai un'ora, / m'infilo in un budello piú stretto, cosí, / fra due cataste, li
voglio far diventare matti. / Ma dove sono? non li sento piú, / non capiscono mica niente, vanno purchessia. / Saranno piú di due ore che sono qui,
/ è da oggi pomeriggio, si fa notte, e loro, / poveracci, cercano sempre, ma
non mi trovano, / e li voglio vedere a trovarmi in questo buco. /

Maybe too they've gotten tired of playing,
for them the game's over, they all went home.
Their loss, I'm standing so still between these boards
that no one's ever going to find me.

E' pò ès ènca ch'i apa pérs la vòia,
che e' zugh u s séa smanè, ch'i séa 'ndè chèsa.
Pézz par lòu, mè a stagh bón tra tótt' stagli asi,
aquè sòtta u n mu n tróva piò niseun.

Può darsi anche che abbiano perso la voglia, / che il gioco si sia smagliato,
che siano andati a casa. / Peggio per loro, io sto buono fra tutte queste assi,
/ qui sotto non mi trova piú nessuno.

The Bypass

Me too, if I could, I'd like to live
on that bypass that rings the town.
Here at Tavernello it's always dark,
a little small talk here and there
but I'm old
and if I talk no one listens.
On top of it, it's hard for me to walk
and when the weather's bad
I don't even get out.
I stay in the room downstairs,
the big one, such humidity the walls swell
and every so often, I squash a roach.

But almost every Sunday, Luisín or Giancarlo
will come to pick me up in his *seicento*
and take me to Zita's, my niece's,
hers is an apartment, the one at the top,
marble and parquet,
in Pozzi's apartment building.
And when I get there, they already know
to open the glass door to the balcony

La circunvulaziòn

Enca mè, s'a putéss, u m pisarébb
d'andè stè ma la circunvalaziòun.
Aquè te Tavarnèl l'è sémpra schéur,
t fé cal do ciacri,
mo mè a so tropa vècia
e s'a zcòrr u n mu n sta a sintéi niseun.
Par di piò a faz fadéiga a caminé
e quant che l'è e' tèmp brótt
a n scap e gnénca.
A stagh tla cambra ad sòtta,
granda, sl'umidità ch' la gònfia i méur
e d'ogni tènt a zach un furnaréin.

Mo guèsi tótt' al dmènghi i m vén a tó
Luisín o Giancarlo sla sizént.
I m pórta da la Zita, la mi anvòuda.
Quèll l'è l'apartamént, e' piò d'in èlt,
sa mèrum e palchè,
te condominio ad Pozzi.
Mè quant ch' aréiv
i l sa zà, i m vérz la bóssla dla teràza

La circonvallazione. Anch'io, se potessi, mi piacerebbe / d'andare a stare alla circonvallazione. / Qui nel Tavernello, è sempre buio, / fai quelle due chiacchiere, / ma io sono troppo vecchia / e se parlo non mi sta a sentire nessuno. / Per di piú faccio fatica a camminare / e quando è tempo brutto / non esco neanche. /Sto nella stanza di sotto, / grande, con l'umidità che gonfia i muri / e ogni tanto schiaccio uno scarafaggio. // Ma quasi tutte le domeniche mi vengono a prendere / Luisín o Giancarlo con la seicento. / Mi portano dalla Zita, la mia nipote. / Quello, sí, è l'appartamento, il piú in alto, / con marmi e parquet, / nel condominio di Pozzi. / Io quando arrivo / lo sanno già, / mi aprono la porta a vetri del balcone /

that looks right over the bypass.
I sit and I stay put for hours.
What commotion down there, what things, what noise.
        I sit completely still, my hands clutching the railing
        and I see the world passing by.

ch' la dà própia sla circunvalazióun.
A m mètt alè disdài e a i stagh dagli òuri.
E' muvimént ch'u i è, la roba, e' cias.
Mè zétta, a téngh al mèni sla ringhira
e a guèrd ch'e' pasa e' mònd.

che dà proprio sulla circonvallazione. / Mi metto lí a sedere e ci sto delle ore.
/ Il movimento che c'è, la roba, il chiasso. / Io zitta, tengo le mani sulla
ringhiera / e guardo che passa il mondo.

The Cat

We didn't give it a thought, that cat we left behind,
when we went to live at Mercatino.
Then they told us it stayed there days and days,
wandering outside the house, meowing in the garden,
scraping at the door,
until Rigo di Faréll picked it up
and took it home and ate it.

È gat

Che gat ch'a se sémm zcórd, a n gn'avémm péns
quant a sémm avnú stè me Marcadéin,
dop i s'à détt che l'è stè dè e dè
a ziré tònda chèsa, a gnulé tl'órt,
a raspè ma la pórta,
fintènt ch'u n l'à tólt sò Rigo 'd Faréll
e ch'u l'à pórt ad chèsa e u s l'è magnè.

Il gatto. Quel gatto che ci siamo dimenticati, non ci abbiamo pensato /
quando siamo venuti ad abitare a Mercatino, / dopo ci hanno detto che è
stato giorni e giorni / a girare intorno a casa, a miagolare nell'orto, / a
raspare alla porta, / finché non l'ha raccolto Rigo di Faréll / e l'ha portato a
casa e se l'è mangiato.

The Comedy

The rehearsals had been going so well,
I was one of the best, but tonight,
I don't even know myself, what's going on with me?
I'm all muddled up inside,
the people, I'm looking through a hole, have already arrived
they're saying hello to each other, just chatting away,
it's already full, we start in just a few minutes,
Gege comes over to ask if we're set,
I don't dare speak a word, the curtain goes up,
from the audience it's all whispering,
Piero enters with Rina, they're talking fast,
they're bickering, a zinger then a quip, they're laughing,
I'm on soon,
I'm looking all around, everything's jumbled,
it's nerves, it's nothing, it'll go away,
so, so I go on and I say,
wait, no, what am I supposed to say?
let me think, it's coming to me, so I come in
and I say, son of a bitch, what do I say?
I don't know, what do I say? I don't know anything anymore,

La cumedia

Ch'agli era 'ndè piò bén al próvi, a séra
tra i piò brèv, mo stasàira,
a n'e' so gnénca mè, cs'èll ch'u m suzéd?
a m sint dréinta un smasír,
la zénta, a guèrd da un béus, i aréiva zà,
i s saléuta, i ciacara,
l'è bèla pin, u i amènca piò póch,
Gege e' vén a dmandè s'a sémm tótt préunt,
a n m'aréisgh ad dí gnént, i èlza e' telòun,
de la sèla l'aréiva un gran susórr,
Piero l'éintra sla Rina, i zcòrr da fétt,
i s fa rabiè, bota e risposta, i réid,
tra un pó u m tòcca mu mè,
a m guèrd datònda, a vèggh tótt imbruièd,
l'è nervòus, u n'è gnént, adès u m pasa,
piotòst, ècco, dòunca mè aréiv e a déggh,
spétta, no, cs'èll ch'a déggh?
fam pensè, adès u m vén, dòunca mè aréiv,
e a déggh, porca putèna, cs'èll ch'a déggh?
a n'e' so, cs'èll ch'a déggh? a n so piò gnént,

La commedia. Che erano andate cosí bene le prove, ero / tra i piú bravi, ma
stasera, / non lo so nemmeno io, cosa mi succede? mi sento dentro un
guazzabuglio, / la gente, guardo da un buco, arrivano già, / si salutano,
chiacchierano, / è ormai pieno, ci manca piú poco, / Gege viene a chiedere
se siamo tutti pronti, / non m'arrischio a dir niente, alzano il telone, / dalla
sala arriva un gran sussurro, / Piero entra con la Rina, parlano fitto, / litigano, botta e risposta, ridono, / fra un po' tocca a me, / mi guardo attorno,
vedo tutto imbrogliato, / è nervoso, non è niente, adesso mi passa, /
piuttosto, ecco, dunque io arrivo e dico, / aspetta, no, cosa dico?/ fammi
pensare, adesso mi viene, dunque io arrivo / e dico, porca puttana, cosa
dico? / non lo so, cosa dico? non so piú niente, /

my part, I can't remember, not one, not one single word,
and Piero, listen, with Rina, they're really going at it,
Gege gives me the high sign, you're on next, he comes up,
taps my shoulder, I'm shaking,
my voice is hoarse: "Gege, I can't,"
his eyes are popping out of his head: "What do you mean you
[can't?"
I try to say my mind's fogged up
I'm not feeling well, it would be better if someone else takes my
[place,
he shakes me: "Have you lost your mind?"
I look at the floor, my mouth's as dry
as the page of a book, my hands are sweaty,
just to do something, I run the comb through my hair,
but I forget I've got white powder there,
now I've done it,
doesn't someone around here have a mirror?
Alba's got a round, celluloid one,
just look, the wrinkles are all smudged
and the tip of the mustache is coming loose,
give me some glue, to top it off I'm drenched in sweat,
where's a towel?
I touch up all over with grease paint,

vàirzna, si ócc cièr, puléida,
e ò vú furtéuna.
La à una gran pazinzia, la sparagna,
la m dà una mèna ènca tla butàiga,
e chi burdéll i téira tótt da li.

Mè a magn, a so dvént lòvv, a m so ingrasè,
a zugh e' lòt, d'ogni tènt a i inzècch,
an s'un amb ò véint trezentmélla frènch.

vergine, con gli occhi chiari, pulita, / e ho avuto fortuna. / Ha una gran
pazienza, risparmia, / mi dà una mano anche in bottega, / e quei bambini
somigliano tutto a lei. // Io mangio, sono diventato goloso, mi sono
ingrassato, / gioco al lotto, ogni tanto ci azzecco, // l'anno scorso con un
ambo ho vinto trecentomila lire.

Be Content

It's been thirty years I've shit like clockwork,
it could be because I always wear a support belt
and long underwear summer and winter,
because three or four times a night
I have to get up to pee a drop.

As for my eating, I'm careful, and even then I don't care for it.
Some broth, a little veal, a couple of spinach leaves,
a slice a stracchino, not much at all,
half a pear, a breadstick, a glass of water,
and I'm set. Pork, I can't stand,
it's been years and years since I've eaten crackling
I don't care for prosciutto, wine –
a quarter of a glass because it gives me acid indigestion,
fish, sole, mullet, the small calamari,
I don't like much, tagliatelle
binds me,
And then it's all stuff
that burns, and I, pardon me for saying this but

Cuntantès

Mè l'è trent'an ch'a chégh cumè un arlózz,
e' sarà ch'a pórt sémpra la pancera
e instèda e invéran al mudandi lònghi,
ènca parchè la nòta ò da stè sò
tre quatar vólti pr'andè fè un gòzz d'aqua.

Se magnè a stagh aténti e pu a n'i téngh.
Un bród, un pó 'd vidèl e du spinàz,
una fètta 'd strachéin, mo quant e' sègna,
mèza pàira, un grissino, un bicír d'aqua,
e me a so a pòst. E' baghéin u m fa schiv,
l'è an e an ch'a n'ò magnè un grasúl,
te parsótt a n'i dagh, e' véin a n bèggh
do dàidi tl'aqua parchè u m fa vní e' gréis,
me pèss, sfòi, rusúl, calamarétt,
a n'i faz una masa, al taiadèli
a m fa e' palòt.
                    E pu l'è tótta roba
ch' la arschèlda trop, e mè, con bón rispèt,

Contentarsi. Io sono trent'anni che caco come un orologio, / sarà che porto
sempre la pancera / e d'estate e d'inverno le mutande lunghe, / anche perché
la notte devo alzarmi / tre quattro volte per andar a fare un goccio d'acqua.
// Sul mangiare sto attento e poi non ci tengo. / Un brodo, un po' di vitello
e due spinaci, / una fetta di stracchino, / ma appena un segno, / mezza pera,
un grissino, un bicchier d'acqua, / e sono a posto. Il maiale mi fa schifo, /
sono anni e anni che non ho mangiato un cicciolo, / nel proscuitto non ci do,
il vino ne bevo / due dita nell'acqua perché mi fa venire l'acidità, / al pesce,
sogliole, triglie, calamaretti, / non ci faccio molto, le tagliatelle / mi fanno il
nodo. – E poi è tutta roba / che riscalda troppo, e io, con buon rispetto, /
se non sto attento, già che soffro di emorroidi / che mi s'ingrossano che
diventano delle patate, / e, dico la verità, non ne ho voglia io /

if I'm not careful, I already suffer from hemorrhoids,
which have gotten as big as potatoes,
and, I'm telling the truth, I have absolutely no desire
to go under the knife, I've been there enough,
twice already, once for the liver,
I couldn't take it anymore, there were nights
when it was going wild, I was climbing
the walls, and I knew it myself, they told me later on
that when they opened me up they found a river's worth of stuff,
they'd never seen such a thing before, they took out a bucket of
                                                    [stones
from inside me, and then, the hernia,
and there, I don't know what happened,
anyway, it came back again two years ago, I have to wear the belt,
which would be no big deal, but they botched it,
it itches all over,
and now I haven't got enough money to buy a new one,
because, damn them all, I don't have insurance, I worked my
                                                    [whole life,
ever since I was a boy it's been me carrying the whole load,
but because I'm a tradesman,
I'm the employer, and I'm not entitled,
employer my ass,
and to think that by doing all that work,
I was a housepainter, I've got arthritis
that's eating me alive, and the money for the medicine,
I'm the only one who knows how much it costs me, a fortune.
And then the ointments, because the lime

s'a n stagh aténti, zà ch'a iò al muròidi
ch'a m s'ingròsa ch'al dvénta dal patèti,
e, a déggh la verità, a n n'ò vòia mè
d'andè piò sòtta i férr, a n n'ò vú basta,
a i so stè zà dò vólti, préima e' fegat,
ch'a n nu n putéva piò, u i era dal nòti,
quant ch'u ciapéva e' mat, ch'a m'agrapéva
mi méur, e a l so ènca mè, dop i m'à détt
che quant i à vért i à tróv una Marèccia,
una robba mai vista, i m'à cavè
una caplètta ad calcoli, e pu l'érgna,
che alè a n'e' so cs'èll ch' l'è suzèst, insòmma
la m s'è 'rfata, du an fa, e a chin purtè e' cint,
ch'u n sarébb gnént, mo i m l'à fat senza grèzia,
u m ròusga tótt,
e adès a n gn'ò quenggmélla frènch da spènd

ènca parchè, ch'u i végna un azidént,
a n'ò la mutua, ò lavurè una véita,
l'è da burdèl che mè a so ma la calce,
mo sicome ch'a sera un artigèn,
datore di lavoro, a n gn'éintar gnént,
datore ad du quaiéun, ch'a fórza ad dèi,

d'andare piú sotto i ferri, / ne ho avuto abbastanza, / ci sono stato già due
volte, prima il fegato, / che non ne potevo piú, c'erano delle notti, / quando
gli prendeva il matto, che m'arrampicavo / sui muri, e lo so anch'io, dopo
m'hanno detto / che quando hanno aperto hanno trovato una Marecchia, /
una roba mai vista, mi hanno tolto / una secchia di calcoli, e poi l'ernia, / che
lí non so cos'è successo, insomma / mi si è rifatta, due anni fa, e devo
portare il cinto, / che non sarebbe niente, ma me l'hanno fatto senza grazia,
/ mi raspa tutto, / e adesso non le ho quindicimila lire da spendere // anche
perché, gli venga un accidente, / non ho la mutua, ho lavorato una vita, / è
da bambino che io tiro la carretta, / ma siccome ero un artigiano, / datore
di lavoro non c'entro niente, / datore di due coglioni, che a forza di darci /

burned my skin, I got
a form of eczema, not eczema exactly,
I've got red hands, and a little on my arms too,
the doctor said sooner or later
we'll be able to cure it, but
in its own good time, these things proceed slowly,
then all these different ointments, this one's no good,
let's try this other one which is a little more yellow,
I know a thing about them, it's enough if it doesn't burn.
Now it's just itcy, I'm telling you it's a bitch,
what can you do, it itches, you scratch.

Anyway, just look around
and you won't feel liking complaining anymore
with all that's happening, with what you see out there,
things that would take the taste out of bread,
so then, let's just be content. If I have debts,
I'll pay them, if not, they'll wait,

ch'a féva l'imbianchéin, a iò un'artrite
ch' la m magna véiv, e i sóld dal midizéini
a l so sno mè quant ch'u n gn'u vó, l'è un céns.

E pu al pumèdi, parchè sla calzéina
u m s'è brusé la pèla, u m'à ciapè
una forma di coso, u n'è un egzéma,
ò al mèni ròssi, e ènca un pó sal brazi,
e' profesòur l'à détt che préima o dop
lo dobiamo guarire, mo però
u i vó e' su témp, l'è robi lénti, pu
sa stal pumèdi, questa la n va bén,
pruvémma st'èlta ch' la è pió zala, mè
a n mu n'intènd, mo basta ch'u n mu n bréusa,
adès l'è sno scadòur, che quell l'è un mèl,
cma fét? u t schèd, ta t grat.

E de rest a guardès un pó datònda
la t va véa la vòia ad lamantèt,
sa tótt quèll ch'e' suzéd, ch'u s vaid in zéir,
zérti robi ch'al tó l'umòur me pèn,
e alòura cuntantésmi, s'a iò i débit
a i pagarò, se no i aspitarà,

che facevo l'imbianchino, ho un'artrite / che mi mangia vivo, e i soldi delle medicine / lo so solo io quanti ce ne vuole, è un censo. // E poi le pomate, perché con la calcina / mi s'è bruciata la pelle, mi ha preso / una forma di coso, non è un eczema, / ho le mani rosse, e anche un po' sulle braccia, / il professore ha detto che prima o dopo / lo dobbiamo guarire, ma però / ci vuole il suo tempo, sono cose lente, poi / con 'ste pomate, questa non va bene, / proviamo quest'altra che è piú gialla, io / non me n'intendo, ma basta che non mi bruci, / adesso è solo prurito, che quello è un male, / come fai? prude, ti gratti. // E del resto a guardarsi un po' intorno / ti va via la voglia di lamentarti, / con tutto quel che succede, che si vede in giro, / certe cose che tolgono il sapore al pane, / e allora contentiamoci, se ho i debiti / li pagherò, se no aspetteranno, /

but debts or no debts, its all the same,
enough said, case closed. I'm tired of struggling.

And it's not the debts causing my head to hurt,
it's a problem I've always been prone to,
there's a circle around my forehead that even blurs
my vision. So then I get up
and I take long walks,
from the station to the Capuccin monastery,
and in summer, when it's cool, I can go
all the way to below Spinalbeto.

And I can't say that it's due to cigarettes,
smoking, I haven't smoked since nineteen forty-one,
my only vice is having two or three pieces
of rhubarb candy every day, they have that bitterness
that I like, plus they're good for you, and every so often
I drink a limeade, but not,
not too cold – No, it's however someone is made,
I'm, I've got one of those heads that's not put together quite right.
Could this be why I never got married?

And it's not that I didn't want to, there was one I courted
for more than a year, I was almost part of the family,
but it always seemed like she was walking on glass,
and I understood why later,
when she became a nun.

mo débit o no débit l'è l'istèss,
basta, chiuso, a m so stóff ad bazilé.

E u n'è pr'i débit quant u m dól la testa,
l'è un distéurb ch'a i so sémpra andè sogèt,
u m s fa un zirc ma la fròunta ch'u m s'anèbbia
ènca la vésta. Alòura mè a ciap sò
e a faz dal caminédi sémpra grandi,
ma la staziòun e pu mi Capuzéin,
e d'instèda, pr'e' frèsch, a so capèzi
d'arivé fina sòtta Spinalbàid.
E a n pòs dí gnènca ch' séa pr'al zigarètti,
fumé a n fómm piò da e' novzentquarentéun,
l'ónich véizi l'è do tre caramèli
ad rabarbaro e' dè, sa cl'amartín
ch'u m pis, e pu al fa bén, e d'ogni tènt
a bèggh un cedrata, mo però
ch' la n séa giazéda.
                    No, l'è cm'u s'è fat,
mè u s vaid ch'a iò la testa fata mèl.
Che séa par quèst ch'a n mu n so mai spusè?

ma debiti o non debiti è lo stesso, / basta, chiuso, mi sono stancato di
tribolare. // E non è per i debiti quando mi duole la testa, / è un disturbo al
quale sono andato sempre soggetto, / mi si fa un cerchio alla fronte che mi
s'annebbia / anche la vista. Allora prendo su / e faccio delle gran camminate,
/ alla stazione e poi ai Cappuccini, / e d'estate, per il fresco, sono capace /
d'arrivare fin sotto Spinalbeto. / E non posso dire neanche che sia per le
sigarette, / fumare, non fumo piú dal novecentoquarantuno, / l'unico vizio
sono due tre caramelle / di rabarbaro al giorno, con quell'amarognolo / che
mi piace, e poi fanno bene, e ogni tanto / bevo una cedrata, ma però / che
non sia ghiacciata. – No, è come si è fatti, / io si vede che ho la testa fatta
male. / Che sia per questo che non mi sono mai sposato? /

I couldn't say a thing about it, but I took it hard,
I was attached to her. Then when I was older
I'd talk all the time to another one, but I knew she wasn't in
[good health

and I fell out of love,
desire went away. When you get down to it,
who knows, it might be better off like this,
a more orderly life, and without children,
because today there's a lot to worry about,
it's not like when we were young.

                                    Enough. Now I've got
a little house beyond the old station,
half an acre, just a little bit of land
where I grow whatever the hell I want.
Me, with one good arm,
I prune branches, plant cantaloupes, I hoe,
I water the tomatoes, pick the peaches,
I only cut the early radicchio.
Sometimes I get tired without realizing it.

E u n'è ch'a n vléss, ma óna a i so 'ndè dri
piò d'un an, a i andéva guèsi ad chèsa,
mo e' pareva ch' la stéss sémpra sal spéini,
e ò capí dop, quant la s'è fata sóra.
Mè a n'ò putú dí gnént, mo a so 'rvènz mèl,
a m séra afezionè. Pu da piò anzièn
ò zcòurs un pó s'un'èlta, mo ò savéu
ch' la n'éva la saléuta, e a m so sgusté,
u m'è 'ndè véa la vòia. Che pu in fònd,
chi lo sa, e' pò ès stè mèi, acsè,
véita piò regolèda, e senza fiúl,
che òz l'è di pansír, u n'è cmè quant
a sérmi zóvan néun.
                                    Basta, mè 'dès
a iò un casètt adlà dla staziòun vècia,
s'un pó 'd tèra, una mèza turnadéura
ch'a i chèv l'ira di Dio. Mè se braz bón
a pòud la véida, a sémn i mléun, a sap,
a daqv i pumidór, a còi al pésghi,
e di radécc a faz sòul e' prim tai.
Dal vólti a m strach, mo a n mu n'incórz e gnénca,
a guèrd e' sòul, a vèggh ch' l'è pas agli òuri.

E non è che non volessi, a una ho fatto la corte / piú d'un anno, ci andavo
quasi in casa, / ma pareva che stesse sempre sulle spine, / e ho capito dopo,
quando s'è fatta suora. / Io non ho potuto dire niente, ma sono rimasto
male, / m'ero affezionato. Poi da piú anziano / ho parlato un po' con
un'altra, ma ho saputo / che non aveva salute, e mi sono disamorato, / m'è
andata via la voglia. Che poi in fondo, che lo sa, può essere stato meglio cosí,
/ vita piú regolata, e senza figli, / che oggi sono dei pensieri, non è come
quando / eravamo giovani noi. — Basta, io adesso / ho una casetta di là dalla
stazione vecchia, / con un po' di terra, una mezza tornatura / che cavo l'ira
di Dio. Io col braccio buono / poto la vite, semino i meloni, zappo, /
innaffio i pomodori, raccolgo le pesche, / e dei radicchi faccio solo il primo
taglio. /

I look at the sun, I see that hours have gone by.
And in the evening when I'm present and accounted for,
                              [that's everyone.
I chain the door, take the drops
for high blood pressure, the horse pill, and I go to bed.

Isn't that good? Who said I have to change?
For me, all I need is to lean back in a chair
and immediately I'm sleeping like a baby.
And the intestines keep going, and it's thirty years
that I've shit like clockwork.

E la sàira quant a i so mè a i sémm tótt,
a mètt la carnazéina, a tóggh al gòzzli
par la presiòun, la pérla, e a vagh a lèt.

U n va bén? chi l'à détt ch'ò da cambiè?
mu mè u m basta puzèm s'una scaràna
ch'a m'indurmént ad bot mèi d'un burdèl.
E l'intestéin e' mèrcia, l'è trent'an
ch'a chégh cumè un arlózz.

A volte mi stanco, ma non me n'accorgo nemmeno, / guardo il sole, vedo
che sono passate le ore. / E la sera quando ci sono io ci siamo tutti, / metto
il catenaccino, prendo le gocce / per la pressione, la pillola, e vado a letto. //
Non va bene? chi l'ha detto che devo cambiare? / A me mi basta
appoggiarmi su una sedia / che m'addormento di botto meglio d'un
bambino. / E l'intestino marcia, sono trent'anni / che caco come un
orologio.

Bats

I shouldn't have left the window open
because now I've got bats in here,
they're flying around everywhere, hissing,
swooping down low, they brush against my face,
I bang the window, go at them with a rag,
I get a few, but others are getting in.

It works better with a sheet. I twist it
like a rope,
I swing it like a windmill, above my head,
it opens up, and where it hits, it makes a clean sweep,
but others always get in
there must be a call,
what could it be, an odor?
the radio? those two peaches
I put on top of the bureau? me?

My arms are almost broken, I can't do this anymore
and it seems like they know it, if I stop
they come right at me, they get into my hair,
they fly through my fingers, at my ears.

I nóttal

A n'éva da lasè vért' la finestra,
adès u m'è éintar i nóttal.
I vòula dimpartótt, i fa di céul,
i vén da bas, i m stréssa ma la faza.
Mè a sbat i véidar, a i dagh s'un straz,
qualchedéun a l'aciàp, mo u n'éintra d'ilt.

U s fa mèi se lanzúl, a l'inturtéi
cmè una córda,
a l zéir a mulinèl sòura la testa,
léu u s'éirva
e dò ch'e' ciapa e' puléss.
Mo u n'éintra sempra d'ilt,
e' pèr ch'u i séa un arcèm,
cs'èll ch'e' sarà, un udòur?
l'è la radio ch' la sòuna? cal do pésghi
ch'ò puzè se cumò? o ch'a séa mè?

Sa sté lanzúl
a m so s-cènt bèla al brazi, a n nu n pòs piò,
e lòu e' pèr ch'i l sapa, s'a m'aférum
i m vén còuntra, i m s'instècca ti cavéll,
i m s'inféila tra 'l dàidi, tagli urècci.

I pipistrelli. Non dovevo lasciar aperta la finestra, / adesso mi sono entrati i pipistrelli. / Volano dappertutto, fanno dei sibili, / vengono bassi, mi sfiorano la faccia. / Io sbatto i vetri, ci do con uno straccio, / qualcuno lo prendo, ma ne entrano altri. // Si fa meglio col lenzuolo, l'attorciglio / come una corda, / lo giro a mulinello sopra la testa, / lui si apre / e dove prende fa piazza pulita. / Ma ne entrano sempre altri, / pare che ci sia un richiamo, / cosa sarà? un odore? / è la radio che suona? quelle due pesche / che ho appoggiato sul comò? o che sia io? // Con questo lenzuolo / mi sono ormai rotto le braccia, non ne posso piú, / e loro pare che lo sappiano, se mi fermo / mi vengono contro, mi si ficcano nei capelli, / mi s'infilano tra le dita, nelle orecchie. /

And now, because I'm so tired from taking swings at them
I've broken the lamp.
The dark is where they live,
they're never going away.
I'm kneeling in a corner, against the wall,
I'm covering my head with my hands, completely still,
waiting, but nothing happens.

I jump into bed under the covers,
even my head is buried.
I'll sit tight here until they get worn out,
until daylight, when they're dazed, blind,
and they go to sleep. In the morning we'll have a good laugh
                                                    [about it.
But it's only ten and the night is a long time
to stay still in the dark
curled up at the foot of the bed,
silent, by myself,
and they are flying, chasing again, they're hissing.

So what's with this big fear?
because there are lot of them? because they never stop
                              [coming? because
there are always more?
yes, that's a given, I'm the exterminator,
but, in here, between the walls

Adès te sbat,
par la strachèzza, ò ròtt la lampadéina,
te schéur lòu l'è e' su stè, i n va véa piò.
A m mètt d'inznòc t'un cantòun, còuntra e' méur,
al mèni, a m cruv la testa, a stagh alè,
aspétt, mo u n suzéd gnént.

Alòura a m bótt te lèt,
sòtta la cvérta, ènca sla testa, spléid,
a vói stè bón aquè, ch'i s stóffa lòu,
ch'e' vénga e' dè, quant i è invurnéid, i è zigh,
e i s'indurménta. Admatéina a ridémm.
Mo l'è sno 'l dis e la nòta la è lònga
a stè férum, te schéur,
scartuzèd aquazò mi pi de lèt,
zétt, da par mè,
e lòu ch'i vòula, ch'i s da dri, ch'i céula.

Mo parchè pu mè ò tótta sta paéura?
parchè i è tint, i n finéss mai, i crèss sémpra?
sè, va bén, i è un strabéigh,
mo aquè dréinta, tra i méur,

Adesso nello sbattere, / per la stanchezza, ho rotto la lampadina, / nel buio
è il loro stare, non vanno via piú. / Mi metto in ginocchio in un angolo,
contro il muro, / le mani, mi copro la testa, sto lí, / aspetto, ma non succede
niente. // Allora mi butto nel letto, / sotto la coperta, anche con la testa,
sepolto, / voglio star buono qui, che si stanchino loro, / che venga giorno,
quando sono intontiti, ciechi, / e s'addormentano. Domattina ridiamo. / Ma
sono solo le dieci e la notte è lunga / a star fermo, al buio, / accartocciato
quaggiú ai piedi del letto, / zitto, solo, / e loro che volano, che si rincorrono,
che sibilano. // Ma perché poi ho tutta questa paura? / perché sono tanti?
non finiscono mai? crescono sempre? / sí, va bene, sono uno sterminio, / ma
qui dentro, tra i muri, /

maybe they feel trapped,
they're worse off than me,
they fight among themselves.
But they're not biting each other, nipping at each other.
It could be they're content, that they like it like this,
being in a swarm, flying, giving each other little shoves,
no really, if all they wanted was to laugh,
and they're looking for me, are they upset because I'm hidden?
I've never even seen them up close,
they've always disgusted me,
but maybe I'm mistaken,
velvet makes me feel that way too,
so I never touch it.
also, they're so black, things with wings, like umbrellas,
what can I say, it gives me the willies.
But is that their fault? they fly, they,
they don't do it on purpose, they're not mean,
and when it comes down to it moths around lights
act crazier, and what can they do to you?
they eat gnats,
they've got bad eyes, no beaks, not even claws,
go ahead and see if they don't make you feel a little more patient,
you could tame them, keep them in a cage.

forse i s sint cmè intraplèd,
i sta pézz ca nè mè, i ragna tra 'd lòu.

Però i n s dà 'd mórs, in n s pézga.
E s'e' fóss ch'i è cuntént, ch'u i pis acsè,
ès un róbbi, vulè, dès dal spatasi,
mo dabón, se i avéss sno vòia ad réid,
e i m zirca, e i è 'rvènz mèl ch'a m so masè?
Me da davséin a n gn'ò gnénca mai vést,
i m'à sémpra fat schiv,
mo magari a sbai mè,
mè u m fa séns ènca e' vléut, ch'a n'e' tòcch mai.
Pu acsè nir, e s' cagli èli cmè un'umbrèla,
cs'òi da déi, i m fa vnéi la chèrna pléina.
Però l'è còulpa sóvva? i vòula, lòu,
i n'e' fa mégga pòsta, i n'è catéiv,
in fònd, agli è piò mati al pavaiòti
tònda mi lómm, e pu cs'èll ch'i t pò fè?
magnè, i magna i musléin,
i n'à i ócc bón, bèch gnént, e gnénca agli óngi,
va vdai che s' ta t'i mètt s'un pó 'd pazinzia,
ta i pò domestichè, ta i tén tla ghèbia.

forse si sentono come intrappolati, / stanno peggio di me, litigano fra di loro. / Però non si danno morsi, non si pizzicano. / E se fosse che sono contenti, che gli piace cosí, / essere uno stormo, volare, darsi delle spinte, / ma davvero, se avessero solo voglia di ridere, / e mi cercano, e sono rimasti male che mi sono nascosto? / Io da vicino non li ho neanche mai visti, / mi hanno sempre fatto schifo, / ma magari sbaglio io, / a me mi fa senso anche il velluto, che non lo tocco mai. / Poi cosí neri, e con quelle ali come un ombrello, / cosa devo dire, mi fanno venire la pelle d'oca. / Però è colpa loro? / volano loro, / non lo fanno mica apposta, non sono cattivi, / in fondo sono piú matte le farfalle / attorno ai lumi, e poi cosa ti possono fare? / mangiare, mangiano i moscerini, / non hanno gli occhi buoni, niente becco, e neanche le unghie, / vai a vedere che se ti ci metti con un po' di pazienza, / li puoi addomesticare, li tieni in gabbia. //

But the cages will come later, what's needed now
is to just find a way to make yourself understood,
to let them know that I don't want to hurt them,
that, if, all in all, they want to stay in the bedroom,
if they like this place, they can stay here as long as they want,
as for my sleeping, we'll see
let's just come to an agreement,
understand each other,
but how can you have a discussion, they're not paying attention,
a hundred bucks for whoever gets them,
they're going every which way, like drunks,
they're only good for hissing.
True, but what if this is their only way of speaking,
and they can't explain themselves any better,
if when they were in my hair,
they were trying to tell me: listen up, I'm talking to you.
But even if you pay attention, all you hear is their hissing,
I don't understand anything, who knows what they're telling me,
listen to how they're screaming. And what if I, me, give them
                                                              [voice?
I'm making more hisses, like them, some shrill cries, but soft,
I'm starting to talk like them. I'm trying now.
And if someone truly answers?

Mo la ghèbia u i è témp, quèll ch'u i vó 'dès
l'è sno da truvè e' módi d' fès capéi,
da fèi savài che mè a n'i ví de mèl,
che, quant l'è tl'éultum, s'i vó stè tla cambra,
s'u i pis e' pòst, ch'i staga quant i vó,
pr'e' durméi u s'avdirà,
basta mèttsi d'acórd, ch'a s'intendémma,
mo cmè ch'u s fa a fè un zcòurs, ch'i n sta d'aténti,
quéi, zént schéud chi i aciapa,
i va d'in quà e d'in là cmè di imbariégh,
i è bón sno d' fè di céul.
Zà, mo s'e' fóss e' su módi ad dizcòrr,
e i gne la fa a spieghès,
se quant i m'instichéva ti cavéll
i m vléva déi: sta 'ténti, a zcòrr sa tè?
mo sta pò 'ténti, mè a sint di gran céul,
a n capéss gnént, chi sa quèll ch'i m racòunta,
sint cmè ch'i rógg. E s'a i déss vòusa mè?
a faz d'ilt céul, cmè i sóvv, di sgréss, mo stil,
a m mètt a zcòrr cmè lòu. Adès a próv.
Se dabón qualchedéun u m'arspundéss?

Ma per la gabbia c'è tempo, quel che ci vuole adesso / è solo trovare il modo
di farsi capire, / di fargli sapere che io non gli voglio del male, / che, alla fin
fine, se vogliono stare nella camera, / se gli piace il posto, ci stiano quanto
vogliono, / per il dormire si vedrà / basta mettersi d'accordo, che
c'intendiamo, / ma come si fa a fare un discorso, che non stanno attenti, /
quelli, cento scudi chi li acchiappa, / vanno di qua e di là come ubriachi, /
sono capaci solo di far dei sibili. / Già, ma se fosse il loro modo di parlare,
/ e non ce la fanno a spiegarsi, / se quando mi si ficcavano nei capelli /
volevano dirmi: sta' attento, parlo con te? / ma stai pur attento, io sento dei
gran sibili, / non capisco niente, chi sa quello che mi raccontano, / senti
come urlano. E se gli dessi voce io? / faccio altri sibili, come i loro, degli
stridi, ma sottili, / mi metto a parlare come loro. Adesso provo. / Se
davvero qualcuno mi rispondesse?

His Father

Why don't I say anything?
you think I don't see that my Adriano
looks like the Panartéuns?
that he's the spitting image of Ferruccio, come on now, that
[it's his son,
and what am I supposed to do?
kill his mother,
who's forty-eight years old
and the years have affected her head
and at night she doesn't sleep,
during the day she gets hot flashes, she forgets things,
she cries for no reason, what can I do, grab her by the shoulders,
yell? tell her she was a whore?
and me? what was I?

And then later tell Adriano too?
and tell him what? that's he's my son, but I'm not his father?
what does it have to do with him?
He cares a ton for me,
he confides, he tells me everything,
and he's cheerful, he's got a desire to work,

E' su bà

Parchè a stagh zétt?
t vu ch' a n'e' vègga che e' mi Driano
u s'asarméa mi Panartéun?
ch' l'è Feruccio spudéd, zò, ch' l'è e' su fiùl?
e alòura cs'òi da fè?
amazè la su mà,
ch' la à quarentòt an
e ch'i i è 'ndè tla testa,
e la nòta la n dórma,
e' dè u i vén i caldéun, la s zcórda al robi,
la piànz par gnént, cs'èll, a la ciap pr'e' còl,
a rógg, a i déggh ch' la è stèda una putèna?
e mè? cs'èll ch'a so stè?

E dop a i e' déggh ènca ma Driano?
e cmè ch'a i déggh?
che l'è e' mi fiúl, però mè a n so e' su bà?
mo léu csa i éintral? ch'u m vó un bén che mai,
u s cunféida, u m dí tótt,
pu l'è ligar, l'à vòia 'd lavurè,

Suo padre. Perché sto zitto? / vuoi che non veda che il mio Adriano / somiglia ai Panartéun? che è Feruccio sputato, dai, che è suo figlio? / e allora cosa devo fare? / ammazzare sua madre, / che ha quarantotto anni / e le sono andati in testa, / e la notte non dorme, / il giorno le vengono le caldane, si dimentica le cose, / piange per niente, cosa faccio, la prendo per il collo, / urlo, le dico che è stata una puttana? / e io cosa sono stato? // E dopo lo dico anche ad Adriano? / e come gli doco ? / che è mio figlio, però io non sono suo padre? / ma lui cosa c'entra? che mi vuole un bene, / si confida, mi dice tutto, / poi è allegro, ha voglia di lavorare, / è piú allegro di me, e meno testone, /

he's more cheerful than me, and less hard-headed,
less testy,
that's why his friends all love him,
at work too,
how could you not love my Adriano,
with those eyes that have never told a lie;
but it's not like he's asleep at the switch,
he understands things, he has conversations
which even I don't have, me who's his father.

l'è piò ligar ch' nè mè, e mènch zucòun,
mènch parmalòus,
l'è par quèll che i su améigh i i vó bén tótt,
e ènca se lavòur,
mo cum s fal no vlí bén me mi Driano,
sa chi ócc ch'u n m'à mai détt una buséa,
però mégga indurmént,
al robi u li capéss, e' fa di zchéurs
ch'a n'i faz gnénca mè ch'a so e' su bà.

meno permaloso, / è per questo che i suoi amici gli vogliono bene tutti, / e anche sul lavoro, / ma come si fa a non voler bene al mio Adriano, / con quegli occhi che non m'ha mai detto una bugia, / però mica addormentato, / le cose le capisce, fa dei discorsi / che non li faccio nemmeno io che sono suo padre.

Winter

The days have gotten so short.
At five there's no light at all.
For me, it turns to night
at ten-thirty in the morning.
I can't find the switch.
It's not even day anymore.

L'invéran

Cumè ch'al s'è zchéurti al zurnèdi!
al zéinch u n s vaid bèla piò lómm.

Mu mè u m'è vnú nòta
al dis e mèz dla matéina.
A n tróv la pirètta dla luce.
U n s fa ancòura e' dè.

L'inverno. Come si sono accorciate le giornate! / alle cinque non si vede
ormai piú lume. // A me mi è venuta notte / alle dieci e mezzo della
mattina. / Non trovo la peretta della luce. / Non si fa ancora giorno.

The Pine Grove

For two nights now I've been dreaming about Fedora.
I don't even know why myself,
maybe because I heard about her sister,
the other evening,
that she's come back from France.
Fedora, the Gianólas, you don't remember her?
stark raving mad, with freckles, and those eyes
that made it seem like she always had a fever.
She lived on the via Costa, above the Fusi's,
she liked hot chocolate
and mint drinks with ice.
Dead at twenty-two in thirty-seven.

It seems like today, that summer at the shore,
we were swimming with the others,
and then, quietly, quietly, we slipped off to the pine grove.
She was never satisfied,
a few times,
when I was stretched out near a cabana,
she would come up right next to me,
she would tousle my hair with her hands,
she would whisper in my ear: "Pippo, are we going?"

La pinàida

L'è do nòti ch'a insógni la Fedora.
A n'e' so gnénca mè,
forse parchè ò sintéi dla su surèla,
l'altrasàira,
ch' la tòurna da la Frènza.
La Fedora ad Gianóla, ta n la arcórd?
Mata s–cènta, se rèmal, e sa chi ócc
ch'e' pareva ch' la avéss sémpra la févra.
La stéva ma la Costa, sòura al Fusi,
u i pieséva la cecolèta in taza
e la menta se giaz.
Mórta a vintidú an de trentasèt.

U m pèr cmè 'dès, l'ultm'instèda a maréina,
a fémmi e' bagn sa ch'ilt
e pu zétt zétt amdémmi tla pinàida.
La n'era mai cunténta,
zérti vólti,
ch'a séra alè stuglèd vsina un capàn,
la m'avnéva tachèd,
la m scavcéva sal mèni,
la m géva t'un'urèccia: "Pippo, andémm?"

La pineta. Sono due notti che sogno la Fedora. / Non lo so nemmeno io, / forse perché ho sentito di sua sorella, / l'altra sera, / che torna dalla Francia. / La Fedora di Gianóla, no te le ricordi? / matta da legare, con le lentiggini, e con quegli occhi / che pareva avesse sempre la febbre. / Stava alla Costa, sopra le Fusi, / le piaceva la cioccolata in tazza /e la menta col ghiaccio. / Morta a ventidue anni nel trentasette. // Mi pare come adesso, l'ultima estate a marina, / facevamo il bagno con gli altri / e poi zitti zitti andavamo nella pineta. / Non era mai contenta, / certe volte, / che ero sdraiato vicino a un capanno, / mi veniva accanto, / mi spettinava con le mani, / mi diceva in un orecchio: "Pippo, andiamo?" //

83

And even now, at night, she says to me:
"Pippo, come on, come on, let's go to the pine grove."
And I see her, she's twenty-two years old,
she's still young,
me, on the other hand, I'm tired,
and when she starts running I don't catch up with her.
But then besides I don't even feel like it,
at this point,
all I like to do is play briscola and have a glass of wine.

E ènca adès, la nòta, la m'e' déi:
"Pippo, dài, dài, andémma tla pinàida".
E mè a la vèggh, la à vintidú an,
la è sémpra zóvna,
invíci mè a so strach
e quant la s mètt a córr a n'i stagh dri.
Mo pu a n n'ò gnénca vòia,
ormai mu mè
u m pis da zughé a bréscla e un bicír 'd véin.

E anche adesso, la notte, me lo dice: / "Pippo, dai, dai, andiamo nella
pineta". / E io la vedo, ha ventidue anni, / è sempre giovane, / invece io
sono stanco / e quando si mette a correre non le sto dietro. / Ma poi non ne
ho nemmeno voglia, / ormai a me / me piace giocare a briscola e un
bicchiere di vino.

In Front of the Mirror

He never knew it, I never said a word,
that time he slept over at my house,
and we made up a bed for him on the sofa in the sitting room.
By mistake, that evening, after saying good night,
I opened the door to go and get something
I'd forgotten. Opened, in a manner of speaking,
a crack. And I just stood motionless,
when I saw him completely nude in front of the mirror.
He was there
looking at himself with eyes half-closed, as if from a distance.
Then he moved, he took three or four steps,
he stopped and stood sideways,
and he looked at himself a good long while out of the corner of
[his eye.
He went closer. He stretched out his arms.
He made muscles.
He studied himself down below, he touched himself,
he played with himself.
He sucked in his snot. Took a deep breath.
With his chin on his chest which was all puffed out,
he raised his head.

Te spèc

Léu u n l'à savù mai, a n gne l'ò détt,
cla vólta ch' l'à durméi ma la mi chèsa,
e a i fésmi e' lèt tla sèla se sofà.
Para sbai, la sàira, dop la bonanòta,
ò vért la pórta pr'andè tó una roba
ch'a m séra zcórd. Vérta par módi 'd déi,
una fiséura, ch'a m so férm ad bot
quant ch'a l'ò vést tótt néud davènti e' spèc.
E' stéva alè d'impí,
u s guardéva si ócc strétt, cmè da dalòngh,
pu u s'è mòs,
l'à fat tri quatar pas,
u s'è férum di fiènch
e u s'è guèrs un bèl pó sla còuda dl'òc.
L'è tòuran piò davséin, l'a slèrgh al brazi,
l'à fat i móscal,
u s'è guardè da bas, u s'è tuchè,
l'à zugarlé.
L'à tiràt sò pr'e' nès, un gran respéir,
se barbètt còuntra e' pèt ch'u s'i gunfiéva.

Allo specchio. Lui non l'ha mai saputo, non gliel'ho detto, / quella volta che ha dormito a casa mia, / e gli facemmo il letto nel salotto sul sofà. / Per sbaglio, la sera, dopo la buonanotte, / ho aperto la porta per andare a prendere una cosa / che avevo dimenticato. Aperta per modo di dire, / una fessura, che mi sono fermato di botto, / quando l'ho visto tutto nudo davanti allo specchio. / Stava lí in piedi, si guardava con gli occhi semichiusi, come da lontano, / poi s'è mosso, / ha fatto tre quattro passi, / s'è fermato di fianco / e s'è guardato un bel po' con la coda dell'occhio. / E' tornato piú vicino, ha allargato le braccia, / ha fatto i muscoli, / s'è guardato da basso, s'è toccato, / ha giocherellato. / Ha tirato su per il naso, un gran respiro, / col mento contro il petto che gli si gonfiava. /

He ran his hand through his hair,
and he remained still, in just that position.
Then he gave a little shudder,
got back into bed, and turned out the light.

He must have been about twenty-three
or twenty-four.
He was with Pierina Torri,
who then hooked up with Anita's Geo,
he never was one to strut his stuff,
tall, lean as hunger,
which is why they called him Wire.

L'à 'lzè la testa,
u s'è pas una mèna ti cavéll,
l'è 'rvènz férum acsè.
Pu u i è vnù un strémal,
u s'è infilé te lèt, l'à smórt la luce.

E' géve 'vai alòura
vintitrì vintquatr'an,
e' feva l'amòur sla Pierina Torri,
che pu da li u i andéva ènch' Geo dla Nita,
quèll se pèt a capòun,
sècch spènt, lòngh cmè la fèma,
ch'i l ciaméva Spranghín.

Ha alzato la testa, / s'è passato una mano nei capelli, / è rimasto fermo cosí.
/ Poi gli è venuto un brivido, / s'è infilato nel letto, ha spento la luce. //
Doveva avere allora / ventitre ventiquattr'anni, / faceva l'amore con la
Pierina Torri, / che poi da lei ci andava anche Geo dell'Anita, / quello col
petto a cappone, magrissimo, lungo come la fame, / che lo chiamavano
Spranghín.

Quiet

You want to say something to me?
no? but you're looking at me with those eyes, you've been
[waiting too long?

it's got everything, look around, why are you looking at me?
here, it's here where you should be looking, don't you see all the
[amenities?

what's not right? I did what you said,
like all the other times, did I not understand?

are you afraid, no, stay calm,
I didn't touch anything, nobody has touched anything,

help me understand, did I make a mistake, speak, say something,
it's for your sake, too, if you tell me where I went wrong,
the next time, I'll do it better, is my thinking out of line here?
what's wrong? are you angry? are you exasperated with me?

because I, you know I even thought, I was expecting
that you'd be singing my praises, at any rate, what did I do?
what should I have done?
answer, if I'm the only one talking, what does it cost
to say something?
we're spending the night here, so are you talking or not?

Zétt

Ta m vlévi dí qualquèl?
no? mo ta m guèrd sa di ócc, t'é spitè tròp?

però i è tótt, guèrda, ta m guèrd mu mè?
l'è què ch' t'é da guardè, ta n vaid la roba?

cs'èll ch'u n va bén? ò fat cmè ta m'é détt,
cmè tótt' cagli èlti vólti, ò capì mèl?

o t'é paéura che, no, sta tranquéll,
a n'ò tòcch gnént, u n'à tòcch, gnént niseun,

fam capéi, ò sbaiè? zcòrr, dí qualquèl,
l'è 'nca par tè, s' ta m déi dò ch'ò sbaiè,
st'èlta vólta a faz mèi, a ragiòun mèl?
mo cs'èll t'é? t si incaplèd? ta la é sa mè?

che mè, fighéurt, a m'aspitéva che
ta m féss i elogi, insòmma cs'èll ch'ò fat?
cs'èll ch'éva da fè? 'rspònd, s'a zcòrr sno mè?
mo cs'èll ch'u t gòsta zcòrr?
aquè a fémm nòta, alòura t zcòrr o no?

Zitto. Mi volevi dire qualche cosa? / no? ma mi guardi con degli occhi, hai aspettato troppo? // però c'è tutto, guarda, guardi me? / è qui che devi guardare, non vedi quanta roba? // cos'è che non va bene? ho fatto come m'hai detto, / come tutte le altre volte, ho capito male? // o hai paura che, no, sta' tranquillo, / non ho toccato niente, non ho toccato niente nessuno, // fammi capire, ho sbagliato? parla, di' qualcosa, / è anche per te, se mi dici dove ho sbagliato, / quest'altra volta faccio meglio, ragiono male? / ma che cos'hai? sei arrabbiato? ce l'hai con me? // che io, figurarsi, m'aspettavo che / mi facessi gli elogi, insomma cosa ho fatto? / cosa dovevo fatto? / cosa dovevo fare? rispondi, se parlo solo io, / ma cosa ti costa parlare? / qui facciamo notte, allora parli o no? //

if not, I'll talk,
and if I talk, then I don't know, come on, sit up,
say what you've got to say, tell me whatever you're thinking,
let me hear your voice, one word,
give me just a single sign, with a finger.

Okay. Fine. I'll talk: you're right.
I did everything wrong, I wanted it all my way,
it's always like this with me, I always mess up with my hands
and I'll never learn, I'm ambitious,
I get way ahead and I fumble,
I want to be brilliant at things, I go on instinct,
and it always turns into a big mess,
even bills with all those numbers, all the adding and subtracting,
I don't stay on top of it, I get all riled up,
with places, I don't ask, then I get lost, with people, in the piazza,
I don't know anything but I always want to give my opinion.
I don't even know what it is I like, what I don't like,

but you, you understand everything at a glance,
you see things so clearly,
you don't get swayed by what someone is saying, you see right
[through it,
you do the right thing,

se no a zcòrr mè,
e s'a zcòrr mè, dop a n'e' so, dài, zò,
dí quèll ch' ta m'é da déi, dí quèll ch'u t pèr,
ch'a sinta la tu vòusa, una paróla,
fam ènch' sno un sègn, s'un daid,

e' va bén, a zcòrr mè: t'é rasòun tè,
ò sbaiè tótt, ò vlú fè 'd testa méa,
sémpra acsè, mè, a m fràigh sémpra sal mi mèni,
e a n'impararò mai, a so imbiziòus,
a ví guardè dalòngh e a m'imbarbai,
tal robi a ví ès brilènt, a i dagh a òc,
e pu e' vén sémpra fura di caséin,
ènca i chéunt, tótt chi nómar, chèva, mètt,
a n'i stagh dri, a m'imbròi,
ti póst, a n dmand, e a m pérd, sla zénta, in piaza,
a n so gnént, mo a ví sémpra dí la méa,
a n so gnénch' quèll ch'u m pis, quèll ch'u mu n pis,

invíci tè, s'n'ucèda t capéss tótt,
tè bén t si 'lè sla testa,
ta n sté a sintí niseun, ta i inzècch sémpra,

se no parlo io, / e se parlo io, dopo non lo so, dai, su, / di' quello che mi
devi dire, di' quello che ti pare, / che senta la tua voce, una parola, / fammi
anche solo un segno, con un dito, // e va bene, parlo io: hai ragione tu, / ho
sbagliato tutto, ho voluto fare di testa mia, / sempre cosí, io, mi frego sempre
con le mie mani, / e non imparerò mai, sono ambizioso, / voglio guardare
lontano e m'imbarbaglio, / nelle cose voglio essere brilliante, ci do a occhio,
/ e poi vengono sempre fuori dei casini, / anche i conti, tutti quei numeri,
cava metti, / non ci sto dietro, / m'imbroglio, / nei posti, non domando, e
mi perdo, con la gente, in piazza, / non so niente, ma voglio dire sempre la
mia, / non so neanche quel che mi piace, quel che non mi piace, // invece
tu con un'occhiata capisci tutto, / tu ci sei con la testa, / non stai a sentire
nessuno, c'indovini sempre, /

there's so much to learn from you even if you don't say a thing,
but you have to be patient with me,
I can't make it by myself,
I have this passion for doing things, I try everything,
but what I need is someone to give the orders,
what I need is you, me with you, I can feel it, I would go to the
                                             [ends of the earth,

and now, maybe, come on, what are we waiting for?
I'm more than ready; you command, I obey.
you're lowering your head? are you saying yes? it's all right? really?
from this moment on, this is it, I'm in your hands,
tell me everything, what I should do, where I should go,

and now, that's enough, I've talked too much, it's the last time,
I'm not saying anything else, I'll talk when you say to.

da tè u i è da imparè ènch s' ta n dí gnént,
mo mè, sa mè tè t'é d'avài pazinzia,
da par mè a n mu n sgavagn,
mè ò pasiòun da fè al robi, agli a mètt tótta,
però u m vó qualcadèun ch'e' daga i cmand,
ta i vu tè, mè sa tè, a m'e' sint, andrébb
in chèva e' mond,

e alòura, forza, dai, cs'èll ch'aspitémm?
mè a so zà pròunt, tè t cmand e mè a faz mód,
t bas la tèsta? t dí 'd sè? ta i sté? dabón?
da sté mumént, ecco, a so tal tu mèni,
déim tótt, quèll ch'ò da fè, dò ch'ò d'andè,

e pu basta, ò zcòurs trop, l'è l'éultma vólta,
a n déggh piò gnént, a zcòrr quant ta l dí tè.

da te c'è da imparare anche se non dici niente, / ma io, con me tu devi aver
pazienza, / da solo non me la cavo, / io ho passione a fare le cose, ce la
metto tutta, / però mi ci vuole qualcuno che dia gli ordini, / ci vuoi tu, io
con te, lo sento, andrei / in capo al mondo, // e allora, forza, dai, cosa
aspettiamo? / io sono già pronto, tu comandi e io obbedisco, / abbassi la
testa? dici di sí? ci stai? davvero? / da questo momento, ecco, sono nelle tue
mani, / dimmi tutto, quel devo fare, dove devo andare, // e poi basta, ho
parlato troppo, è l'ultima volta, / non dico piú niente, parlo quando lo dici
tu.

Her Mother

It never even crossed my mind
that one day she might
look just like her mother.
Thin, skin like fine silk,
hair always messed up,
and then
all that nervousness. She was too different.

But then, no, little by little,
without my being aware of it, she put on weight,
there's almost a quivering when she walks,
she's even got her mannerisms,
seeing her from behind, it's the spitting image,
then the voice, it's even her way of talking,
she's all her mother, that ignorant woman,
Sina, who I remember,
when she ended up that evening
in the warehouse, at the back, among
the piles of dried codfish, and she started crying
among the baccalà, there was such a stench,
baccalà and sardines,

La su mà

Mè a n'i penséva gnénca
che u n dè la avrébb putéu
sarmiés ma la su mà,
Stila, la pèla féina cmè la sàida,
i cavéll cmè ch' la fóss sémpra scavcèda,
e pu tótt che nervòus. Tropa diversa.

E invíci no, pièn pièn,
senza ch'a m n'incurzéss, la s'è incurpéida,
adès te caminé guèsi la nénna,
la à ciap ènca e' su fè,
a vdàila da di dri l'è li spudéda,
pu la vòusa, parsìna e' módi 'd zcòrr,
l'è tótta cl'ignurènta dla su mà,
la Sina, ch'a m la arcórd,
quant ch' la s truvétt cla sàira
te magazéin, in fònd, tramèza al bali
de becalà, e la s mitétt a piànz.
Mè a m striséva sal dàidi sòtta e' nès
e a géva sémpra ad sè,
che invíci l'era da s-ciupè de réid,
tra tótt che becalà, u i era una pózza,
becalà e rènghi,

Sua madre. Io non ci pensavo nemmeno / che un giorno avrebbe potutuo
somigliare a sua madre. / Sottile, la pelle fina come la seta, / i capelli come
fosse sempre spettinata, / e poi tutto quel nervoso. Troppo diversa. // E
invece no, piano piano, / senza che me n'accorgessi, s'è ingrossata, / adesso
nel camminare quasi tremola, / ha preso anche il suo fare, /a vederela da
dietro è lei sputata, / poi la voce, persino il modo di parlare, / è tutta
quell'ignorante di sua madre, / la Sina, che me la ricordo, / quando ci trovò
quella sera / nel magazzino, in fondo, tra le balle / del baccalà, e si mise a
piangere. /

for more than a week I was on top of her,
always said yes to make her happy,
keeping one eye on the door.
Outside, it was a different thing all together,

a wave to her father,
who was something of an oddball,
he was always off by himself, always quiet,
he didn't even wave back,
always sitting there cleaning his double-barrelled shotgun.

ch'a la ò véuda madòs piò d'una stmèna.
Mè a géva sémpra ad sè par cuntantèla,
mo a guardéva la pórta,
fura dla porta, dop, l'era un èlt zcòurs,

salvo par e' su bà,
ch' l'era un tip un pó strambal,
e' stéva par còunt sóvv, sémpra da zétt,
u n salutéva gnénca,
e l'era sémpra dri a puléi la s-ciòpa.

Io mi strofinavo le dita sotto il naso / e dicevo sempre di sí, / che invece era
da scopiar dal ridere, / fra tutto quel baccalà, c'era una puzza, / baccalà e
aringhe, / che l'ho avuto addosso piú di una settimana. / Io dicevo sempre
di sí per accontentarla, / ma guardavo la porta, / fuori della porta, dopo, era
un altro discorso, // salvo per suo padre, / che era un tipo un po' strambo,
/ stava per conto suo, sempre zitto, / non salutava neanche, / ed era sempre
dietro a pulire la doppietta.

The Wife

At my age, I'm giving them a good laugh? Let them talk.
I'm fifty-five years old, she's twenty-three.
She's brand new. She hasn't got a single wrinkle,
Sometimes I'm there watching her
like some kind of idiot, she's mine,
and I start to tremble all over.
They're also saying that I've lost my mind.
It's a nice place to be, losing your mind,
you never want to leave, but they don't know,
they've never seen Loredana naked
on the bed, eyes closed, hands in her hair,
playing with the curls in that half-light,
in the afternoon, with the blinds slightly opened,
and up above on the ceiling a shadow moving.
They haven't seen her sleeping, when she's hot,
with that veil of sweat that looks like frost.
I'm giving them all a good laugh? It makes me cry
when she's wrapped herself around me,
that she wants to be with me,
and she touches my face with a hand,

La mòi

A la mi età a faz réid? lasa ch'i dégga.
Mè a n n'ò zinquentazéinch, li vintitréi,
la è nóva, la n'à gnénca una péiga,
dal vólti a stagh alè, férm, a guardèla,
cmè un cuchèl, l'è la méa,
e u m vén da tremè tótt.
I déi ènca ch'a so 'ndè tal bumbòzi,
l'è un bèl pòst, tal bumbòzi, u s'i sta bén,
ta n vrébb vnì véa mai vésta néuda,
se lèt, i ócc céus, al mèni ti cavéll,
ch' la zuga si rézz ad cla mèza luce,
e' dopmezdè, sal persièni, custèdi,
e u su sint sla strèda d'ogni tènt un pas
e te sufétt, d'in èlt, u s móv un'òmbra.
I n la à vésta ch' la dórma, quant la à chèld,
sa che vail ad sudòur ch'e' pèr dla bréina.
A faz réid? mu mè invíci u m vén da piànz
quant a la sint che la s'ataca tótta,
che la vó stè sa mè,
e la m tòcca la faza s'una mèna,

La moglie. Alla mia età faccio ridere? lascia che dicano. / Io ne ho cinquantacinque, lei ventitre, / è nuova, non ha neanche una piega, / delle volte sto lí fermo a guardarla, / come uno scimunito, è la mia, / e mi viene a tremare tutto. / Dicono anche che sono andato in bambola, / è un bel posto, in bambola, ci si sta bene, / non vorresti venir via mai, ma loro non lo conoscono, / la Loredana non l'hanno mai vista nuda, / sul letto, gli occhi chiusi, le mani nei capelli, / che gioca con i riccioli in quella mezza luce, / il pomeriggio, con le persiane accostate, / e sulla strada si sente ogni tanto un passo, / e sul soffitto, in alto, si muove un'ombra. / Non l'hanno vista che dorme, quando ha caldo, / con quel velo di sudore che pare brina. / Faccio ridere? a me invece mi viene da piangere / quando la sento che s'attacca tutta, / che vuol stare con me, / e mi tocca la faccia con una mano, /

101

runs her fingers along my mouth,
my nose, then over the eyes, as if she didn't see.

The only worry is Olga and the girls,
who are both against me.
I love her, Olga, she didn't do a thing to me,
I know it's not her fault,
I don't want to know how it's all going to end up.
Go back? I won't do it. I'll move forward.
but I don't want to hurt her.
I, I didn't want to, and this,
this is the worm gnawing away in my brain,
since that evening with Loredana,
under the porticoes, in Verucchio.
I put a hand on her shoulder
and she put her hand on top of mine.

But every so often I come back,
I want to talk, I don't want to hide anything.
I want her to understand how it happened,
that I love her, but that with the other one it's different.
She's there, I see her, she doesn't want to hear it,
she moves from here to there. She dusts.
She folds laundry. She irons.
I wait a week, then there I am again,

la m caméina sal dàidi da la bòcca
me nès, pu sòura i ócc, cmè ch' la n m'avdéss.

L'ónich pensìr l'è Olga e cal burdèli,
ch'al m'è còuntra tutt' do.
Mè ma l'Olga a ví bén,
la n m'à fat gnént, a l so, u n'è còulpa sóvva,
e cmè ch'la andrà a finí a n'e' ví savài,
turnè indrì a n gne la faz, a vagh avènti,
mo a n vléva fèi da mèl, mè, a n vléva, e quèst
l'è e' tèral ch'u m lavòura te zarvèl
da pu cla sàira che sla Loredana,
sòtta i pórtich, a Vrócc,
a i ò mèss una mèna s'una spala
e li la i à mèss sòura la su mèna.

Mo d'ogni tènt a tòuran,
a ví zcòrr, a n'i ví tnai masèd gnént,
a zirch da fèi capéi cumè ch' la è 'ndèda,
ch'a i ví bén, mo sa cl'èlta l'è divérs.
Li la sta 'lè, a la vèggh, la n vó sintéi,
la va d'in quà e d'in là, la dà la pòrbia,
la móccia i pan, la stéira.
Mè aspétt 'na stmèna, pu a so 'ncòura alè,

mi cammina con le dita dalla bocca / al naso, poi sopra gli occhi, come se
non mi vedesse. // L'unico pensiero è l'Olga e quelle bambine, / che mi
sono contro tutt'e due. / Io all'Olga le voglio bene, / non m'ha fatto niente,
lo so, non è colpa sua, / e come andrà a finire non lo voglio sapere, / tornare
indietro non ce la faccio, vado avanti, / ma non volevo farle del male, io, non
volevo, e questo / è il tarlo che mi lavoro nel cervello / da quella sera che
con la Loredana, / sotto i portici, a Verucchio, / le ho messo una mano sulla
spalla, / e lei ci ha messo sopra la sua mano. // Ma ogni tanto torno, /
voglio parlare, non le voglio tener nascosto niente, / cerco di farle capire
com'è andata, / che le voglio bene, ma che con quell'altra è diverso. / Lei sta
lí, la vedo, non vuol sentire, / va in qua e in là, dà la polvere, / ammucchia
i panni, stira. / Io aspetto una settimana, poi sono ancora lí, /

and I start to talk. She sits on the couch
sewing buttons back on a pillowcase,
but every once in awhile she lifts her head
and gives me a look like a bolt of lightening.
What does she want me to say?
I only see eyes that have deep shadows,
a wrinkled, flowered skirt,
a bulky red sweater, a gold necklace,
even her hands are red, they say nothing,
and the wedding ring has blackened the space between her fingers.
I argue, I state my case, I lose my train of thought.
She's quiet. At least if she would shout,
cry, take what's in her hands and throw it at me,
but no, she threads the needle,
fumbles around in the sewing basket for buttons,
and I start screaming, but to myself,
why didn't you ever spread out naked
in front of me? I bite my tongue,
I would only make her cry,
she can't understand, and now it's just too late.

e avènti a zcòrr, li la sta sla tumèna,
la taca di butéun m'una fudrètta,
mo d'ogni tènt u i vén d'alzè la testa
e la m dà dagli ucèdi cmè saètti.
Cs'èll ch' la m vó déi? mè a vèggh sno du ócc pést,
una sutèna spigazéda, a fiéur,
e' maiòun ròss, la culanina d'ór,
ènca al mèni, la n s dà gnént, la gli à ròssi,
e la varghètta la i fa e' nir tra 'l dàidi.

Mè a ragiòun, a ragiòun, a pérd e' féil,
li sémpra zétta, emènch che la rugéss,
ch' la pianzéss, ch' la m tiréss quèll ch' la à tal mèni,
mo no, la péunta l'ègh,
la smèsa tla cassètta di butéun,
e u m vén da rógg mu mè:
parchè tè ta n t si mai spuièda néuda
davènti mè? mo a m dagh ad mórs ti labar,
a la farébb sno piànz,
la n pò capéi,
                    e pu ormai l'è trop tèrd.

e avanti a parlare, lei sta sul divano, / attacca dei bottoni a una federa, / ma ogni tanto le viene da alzare la testa / e mi dà delle occhiate come saette. / Cosa mi vuol dire? io vedo sole due occhi pesti, / una sottana spiegazzata, a fiori, / il maglione rosso, la collanina d'oro, / anche le mani, non si dà niente, le ha rosse, / e la vera le fa il nero fra le dita. // Io ragiono, ragiono, perdo il filo, / lei sempre zitta, almeno urlasse, / piangesse, mi tirasse quel che ha nelle mani, / ma no, punta l'ago, / fruga nella cassetta dei bottoni, / e mi vieni da urlare a me: perché non ti sei mai spogliata nuda / davanti a me? ma mi mordo le labbra, / la farei solo piangere, / non può capire, – e poi ormai è troppo tardi.

Nothing

He living seventy-one years without doing a thing
because he married
Oreste Matassoni's sister.
All he had to do was sign the papers
witness the will
and keep quiet.
But he didn't put on any airs.
He'd come and go, he'd stop to talk.
He'd walk around carrying plastic shopping bags,
he'd play rummy, even with us.

And he didn't feel like he was useless,
he didn't concoct something to do
just to give the day some color,
just so they wouldn't say he thought he was better than
everyone else.
But he didn't laugh that much. He was always serious
in a way that made it seem
like he always had a lot of things to be concerned about.

His wife brought three or four fields,
and a house at the sea.
The house on the road
was his. That was his.
And he even had a free train pass

Gnént

L'à campè stentún an senza fè gnént
parchè l'éva spusè
la surèla d'Oreste Matassoni.
L'éva sno da firmé sòtta dal chèrti,
da fè da testimóni, da stè zétt.
Mo u s déva dl'impurtènza,
l'andéva, e' vnéva, u s'afarméva a zcòrr,
e' camiéva s'un scartòz tal mèni,
e' zughéva a ramino ènca sa néun.

E u n s sintéva 'd di piò,
u n s'inzgnéva 'd fè quèl
par dè culòur me témp,
pòsta ch'i n géss ch' l'éva tach sò e' capèl.
Però e' ridéva póch, e' stéva séri,
in módi ch'e' pareva
cumè se l'avéss sémpra un gran dafè.

La mòi la i éva pórt tri quatar fónd
e una vélla a maréina.
La chèsa se stradòun
l'era la sóvva ad léu. E l'éva ènca
e' permanent se treno

Niente. Ha campato settantun'anni senza far niente / perché aveva sposato / la sorella di Oreste Matassoni. / Aveva sola da firmare sotto delle carte, / da far da testimone, da star zitto. / Ma non si dava importanza, / andava, veniva, si fermava a parlare, / camminava con un cartoccio nelle mani, / giocava a ramino anche con noi. // E non si sentiva inutile, / non ingegnava di far qualcosa / per dar colore al tempo, / perché non dicessero che aveva attaccato il cappello. / Però rideva poco, stava serio, / in modo che pareva / come se avesse sempre un gran da fare. // La moglie gli aveva portato tre quattro fondi / e una villa al mare. / La casa sullo stradone / era la sua, di lui. E aveva anche / il permanente sul treno /

which was hard to understand
because the thing of it is
he didn't like to travel.
He never budged.
He'd go hunting often,
fishing too.
He had a hound that was a real beauty.
But what he bragged about were his teeth,
he'd open his mouth wide,
run his tongue across his teeth,
he could chew as well as a horse with those teeth,
he'd say that he still had all of them,
that they never hurt,
it seemed like with all those teeth
he would never die.

And with the dying, too, that didn't give him much difficulty
either.
He died in his sleep.
One morning, his wife
was supposed to wake him up before nine
to go to the tailor. It didn't happen.
     He'd passed away
     who knows,
     in a dream,
     and still doesn't know he's dead.

ch'u n putú capéi mai e' parchè,
e de rest ad viazè u n'i pieséva,
u n s'è mai mòs. L'andéva a caza spèss,
ènca a pischè.
L'aveva un brach che l'era una belèzza.
Mo quèll che léu u s stiméva l'era i dint,
e' slarghéva la bòcca,
l'andéva in zéir sla lèngua,
e' mastighéva sècch cumè un cavàl,
e' géva ch'u i avéva ancòura tótt,
ch'i n gn'era mai duléu,
e' pareva cmè se sa tótt chi dint
u n duvéss murí mai.

Che pu ènca a muréi
l'à fat póca fadéiga.
L'è mort te sònn. La su mòi 'na matéina
la l duvéva svigé prima dal nóv
par andè de sartòur. La n gne la à fata.
Léu l'era pas adlà,
chi lo sa, t'un insógni.
E u n sa ancòura ch' l'è mort.

che non s'è mai potuto capire perché, / e del resto viaggiare non gli piaceva, / non s'è mai mosso. Andava spesso a caccia, / anche a pescare. / Aveva un bracco che era una bellezza. / Ma quello di cui si vantava erano i denti, / allargava la bocca, / andava in giro con la lingua, / masticava secco come un cavallo, / diceva che li aveva ancora tutti, / che non gli erano mai doluti, / pareva come se con tutti quei denti / non dovesse morire mai. / / Che poi anche a morire / ha fatto poca fatica. / È morto nel sonno. Sua moglie una mattina / lo doveva svegliare prima delle nove / per andare dal sarto. Non ce l'ha fatta. / Era passato di là, / chi lo sa, in un sogno. / E non sa ancora ch'è morto.

Night Swim

It was an evening in July, with a yellow moon,
we were at Passeggio, and we got the urge
to go swimming.
Half an hour later we had already crossed over the tracks
at the old station,
we were pedaling quietly surrounded by crickets
until a toad
crossed the road in front of Lidia
and she let out a yell,
all the lights went on in a peasant's house.
We passed la Torre, then Bordonchio,
and from there went straight all the way to Castellabate
where there wasn't a soul.
Our bicycles skidded in the sand,
pedals in the air,
the water was immense,
clear and black as tar,
the waves rolled,
slowly, in a whisper,
and were warm around our feet.

È bagn ad nòta

L'è stè una sàira ad lói, sla léuna zala,
a sérmi me Pasègg, u s'è vnú vòia
d'andè a fè e' bagn.
Mez'òura dop a pasémmi zà al sbari
dla staziòun vècia,
a pedalémmi da zétt framèza i gréll,
fintènt che un bòtal
l'à travarsè la strèda ma la Lidia
e li la à fat un rógg
che m'una chèsa ad cuntadéin
i à zais la luce.
A sémm pas par la Tòrra, pu a Burdòuncia,
e da 'lè drétt fina Castelabèt,
dvò ch'u n gn'era niseun.
Al biciclètti agli è sguilé tla sabia
si pedèl pr'aria,
l'aqua la era granda,
lócida e nira cmè ch'e' fóss catràm,
agli òndi al s'arugléva
pièn, t'un susórr,
e al s'arivéva tévdi fina i pi.

Il bagno di notte. È stato una sera di luglio, con la luna gialla, / eravamo al Passeggio, c'è venuta voglia / d'andare a fare il bagno. / Mezz'ora dopo passavamo già le sbarre / della stazione vecchia, / pedalavamo zitti in mezzo ai grilli, / finché un rospo / ha attraversato la strada alla Lidia / e lei ha fatto un urlo / che a una casa di contadini / hanno acceso la luce. / Siamo passati per la Torre, poi a Bordonchio, / e da lí dritto sino a Castellabate, / dove non c'era nessuno. / Le biciclette sono scivolate nella sabbia / con i pedali in aria, / l'acqua era grande, / lucida e nera come fosse catrame, / le onde rotolavano / piano, in un sussurro, / e ci arrivavano tiepide fino ai piedi. /

Then we scattered
among the tamarisks and in the gullies to get undressed,
it didn't take long, Ghigo whistled
and everyone started running
but in the moonlight, I thought I was seeing,
and the others saw it too,
we stood there looking at her
with our mouths hanging open,
Daria, who was running, completely naked,
like a crazy girl,
she ran right through the middle and didn't see us,
on top of it all she wasn't wearing her glasses,
but that wasn't the reason,
she entered the water
in a storm of splashing,
she was still running, then she turned around,
she waved,
and laughed, we started to laugh too,
but we stayed right where we were
and then she was swimming,
she was swimming hard,
she had made it well past the first drop-off.

Dop a s sémm sparguié
tra i tamaréisgh e al béusi par spuiès,
u i è vlú póch, Ghigo l'à fat un fés-ci
e l'è stè tótt un córr,
mo me léun 'd léuna mè u m'è pèrs d'avdài,
e i la à vésta ènca ch'ilt,
e a s sémm férm a guardèla
cumè di bucaléun,
la Daria ch' la curéva tótta néuda,
la pareva una mata,
la s'è pasa te mèza a la n s'avdéva,
ènca parchè la era senza ucèl,
mo u n gn'impurtéva gnént,
la è éintra tl'aqua
t'una tempesta ad squézz,
la à chéurs ancòura, pu la s'è 'rvólta indrí,
la à fat un sègn sal mèni
e la rideva, neun a s sémm mèss a réid
ènca neun, mo a stémmi sempra alè,
e li ormai la nudéva,
la andéva fórt,
la era bèla piò in là dla prima fosa.

Dopo ci siamo sparsi / fra i tamerischi e le buche per spogliarci, c'è voluto
poco, Ghigo ha fatto un fischio / ed è stato tutto un correre, / ma al lume
della luna a me m'è parso di vedere, / e l'hanno vista anche gli altri, / e ci
siamo fermati a guardarla / come dei boccaloni, / la Daria che correva tutta
nuda, / pareva una matta, / c'è passata in mezzo e non ci vedeva, / anche
perché era senza occhiali, / ma non le importava niente, / è entrata
nell'acqua / in una tempesta di spruzzi, / ha corso ancora, poi s'è voltata
indietro, / ha fatto un segno con le mani / e rideva, ci siamo messi a ridere
/ anche noi, ma stavamo sempre lí, / e lei ormai nuotava, / andava forte, /
era già oltre la prima fossa.

An Eye on Things

Signor Leo goes almost every day
to see Veglio Betti in his shop.
If the weather's good he sits by the door
with his hands crossed on top of his cane,
he chats a little or is quiet.
He's got sunglasses for bright days and sometimes
he brings along the newspaper.
He goes there to have some company,
he and Veglio's father were pals from the time they were young,
and also because four years ago he lent Veglio
twelve million to buy the building.
It's not that he gets on his back about it, that he says anything at all,
he just comes to keep an eye on things.

L'ucèda

E' sgnòr Leo e' va guèsi tótt i dè
a truvè Veglio 'd Betti tla butàiga.
Se e' témp l'è bón u s mètt disdài sla pórta,
e' tén al mèni incrusèdi se bastòun,
e' fa do ciacri o e' sta zétt.
Pr'e' sòul l'à i ucèl nir e u i è dal vólti
ch'u s pórta dri e' giurnèl.
E' va 'lè par stè un pó in cumpagnéa,
se bà 'd Veglio da zóvan i era améigh,
e énca parchè ma Véglio quatr'an fa
u i à imprèst dògg migliéun par cumprè i méur.
Mo u n'è ch'u i stàga adòs, ch'e' dégga gnént.
E' vén a dè un'ucèda.

L'occhiata. Il signor Leo va quasi tutti giorni / a trovare Velio Betti in
bottega. / Se il tempo è buono si mette a sedere sulla porta, / tiene le mani
incrociate sul bastone, / fa due chiacchiere o sta zitto. / Per il sole ha gli
occhiali neri e certe volte / si porta dietro il giornale. / Va lí per stare un po'
in compagnia, / lui e il babbo di Velio da giovani erano amici, / e anche
perché a Velio quattro anni fa / ha prestato dodici milioni per comprare i
muri. / Ma non è che gli stia addosso, che dica niente. / Viene a dare
un'occhiata.

In the Shop

He always asked me: "And you, aren't you tired yet?"
I don't follow, and I say to him, "Of what Fafin?"
he'd stand there shaking his head and then he'd laugh:
"You, Mario, you see, have a great deal of patience."
I laughed too, but for the sake of playing along:
"If patience was all you needed for the bills!"

Yesterday afternoon they found him in the shop.
His brother-in-law opened up.
He'd put a rifle,
from what can be gathered, underneath his chin
and he shot it off.

They were zero-gauge pellets, they mangled him.
Some of the matter was still in his hat.

Tla butàiga

U m géva sémpra: "Ta n t si ancòura stóff?"
e mè a n capéva, a i géva: "Ad chè, Fafin?"
leu e' sculéva la testa e pu e' rideva:
"Tè, vitti, Mario, t'é una gran pazinzia".
A rideva ènca mè, mo un pó a cardénza:
"S'e' bastéss la pazinzia pr'al cambièli!"

Ir dopmezdè i l'à tróv céus tla butàiga.
L'à vért e' su cugnèd.
U s'era mèss la s-ciòpa,
da quèll ch'u s'è capéi, sòtta e' barbètt.

L'era paléin de zero, i s l'è magnè.
Un pó 'd roba la è 'rvènza te capèl.

Nella bottega. Mi diceva sempre: "Non ti sei ancora stufato? " / e io non capivo, gli dicevo: "Di che, Fafin?" / lui scuoteva la testa e poi rideva: / "Tu, Mario, vedi, hai una gran pazienza". / Ridevo anch'io, ma un po' a credenza: / "Se bastasse la pazienza per le cambiali!" / / Ieri pomeriggio l'hanno trovato nella bottega. / Ha aperto suo cognato. / S'era messo il fucile, / da quel che s'è capito, sotto il mento. / E ha tirato. // Erano pallini dello zero, se lo sono mangiato. / Un po' di roba è rimasta nel cappello.

117

The Will

You could tell she felt it coming.
Tuesday morning she called Elvira
and had her write down on a piece of paper
a whole long list:
three hundred to Aurora
for a head of lettuce
and a half kilo of oranges,
fourteen hundred to the guy from Forlì
for kerosene, nine hundred to Bréina
for artichoke oil
six hundred to Ofelia
for needles, two spools, mothballs,
four hundred twenty-five to Rafaél
for candlesticks and a votive candle.
And then Thursday the attack,
she called out, mama,
and died in an instant like a fledgling sparrow.

È testament

U s vaid ch' la s la sintéva.
E' mèrt matéina la a ciamè l'Elvira
e la i à fat mètt zò s'un fòi ad chèrta
tótt' una lésta:
trezént frénch ma l'Aurora
pr'un casp ad insalèda
e mèz chéll 'd melarènzi,
melaquatarzént frènch me Furlivàis
pr'e' cherosene, novzént frènch ma Bréina
par l'óli di scarcióffal,
sizént frénch ma l'Oféglia
pr'agli èghi, du ruchétt, la naftalina,
quatarzentvintzínch frènch ma Rafaél
pr'al candàili e un luméin.
E pu zóbia u i à ciap un sèra sèra,
la à détt: oh mama!
e la è mórta t'un sbréss cmè un pasaròt.

Il testamento. Si vede che se la sentiva. / Il martedí ha chiamato l'Elvira / e le
ha fatto metter giú su un foglio di carta / tutta una lista: / trecento lire
all'Aurora / per un cespo d'insalata / e mezzo chilo di arance, / millequat-
trocento lire al Forlivese / per il cherosene, novecento lire a Bréina / per
l'olio dei carciofi, / seicento lire all'Ofelia / per gli aghi, due rocchetti, la
naftalina, / quattrocentoventicinque lire a Raffaele / per le candele e un
lumino. / E poi giovedí le ha preso un serra serra, / ha detto: oh, mamma!
ed è morta in un soffio come un passerotto.

119

Yarn

They can never do anything the easy way,
to get out a little bit of yarn,
they mess up two or three balls.
Who got into it?
Just look at all that stuff, what did they do?
everything's upside down,
I'd like to see you here now fixing it
and that one upstairs, grumbling.
Where do you start?
it's all one big snarl,
one big tangle, and full of knots to boot,
you'd have to have fingernails like Libero the barber,
then with this cold, you can't even feel your fingers anymore,
you could use your teeth, but the front ones,
two or three of them are loose,
no, the only way is to go at it is with patience,
spread it all out on the floor,
make the loops bigger, the yarns that are twisted,
and work on one end, the only thing is, it's dark down here,

La sparzéina

I n'è bón da fè un pchè ch l'apa grèzia,
par tó un pó 'd sparzéina,
i à guàst du tri ghéffal chi è l'è stè?
vè ch' roba, mo cma s fal? u n s cnòss piò gnént,
aquè 'dès a t ví vdai rimidiéla,
e cl'èlt ad sòura ch'e' ragna.
Da dò t ravéi? l'è tótt un smanadézz,
tótt un invrócc, l'è 'nca pin 'd néud, marébb
avài agli óngi ad Libero e' barbír,
pu sa sté frèdd a n sint gnénca piò al dàidi,
u s putrébb fè si dint, mo quéi davènti
a n n'ò du tréi ch'i zóccla,
no, l'ónica l'è mèttsi sa pazinzia,
sparguié tótt par tèra,
slarghè al nasètti, i féil incavalèd,
e fès d'un chèv, sno ch' l'è un schéur aquè 'd sòtta,
u i è che finistréin, 'lasò d'in èlt,
mo u s'i è ròtt tótt i véidar e i i à mèss
di gran pézz ad cartòun,
e t'é vòia a smaiè, t'é vòia a stènd,

Il refe. Non son capaci di fare un peccato con grazia, / per prendere un po'
di refe / hanno guastato due tre gomitoli, che è stato? / ve' che roba, ma
come si fa? non si capisce piú niente, / qui adesso ti voglio vedere a
rimediarla, / e quell'altro di sopra che rogna. / Da dove cominci? è tutto un
arruffio, / tutto un viluppo, è anche pieno di nodi, bisognerebbe / avere le
unghie di Libero il barbiere, / poi con questo freddo non sento neanche piú
le dita, / si potrebbe fare con i denti, ma quelli davanti / ne ho due tre che
dondolano, / no, l'unica è mettersi con pazienza, / sparpagliare tutto per
terra, / allargare i cappi, i fili accavallati, / e farsi da un capo, solo che è un
buio qui di sotto, / c'è quel finestrino lassú in alto, / ma gli si son rotti tutti
i vetri e ci hanno messo / dei gran pezzi di cartone, / e hai voglia a smagliare,
hai voglia a stendere, /

there's that little window there up above,
but all the glass got broken and they put up
some big pieces of cardboard,
and there's no way to unravel it, there's no way to stretch it out,
I've almost covered the whole floor,
not counting the wads, and there's still more,
I'm beginning to suspect
it's not just a matter of two or three balls, this is what happens
when you're working away,
you're there untangling one big knot, the yarn
feels like it's giving, you go under,
over, then under, you pick it up again,
you see where you're going with it,
progress, but you don't pay attention to where you've put your
[feet,
you drag in an end that you've already untangled,
you make a big jumble of it, tangle it more than it was at the
[beginning,
and when you realize it, you just want to eat all that yarn,
that's enough, damn it all anyway, here's where you go crazy,
I wasn't even the one who made this whole big mess,
you fix it.

ò bèla cvért ma tèra,
senza cuntè i palótt, e u n gne n'è 'ncòura,
e mè u m vén e' suspèt
ch'u n séa mèl 'd du tri ghéffal, pu u t suzéd
quant t si 'lè che t lavòur,
che t sté par s-ciòi tótt un patòun, e' féil
t sint ch'e' zéd, ta i vé dri,
ta l pas sòura, pu sòtta, ta l'arciàp,
t vaid dò ch'e' va a finéi,
t vé 'vènti, mo ta n bèd dò t mètt i pi,
t strascéin un chèv ch' ta l'évi za svrucé,
ta l'amócc, ta l'imbròi piò ca nè préima,
e quante ta t n'incórz,
u t vén vòia 'd magnètla cla sparzéina,
basta, porca putèna, aquè a dvént mat,
ch'a n so gnénca stè mè a fè sté caséin,
arangév. Pu la t pasa,
e ciapèla cm'e' fóss un badalócch?
in fònd aquè u i vó sno de témp, e témp
u i n'è, u n t dà dri niseun, t bótt l'òc ma tèra,
ècco, l'è sa sté chèv ch'a m so freghè,
spetta, alà però l'è piò rèd, t'artàch,

ho quasi coperto per terra, / senza contare i batufoli, e ce n'è ancora, / e a
me mi viene il sospetto / che non sia affare di due tre gomitoli, poi ti succede
/ quando sei dietro a lavorare, / che stai per sciogliere tutto un groviglio, il
filo / senti che cede, gli vai dietro, / lo passi sopra, poi sotto, lo riprendi, /
vedi dove va a finire, / vai avanti, ma non badi a dove metti i piedi, / trascini
un capo che avevi già districato, / l'ammucchi, l'imbrogli piú di prima, / e
quando te n'accorgi, / ti vien voglia di mangiartelo quel refe, / basta, porca
puttana, qui divento matto, / che non sono nemmeno stato io a fare 'sto
casino, / arrangiatevi. Poi ti passa, / e prenderla come fosse un badalucco?
/ in fondo, qui ci vuole solo del tempo, e tempo / ce n'è, non t'insegue
nessuno, butti l'occhio a terra, / ecco, è con questo capo che mi sono
fregato, / aspetta, là però è piú rado, ricominci, /

Then you calm down,
and if you just treated it like it's a little pastime?
after all, what you need here is just time, and time
I've got, no one's chasing after you to do it, stare down at it,
there, I screwed up this end.
wait, it's looser there, you start over,
you really get going, you're starting to enjoy it,
you could be doing needlework,
fine, but even if it's needlework, how much more can there be?
wherever you look, there's yarn,
you're there with your arms hanging, your head lowered,
dead end, oh come on now, you're never going to finish.
The point is this though, if you think about it,
this is what happens with whatever you do, there are ups and
[downs,
today you're doing just fine, tomorrow you're stuck,
the day after that you've got the world by the tail,
the next day you're throwing the chair against a wall.
The chair. If it were a chair,
the caning would be shot, the legs would creak,
it's not sturdy, you could get hurt.
And just look at what I've gotten myself into,
hunched over for hours and hours, I'll wreck my back,
and when I stand up, it feels like I'm drunk.
I must really be an idiot, things,

ta t'arschèld, ta i ciap góst,
u t pèr da fè un richèm,
sno che richèma pò, mo quant u i n'è?
dò che t guèrd l'è sparzéina,
t sté 'lè, brazi spandléun, a testa basa,
gnént, aqué, mo va là, u n s finéss piò.
Ch' l'è un zcòurs, però, s' ta i péns,
l'è 'csè d' tótt i lavéur, l'è di èlt e bas,
òz la va bén, admèn t si incarugnéid,
e' dé dop t dmand se Roma la è da vènd,
cl'èlt dè t téir la scaràna còuntra e' méur.
La scaràna. Ch'e' fóss una scaràna,
la pivira la è 'ndèda, al gambi al scrécca,
u n gn'è méggh' da fidés, u i è da fès mèl.
Mo vèrda ad che lavòur ch'a m so 'ndè mètt,
òuri e òuri cuvéun, ch'a m ròmp la schéina,
e quant a stagh sò, u m pèr d'ès imbariègh,
a sarò pò un pataca, mè tal robi
a m'i bótt, a m'adàn, a n so cuntént
fintènt ch'a n mu n li so cavè dal mèni,
ch' l'è un sbai, al robi, s' ta t'incapunéss,
t n'armédi gnént, bsògna nu pensèi trop,
ciapèli sòtta gamba, t'un zért séns

ti accalori, ci prendi gusto, / ti pare di fare un ricamo, / solo che ricama pure,
ma quanto ce n'è? / dove guardi è refe, / stai lí, braccia penzoloni, a testa bassa,
/ niente, qui ma va' là, non si finisce piú. / Che è un discorso, però, se ci pensi,
/ è cosí in tutti i lavori, sono degli alti e bassi, / oggi va bene, domani sei
incarognito, / il giorno dopo domandi se Roma è da vendere, / l'altro giorno
tiri la sedia contro il muro. / La sedia. Fosse una sedia, / l'impagliatura è
andata, le gambe scricchiolano, / non c'è mica da fidarsi, c'è da farsi male. / Ma
guarda in che impresa mi sono andato a cacciare, / ore e ore chinato, che mi
rompo la schiena, / e quando mi alzo, mi pare d'essere ubriaco, / sarò pure un
coglione, io nelle cose / mi ci butto, mi ci danno, non sono contento / finché
non me le sono cavate dalle mani, / che è uno sbaglio, le cose, se t'incaponisci,
/ non rimedi niente, bisogna non pensarci troppo, / prenderle sotto gamba,
in un certo senso /

I throw myself in, they take me over, I'm not happy
until I'm finished
which is a mistake, with things, if you dig in your heels,
you don't get anything out if it, it's best not to think about them
[too much,
it's better to play them down a little, in a way,
let them work themselves out
you get less tired out and they turn out better.
It's just that I'm thinking about the guy upstairs too,
the one, who can figure him out,
because this yarn
however you want to think about it, it's going to be put back in
[order,
all these balls of yarn are going to be rewound, even
all these tangles, but the best would be
to reach up to that little window up there,
I've been thinking about this awhile now,
pull down the cardboard, cut it up,
then make some spools, wrap it around them,
you'll end up with a ball of yarn with a hole in the middle
which is better than just one big ball.
Except that, nothing changes, just try to talk with him,
with him you never know, it depends on the day,
if some morning he gets up with a bee up his ass,
it seems like I can hear him, he's scratching his neck a little,
he looks at you with the whites of his eyes over his glasses.
"What's with all this yarn? and do what with it?"

agli à d'avnéi 'd su pi,
t fadéigh mènch e al vén mèi.
L'è che mè a péns ènca ma cl'èlt ad sòura,
che quèll, val a capéi,
parchè què sta sparzéina,
ciapla cmè t vu, mo la va radanèda,
e' va 'rfat tótt i ghéffal, o magari
dal matasi, mo e' masum e' sarébb
putài rivé 'lasò me finistréin,
l'è un pó ch'a i péns, tó zò i cartéun, taièi,
pu t fé di rudal, ta glia invrócc datònda,
e' vén dal bóbbli, ch'agli è mèi di ghéffal.
Sno ch'a sémm sempra alè, va a zcòrr sa léu,
che léu, ta n'e' sé mai, sgònd la zurnèda,
se cla matéina l'è stè sò a cul drétt,
u m pèr d' sintéil, u s grata un pó la còppa,
u t guèrda sa chi ócc biènch sòura i ucèl:
"Mo cs'èll tótt sta sparzéina? da fè chè?"

devono venir fuori da sole, / fatichi meno e vengono meglio. / È che io
penso anche a quell'altro di sopra, / che quello, vallo a capire, / perché qui
questo refe, / prendila come vuoi, ma va rimesso in ordine, / vanno rifatti
tutti i gomitoli, o magari / delle matasse, ma il massimo sarebbe / poter
arrivare lassú al finestrino, / è un po' che ci penso, tirar giú i cartoni, tagliarli,
/ poi fai dei rotoli, e glielo avvolgi attorno, / vengono dei gomitoli bucati,
che sono meglio di quelli tondi. / Solo che, siamo sempre lí, va' a parlare con
lui, / che lui, non lo sai mai, secondo la giornata, / se quella mattina s'è
alzato a culo dritto, / mi pare di sentirlo, si gratta un po' la nuca, / ti guarda
con quegli occhi bianchi sopra gli occhiali: / "Ma cos'è tutto questo refe? da
far che?"

Fussbudget

Someone that fussy I've never met.
He'd be there all day washing his hands.
He'd hold the handle of the coffee cup
away from his face, across from his nose,
he'd drink from where nobody else did.
In summer, he always used
a straw for his orange drink.
And God forbid if the glasses got switched
at a crowded party,
everything disgusted him,
his spoon fell on the floor
one New Year's Eve,
and he left half the zupp'inglese uneaten.
He wouldn't shake anybody's hand,
he always stood apart from people,
and if someone got all worked up,
talking, and got too close,
and maybe spat a little,
he'd pass his hand over his face,
like he wasn't aware he was doing it,
like you'd scratch your beard,
and then, his hand
would stop and open underneath his nose

Spulicréd

Éun acsè spulicréd a n l'ò mai vést.
Tótt e' dè l'era dri a lavès al mèni.
E' tnéva e' mangh dla taza de cafè
vérs d'in èlt, drétt me nès,
e' bivéva dvò ch'u n bivéa niseun.
D'instèda l'aranciata
u la tuléva sémpra sla paiètta.
E ènca tal giuvàchi
guai a sbaiè 'd bicír,
léu l'era schiv ad tótt, un éultum dl'an,
ch'u i era casch ma tèra e cuciaréin,
l'à las alè a mità la sopinglàisa.
U n strinzéva la mèna ma niseun,
sla zénta e' stéva sémpra un pó dalòngh,
e quante qualcadéun u s'arscaldéva
te dizcòrr e u i avnéva trop davséin,
e par di piò magari
e' spudacéva un pó,
léu u s striséva la faza s'una mèna,
cmè non volénd, cmè ch'u s gratéss la bèrba,
e pu invíci la mèna
u s la farméva vérta sòtta e' nès,

Schifiltoso. Uno cosí schifiltoso non l'ho mai visto. / Tutto il giorno era dietro
a lavarsi le mani. / Teneva il manico della tazza del caffè / verso l'alto, dritto
al naso, / beveva dove non beveva nessuno. / D'estate l'aranciata / la
prendeva sempre con la cannuccia. / E anche nelle baldorie / guai a sbagliare
bicchiere, / aveva schifo di tutti, un ultimo dell'anno, / che gli era caduto per
terra il cucchiaino, / ha lasciato lí a metà la zuppa inglese. / Non stringeva
la mano a nessuno, / con la gente stava sempre un po' lontano, / e quando
qualcuno si riscaldava / nel parlare e gli veniva troppo vicino, / e per di piú
magari / sputacchiava un po', / lui si strisciava una mano sulla faccia, / come
non volendo, come se si grattasse la barba, / e poi invece la mano / se la
fermava aperta sotto il naso, /

against his mouth.
And sitting down
on a warm chair
where someone else had just gotten up?
he rather keep standing.
On a train,
he never touched anything,
coming down the steps
he'd press the handrail with two fingers.
Every once in awhile he'd have his head shaved
so his hair would grow back thicker
but also because hair was a receptacle
for dust, dirt and microbes.
He was always afraid of infections
of getting some illness, that he'd catch something.
He often cited the example of Tina Ziol', who as a girl
scratched a pimple with dirty hands until it bled,
three days later she spiked a fever
and there was nothing they could do.
As far as a dog, never once
did he pet one,
they never once saw him lick a stamp in the shop.

còuntra la bòcca.
Che nè mèttsi disdài
s'una scaràna chèlda
che l'era stè sò 'lòura qualcadéun
u s tuléva piotòst da stè d'impí.
Quant e' viazéa se treno
u n tuchéva mai gnént, e te smuntè
u s ciapéva me mènfar sa do dàidi.
D'ogni tènt u s faséva tusè plèd
par rinfurzè i cavéll,
mo ènca parchè i cavéll l'éra un ardótt
'd pòrbia, 'd spurchèra, 'd microbi.
L'éva sémpra paéura dagli infeziòun,
ad ciapè al malatéi, ch'i gli atachéss.
E' numinéva spèss la Tina ad Zioli
che da burdlàza
te gratès un zgagnúl sal mèni spórchi
la s'era fata vní e' sangh
e tri dè dop la éva quarènta ad févra
e u n gn'è stè gnént da fè.
M'un chèn u n gn'à mai fat una carèzza,
te spazi i n l'à mai vést liché un frencbòll.
L'era sémpra puléid,

contro la bocca. / Che mettersi a sedere/ su una sedia calda / da cui s'era
appena alzato qualcuno / preferiva piuttosto stare in piedi. / Quando
viaggiava in treno / non toccava mai niente, e nello scendere / si prendeva
alla maniglia con due dita. / Ogni tanto si faceva rapare a zero / per
rinforzare i capelli, / ma anche perché i capelli erano un ricetto / di polvere,
di porcheria, di microbi. / Aveva sempre paura delle infezioni, / di prendere
le malattie, che gliele attaccassero. / Nominava spesso la Tina di Zioli / che
da ragazza / nel grattarsi un foruncolo con le mani sporche / s'era fatta
venire il sangue / e tre giorni dopo aveva quaranta di febbre / e non c'è stato
niente da fare. / A un cane non ha mai fatto una carezza, / nello spaccio non
l'hanno mai visto leccare un francobollo. / Era sempre pulito, /

He was always clean, slightly perfumed,
because perfume, after all, disinfects.

And over time people got the message,
they didn't go near him,
the barber had a razor set aside for him,
nobody asked to borrow his newspaper.
But it wasn't enough. He died of T.B at thirty.

ènca un pó profuméd,
parchè e' parfómm in fònd e' disinfèta.

E se témp pu la zénta i à capéi,
i n'i stéva tachèd,
e' barbír l'éva un raséur snò par léu,
i n'i dmandéva in prèst gnénca e' giurnèl.
Mo u n'è bastè. L'è mórt téisgh a trent'an.

anche un po' profumato, / perché il profumo in fondo disinfetta. // E col
tempo poi la gente ha capito, / non gli stavano vicino, / il barbiere aveva
un rasoio solo per lui, / non gli domandavano in prestito nemmeno il
giornale. / Ma non è bastato. È morto tisico a trent'anni.

Absolution

Father Paolo couldn't see anything up close
and he didn't notice when he stained his clothes
with a splash of broth,
with spaghetti sauce, with caffelatte.
He never brushed his teeth,
there weren't many left,
some of them were just barely hanging on, they were green,
they looked like moss.
Big bunions had grown on his feet
and to give them more room
he'd cut open his shoes.
Father Paolo was old,
the housekeeper Rosina's bones ached,
her mind wasn't clear anymore, she would forget
to heat up his water, to empty the sink.

And kneeling against the wall in that corner
of the sacristy, underneath the picture of the Pope,
when he leaned closer
so he wouldn't have to yell,
telling you to not do it anymore,
and giving you absolution,

L'asoluziòun

Don Pèval u n'andéva da davséin
e u n s'incurzéva
quant ch'u s macéa la vèsta
s'un gòzz 'd bród, se rogò, se cafelàt.
I dént u n s'i era mai lavè,
u i éva rèd,
qualchedéun e' zucléva, i éra véird,
i éva fat cumè un mós-ci.
Ti pi u i era criséu dal gran patèti
e léu per fèi e' pòst
l'aveva taiè al schèrpi.
Don Pèval l'era vèc,
la Rusina u i duléva tótt' agli òsi,
la n gn'era piò sla testa, la s zcurdéva
ad scaldèi l'aqua,
'd rimpéi la caldarètta.

E d'inznòc còuntra e' méur, at che cantòun
dla sagrestéa, sòtta e' ritràt de pèpa,
quant l'avnéva tachèd
pòsta che ta n rugéss,
ch'u t géva d' no fèl piò
e u t déa l'asoluziòun,

L'assoluzione. Don Paolo non vedeva da vicino / e non s'accorgeva / quando si macchiava la veste / con un goccio di brodo, col ragú, col caffelatte. / I denti non se li era mai lavati, / li aveva radi, / qualcuno dondolava, erano verdi, / avevano fatto come un muschio. / Nei piedi gli erano cresciute delle gran patate / e lui per fargli il posto / aveva tagliato le scarpe. / Don Paolo era vecchio, / la Rosina le dolevano tutte le ossa, / non c'era piú con la testa, / si dimenticava di scaldargli l'acqua, / di riempire la bacinella. // E in ginocchio contro il muro, in quel cantone / della sacrestia, sotto il ritratto del papa, / quando veniva vicino / perché non urlassi, / che ti diceva di no farlo piú /

you'd feel lighter,
you'd be in God's grace,
if you died, you'd go to Heaven,
but that grace had a something,
an odor of wine, of socks,
of sweat that was already old,
of sweaters unravelling at the wrists,
of dandruff on the collar.
And if it was summer,
you'd see in the darkness of that sacristy
a ray of sunlight with dust motes dancing around,
and when you went outside
you'd have to close your eyes,
and you'd go into the woods
with its odor of linden trees
or on the big wall where a hint
of sea breeze would hit your face
and from down below, like clockwork,
you'd hear the banging from the ones playing tamburello,
and from above,
around the cornice of the Collegiata,
the screeching of swallows.

ta t sintévi lizír,
t séri in grèzia di Dio, se t murèvi
t'andévi in paradéis,
mo cla grèzia la éva un chè,
un fiè 'd véin, ad calzétt,
ad sudédi ormai vèci,
ad mài sfilazédi tònda i péuls,
ad scaia sòura e' bèvar.
E se l'era d'instèda,
u s'avdéva te schéur dla sagrestéa
un raz ad sòul sla pòrbia ch' la baléva,
e quant t scapévi 'd fura
u t tuchéva céud i ócc,
e t'andévi tla Bósca
sl'udòur ti tigli
o sla Méura ch' l'avnéva da maréina
un pó 'd bura tla faza,
e u t'arivéva da 'd sòtta, cmè un arlózz,
al bòti 'd quéi ch'i zughéva a tamburèl
e da 'd sòura,
datònda e' curnisòun dla Colegèta,
i sgréss dal ròndi.

e ti dava l'assoluzione, / ti sentivi leggero, / eri in grazia di Dio, se morivi /
andavi in paradiso, / ma quella grazia aveva un che, / un odore di vino, di
calze, / di sudate ormai vecchie, / di maglie sfilacciate ai polsi, / di forfora
sul bavero. / E se era d'estate, / si vedeva nel buio della sacrestia / un raggio
di sole con la polvere che ballava, / e quando uscivi all'aperto / dovevi
chiudere gli occhi, e andavi nella Bosca / con l'odore dei tigli / o sulla Mura
dove veniva dal mare un po' di brezza in faccia, / e t'arrivavano da sotto,
come un orologio, / i botti di quelli che giocavano a tamburello / e da sopra,
/ intorno al cornicione della Collegiata, / gli stridi delle rondini.

Hair

Off. He's always been off.
But ever since his hair started falling out
he walks right by
and doesn't say hello to anyone.

I cavéll

Mat, l'è sémpra stè mat.
Mo da quant ch'u i à ravié a caschè i cavéll
e' pasa drétt
e u n saléuta niseun.

I capelli. Matto, è sempre stato matto. / Ma da quando gli sono cominciati a
cadere i capelli / passa dritto / e non saluta nessuno.

The Storm

There was a killer sirocco.
Maria's cat rolled around
in the tiny carnations, she sensed the weather.
Toward Verucchio the clouds had started to be lit up again,
at the sea coast you could see cumulus clouds
the color of ash, the air above the road
was still and clear as a piece of glass.

Between Verucchio and Spinalbeto,
the clouds were almost pink,
from the coast they were swirling bigger,
it had already come up above San Vito,
black as ink.
Then from the direction of Milécch and the old station
a great dust storm rose up,
on the piazza you could hear windows banging,
someone yelled,
people hugged the walls,
held down their hats,
Natalina folded up the chairs,
Michele turned the crank and took down the awning,

E' temporèl

L'era curéina fràida,
la gata dla Maria la s'arugléva
tra la garufanéina, la sintéva e' témp.
Vérs Vrócc al nóvli agli éva cméinz a léus,
a maréina u s'avdéva di ruchéun
culòur dla zèndra, l'aria se stradòun
la era férma e cièra cumè un vàidar.

Fra Vrócc e Spinalbàid
al nóvli adès agli era guèsi rósa,
mo da maréina e' gunfiéva sémpra piò,
l'era bèla rivàt sòura San Véid
e nir cumè l'inciòstar.
Pu da Milécch e da la staziòun vècia
u s'è 'lzè un gran purbiòun,
sla piaza u s'è sintéi sbat al finestri,
qualcadéun l'à rugéu,
la zénta i caminéa tachèd mi méur,
la mèna se capèl,
la Natalina la ciudéa al scaràni,
Michél sla manuvèla

Il temporale. Era scirocco fradicio, / la gatta della Maria si rotolava / fra la garofanina, sentiva il tempo. / Verso Verucchio le nuvole avevano cominciato a rilucere, / a marina si vedevano dei cumuli / color cenere, l'aria sullo stradone / era ferma e chiara come un vetro. // Fra Verucchio e Spinalbeto / le nuvole adesso erano quasi rosa, / ma da marina gonfiava sempre piú, / era ormai arrivato sopra San Vito / e nero come l'inchiostro. / Poi da Milécch e dalla stazione vecchia / s'è alzato un gran polverone, / sulla piazza si sono sentite sbattere le finestre, / qualcuno ha urlato, / la gente camminava vicino ai muri, / la mano sul cappello, / la Natalina chiudeva le sedie, / Michele con la manovella /

the canaries in the cage went silent.
Then the whole piazza lit up
with a dry gunshot.
The women made the sign of the cross.
There was a great commotion outside
and the mare that belonged to Fin
went running by, terrified, with the cart still attached.
She came up from the Mulini, she passed under
the Arch, passed in front of the shop,
she got as far as the Big Curve and was out of sight.

The wind flipped three or four bicycles,
the first drops splattered on pavement,
it was like the end of the world,
then it just stopped. But Fin's mare kept going,
she got as far as San Martino,
at which point she collapsed
right in front of the barber's window.

e' tiréva sò al tèndi,
i canaréin tla ghèbia i stéva zétt.
Pu u s'è zais tótt la piaza
s'una s-ciuptèda sècca e pina 'd ténga,
cal dòni al s'è fàti e' sègn dla cròusa,
da 'd fura u s'è sintéi un gran scatramàz,
l'era la cavàla 'd Fin de Plèd
ch' la s'era spavantèda e la curéva
se baruzéin tachèd.
La avnéva di Muléin,
la è pasa sòtta l'Èrch, davènti e' spazi,
fina la curva, e la n s'è vésta piò.

E' vént l'à arbórt tre quatar biciclètti,
al primi gòzzli agli à macè e' catràm,
e' pareva ch'e' vléss fè l'univérs,
e pu u s'è férm alè.
Mo la cavàla 'd Fin la à tiràt drétt,
la è rivàta fina San Martéin
e pu la è s-ciòpa
davènti la vedréina de barbír.

tirava su le tende, / i canarini nella gabbia stavano zitti. / Poi s'è accesa tutta
la piazza / con una schioppettata secca e rabbiosa, / quelle donne si sono
fatte il segno della croce, / da fuori s'è sentito un gran fracasso, / era la
cavalla di Fin de Plèd / che s'era spaventata e correva / col barroccino
attaccato. / Veniva dai Mulini, / è passata sotto l'Arco, davanti allo spaccio,
/ sino alla curva, e non s'è vista piú. // Il vento ha ribaltato tre quattro
biciclette, / le prime gocce hanno macchiato il catrame, / pareva che volesse
fare il finimondo, / e poi s'è fermato lí. / Ma la cavalla di Fin ha tirato dritto,
/ è arrivata fino a San Martino / e poi è scoppiata / davanti alla vetrina del
barbiere.

Snow

LA NÀIVA

Grandpa

Go to the café?
For what particular purpose?
I'm better off here
in my own house
playing with the kids,
playing games
I never learned.
Plus, I enjoy losing.

E' nòn

Te cafè? da fè chè a stagh mèi chèsa,
a zugh sa cal burdèli,
i zugh ch'ò imparè mai! e u m pis da pérd.

Il nonno. Al caffè? da far che? / sto meglio a casa, / gioco con quelle bambine, / i giochi che ho imparato mai! e mi piace perdere.

Stricken

"She's dead," he spoke. "She's dead."
Go to Rafaél's, four candles,
have him pick out the best ones.
And a sung mass. With violins."
Then he went back to the bed, he looked at her,
he spoke to her, "Rita, where did you go?"
until those ladies arrived to say the rosary,
then he stopped talking. Even the next day, .
still silent.
At the office, he wouldn't even respond,
and one morning when he heard Sacchini behind him
blustering,
he threw on his raincoat and went home.

For two or three days they saw him in the garden watering,
then he never came out again, he wouldn't open up for anyone,
only for his sister who brought him a few swallows
of lukewarm soup in a pan.
But he'd lost his appetite,
he'd mash a hard-boiled egg,
he'd fiddle with a baked apple,
he had always been thin, but now it was like
he'd withered away, it seemed like he was shrinking inward.
In bed, he'd work himself into a frenzy,
he'd thrash his legs around trying find a cool spot,
but his feet never could, in any position all.

La pasiòun

"La è mórta! la è mórta", l'à rugéu,
"andé da Rafaél, quatar candàili,
ch'e' capa piò beli,
e la mèssa cantèda si viuléin".
Pu l'è tòuran me lèt, u la guaradèva,
u la ciaméva: "Rita, dvò t si 'ndèda?",
fintènt ch' l'è vnú cal dòni pr'e' rusèri,
alòura u n'à zcòurs piò, ènca e' dè dop
sémpra zétt,
ènca tl'uféizi, u n'arspundéva gnénca,
e una matéina ch' l'à sintéi di dri
Sachini ch'e' sufiéva,
l'à ciap sò e' spolverino e l'è 'ndè chèsa.

Par du tri dè i l'à vést tl'órt a daquè,
pu u n'è scap piò, u n'arvéva ma niseun,
sno ma la su surèla ch' la i purtéva
un gòzz 'd minestra tévda t'un giaméin.
Mo l'éva pérs la ptéita,
e' sbuzéva un óv déur,
e' paciughéva un pó s'na màila còta,
e pu e' laséva alè.

Il dolore. "È morta! è morta!" ha gridato, / "andata da Raffaele, quattro candele, / che scelga le piú belle, / e la messa cantata coi violini". / Poi è tornato al letto, la guardava, / la chiamava: "Rita, dove sei andata?" / finché sono venute quelle donne per il rosario, / allora non ha parlato piú, anche il giorno dopo / sempre zitto, / anche in ufficio, non rispondeva neanche, / e una mattina che ha sentito dietro di sé / Sacchini che sbuffava, / ha preso su lo spolverino ed è andato a casa. // Per due tre giorni l'hanno visto nell'orto a innaffiare, / poi non è uscito piú, non apriva a nessuno, / solo a sua sorella che gli portava / un goccio di minestra tiepida in un tegamino. / Ma aveva perso l'appetito, / sgusciava un uovo sodo, / pasticciava un po' con una mela cotta, / e poi lasciava lí. /

Every so often he'd feel like he had to vomit,
he'd try, but only bile would come up,
then his heart went haywire,
he could feel it beating in his armpit.
Sunk into that pillow, he was all nose,
with hair like yarn that needs untangling,
and getting even more shrunken.

He died about midnight, by himself,
with the light turned on,
and dead he seemed even smaller.
It only took two to carry his coffin downstairs,
but even that wasn't necessary,
they could have carried him away in a gunny sack.

L'era sémpra stè sècch, mo adès u s'era
cmè ingiangléi, e' paréa ch'u s'artiréss.
Te lèt l'éva la smènga,
e' dvanéva sal gambi a zarchè e' frèsch,
mo si pi ormai u n'arivéva invéll.
D'ogni tènt u i avnéva i sfórz de vòmit,
e' pruvéva, mo e' féa dla spudarèla.
Pu e' cór u s'i è smanè,
l'è rivàt ch'u batéva sòtta braz.
D'indrí sa che cuséin l'era tótt nès,
si cavéll cmè la lèna da scarmié,
e sémpra piò ingranznéid.

L'è mórt vérs mezanòta, da par léu,
sla luce zàisa,
e da mórt e' pareva ènca piò znin.
I è bastè in déu mal schèli par la casa,
mo u n gn'era gnénca bsògn,
i l putéva purtè véa t'na ligàza.

Era sempra stato magro, ma adesso si era / come rinsecchito, pareva che si
ritirasse. / Nel letto aveva la smania, / dipanava con le gambe a cercare il
fresco, / ma coi piedi ormai non arrivava da nessuna parte. / Ogni tanto gli
venivano gli sforzi del vomito, / provava, ma faceva della saliva. / Poi il cuore
gli si è scombussolato, / è arrivato che gli batteva sotto il braccio. /
Sprofondato in quel cuscino era tutto naso, / coi capelli come la lana da
sciogliere, / e sempre più rattrappito. // È morto verso mezzanotte, da solo,
/ con la luce accesa, / e da morto pareva anche più piccolo. / Sono bastati in
due giù dalle scale per la cassa, / ma non ce n'era neanche bisogno, / lo
potevano portar via in una bisaccia.

Thieves

You've just got to pray they don't come, but if they do come,
it's something, my friends, thieves in your house,
it's not so much what they steal, it's what they leave,
like a storm that blew through,
they smash, they shatter, they shit, I, in my,
they crapped, out of spite, they did, in the living room,
if you don't see it yourself, certain things,
you'd have to see it to believe it, I'll never ever forget it,
that Wednesday evening, it was the end of May,
I knew right away, when I'd taken a walk to the Roccolo,
when I saw the light on in a bedroom
and the door ajar, swinging,
I just stood there steadying myself against the wall
like I'd been nailed in place,
I didn't dare go inside, what if they were still in there?
I waited a good long while,
then luckily Cornelio came up,
he saw everything, he knew,
he wanted to go in first, then he called me,
and what I found, this is my house? this?

I lèdar

Bsògna preghè ch'i n vénga, mo s'i vén,
l'è una roba, burdéll, i lèdr' ad chèsa,
u n'è gnénch' quèll ch'i róbba, quèll ch'i lasa,
cm'e' fóss pas la tempesta,
i spaca, i sbrènca, i chéga, mè, da mè,
i a caghé, par dispèt, cumè, tla sèla,
no, s' ta n li próv, zért' robi
bsògna pruvèli, a n me zcurdarò mai
che mircal sàira, l'è stè a la féin 'd maz,
ò capì sóbit, quant ó vólt da e' Ròcal,
ch'ò vést la luce zàisa t'una cambra
e la pórta custèda ch' la ninéva,
a m so férum alè tachèd me méur
cmè ch'i m'éss inciudè,
a n m'arisghéva antrè, s'i i era ancòura?
ò spité 'lè un bèl pèz,
pu par furtéuna l'è vnù sò Corneglio,
l'à vést tótt, l'à capéi,
l'è vlù 'ndè 'vènti léu, pu u m'à ciamè,
e quèll ch'ò tróv, l'è la mi chèsa, quèsta?

I ladri. Bisogna pregare che non vengano, ma se vengono, / è una cosa, ragazzi, i ladri in casa, / non è neanche quel che rubano, quello che lasciano, / come fosse passata la tempesta, / spaccano, rompono, cagano, io, da me, / hanno cagato, per dispetto, davvero, nel salotto, / no, se non le provi, certe cose / bisogna provarle, non me lo dimenticherò mai / quel mercoledí sera, è stato alla fine di maggio, / ho capito subito, quando ho girato al Roccolo, / che ho visto la luce accesa in una camera / e la porta accostata che dondolava, / mi sono fermato lí appoggiato al muro / come se m'avessero inchiodato, / non m'arrischiavo a entrare, se c'erano ancora? / ho aspettato un bel pezzo, / poi per fortuna è venuto su Cornelio, / ha visto tutto, ha capito, / è voluto andare avanti lui, poi mi ha chiamato, / e quel che ho trovato, è la mia casa, questa? /

you couldn't make any sense of it, the end of the world,
and what can you do about it, cry? I took off my sport coat,
I moved past the entryway, past the dresser,
they'd emptied it out, everything strewn all over,
then the hallway, the bedrooms,
it was a good thing Dina was away,
she was in Rimini, visiting her sister,
she was spending the night there too,

I was awake all night, at three,
oh, it's all right now, it's still my house,
and when it finally got to be morning,
yes, they'd broken some plates, a soup tureen,
two or three glasses, the glass on the diploma,
they'd even cut up the throw-pillows on the sofa,
who knows what they were thinking,
that we still hide money under the mattress,
at eight Seconda's Curio came by
to repair the lock;
anyway, she still didn't know anything about it,
she had a bunch of flowers, she went straight into the kitchen,
she set them in the sink, she ran the water,
she was muttering that I'd kept the house all closed up,
she put things away in the cupboard,

u n s capéva piò gnént, e' finimònd,
e 'lè, t vu piànz? a m so cavè la sèrga,
a m so fat da l'antrèda, da e' cassòun,
ch'i l'éva sgòmbar, tótt' la roba in zéir,
pu e' curidéur, al cambri,
e 'ta bón che la Dina la era fura,
a Rémin, a truvè la su surèla,
la i stéva 'nca a durméi,

a so 'ndè 'vènti tótt' la nòta, al tre
oh, adès a i sémm, l'è 'ncòura la mi chèsa,
e la matéina dop, quant la è rivata,
sè, i éva ròtt di piat, una supira,
du tri bicír, e' vàidar de diploma,
i éva ènca sbrènch i cuscéin dla tumèna,
chi sa quèll ch'i s cridéva,
ch'a tnéssmi i bócch ancòura tla calzètta,
agli òt l'era vnú Curio dla Secònda
a cundè la sradéura,
insòmma, li la n s'era incórta ad gnént,
la éva un maz 'd fiéur, l è 'ndè drétt tla cuséina,
la i à pòuns te cadéin, la à fat córr l'aqua,
la à sbruntlè un pó ch'aveva tnéu tótt céus,
la à mèss a pòst dal robi sla cardénza,

non si capiva piú niente, il finimondo, / e lí, vuoi piangere? mi sono tolto la
giacca, / mi sono fatto dall'ingresso, dal cassettone, / che l'avevano svuotato,
tutta la roba in giro, / poi il corridoio, le camere, / e sta' buono che la Dina era
fuori, / a Rimini, a trovare sua sorella, / ci stava anche a dormire, // sono
andato avanti tutta la notte, alle tre, / oh, adesso ci siamo, è ancora la mia casa,
/ e la mattina dopo, quando è arrivata, / sí, avevano rotto qualche piatto, una
zuppiera, / due tre bicchieri, il vetro del diploma, / avevano anche squartato
i cuscini del divano, / chi sa quel che credevano, / che tenessimo i soldi ancora
nella calza, / alle otto era venuto Curio della Seconda / a riparare la serratura,
/ insomma, lei non s'era accorta di niente, / aveva un mazzo di fiori, è andata
dritto in cucina, / li ha posati nel catino, ha fatto correre l'acqua, / ha
brontolato che avevo tenuto chiuso, /

and I was quiet, I was waiting for the right moment,
I didn't want to scare her,
but Morena walked in, oh my God the end of the world,
screams, exclamations,
I told her that's enough now, Dina had turned
white as a bleached sheet,
she patted her necklace, her bracelets,
she looked all around,
she went into our bedroom,
she opened everything up, she was a detective at the crime scene,
then in the other bedrooms, she counted covers,
sheets, pillows, tablecloths, towels,
shirts, jackets, everything, she counted, she re-counted,
nothing was missing,
she fell into a chair,
serious, then all of a sudden, a laugh,
"It took thieves, these throw-pillows, come on,
they were shot, and we'll get a new sofa too,
this one's just had it, plus I was tired of it,
and you, what do you say?" "That you're right,"
then I went out, I got to the piazza,
there must have been a hundred who came up to talk to me,
and that evening we went out to eat, in spite of the thieves,

e mè zétt, a spitéva e' mumént bón,
a n vléva spavantèla,
mo l'è vnú la Morena, apriti cielo,
i spatéran, i sclèm,
ch'a i ò ragnè, la Dina la era dvénta
biènca cmè un pan lavèd,
la s'è tòcch' la culèna, i brazalétt,
la s'è guèrsa datònda,
la è 'ndè tla nòstra cambra,
la arvéva tótt, l'era un carabinìr,
pu tagli èlt' cambri, la cuntéva, cvérti,
lanzùl, fudrètti, tvài, sugamèn,
caméisi, sèrghi, tótt, la à còunt, la à 'rcòunt,
u n gn'amanchéva gnént,
la s'è bótta disdài s'una scaràna,
seria, pu tótt t'un bot 'na sbacarèda:
"U i vléva i lèdar, chi cuscéin, va là,
i era 'ndèd, e a cambiémm ènch' la tumèna,
quèsta la n nu n pò piò, pu la m'à stóff,
tè csa déit?" "Che t'é rasòun",
dop a so scap, a so rivàt a piaza,
ch'i m'avrà férm in zént,
e la sàira a sémm andè a magnè fura,
a la faza di lèdar,

ha messo a posto delle cose sulla credenza, / e io zitto, aspettavo il momento
buono, / non volevo spaventarla, / ma è venuta la Morena, apriti cielo, / gli
strilli, le esclamazioni, / che l'ho sgridata, la Dina era diventata / bianca come
un panno lavato, / s'è toccata la collana, i braccialetti, / s'è guardato attorno,
/ è andata nella nostra camera, / apriva tutto, era un carabiniere, / poi nelle
altre camere, contava, coperte, / lenzuoli, federe, tovaglie, asciugamani, /
camicie, giacche, tutto, ha contato, ha ricontato, / non mancava niente, / s'è
buttata a sedere su una sedia, / seria, poi di colpo una risata: "Ci volevano i
ladri, quei cuscini, va là, / erano andati, e cambiamo anche il divano, / questo
non ne può piú, poi m'ha stufato, / tu cosa dici?", "Che hai ragione", / dopo
sono uscito, sono arrivato in piazza, / che m'avranno fermato in cento, / e la
sera siamo andati a mangiare fuori, / alla faccia dei ladri, //

but the next day I thought about it again, everything a wreck,
for nothing? they came for nothing?
think about it, these were people who had cased it out
before making a move, it was a foolproof plan,
they took from here, I don't know what,
but they very well know what,
and it's been awhile since, I haven't said a thing to Dina,
but when she's not here, when she goes out,
I walk through the whole house, I look, I touch,
I try to put myself in their shoes, the thieves',
what was here that they wanted?
but which isn't here anymore?
sometimes I try an experiment, I stand with my eyes closed,
for awhile, then I open them all of a sudden, because this way,
in my opinion, you can better see if something isn't in place,
I'm even thinking about writing it all down in a notebook,
room by room, everything, right down to the last paper clip,
which I'm still not sure what good it would do,
but anyway, when all's said and done,
which then they, who knows, maybe they took
something that I thought was worthless,

mo e’ dè dop a i ò ’rpéns, tótt sté caséin
par gnént? i è vnú par gnént?
che fighéurt, quéi l’è zénta ch’i la stéudia,
préima da móvsi, i va a bota sichéura,
lòu aquè i à tólt sò, che mè a n’e’ so,
mo i l sa bén lòu,
e l’è un pó che, la Dina, a n gn’ò détt gnént,
mo quant la n gn’è, ch’ la scapa,
a vagh par tótt’ la chèsa, a guèrd, a tòcch,
a zirch da mèttmi ti su pan, di lèdar,
csa i éral aquè ch’u putéva pis?
e che adès u n gn’è piò?
dal vólti a faz ’na próva, a stagh a ócc céus
un pèz, pu a i éirv ad bot, che acsè sgònd mè
u s vaid mèi se qualquèl u n’è a e’ su pòst,
ò in amént ènch’ da mètt zò t’un quadéran,
cambra par cambra, tótt, fina un butòun,
ch’a n’e’ so ’ncòura quèll ch’ putrà sarvéi,
mo intènt, quant l’è tótt scrétt,
ch’ pu lòu, chi sa, magari, i à tólt sò
qualquèl che mè a n’i féva nisun còunt,
ch’a n savéa gnénch d’avàil,
e invici lòu, par lòu l’era un valòur,

ma il giorno dopo ci ho ripensato, tutto questo casino / per niente? sono
venuti per niente? / che, figurati, quelli sono gente che la studia / prima di
muoversi, vanno a colpo sicuro, / loro qui hanno preso, che io non lo so, / ma
lo sanno ben loro, ed è un po’ che, alla Dina non ho detto niente, / ma quando
non c’è, che esce, / vado per tutta la casa, guardo, tocco, / cerco di mettermi
nei loro panni, dei ladri, / cosa c’era qui che gli poteva piacere? / e che adesso
non c’è piú? / delle volte faccio una prova, sto con gli occhi chiusi / un bel po’,
poi li apro di colpo, che cosí, secondo me, / si vede meglio se qualcosa non è
al sùo posto, / ho in mente anche di metter giú su un quaderno, / camera per
camera, tutto, sino a un bottone, / che non so ancora a cosa potrà servire, / ma
intanto, quando è tutto scritto, / che poi loro, chissà, magari hanno preso / una
cosa che io non ci facevo nessun conto, / che non sapevo nemmeno d’averla,
/ e invece loro, per loro era un valore, /

159

that I didn't even know I had,
but which they, on the other hand, for them, was valuable,
it's just that to search blindly,
but I'm always searching, there's no peace, days pass,
sometimes I say: and write them? if you could,
the thieves, a letter,
but you can't, where would you send it?
or if not, a flier, for Christ's sake,
I hadn't even thought of that, I hadn't, a flier,
on colored paper,
I'll circulate it, sooner or later they'll read it,
printed in big, bold letters, saying to them: about what happened,
we won't talk about it, I don't want anything back,
it's yours now, it's over, done,
but give me the satisfaction, just one question,
which only you can answer:
what did you carry away, what did you steal from me?

sno che zarchè a la ziga,
mo a zirch sémpra, a n'ò pèsa, e' pasa i dè,
dal vólti a déggh: e' scréivi? s'u s putéss,
mi lèdar, una lèttra,
mo u n s pò, dò ta glia mand?
o se no un vulantéin, porca putèna,
a n gn'éva péns, dabón, un vulantéin,
ad chèrta culurèda,
ta l las in zéir, quèll préima o dop i l lèz,
scrétt bén in grand, da déii: quèll ch' l'è suzèst
a n nu n zcurémm, a n ví indrì gnént, adès
l'è roba vòsta, ormai la è fata, chiuso,
mo dém sodisfaziòun, 'na dmanda sno,
ch'a m putí 'rspònd sno vuílt:
cs'avéiv pórt véa, cs'èll ch'a m'aví rubé?

solo che cercare alla cieca, / ma cerco sempre, non ho pace, passano i giorni,
/ delle volte dico: e scrivergli? se si potesse, / ai ladri, una lettera, / ma non si
può, dove gliela mandi? / o se no un volantino, porca puttana, / non ci avevo
pensato, davvero, un volantino, / di carta colorata, / lo lasci in giro, quello
prima o poi lo leggono, / scritto bene in grande, da dirgli: quel che è successo
/ non ne parliamo, non voglio indietro niente, adesso / è roba vostra, ormai è
fata, chiuso, / ma datemi soddisfazione, una domanda sola, / che mi potete
rispondere solo voi: / cosa avete portato via? cosa m'avete rubato?

Piece of Land

Just think about it, how big the world is,
and then the moon, the stars, the universe
that never ends, and there's a little bit that's mine,
that little piece below Torriana,
about seven-and-a-half *tornature*, nothing really,
it's even good soil,
but the peasant left, it rains inside the house,
I'd like to have a vegetable garden, if I can find
someone for day-work, or even just make it a vineyard,
but it's so much work figuring it all out,
today, with land, all you do is pay taxes,
there was an agent, two or three months ago
who came up here to eyeball the place,
but nothing came of it, it was me,
I said no, and then I regretted it,
maybe it really would have been better to sell,
and then, just on a spree, a new Alfa,
take a nice trip,
instead I come here, among all these weeds,
by myself, I go down the footpath,
I get to the spring, under these poplars,
turn along the row,

È pécc

Pensè e' mònd quant l'è grand,
e pu la léuna, al stèli, l'univérs
ch'u n finéss mai, e u i n'è un pzulín ch' l'è e' méi,
che pécc sòtta Scurghèda,
gnént, e' sarà sèt turnadéuri e mèz,
ènch' tèra bóna,
mo e' cuntadéin l'à las, la chèsa u i pióv,
mè a i vrébb fè un pó d'urtlàia, s'a truvéss
éun a zurnèda, o ènca tótta vénga,
mo l'è fadéiga a mètt insén al ròbi,
òz, la campagna, u s pèga sno dal tasi,
u i è stè un mediatòur, du tri méis fa,
ch'u i è vnú dè un'ucèda,
mo u n s'è cumbiné gnént, a so stè mè,
ò détt ad no, pu dop a m so pentéi,
forse dabón e' sarébb mèi a vènd
e pu magnèsi tótt, un'Alfa nova,
fè un bel viàz,
invíci a véngh aquè, tra sti arbazéun,
da par mè, a ciap d'inzò par la calèra,
aréiv ma la surtéa, sòtta chi piópp,
pu dri ma la piantèda

Il poderetto. Pensare il mondo quant'è grande, / e poi la luna, le stelle, l'universo / che non finisce mai, e ce n'è un pezzettino che è mio, / quel poderetto sotto Torriana, / niente, saranno sette tornature e mezzo, / anche terra buona, ma il contadino ha lasciato, la casa ci piove, / io vorrei farci un po' d'ortaglia, se trovassi / uno a giornata, o anche tutta vigna, / ma è fatica mettere insieme le cose, / oggi, la campagna, si pagano solo tasse, / c'è stato un mediatore, due tre mesi fa, / che è venuto a darci un'occhiata, / ma non s'è combinato niente, sono stato io, / ho detto di no, e dopo mi sono pentito, / forse davvero sarebbe meglio vendere / e poi mangiarseli tutti, un'Alfa nuova, / fare un bel viaggio, / invece vengo qui, fra queste erbacce, / da solo, prendo giú per la callaia, / arrivo alla sorgente, sotto quei pioppi, / poi lungo il filare, /

where there's a few sorry bunch of grapes, all shriveled up,
and a few big wasps,
walking across it, I hear grasshoppers
flitting around in front of me,
the property line's there higher up, near that sorb tree,
I stop, I sit down on a bank,
the air's better,
over there, on Bigi's property,
five or six horses are playing,
their backs are shiny,
hours go by, the sun's getting big,
the grass is yellow, up above
it looks like a window's caught on fire,
my God, what's that, it had wings,
a falcon? and where did it go?
it's getting dark, the lights are coming on in Torriana,
in Montebello now too, they're eating inside the houses,
it's night, I'm hearing a trickle of water running,
all around everywhere it's just covered with lights,
above, there's no moon, it's all stars,
the crickets are crying out, I'm lying down, hands
under my head, I look,
and so, when you die, that's
where you end up?

ch'u i è qualche ruspòll, tótt ingranznéid,
e dal gran vèspri,
a vagh 'd travérs, a sint al cavalètti
ch'a m svulàcia davènti,
piò in sò e' pasa e' cunféin, vsina che sórb,
a m'aférum, a m mètt disdài s'na spònda,
u i è una piò bel'aria,
adlà, tla tèra ad Bigi,
zéinch si cavàl i zuga, u i léus la schéina,
e' pasa agli òuri, e' sòul e' dvénta grand,
l'erba la è zala, alasò una finestra
e' pèr ch' la apa ciap fugh,
orca, mo quèll cs'ell ch' l'è? l'éva dagli èli,
un fèlch? e dò ch' l'è 'ndè?
e' vén schéur, a Scurghèda i zènd al luci,
adès ènca a Mountbèl, tal chèsi i magna,
u s'è fat nòta, a sint córr un féil d'aqua,
datònda dimpartóttt l'è pin ad lómm,
d'in èlt, u n gn'è la léuna, l'è tótt stèli,
i gréll i rógg, a so struglèd, sal mèni
sòtta la testa, a guèrd,
e alòura quant u s mór u s va 'lasò?

che c'è qualche raspollo, tutto raggrinzito, / e delle gran vespe, / vado attraverso, sento le cavallette, / che mi svolazzano davanti, / piú in su passa il confine, vicino a quel sorbo, / mi fermo, mi metto a sedere su una sponda, / c'è una piú bell'aria, / di là nella terra di Bigi, / cinque sei cavalli giocano, gli riluce la schiena, / passano le ore, il sole diventa grande, / l'erbe è gialla, lassú una finestra / sembra abbia preso fuoco, / orca, ma quello cos'è? aveva delle ali, / un falco? e dov'è andato? viene buio, a Torriana accendono le luci, / adesso anche a Montebello, nelle case mangiano, / s'è fatta notte, sento scorrere un filo d'acqua, / intorno dappertutto è pieno di lumi, / in alto, non c'è la luna, sono tutte stelle, / i grilli urlano, sono sdraiato, con le mani / sotto la testa, guardo, / e allora quando si muore si va lassú?

The Lady

She was always a lady, right up till the end.
On Sundays, when she'd come to eleven
o'clock Mass, at the Collegiata,
after dismissal, she'd hired a cab,
the biggest one, Rosolino's Lancia,
which he kept like a mirror, and himself as well,
always polished, a black leather jacket
his hair all slicked back,
muttering under his breath,
but he never did have the courage to refuse her,
he would take her as far as the main entrance,
as far as the front stairs,
he'd open the door for her, she would step out,
she would smile at him, she would thank him,
then she would walk right in,
she wouldn't even acknowledge the nuns,
she would enter, into the dark, without looking back.

Sgnòura

L'è stè sémpra una sgnòura, fina tl'éultum,
la dmènga, quant la avnéva
a la mèssa dagli óngg tla Colegèta,
dop, te scapè, la tuléva un vtéura,
la piò granda, la Lancia ad Rosolino,
ch'u la tnéva cmè un spèc, e ènch léu
sémpra sfurbéid, giacòun ad pèla nira
e i cavéll tótt tiràt,
e' sbruntléva tra i dint,
mo u n'à mai vú e' curàg da déii ad no,
u la purtéva fina se purtòun,
ma la scalètta,
u i arvéva e' spurtèl, li la smuntéva,
la i féa bòcca da réid, la i géva grazie,
pu la andéva sò drétta, ma la sóra
la n'i badéva gnénca,
la antréva, te schéur, senza vultès.

Signora. È stata sempre una signora, fino all'ultimo, / la domenica, quando veniva / alla messa delle undici nella Collegiata, / dopo, all'uscita, prendeva una vettura di piazza, / la piú grande, la Lancia di Rosolino, / che la teneva come uno specchio, e anche lui, / sempre forbito, giaccone di pelle nera / e i capelli tutti tirati, / brontolava fra i denti, / ma non ha mai avuto il coraggio di dirle di no, / la portava fino sul portone, / alla scaletta, / le apriva lo sportello, lei scendeva, / gli sorrideva, gli diceva grazie, / poi andava su dritta, alla suora, / non ci badava neanche, / entrava, nel buio, senza voltarsi.

Here's My Advice

Don't say anything to anyone, I'm advising
you say it was dark,
that you were right on your own street,
say that you never saw me,
no, better yet,
that you never mentioned my name,
not even by mistake,
you, if it comes up in conversation, just listen,
if they ask you, act confused, you ask too,
because they're things that don't matter to anyone anyway,
but it's best not to draw things out,
keep to yourself,
if two of them sitting at the Monument are talking
and you hear they're discussing me and arguing,
don't defend me,
it's okay for you just to be quiet,
if someone in the piazza says my name
and shoots you a look, pretend you don't understand,
try to distance yourself, but without rushing,
walk around a little, like it's nothing, be smart about it,
don't go where there are lots of people,

A m'aracmànd

Nu dí gnént ma niseun, a m'aracmànd,
dí ch' l'era schéur,
che tè t'andévi drétt par la tu strèda,
dí ta n m'é vést,
ènzi no, par fè mèi,
mu mè tè n m'é mai da luminè,
gnénca par sbai,
tè, s'i vén in dizcòurs, sta sno a sintéi,
s'i t dmanda fa e' zcurdèd, dmanda ènca tè,
ch' pu l'è robi ch'u n gn'arimpórta gnént
ma niseun, mo l'è mèi no fèla lònga,
sta par còunt tóvv,
se déu, disdài me Monumént, ta i sint
ch'i zcòrr ad mè e i s'aràgna,
tè nu ciapa al mi pèrti, lòu magari
i l fa pòsta, chi sa quèll, ch'i à in amént,
mo tè bast' t staga zétt,
se qualcadéun in piaza e' fa e' mi nóm
e u t scrécca un òc, fa féinta 'd no capéi,
e zirca 'd sluntanèt, mo senza préssia,
zéira piò in là, cmè gnént, fala da féurb,
nu va dvò ch'i una masa,

Mi raccomando. Non dire niente a nessuno, mi raccomando, di' che era buio, /
che tu andavi dritto per la tua strada, / di' che non m'hai visto, / anzi no, per
far meglio, / a me tu non mi devi mai nominare, / neanche per sbaglio, / tu,
se vengono in discorso, stai solo a sentire, / se ti chiedono, fai lo smemorato,
chiedi anche tu, / che poi son cose che non gli'importa niente / a nessuno, /
ma è meglio non farla lunga, / stai per conto tuo, / se due, seduti al
Monumento, li senti / che parlano di me e litigano, / tu non prendere le mie
parti, loro magari / lo fanno apposta, chi sa quel che hanno in mente, / ma tu
basta che stia zitto, / se qualcuno in piazza fa il mio nome / e ti strizza un
occhio, fa' finta di non capire, / e cerca d'allontanarti, ma senza fretta, / gira
piú in là, come niente, falla da furbo, / non andare dove sono in molti, /

and don't walk along the walls either,
if someone rude from the Borgo comes up to you
and blows smoke in your face and says to you that you know me,
shake your head no and keep walking,
if others come up, if they gather around you,
do what you can, say that we sometimes ran into each other at
                                                    [the cafe,
that we said hello to each other,
but there was nothing between us,
and if they're still there not budging
and crowding you, with their hands in their pockets,
don't let yourself get unnerved, say that last evening
I was at home early, with a fever,
that on top of it you don't even know where I am,
if you see they're getting mad,
if they call you a liar,
you don't have to get angry,
I've known them a long time,
they're guys, it's all just a lot of noise, their yelling,
but they get bored right away,
and who says they were really serious anyway?
it could be they might even just be staging
a big show, but you just don't act like you're afraid,
if they step into your path under the arcades,
say that you have to go to the store, that you're in a hurry,
that they're expecting you at home for dinner,

e gnénch' tachèd mi méur,
se un pataca te Bòurgh u t vén incòuntra
e u t bótta e' fómm tla faza e u t déi ta m cnòss,
fa sègn ad no e va drétt,
s'u n vén d'ilt, s'i s'amóccia, fa cmè t pò,
dí ch'a s'avdémm dal vólti te cafè,
ch'a s salutémm,
mo ch'a n'avémm nisuna cunfidenza,
e s'i sta 'lè ch'i n s móv
e i t vén tachèd sal mèni tla bascòza,
nu fat avní e' nervòus, dí ch'irisàira
a so 'ndé chèsa prèst, ch'éva la févra,
che pu tè ta n sé gnénca dvò ch'a stagh,
s' ta i vaid ch'i s'incapèla,
s'i t déi che t si un biséin,
ta n t si da spavantè, mè a i cnòss da mò,
lòu l'è burdlàz, l'è tótta boba, i rógg,
mo i s stógga prèst,
e pu chi è chi l'à détt ch'i fa se séri?
e' pò ès ènca ch'i apa mèss impí
tótt' 'na cumédia,
mo tè nu fat avdài cmè t'éss paéura,
s'i t'à taiè la strèda sòtta i pórtich,
déi ch' t'é d'andè te spazi, che t'é préssia,
che ma chèsa i t'aspétta par magnè,

e neanche lungo i muri, / se uno stupido nel Borgo ti viene incontro / e ti butta
il fumo in faccia e ti dice che mi conosci, / fa' segno di no e va' dritto, / se ne
vengono altri, se si ammucchiano, fa' come puoi, / di' che ci vediamo delle
volte al caffè, / che ci salutiamo, / ma che non abbiamo nessuna confidenza,
/ e se stanno lí che non si muovono / e ti vengono vicino con le mani in tasca,
/ non farti venire il nervoso, di' che ieri sera / sono andato a casa presto, che
avevo la febbre, / che poi tu non sai neanche dove sto, / se vedi che s'arrabbiano, / se ti dicono che sei un bugiardo, / non devi spaventarti, io li conosco
da tanto, / sono ragazzi, è tutto chiasso, urlano, / ma si stufano presto, / e poi
chi l'ha detto che fanno sul serio? / può essere anche che abbiano messo in
piedi / tutta una commedia, / ma tu non farti vedere come se avessi paura, /
se ti hanno tagliato la strada sotto i portici, / di' che devi andare allo spaccio,
che hai fretta, / che a casa ti aspettano per mangiare, /

171

in any event, act indifferent,
because, even with jokes, sometimes you never know,
try not to even go out, where do you need to go?
if they start in with comments,
if they kick you, if they rough you up, try for awhile
to look them in the eye, glare at them,
it'll make someone start to laugh,
and if they don't laugh, if it's not a game,
if you hear that they're starting to talk about coming to get me,
say that I'm shut up in the house and I've gotten out all the
                                                    [knives
and I'm on lookout at the window,
say that and see what happens,
you want to bet they rethink the whole thing, that they quit?
and if they don't quit, same thing, if they mean it
and they've pushed you out of the way,
you just take off, walk naturally,
don't try to walk slowly, don't tell them off,
do whatever they want, but grant me this one thing,
they want to come up on me when I'm not expecting it,
and they walk very quietly, with rubber-soled shoes,
they've stubbed out their cigarettes, they use hand signals,
but you, I'm asking you just this, before they get here,

mo fa l'indiferent,
parchè 'nca i schérz, dal vólti, u n s pò savài,
scapè nu próva gnénca, dvè t vu andè?
s'i cméinza sal spatàsi,
s'i t dà 'd chélz, s'i t sagàta, tè pr'un pó
zirca 'd guardèi tla faza, guèrdi féss,
che qualcadéun magari u i vén da réid,
e s'i n réid, s'u n'è un zugh,
se t sint ch'i ravéa a zcòrr d'avnéim a tó,
déi ch'a m so céus ad chèsa e ò tiràt fura
tótt i curtéll
e a stagh 'd vedètta spèsa la finestra,
tè dí 'csè e sta d'avdài,
vut scumètt ch'i i arpénsa, ch'i s'aférma?
e s'i n s férma l'istèss, s'i dí dabón
e i t'à zà mèss davènti par fè strèda,
tè avéiti pò, caméina naturèl,
nu zirca d'andè pièn, da fèt ragnè,
va cm'i vó lòu, mo t m'é da fè un reghèl,
mè bsògna ch'i n m'arcnòssa,
parchè a l so, e' sarà 'd nòta,
i m vó rivé madòs ch'a nu m l'aspèt,

ma fa' l'indifferente, / perché anche gli scherzi, delle volte, non si può sapere, / scappare non provarci neanche, dove vuoi andare? / se cominciano con le spinte, / se ti danno calci, se ti malmenano, tu per un po' / cerca di guardarli in faccia, guardali fisso, / che a qualcuno magari gli viene da ridere, / e se non ridono, se non è un gioco, / se senti che cominciano a parlare di venirmi a prendere, / di' che mi sono chiuso in casa e ho tirato fuori / tutti i coltelli / e sto in vedetta dietro la finestra, / tu di' cosí e stai a vedere, / vuoi scommetere che ci ripensano, che si fermano? / e se non si fermano lo stesso, se dicono sul serio / e ti hanno già messo davanti per far strada, / tu avvíati pure, cammina naturale, / non cercare d'andar piano, da farti sgridare, / va' come vogliono loro, ma mi devi fare un regalo, / io bisogna che non mi riconoscano, / perché lo so, sarà di notte, / mi vogliono arrivare addosso che non me l'aspetto, / e camminano zitti, hanno le scarpe di gomma, / hanno spento le sigarette, parlano con le mani, / ma tu, io ti chiedo solo questo, prima d'arrivare /

give me a sign, but one they don't understand,
one that's not going to drag you into the middle of it,
whatever signal, pretend that you trip,
that you twist an ankle,
yell out, but right away put your hand
over your mouth
and lie there a minute, maybe two,
that's all I need to put on my dark glasses
and draw on the charcoal mustache.

e i caméina da zétt, i à 'l schèrpi ad gòmma,
i à smórt al zigarètti, i zcòrr sal mèni,
mo tè, mè a t dmand sno quèst, préima 'd rivé
fam un segnèl, però che lòu i n capéssa,
ch' ta n'i vaga di mèzi,
un sègn purséa, fa féinta ad scapuzé,
d'andè zò mèl s'un pi,
fa un rógg, mo mèt-ti sóbit
una mèna sla bòcca,
e férmti alè un mumént, gnént, du minéut,
par mè l'è tótt,
mè u m vó sno e' témp da mèttmi i ucèl nir
e d' piturém i bafi se carbòun.

fammi un segnale, però che loro non capiscano, / che tu non ci vada di mezzo,
/ un segno purchessia, fa' finta d'inciampare, / d'andar giú male con un piede,
/ fa' un urlo, ma mettiti subito / una mano sulla bocca, / e fermati lí un
momento, niente, due minuti, / per me è tutto, / a me mi ci vuole solo il tempo
di mettermi gli occhiali neri / e di pitturarmi i baffi col carbone.

Easily Chilled

The cold always goes right through me, even in summer,
if there's the hint of a breeze
and I don't put my scarf on when I go out,
the next day I get hit, I have a sore throat.
It's not that I go around all bundled up,
just once around the neck, and then I tuck it
under my jacket, you can't even see it.
Towards evening, when I go for a stroll,
I toss my overcoat over my shoulders,
at night on my bed, I keep
the usual quilt,
but without the down comforter,
just a light cover over the feet,
thin as onion skin,
for early in the morning when you feel the chill.
To tell you the truth, I've even tried
fewer covers,
something really bold,
but you see how then afterwards I paid,
I got sick, with a fever, bronchitis.

Fridulòus

Mè u m córr sémpra dri e' frèdd, ènca d'instèda,
s'u i è un pó 'd bura
e a n mu n mètt la scialètta quanta a scap,
e' dè dop a m n'incórz, a iò e' rusghéin.
Méggh' ch'a vaga gulpéd,
un zéir sno tònda e' còl, e pu a m la instècch
sòtta la sèrga, che la n s vaid e gnénca.
Vérs sàira quant a vagh a fè du pas
a m bótt e' spolverino sòura al spali,
se lèt la nòta a téngh
la solita imbutéida,
mo senza cuscinòun,
sno una cvérta lizíra sòura i pi,
un vail ad zvòlla,
par la matéina prèst ch'u s sint cla péunta.
A dí la verità, a iò ènca próv
dal vólti andè piò zcvért,
ò fat qualche bravèda,
mo t'avdiré che dop a la ò paghèda,
a so stè mèl, sla févra, una bronchite.

Freddoloso. A me mi corre sempre dietro il freddo, anche d'estate, /se c'è un po' di brezza / e non metto la sciarpa quando esco, / il giorno dopo me n'accorgo, ho la raucedine. / Mica che vada imbacuccato, / un giro solo intorno al collo, e poi me la ficco / sotto la giacca, che non si vede nemmeno. / Verso sera, quando vado a fare due passi, / mi butto lo spolverino sulle spalle, / sul letto la notte tengo / la solita trapunta, / ma senza piumino, / solo una coperta leggera sui piedi, / un velo di cipolla, / per la mattina presto che si sente quella punta. / A dire la verità, ci ho anche provato / delle volte ad andare piú scoperto, / ho fatto qualche bravata, / ma vedrai che dopo l'ho pagata, / sono stato male, con la febbre, una bronchite. /

then I ask myself: Why is it I get so cold?
I like warmth,
is keeping oneself covered up anything to be ashamed of?
Sometimes I do sweat, it's true,
but sweating is healthy,
it's good for the skin, and the blood too,
it's hard enough staying out of a draft,
but I always position myself on the sunny side,
and in the afternoon, in the shade, under the porticoes,
I'm there watching them laying down cards,
I feel that dazed feeling,
I nod off,
I don't even try to fight it, my head drops,
and I take a little nap,
the others don't even notice,
they're playing, and I'm plenty of company.

Mo pu mè a déggh: parchè ò da ciapè frèdd?
mè u m pis e' chèld,
u i è da vargugnès a stè ciutèd?
Dal vólti a séud, l'è vèrra,
mo sudé l'è saléuta,
e' fa bén ma la péla, ènca me sangh,
l'è tótt vlén ch'e' va fura,
basta stè 'ténti 'd no mèttsi tla corénta,
mo mè a stagh sémpra férum ma la bdòsa
e e' dopmezdè ma l'òmbra sòtta i pórtich,
a stagh alè d'avdài ch'i zuga a schèla,
pu a sint cl'invurnimént,
u m vén dal bonanòti,
mo a n zirch mégga ad tnai bota, a dagh e' còl
e a m'imparluzéss,
ch'ilt i n s n'incórz e gnénca,
lóu i zuga e mè a stagh in cumpagnéa.

Ma poi io dico: perché devo prendere freddo? / a me mi piace il caldo, / c'è da
vergognarsi a stare coperti? / Delle volte sudo, è vero, / ma sudare è salute, /
fa bene alla pelle, anche al sangue, / è tutto veleno che va fuori, / basta stare
attenti a non mettersi nella corrente, / ma io sto sempre fermo sul lato al sole
/ e il pomeriggio all'ombra sotto i portici, / sto lí a vedere che giocano a scala,
/ poi sento quell'intontimento, / mi cade la testa, / ma non cerco mica di tener
botta, do il collo / e m'appisolo, / gli altri non se n'accorgono nemmeno, / loro
giocano e io sto in compagnia.

That Evening

Renata, that evening.
Four dances in a row, without saying a word,
I took her by the hand,
and she followed behind, just like a young girl,
as far as Bosca,
we were quiet the whole way,
I explored her in the dark, I couldn't believe it,
I felt her everywhere,
and that mouth, that perfume, the unbuttoned
blouse, I trembled,
and underneath, nothing, it was just her,
she came down slowly, gently, with eyes closed.
The next Sunday, she got married.

Cla sàira

La Renata, cla sàira.
Quatar bal atachàd, senza dí gnént,
a i ò ciap una mèna
e la m'è vnéuda dri cmè una burdèla,
fina la Bosca, a stémmi sémpra zétt,
a la ò zirca te schéur, a n'i cridéva,
a la ò sintéida tótta,
e cla bòcca, cl'udòur, la camisètta
sbutunèda, a treméva,
e sòtta senza gnént, u i era li,
la è vnéuda zò pianín, dòuzla, si ócc céus.
E pu la dmènga dop la s'è spusèda.

Quella sera. La Renata, quella sera. / Quattro balli di seguito, senza dire niente, / le ho preso una mano / e mi è venuta dietro come una bambina, / fino alla Bosca, stavamo sempre zitti, / l'ho cercata nel buio, non ci credevo, / l'ho sentita tutta, / e quella bocca, quel profumo, la camicetta / sbottonata, tremavo, / e sotto senza niente, c'era lei, / è venuta giú piano, dolce, con gli occhi chiusi. / E poi la domenica dopo s'è sposata.

The Cockaigne Tree

The bell's struck one and no one's gotten up there yet.
These are teams we're not familiar with,
not the same as last year, they're all new.
There was one guy climbing up who was small, good too,
he went up like a toad, but he rushed,
he forgot the chalk, and also he was going at it too hard,
same thing with those others, they didn't wipe they way they
                                                    [should,
they didn't know how to adapt, they blew it,
Plus, they put up a taller pole this year,
look at the basket, it's as high as the clock
on the bank,
you've got to have better lungs, and better brains too,
but instead it was just a big hoopla
they wore themselves out and didn't come up with a thing,
It's a little bit too that people weren't concentrating on the game,
they were laughing too much. And then the heat, this heavy air.
But, be patient, one guy's starting up, he's going,
he's gotten to where the grease is,
then he's stopped, perfect,
at the halfway point it's better to catch your breath,

La cucagna

L'à sunè e' tòcch e i gn'è 'ncòura rivàt.
L'è al squèdri ch'a n'i sémm,
u n'è quéi d'an, i è nóv.
Te rapè u i era un znin ch' l'era ènca brèv,
l'andéva sò cmè un ròsp, mo l'éva préssia,
u s zcurdéva de zèss, pu u n déva trop,
e ch'ilt si straz cumpàgn,
i n gn'à savù druvè, i i à strusié.
Par di piò st'an i à mèss un pèl piò lòngh,
vèrda e' gavàgn, l'aréiva ma l'arlózz
dla Casa de Rispèrmi,
u i vó fiè, e u i vó 'nca pió zarvèl,
invici lòu i à fat un gran sò e zò,
i s'è slumbè e i n'à rimidié gnént.
Un pó l'è 'nca la zénta ch'i gn'à fat,
i à ridù trop. E pu e' chèld, st'aria basa.
Però, 'ta bón, éun u s fa sòtta, e' va,
l'aréiva dò ch' l'è spórch,
pu u s'aférma, acsè bén,
a mèza véa l'è mèi ciapè un pó 'd fiè,

La cuccagna. È suonato il tocco e non ci sono ancora arrivati. / Sono le squadre che non ci siamo, / non sono quelli dell'anno scorso, sono nuovi. / Nell'arrampicarsi c'era uno piccolo che era anche bravo, / andava su come un rospo, ma aveva fretta, / si dimenticava del gesso, poi ne dava troppo, / e gli altri con gli stracci lo stesso, / non li hanno saputi adoperare, li hanno sprecati. / Per di più, quest'anno hanno messo un palo più lungo, / guarda il cavagno, arriva all'orologio / della Cassa di Risparmio, / ci vuole più fiato, e ci vuole anche più cervello, / invece loro hanno fatto un gran su e giù, / si sono slombati e non hanno rimediato niente. / Un po' è anche la gente che non s'è spesa, / hanno riso troppo. E poi il caldo, quest'aria bassa. / Però, sta' buono, uno si fa sotto, va, / arriva dov'è sporco, / poi si ferma, / benissimo, / a mezza via è meglio prendere un po' fiato, /

he's pulling out the rag,
he's wiping, he's wiping again, but he's going at it too hard,
you need the chalk, what's he waiting for?
he's going into the sack, he's not starting up again,
he's fumbling around, he's making a mess of it, he dropped the rag,
watch out he doesn't choke now,
what's he doing? holy smoke, the bag ripped,
all the chalk's fallen, you hear him yelling,
coughing, spitting, the air's a big cloud of chalk dust,
Nothing's changing here, it would better to just go home,
but no one's moving, the people
are all quiet, they're waiting. On the bench near the Arch,
the two old Bagiagia girls squeeze together
to make a little room for Norina,
in the window above Pisutlais',
Caterina's waving to someone.
It's a cauldron, you can't breathe, you can't budge,
way up above the weathercocks are there with their mouths hanging
[open,
even they're dying of thirst.
From behind the Collegiata,
the moon's coming out.
On the balcony, Signora Pellacani's
holding her hair up, she's straining her neck,

pu e' téira fura e' straz,
e' puléss, l'arpuléss, mo u i va dri trop,
u i vó e' zèss, cs'èll ch' l'aspétta?
e' va ma la malètta, u n tróva e' vérs,
e' sfurgata, e' paciéuga, u i casca e' stràz,
bast' ch'u n s mètta e' nervòus,
csa fal? a fórza ad dèi l'à sbrènch e' sach,
e' vén zò tótt e' zèss, u s sint a rógg,
a tòs, a spudé, pr'aria l'è un purbiòun.
Aquè i n cumbina gnént, mèi andè chèsa,
mo u n s móv niseun, la zénta
i sta tótt zétt, i aspétta.
Se sedéili dri l'Èrch al do Bagiagia
a l s strènz par fè un pó 'd pòst ma la Norina,
da la finèstra sòura Pistulàis
la Caterina la fa sègn s'na mèna
ma qualcadéun.
L'è un bulòur ch'u n s'arfièda, u n s móv un féil,
'lasò in zéima i galétt i sta a bèch vért,
ènca lòu i à d'avài 'na bèla arséura.
Di dri dla Colegèta
l'è vnú fura la léuna.
La sgnòura Pelacani se teràz
la s téira sò i cavéll, la stórz e' còl,

tira fuori lo straccio, / pulisce, ripulisce, ma ci va dietro troppo, / ci vuole il gesso, cosa aspetta? / va alla sacca, non trova il verso, / fruga, pasticcia, gli cada lo straccio, / basta che non si metta il nervoso, / cosa fa? a forza di darci, ha rotto la sacca, / viene giú tutto il gesso, si sente urlare, / tossire, sputare, per aria c'è un polverone. / Qui non combinano niente, meglio andare a casa, / ma non si muove nessuno, la gente / stanno tutti zitti, aspettano. / Sulla panchina vicino all'Arco le due Bagiagia / si stringono per fare un po' di posto alla Norina, / dalla finestra sopra Pistulàis / la Caterina fa segno con una mano / a qualcuno. / È un bollore che non si respira, non si muove un filo, / lassú in cima i galletti stanno a becco aperto, / anche loro devono avere una bella arsura. / Da dietro la Collegiata / è venuta fuori la luna. / La signora Pellacani sul balcone / si tira su i capelli, torce il collo, /

fanning herself with her hand,
her husband's searching his pockets:
"You want a mint-ice?"
For a long while nothing happens,
then one of the teammates from Ciola
goes to cook up something with the ones from Casale,
you have to outwit it,
to go up all together, and then split up.
The first to go up is the small one,
a stocky guy, who's doing well, and the others behind,
he's up to where it's greased,
he's drenched in sweat,
he's just dripping, it's getting into his eyes,
he's reached up one arm, it's filthy, it's worse now,
he's changing arms, he can't get a good grip, he's falling,
he' can't go on,
he's feeling for the head of his teammate below,
but he's pushing down too hard,
the one below him's giving, now two of them are falling down,
the others can't take the impact,
they're collapsing, they've piled into a heap of bones.
And people are being patient about it,
a few of them are sneaking into the church,
some have brought out chairs,
and are straddling them,
others have spread out a newspaper, a handkerchief
and sat down on the ground.

la s fa vént sal do mèni,
e' su maréid e' zirca tla bascòza:
"Vut una menta ghiaccio?"
Pr'un bèl pó u n suzéd gnént,
pu éun dla squèdra ad Zula
e' va a confabulè sa quéi 'd Casèl,
bsògna s-ciantèla,
andè sò tótt insén e pu partéi.
E' préim a inviés l'è e' znin,
tracagnòt, ch'e' va bén, e ch'ilt di dri,
l'aréiva dò ch' l'è òunt,
l'è tótt sudéd, e' còula, la i va ti ócc,
u s dà s'un braz, u n s ciapa bén, e' cala,
u n nu n pò piò,
se pi e' zirca la tèsta de cumpàgn,
mo e' chèlca trop,
quèll sòtta e' zéd, adès i va zò in déu,
ch'ilt i n tén bota, i slèma, i fa un mócc d'òsi.
E la zénta i sta bón,
parécc i è 'ndè tla cisa d'ingatéun,
i à tólt una scaràna,
i s'i è mèss a cavàl,
d'ilt i à stais un giurnèl, un fazulètt,

si fa vento con le due mani, / suo marito cerca in tasca: "Vuoi una menta ghiaccio?" / Per un bel po' non succede niente, / poi uno della squadra di Ciola / va a confabulare con quelli di Casale, / bisogna romperla, / andar su tutti insieme, e poi dividere. / Il primo ad avviarsi è il piccolo, / tracagnotto, che va bene, e gli altri dietro, / arriva dov'è unto, / è tutto sudato, cola, gli va negli occhi, / si dà con un braccio, è sporco, adesso è peggio, / cambia braccio, non si afferra bene, cala, / non ne può piú, / con i piedi cerca la testa del compagno, / ma calca troppo, / quello sotto cede, adesso vanno giú in due, / gli altri non tengono botta, franano, fanno un mucchio d'ossa. / E la gente stanno buoni, / parecchi sono andati nella chiesa gatton gattoni, / hanno preso una sedia, / ci si sono mesi a cavallo, / altri hanno steso un giornale, un fazzoletto, /

Almost every baby has fallen asleep.
Underneath the arcades there's a bit of a commotion,
what are they up to? Cin's going up?
really? people are asking, craning their necks,
where is he? you can't see anyone, is he going or is he not going?
It's striking two now,
at the drink stand, Gustavo's
starting to put away the bottles, and one guy from here,
takes off his shirt,
he gives a signal to his friends and then he goes up,
right now he's under the grease, he reaches one arm,
he's making the basket shake, he's not going to get up there like
[that,
he looks below, he's laughing, forget it, he's a moron,
little by little he's slipping down, he's getting everything filthy,
At Batóss's bakery they've already finished the mixing,
Chichín's in his undershirt pulling the shutters closed,
he shakes his head a little and goes back inside.
One baby's awake, he starts to cry,
his mother: "Hush hush, be good now,"
it wakes up another one,
this one's whining: "Are they done yet?" a man's complaining:
"Can't you people make him be quiet?"

e i è 'ndè zò ma tèra.
I burdéll i s'è guèsi indurmént tótt.
Sòtta i pórtich u s sint un pó 'd smasìr,
csa fai? e' va sò e' Cin?
dabón? la zénta i dmanda, i slònga e' còl,
duv'èll? u n s vaid niseun, e' va o ch'u n va?
L'è al do sunèdi,
me barachéin dal bébiti Gustavo
e' cméinza a mètt véa al bòci,
e' céud ènch' quèll di cómbar, se bancòun
u i è do tre fètti ch'i n li vó niseun.
U s fa 'vènti un burdlàz, l'è éun d'aquè,
u s chèva la caméisa,
e fa sègn ma i améigh e pu a e' va sò,
adès l'è sotta l'òunt, e' slònga e' braz,
e' fa tremè e' gavàgn, acsè u n s'i aréiva,
e' guèrda ad sòtta, e' réid, gnént, l'è un pataca,
e' cala zò pianín, u s'è spórch tótt.
Te fòuran ad Batóss i impasta zà,
Chichín in canotira e' chèva i schéur,
e' scrólla un pó la testa, e' tòurna dréinta.
Un burdèl u s'è svégg, e' taca a piànz,
la su mà: "Zò, fa e' bón", u n s svéggia un èlt,
e' sprégnla: "I à finéi?", un òm e' ragna:

e sono andati giú a terra. / I bambini si sono addormentati quasi tutti. / Sotto i portici si sente un po' di trambusto, / cosa fanno? va su il Cin? / davvero? la gente domanda, allungano il collo, / dov'è? non si vede nessuno, va o non va? / Sono le due suonate, / al baracchino delle bibite Gustavo / comincia a mettere via le bottiglie, / chiude anche quello dei cocomeri, sul bancone / ci sono due tre fette che non le vuole nessuno. / Si fa avanti un giovanotto, è uno di qui / si toglie la camicia, / fa un segno agli amici e poi va su, / adesso è sotto l'unto, allunga un braccio, / fa tremare il cavagno, cosí non ci si arriva, / guarda sotto, ride, niente, è un coglione, / cala giú piano piano, s'è sporcato tutto. / Nel forno di Batóss impastano già, / Checco in canottiera toglie gli scuretti, / scuote un po' la testa, torna dentro. / Un bambino s'è svegliato, comincia a piangere, / sua madre: "Su, fai il buono", se ne sveglia un altro, / piagnucola: "Hanno finito?", un uomo protesta: / "Non siete capaci di farlo star zitto?" /

The festival organizers are standing against the
side door of the church, they're whispering,
one of them walks away,
he goes to a light box, he turns out the lights.
Below town hall, you can hear a motorcycle leaving,
two from the Ciola team are going home.
Someone's snoring at the windows,
shifting his weight Gròt fell off the chair
and Anna pulled him up, she got the giggles,
Mino was chuckling too. It rang three o'clock.
Underneath the movie posters, Fulvio Ronchi
was patting all his pockets, he'd finished his cigarettes,
Gioti went to the fountain, turned on the water,
he put his head under and then his back,
someone said, "Me too," others were saying, "Shh!"
the moon at this point is above the Cappuccini,
shining, in it's full splendor. Towards Pozzo Lungo
you can hear the Montanari's dog barking,
and over by the Old Dispensary, another dog replying,
it's a howling match, Bagióll's swearing a blue streak,
Giacommini's yawning, Fiorona's praying:
Our Our, Father Father,"

"A n si bón 'd fèl stè zétt?"
Quéi dla festa, d'impí còuntra e' purtòun
de prit, i zcòrr da fétt, éun u s sluntèna,
e' va m'una casètta, e' smórta i lómm.
Sòtta e' Cuméun u s sint 'viés un mutòur,
l'è déu dla squèdra 'd Zula ch'i va chèsa.
Mal finèstri qualcadéun e' surnèccia,
te cundès Gròt l'è casch da la scaràna,
l'Anna la l téira sò, u s'i smóv la sgrégna,
e' réid pièn ènca Mino. E' sòuna al tre.
Sòtta i cartléun de cino Fuglio 'd Ròunch
u s tasta dimpartótt,
l'à finéi 'l zigarètti.
Gioti e' va ma la pòumpa, l'éirva l'aqua,
u i mètt sòtta la testa e pu la schéina,
éun e' déi: "Enca mè", d'ilt i fa: "Ssst!"
La léuna la è ormai sòura i Capuzéin,
la léus, la è te su bèl. Vérs e' Pòzz Lòngh
u s sint baiè e' chèn ad Montanari,
u i arspònd un èlt chèn de la Dispensa,
l'è un gran baiè, Bagióll e' téira un mòcal,
Giacomini e' sbadàia, la Fiuròuna
la pràiga: "Pater Pater, noster noster",

"Quelli della festa, in piedi contro il portone / del prete, parlano fitto, uno si allontano, / va a una cassetta, spegne le luci. / Sotto il Comune si sente avviarsi una motocicletta, / sono due della squadra di Ciola che vanno a casa. / Alla finestre qualcuno russa, / nell'accomodarsi Gròt è caduto dalla sedia, / l'Anna lo tira su, le prende la ridarella, / ride piano anche Mino. Suonano le tre. / Sotto i cartelloni del cinema Fulvio Ronchi / si tasta dappertutto, / ha finito le sigarette. / Gioti va alla fontana, apre l'acqua, / ci mette sotto la testa e poi la schiena, / uno dice: "Anch'io", altri fanno: "Ssst!" / La luna è ormai sopra i Cappuccini, / splende, è nel suo bello. Verso il Pozzo Lungo / si sente abbaiare il cane di Montanari, / gli risponde un altro cane dalla Dispensa, / è un gran abbaiare, Bagióll tira un moccolo, / Giacomini sbadiglia, la Fiorona / prega: "Pater Pater, noster noster", /

she's putting in an extra Father, "who art in heaven,
who art in heaven," her daughter's muttering,
"What's with all this praying right now, go to sleep instead,"
"I'm praying for you too,"
"What is going on with you, you look terrified."
"It's an air I don't like, can't you feel that it's still?"

la déi un pater dòppi, "quesinceli
quesinceli", la su fióla la sbròuntla:
"Csa i éintral preghè 'dès? durméi piotòst,"
"A pràigh ènca par tè",
"Mo cs'avéiv, sa cla faza spavantèda?"
"L'è un'aria ch' la n mu n pis, ta n sint che férma?"

dice un Pater doppio, "qui es in coelis / qui es in coelis", sua figlia brontola: /
"Cosa c'entra pregare adesso? dormite piuttosto", / "Prego anche per te", / "Ma
cosa avete, con quella faccia spaventata?", / È un'aria che non mi piace, non senti
che ferma?"

193

The Bridge

Here, the road ends here,
and there's the bridge,
what's left of it, where there was
in seventy-five, a flood, at night.
It washed away two arches
and a man on a bicycle.

A bridge, which when it was inaugurated,
in the twenties, the king attended,
long, it went forever,
from over on the other side you felt like an outsider,
even people who lived here, and they talked different over there.
I remember when the flood happened,
they came into the café to tell us, we all ran out,
we were all looking down from above, a thousand of us,
hanging over the wall, it was a sight.
The water came down the color of mud,
widening out, but not rushing,
you lost yourself following a hawthorn
with a tangle of roots
every so often it would make a funnel,
in certain places it would even seem
like it was still, and there was good reason to be afraid,
below it was churning,

E' pòunt

Ècco, la strèda la finéss aqué,
e alè u i è e' pòunt, quèll ch'u i è 'rvènz, l'è stè,
de stentazéinch, una fiumèna, ad nòta,
la à pórt véa do archèdi
e un óm in biciclètta.

Un pòunt che arvéil, de véint, l'era vnú e' rè,
lòngh, ch'u n finéva mai,
e da la pèrta adlà
éun u i pareva d'ès un furistír,
ènch' la zénta, i zcuréva t'un èlt módi.
A m'arcórd quant u i era la fiumèna,
ch'i l géva te cafè, a scapémmi tótt,
andémmi avdài da sòura, a sérmi mélla,
tachèd me parapèt, l'era un spetècal.
L'aqua la avnéva zò culòur dla mèlta,
a brazi vérti,
mo senza préssia,
la s pardéva a zughé s'un marugòun,
s'un ghéffal ad radéisi,
la féva d'ogni tènt un pidriúl,
ad di póst e' pareva 'diritéura
ch' la stéss férma, e u i era d'avài paéura,
sòtta la lavuréva,

Il ponte. Ecco, la strada finisce qui, /e là c'è il ponte, quel che è rimasto, è stato /
nel settantacinque, una piena, di notte, / ha portato via due arcate / e un uomo in
bicicletta. // Un ponte che a inaugurarlo, nel venti, era venuto il re, / lungo, che
non finiva mai, / e dalla parte di là / uno gli pareva d'essere un forestiero, / anche
la gente parlavano in un altro modo. / Mi ricordo quando c'era la piena, / che lo
dicevano al caffè, uscivamo tutti, / andavamo a vedere da sopra, eravamo mille, /
attaccati al parapetto, era uno spettacolo. / L'acqua veniva giú color del fango, /
a braccia aperte, / ma senza fretta, / si perdeva a giocare con una marruca, / con
un gomitolo di radici, / faceva ogni tanto un imbuto, / in certi punti pareva
addirittura / che stesse ferma, / e c'era da aver paura, / sotto lavorava, /

if you had fallen in,
they wouldn't have found a trace.

But that night must have been the end of the world,
from above, it was pounding down in torrents,
and down below it was ripping everything apart,
and the women were screaming
and an old man, poor fellow, was searching with a flashlight,
soaked, drenched, in the middle of the road,
waving at those who were coming to stop.

Then there was a lot of talk,
that no one used it anymore,
that people went the other way.
They built the new bridge up there,
on the way to San Martino.

They only come to the old one
now for the gravel,
with those trucks that spill all over,
and every once in awhile another arch collapses.
The store's still open, the owner
sitting at the door is cleaning radicchio,

se ta i caschévi dréinta
dop i n truvéva piò gnénca un butòun.

Mo cla nòta l'à da ès stè e' finimònd,
sòura e' dluviéva ad vént, sòtta e' rumpéva,
e al dòni ch'al rugéva
e un vèc, purètt, a sfurgatè sla pila,
mòl fraid, te mèz dla strèda,
a fè segn, quéi ch'i avnéa, ch'i s'afarméss.

Pu u i è stè di gran zchéurs,
dis che d'alè u n paséva piò niseun,
che la zénta i andéva t'un èlt vérs.
E' pòunt nòv i l'à fat alasò 'd sòura
par andè a San Martéin.

Adès aquè me vèc
u i vèn sno quéi dla gèra,
sa chi camion ch'i còula dimpartótt,
e d'ogni tènt e' casca un'èlta archèda.
L'è 'ncòura vért e' spazi, la padròuna
disdài sla pórta la chéunza e' radécc,

se ci cadevi dentro, / dopo non trovavano piú neanche un bottone. // Ma quella notte dev'essere stato il finimondo, / sopra diluviava di vento, sotto rompeva, / e le donne che urlavano, / e un vecchio, poveretto, a frugare con la pila, / mollo fradicio, in mezzo alla strada / a far segno a quelli che venivano che si fermassero. // Poi c'è stato un gran parlare, / dice che di lí non passava piú nessuno, / che la gente andava per un altro verso. / Il ponte nuovo l'hanno fatto lassú di sopra / per andare a San Martino. // Adesso qui al vecchio / ci vengono solo quelli della ghiaia, / con quei camion che colano dappertutto, / e ogni tanto cade un'altra arcata. / È ancora aperto lo spaccio, la padrona / seduta sulla porta pulisce il radicchio, /

197

inside she's got piled up on shelves
a few packs of cheap cigarettes,
salt, bleach,
a case of bottled water,
and, standing in a corner, two or three brooms.

If you go down from here, you get to Bornaccino,
if you go beyond the river, above, you run into the Fabbricone.
And going straight from here takes you nowhere.

dréinta la tén, mucéd t'una scanzéa,
un pó 'd pachétt ad Alfa e ad Nazionèli,
e' sèl, la varechina,
una casa ad gazòusi,
e d'impí t'un cantòun do tre garnèdi.

D'instèda u s sint la machina di sas
e vérs novèmbar
u s vaid qualch' operai
te capanòun ch'i lavòura la mnaza.

S' t vé zò d'aquè t'aréiv me Burnazéin,
d'insò, s' t vé dri me fiómm t sbòcch me Fabrécch.
E andè drétt u n s va invéll.

dentro tiene, ammucchiati su una scansia, / un po' di pacchetti di Alfa e di
Nazionali, / il sale, la varechina, / una cassa di gazzose, / e in piedi in un angolo
due tre scope. // D'estate si sente la macchina dei sassi / e verso novembre /
si vede qualche operaio / nel capannone dove lavorano la vinaccia. // Se vai giú di
qui arrivi al Bornaccino, / in su, se vai dietro al fiume, sbocchi al Fabbricone. / E
ad andare dritto non si va da nessuna parte.

Hospital Room

Now in a little while they're coming to get you,
are you afraid? because of the operation.
No, silly, you've already had it, here,
feel right here, but don't push down,
are you feeling the medication?
they're already finished,
aren't you pleased? and then you've got good color,
it doesn't even seem like you went under the knife,
it's being eighteen,
if it had been me it would have taken two.
Don't you talk now, I'll talk, do you know who this is?
This is Palmina, and this? Look at him. It's Rodolfo,
well if you move it hurts, I know, don't move,
and keep your hands still,
give them to me, that's all right, keep them under the blanket,
are you still sleepy? what are you looking at? who knows
where you think you are, we're in the room,
look at Germano down there saying hello,
down there, don't you see him?
it's because they've pulled down the blinds, it's a good thing they did,
it's nice and dark now, and cool,

Te camaròun

Adès, fra un pó i t vén a tó, t'é paéura?
par fèt l'operaziòun.
Mo no, quaiòun, ta la é za fata, tò,
tòcca aquè, mo nu chèlca,
t sint la medicaziòun? i à zà fat tótt,
ta n si cuntént? e pu t si biènch e ròss.
u n pèr mégga che séa stè sòtta i férr,
l'è che pr'avài zdòt an
mè dagli operaziòun a n farébb do.
Tè nu zcòrr, a zcòrr mè, ta la cnòss questa?
l'è la Palmina, e st'èlt? guèrdal, l'è Dolfo,
amo s' ta t móv, a l so, u t fa mèl, nu t móv,
e sta férum sal mèni,
damlí mu mè, va bén, ténli sla cvérta,
t'é ancòura sònn? e dórma,
ta n dórum? dò che t guèrd? ma tè chi sa
dò ch'u t pèr d'ès, a sémm te camaròun,
vèrda alazò Germano ch'u t saléuta,
alazò in fònd, ta n vaid?
l'è ch'i à batù sò i schéur, e i à fat bén,
u i è una piò bèl'òmbra, l'ènca frèsch,

Nel camerone. Adesso, fra un po' ti vengono a prendere, hai paura? / per farti
l'operazione. / Ma no, salame, l'hai già fatta, toh, / tocca qui, ma non spingere,
/ senti la medicazione? hanno già fatto tutto, / non sei contento? e poi sei
bianco e rosso, / non sembra mica tu sia stato sotto i ferri, / è che per avere
diciotto anni / io delle operazione ne farei due. / Tu non parlare, parlo io, la
ĉonosci questa? / è la Palmina, e quest'altro? guardalo, è Rodolfo, / e beh, se
ti muovi, lo so, ti fa male, non muoverti, / e sta' fermo con le mani, / dammele
a me, va bene, tienile sopra la coperta, / hai ancora sonno? e dormi, / non
dormi? dove guardi? e te chi sa / dove ti pare d'essere, siamo nel camerone, /
guarda laggiú Germano che ti saluta, / laggiú in fondo, non vedi? / è che hanno
accostato gli scuri, e hanno fatto bene, / c'è una cosí bell'ombra, è anche
fresco, /

and this one coming in is the nurse,
is it true that everything went all right?
it's Alfonso – the Bréun family – he's got
a motorcycle too, but he goes slow,
he's not a wild man like you, oh now, I should be quiet?
never mind about a next time,
I want to find out about it too, but, then, I'm selling it,
and that'll be the end of it,
what are you saying? I didn't understand, what? a ghost?
there in the middle of the room? no, no, it's Rodi Senior,
in a johnny, he slipped and fell down the stairs,
he's been in a cast for two months
and now Alfonso is going to teach him how to walk.

e quèll ch'e' vén adès l'è l'infermír,
vèrra ch' l'è 'ndè bén tótt? l'è Fonso 'd Bréun,
ènca léu l'à e' mutòur, però e' va pièn,
u n'è mat cumè tè, ah, ò da stè zétta?
va là che st'èlta vólta
a l ví savài 'nca mè, mo pu a t'e' vènd,
e acsè a la fémm finéida,
cs'ét détt? a n'ò capéi, cumè? un fantèsma?
alè te mèz? mo no, l'è Rodi e' vèc
se camisòun, l'à sguilé zò mal schèli,
l'è stè inzisèd du méis,
e adès Fonso u i insegna 'd caminé.

e quello che viene adesso è l'infermiere, / vero che è andato tutto bene? è
Alfonso di Bréun, / anche lui ha la moto, però va piano, / non è matto come
te, ah, devo star zitta? / va' là che un'altra volta / lo voglio sapere anch'io, ma
poi te la vendo, / e cosí la facciamo finita, / cos'hai detto? non ho capito,
come? un fantasma? / lí in mezzo? ma no, è Rodi il vecchio, / col camicione,
è scivolato giú per le scale, / è stato ingessato due mesi, / e adesso Alfonso gli
insegna a camminare.

Meatball

It's an awful thing, you're just sick,
and on top of it all he was religious, Domenico was right,
to have said all those Our Fathers,
he was always in church praying,
in the Suffragio, in San Rocco, in the Collegiata,
I myself saw him one night
saying the rosary in the Little Chapel,
which with those trucks passing by, with all that noise,
all those clouds of dust and exhaust,
it's impossible to be there inside,
and then, the method, what's it all coming to, a man like him,
dead like that, on the street,
but the idea of it, of making yourself a meatball with poison,
like for a dog,
then to walk down the avenue with his paper sack,
he chose the last bench,
he sat there until they were done coming out of the movies,
he spread it out, he laid out a snack,
he stretched out his legs and waited to die,
then later, around two, it started to rain,
and the night watchman, when he bumped into him

La pulpètta

L'è brótti robi, zò, u s'arvènza mèl,
pu l'era ad cisa, l'à rasòun Manghín,
alòura da fè chè tótt chi Patérr,
ch' l'èra sémpra d'inznòc,
te Sufràz, a San Roch, tla Colegèta,
mè una nòta o l'ò vést
parfína ma la Zléina a dí e' ruséri,
che s' chi camion ch'i pasa, fra malàn,
purbiòun e scapamént, u n s'i pò stè,
e pu e' sistéma, andémma, un òm cmè léu
mórt, acsè, par la strèda,
mo e l'idea da fès una pulpètta
invalnèda, cmè quèlli par i chèn,
pu l'è andè zò pr'e' vièl se su scartòz,
l'à cap l'éultum sedéili,
l'è stè alè bón fintènt ch'i è scap de cino,
l'à vért, l'à fat 'n'imbrènda,
l'à slòngh al gambi e l'a spitè 'd muréi,
che pu dop, vérs al do, l'à tach a pióv
e e' guardianòta quant u s'i è imbatéu

La polpetta. Sono brutte cose, dai, si rimane male, / poi era di chiesa, ha ragione Domenico, / allora da far cosa tutti quei Paternoster, / che era sempre in ginocchio, / nel Suffragio, a San Rocco, nella Collegiata, / io una notte l'ho visto / perfino dire il rosario alla Celletta, / che con quei camion che passano, fra rumore, / polverone e scappamento, non ci si può stare, / e poi il sistema, andiamo, un uomo come lui / morto, cosí, per strada, / ma e l'idea di farsi una polpetta / avvelenata, come quelle per i cani, / poi è andato giú per il viale col suo cartoccio, / ha scelto l'ultima panchina, / è stato lí finché non sono usciti dal cinema, / ha aperto, ha fatto una merenda, / ha allungato le gambe e ha aspettato di morire, / che poi dopo, verso le due, ha cominciato a piovere / e la guardia notturna quando ci si è imbattuto /

205

was terrified,
at this man who was glittering under the lamplight
and water rolling down his hat
onto his vest.

u s'è ènca spavantè,
st'òm che luséva tótt sòtta e' lampiòun
e l'aqua ch' la i culéva da e' capèl
sòura e' panciòt.

s'è anche spaventato, / quest'uomo che riluceva tutto sotto il lampione / e
l'acqua che gli colava dal cappello / sul panciotto.

Signature

What is it I've got to sign, which I don't know a thing about?
me, with a pen, come on now, I got to third grade,
can't Guerrino sign? he's my son,
just look at all this stuff, all over a couple of bucks,
they've got no trust? come on, come off it, let's get it over with,
where do I have to sign, down here?
on the line, sure, what do you expect? me, for godsake,
so I can scribble a mess, give me the pen,
and get the ink, is there any?
son of gun, I dipped it too much, look at that blot,
haven't you got another one of these pieces of paper, no?
now what? blotting paper? I haven't got any,
why would I? just leave everything alone, you're not going to find any,
you're just making a big mess, just go get the sports page,
whatever page, Guerrino's already read it,
try with that one,
here we go now, wait, let me sit better,
me, with chairs,
I've got to sit less close, oh, that's good,
so now, *Ta,* with a capital *T,* then *a,*
what is it with this nib, it's gouging,

La firma

Cus'èll ch'ò da firmé ch'a n capéss gnént?
mè, sla pènna, fighéurt, ò fat la térza,
u n pò firmé Guerino? l'è e' mi fiúl,
mo vèrda ach roba par ciapè du bòch,
i n s'aféida? dài, va là, fémma prèst,
dvò ch'ò da sgnè, aquazò?
sla réiga? sè, t'é vòia, mè diogrèzia
ch'a faza un scarabòc, dàm la canètta
e tó l'inciòstra, u i n'è?
orca masóla, ò impuzè trop, vè ch' macia,
ta n n'é un èlt ad sti fói? no? e adès cum s fal?
una chèrta sughènta? mè a n la ò,
's'ut ch'apa, e lasa stè, che ta n tróv gnént,
t fé sno de gran smasír, piotòst tó e' Stadio,
un fòi purséa, Guerino u l'à zà lèt,
próva sa quèll,
e zà ch'a i sémm, aspétta, ch'a m cònd mèi,
mè sla scaràna
ò da stè mènch tachèd, oh, acsè e' va bén,
dòunca Ta, sla T grande, pu la a,
mo cs'àl sté pínni, e' péunta,

La firma. Cos'è che devo firmare, che non capisco niente? / io, con la penna, figurati, ho fatto la terza, / non può firmare Guerrino? è mio figlio, / ma guarda che roba per prendere due soldi, / non si fidano? / dai, va' là, facciamo presto, / dove devo firmare, quaggiú? / sulla riga? sí, hai voglia, io diograzia / che faccia uno scarabocchio, dammi la cannuccia / e prendi l'inchiostro, ce n'è? / orca masóla, ho intinto troppo, ve' che macchia, / non ne hai un altro di questi fogli? no? e adesso come si fa? / una carta asciugante? non ce l'ho, / cosa vuoi che abbia, e lascia stare, che non trovi niente, / fai solo del gran disordine, piuttosto prendi lo Stadio, / un foglio purchessia, Guerrino l'ha già letto, / prova con quello, / e già che ci siamo, aspetta, che mi accomodo meglio, / io con la sedia / devo stare meno vicino, oh, cosí va bene, / dunque Ta, con la T grande, poi la a, / ma cos'ha questo pennino, s'impunta, /

209

is it me pressing too hard? if I don't press, it doesn't mark,
now what have I done? if all you're going to do is criticize,
well I'll just do the best I can,
I've already had enough of it, see how bad I've started off,
and this piece of paper moving all over the place, every which way,

instead of talking, help me hold it still, keep it from slipping,
just put your hand here, fine, now we're set,
the *l* is finished now too, oh just be quiet,
you'll make me lose my place, what is it that's missing?
the *g* where? really? you're exactly right,
how am I going to squeeze it in between here now?
I'll put it above, all right? let's just try and,
look how clumsy, all because I listened to you,
just be patient, it's almost finished,
is this good enough for them,
let's keep going,
the *e*, just be nice a minute,
you've always got to comment, it needs the *i*?
fine, here's the *i*, then the *e*,
there, you see how I can't write?
I have to press down over it again,
it's not the pen, it's the ink,
let me see, it's all slimy, it's covered with grit,
just look at this blot coming through

a so mè ch'a chèlch trop? s'a n chèlch u n dà,
cs'èll ch'ò sbrènch? s' l'è un struncòun,
e pu, ció, a faz cm'a pòs,
che aquè s'a m stóff, da zà ch'ò ravié mèl,
e sta chèrta ch' la va da tótt i chènt,
invíci ad zcòrr aiéutmi a tnàila férma,
basta una mèna aquè, oh, adès a i sémm,
ènch' la elle la è fata, mo sta zétt,
che ta m fé pérd e' féil, cs'èll ch'u i amènca?
la gi? duvò? dabón, t'é pò rasòun,
adès cmè ch'a glia instècch aquè te mèz?
mè a glia faz sòura, no? pruvémma pò,
vè ch' macaròun, par stèt sintéi ma tè,
pazinzia, ormai la è fata,
i s'acuntantarà,
andémma avènti,
la e, mo sta bunéin,
tè t'è sémpra da déi, u i vó la i?
va bén, a faz la i, pu dop la e,
toh, vitt ch'u n dà? u m tòcca arpasèi sòura,
quèst u n'è gnénca e' pínni, l'è l'inciòstra,
fam avdài, mo l'è mèlta, e pin ad tróccal,
vè a ch' patòun ch' l'è vnú sò,
dai 'na puléida tè, che mè a n so fè,

sono io che spingo troppo? se non spingo non segna, / cos'ho sfasciato? se è uno
stronco, / e poi faccio come posso, / che qui se mi stufo, già che ho cominciato
male, / e questa carte che va da tutte le parti, / invece di parlare aiutami a tenerla
ferma, / basta una mano qui, oh, adesso ci siamo, / anche la elle è fatta, ma stai
zitto, / che mi fai perdere il filo, cos'è che ci manca? / la gi? dove? davvero, hai pur
ragione, / adesso come gliela ficco qui in mezzo? / io gliela faccio sopra, no?
proviamo pure, / ve' che maccherone, per stare a sentire te, / pazienza, ormai è
fatta, / s'accontenteranno, / andiamo avanti, / la e, ma stai buonino, / tu hai
sempre da dire, ci vuol la i? / va bene, faccio la i, poi dopo la e, / toh, vedi che non
scrive? mi tocca ripassarci sopra, / questo non è nemmeno il pennino, è
l'inchiostro, / fammi vedere, ma è una melma, e piena di bioccoli, / ve' che grumo
è venuto su, / dacci una pulita tu, che io non so fare, /

211

you give it a good wipe, I don't know how to do it,
and now I'm getting the shakes,
what are you saying? oh sure, I'm going a little bit crooked,
I'm crooked too, my back is already sore,
being all hunched over,
just look this job I'm stuck with,
and they're waiting for me in the piazza, I said seven,
it's already seven-thirty,
did you clean it up? give it here, where was I?
I'm no good anymore at having to concentrate,
what does it still need? the *e*?
then after that the *r*, yeah, I understand,
like in Rosina, I've gotten this far,
can you just be quiet a minute, you're such a know-it-all,
just look at the letters, the farther I go
the bigger they get,
I'm just no good for writing small,
I fiddle around, I fiddle around, and then I make a mistake,
see! look, I made an *n* with two legs,
and you, you too, who's the one making me talk,
it's not a mistake? no? it's the *m* that has two legs,
right, that's true, the *i*, keep going now,
I want to do it quickly, the *o*, see how nice I'm doing it,
but it's sloping down too much,

e pu u m vén i santéssum,
cs'èll t'é da déi? mo sè, a vagh un pó tórt,
a so tórt ènca mè e u m dól zà la schéina
a stè tótt ingubéid,
mo vè at che lavurír ch'a m so andè mètt,
e mè i m'aspétta in piaza, ò détt al sèt,
l'è bèla al sèt e mèz,
t l'é puléi? dam aquè, duvò ch'a séra?
mè a n so mégga piò bón d' stè 'lè sla testa,
csà i vól adès? la e?
pu dop e' vén la erre, sè, ò capéi,
cmè la Rusina, fina 'lè a i aréiv,
mo sta un pó zétt, t saré pò un avuchèd,
tra che stal lèttri
aquè piò a vagh avènti, piò a m vén grandi,
mè a scréiv znin a n so bón,
a zanzéigh, a zanzéigh, pu dop a sbai,
alè, vè, ò fat un enne sa do gambi,
azidént ènch' ma tè che ta m fé zcòrr,
u n'è un sbai, no? l'è l'emme ch' l'à tre gambi,
zà, l'è vèrra, la i, e adès, avènti,
a ví fè prèst, la o, vitt ch'a vagh bén,
però a cal un pó trop,

e poi mi vengono i nervi, / cos'hai da dire? ma sí, vado un po' torto, / sono
torto anch'io e mi duole già la schiena / a stare tutto ingobbito, / ma guarda in
che lavoro mi sono andato a mettere, / e mi aspettano in piazza, ho detto alle
sette, / sono ormai le sette e mezzo, / l'hai pulito? dammi qui, dov'ero? / io
non sono mica piú buono di star lí con la testa, / cosa ci vuole adesso? la e? /
poi dopo viene la erre, sí, ho capito, / come la Rosina, fin lí ci arrivo, / ma stai
un po' zitto, sarai pure un cacasenno, / già che queste lettere / qui piú vado
avanti, piú mi vengono grandi, / io a scrivere piccolo non sono capace, /
cincischio, cincischio, e poi sbaglio, / alè, ve', ho fatto una enne con due
gambe, / accidenti anche a te che mi fai parlare, / non è uno sbaglio? no? è
l'emme che ha tre gambe, / già, è vero, la i, e adesso avanti, / voglio far presto,
la o, vedi che vado bene, / però calo un po' troppo, /

213

I admit it, I'm no good at it,
I've got to come up, it's not so hard, I've got to back curve up,
be patient will you, leave the paper alone, why are you tugging at it?
look at this blot you made me make, are you out of your mind?
this is your idea of helping? nice job,
just let me do it myself,
here you've got to slowly curve back upwards,
would you prefer I draw a ladder?
it's got to be big, it needs its own space,
but it's taking up way too much, I'm not going to get it,
I can't get it to curve,
and he's laughing, what are you laughing about, you're so smart,
and stop crowding me, which in a minute
I'm going to chuck it all out the window,
I'll give you a signature,
it's that I never would have thought,
come off it now, I just can't do it, then these letters,
too big, can't you see? they look like flopping dolls,
and I just can't stop myself, I'm jittery,
I just can't be steady on the paper, go get the newspaper,
put it underneath, spread it out, not like that,
where are you putting it, have you got it set? I went off,
there, you see, now I'm writing on the wood,
it doesn't matter, come on, I want to be done with it,

a zéd ch'a n mu n'incórz,
ò d'andè sò, u n'è gnént, ò da vultè,
'ta bón, lasa stè e' fòi, mo cs'ét tiràt?
vè 'd rasp ta m'é fat fè, u t'è vnú e' mat?
ta m vlévi dè una mèna? un bel lavòur,
mo lasmi fè mu mè,
aquè bsògna andè 'dèsi a dèi e' zéir,
t vu ch'a faza e' scaléin?
la va ciapèda lèrga, u i vó e' su pòst,
però acsè u i nu n vó trop, a n gne la faz,
a n'aréiv a vultè,
e léu e' réid, csà réidti, ch' t si pataca?
e nu vénmi madòs, che aquè a muménti
a bótt tótt pr'aria, a t la dagh mè la firma,
l'è che mè a n mu n cridéva,
mo va là, a n m'indrézz mégga, pu stal lèttri,
tropi grandi, ta n vaid? l'è di bumbózz,
e a n so bón d'afarmèm, ò ciap la léssa,
a n'i stagh piò te fòi, va tó e' giurnèl,
mèttme sòtta, ténal spianèd, no acsè,
dò ta l mètt, ta l fé pòsta? a so 'ndè fura,
ècco, t'é vést, adès a scréiv se lègn,
u n'arimpórta, avènti, a ví finéi,
l'è che ènca e' fòi l'era vnú mèss sla zéima,

cedo che non me n'accorgo, / devo andare su, non è niente, devo voltare, / sta'
buono, lascia stare il foglio, ma cos'hai tirato? / guarda che sgorbio m'hai fatto
fare, t'è venuto il matto? / mi volevi dare una mano? un bel lavoro, / ma
lasciami fare a me, / qui bisogna andare adagio a darci il giro, / vuoi che faccia
lo scalino? / va presa larga, ci vuole il suo posto, / però cosí ce ne vuole troppo, non ce la faccio, / non arrivo a voltare, / e lui ride, cosa ridi, che sei fesso?
/ e non venirmi addosso, che qui a momenti / butto tutto per aria, te la do io
la firma, / è che io non credevo, / ma va' là, non mi raddrizzo mica, poi queste
lettere, / troppo grandi, non vedi? sono dei bambocci, / e non sono capace di
fermarmi, ho preso lo scivolo, / non ci sto piú nel foglio, va' a prendere il giornale, / mettimelo sotto, tienilo spiegato, non cosí, / dove lo metti, lo fai apposta? sono andato fuori, / ecco, hai visto, adesso scrivo sul legno, / non importa,
avanti, voglio finire, / è che anche il foglio era venuto messo sul bordo, /

it's also because the paper was right at the edge,
is the table big enough?
look at how it's sloping down, for christsakes, I'm falling off,
get that cardboard, I'll try to write on top of it,
no, there's too much of a drop, get the ironing board,
it's down there against the wall, come on hurry up,
put it next to it, like this, closer,
hold it still, don't laugh, I've done it like this before,
fine, laugh now all you want, it's just killing you,
just come here next to me, so I can write all the way across,
and then it's still not working, these letters are just swelling up,
I can't keep up with them, they're train cars,
the board, look, I'm already at the edge,
get the cutting board,
we haven't got all day, what are you waiting for, you waiting for
                                                    [pigs to grow wings,
harder now! give it a good shove,
so it'll come out, and bring it here, then the buffet,
bring it all, the problem is, is that it's not enough,
just leave it be, it's doesn't matter,
just take down the ironing board,
I'll finish on the floor,
this fountain pen's not good
for anything anymore, what I need is a shovel
and some plaster or a big fat paintbrush and some mortar,
I want to write on the pavement, open the door,
open it I told you, which if I don't get out of here,
I'm going to go on the street, and then, if that's not enough, the
                                                    [piazza,
this is my name, *you* tell them it, and if they don't understand,

la bastarà la tèvla?
vè cmè ch'a vagh d'inzò, orca, a m'aréugal,
tó che cartòun, ch'a próv da muntèi sòura,
no e' bala trop, tó l'asa da stiré,
la è 'lazò còuntra e' méur, mo fa a la svélta,
còstla, acsè, piò tachèda,
ténla férma, nu réid, a i la ò pò fata,
e adès réid quant u t pèr, ta t'astruzéss,
mo vénmi dri, ch'a pòsa scréiv pr'e' lòngh,
e pu a n'i sémm l'istèss, stal lèttri al gòunfia,
a n gn'aréss a stèi dri, l'è di vaghéun,
l'asa, vè, a so zà sl'òural, tó e' tulír,
chèval dai gàngar, forza! dài 'na bota
ch'e' scapa e pórtl'aquè, pu la cardénza,
pórta tótt, l'è l'istèss, cala zò l'asa,
a vagh ma tèra,
sta canètta che què la n'è piò bóna
d' fè gnént, u m vó un badéil
e de zèss o un pnèl gròs sa dla calzéina,
a ví scréiv se sulèr, éirva la pórta,
éirva, a t'ò détt, che s'a n'i stagh a scap,
a vagh sla strèda e pu, s'u n basta, in piaza,
quèst l'è e' mi nóm, tè déie, e s'i n capéss,

basterà la tavola? / ve' come vado giú, orca, ruzzolo, / prendi quel cartone, che provo a salirci sopra, / no, balla troppo, prendi l'asse da stirare, / è laggiú contro il muro, ma fai alla svelta, / accostala, cosí, piú attacata, / tienila ferma, non ridere, ce l'ho pur fatta, / e adesso ridi quanto ti pare, ti strangolassi, / ma vienimi dietro, che ci possa scrivere per il lungo, / e poi non ci siamo lo stesso, queste lettere si gonfiano, / non riesco a starci dietro, sono dei vagoni, / l'asse, ve', sono già sull'orlo, prendi il tagliere, / càvalo dai gangheri, forza! dacci una botta, / che esca, e portalo qui, poi la credenza, / porta tutto, è che non basta, / lasica stare, è lo stesso, cala giú l'asse, / vado per terra, / questa cannuccia qui non è piú buona / da far niente, mi ci vuole un badile / e del gesso o un pennello grosso e della calcina, / voglio scrivere sul pavimento, / apri la porta, / apri, t'ho detto, che se non ci sto esco, / vado sulla strada e poi, se non basta, in piazza, / questo è il mio nome, tu diglielo, e se non capiscono, /

too bad for them, I'll write it for them as big as possible,
even bigger than the piazza, I want to go
all the way to the fairgrounds, under the wall,
and from up above with just a glance, everyone can see it,
but I've got to do it right away, before it rains,
and people walk all over it,
but then even if they don't get there in time,
if they get there and everything's washed away,
I'm right here, they'll find me right away, at Annibale's
or in the piazza or in the cafe,
I'll tell them what my name is, first name and last,
softly in an ear, if they only want themselves to hear it,
or loud, even, whatever they want,
when *I* yell, they hear me as far as the Mulini,
they can look at me, who I am,
I'll show them the birthmark I've got on my neck,
the little finger without a fingernail
because I had whitlow when I was a boy,
it's me, there's no mistaking it, who once fell
into the millpond at Rancaia,
I must have been sixteen years old,
then a soldier at Sacile
when I saw Norma and Rigoletto, a packed-house,
no one could get into the theater,

pézz par lòu, mè a i e' scréiv piò grand ch'u s pò,
ènca piò grand dla piaza, e ví rivé
fina te canfiré, sòtta la Méura,
e d'alasò s'n'ucèda i l pò vdai tótt,
però i à da fè prèst, préima ch'e' pióva
e che la zénta la i caméina sòura,
mo pu ènca s'i n fa in témp,
s'i aréiva ch'u s'è ormai scasè iniquèl,
a so què mè, i m tróva sóbit, da Nébal
o in piaza o te cafè,
a i e' déggh mè cm'a m cèm, nóm e cognóm
pièn, t'n'urèccia, s'i l vó sintéi sno lòu,
o ènca fórt, cmè ch'u i pèr,
mè quant ch'a rógg i m sint fina i Muléin,
i m pò guardè, chi ch'a so,
a i faz avdài la vòia ch'ò te còl,
e' daid znin senza l'óngia
pr'un ziradàid quant a séra burdèl,
a so mè, u n s pò sbaiè, che un èlt mumént
a m'afughéva te gòurgh dla Rancàia,
a géva avài ségg an,
put ti suldè a Sacile quant ò vést
la Norma e e' Rigulètt che te teètar
da la zénta u n s'i stéva,

peggio per loro, io glielo scrivo piú grande che si può, / anche piú grande della
piazza, voglio arrivare / fino al campo della fiera, sotto la Mura, / e di lassú con
un'occhiata lo possono vedere tutto, / però devono far presto, prima che piova
/ e che la gente ci cammini sopra, / ma poi anche se non fanno in tempo, / se
arrivano che s'è ormai cancellata ogni cosa, / sono qui io, mi trovano subito, da
Annibale / o in piazza o al caffè, / glielo dico io come mi chiamo, nome e
cognome, / piano in un orecchio, se lo vogliono sentire solo loro, / o anche
forte, come gli pare, / io quando urlo mi sentono fino ai Mulini, / mi possono
guardare, chi sono, / gli faccio vedere la voglia che ho sul colo, / il dito piccolo
senza l'unghia / per un patereccio quand'ero bambino, / sono io, non si può
sbagliare, che un altro momento / m'affogavo nella gora della Rancaia, / dovevo
avere sedici anni, / poi soldato a Sacile quando ho visto / la Norma e il
Rigoletto che nel teatro / dalla gente non ci si stava, /

then I was a laborer for the railroad,
and that Sunday, hold on a minute, at Villagrande,
or was it Ponte dell'Uso? I don't remember anymore,
where I pulled out a chub
bigger than this arm,
I'd never seen an animal like that,
it pulled like an ox,
do you understand? then, come on now, would that be enough
                                                     [for them?

but for what purpose, it's all just too much talk,
what do they need, what more do they need than me
which they've got right there in front of them,
me, which they can touch with a hand?

dop ò fat e' manèzz in ferovéa,
e cla dmènga, 'ta bón, a Vilagranda,
o l'è stè me Pòunt dl'Éus? a n m'arcórd piò,
ch'ò tiràt sò un cavéidal
piò gròs ca nè sté braz,
'n'animèli ad cla fata a n l'ò mai vést,
e' tiréva cmè un bò,
t'é capéi? pu, t'é vòia, u i nu n sarébb,
mo da fè chè, l'è tótt zchéurs ad di piò,
cs'ài bsògn, piò ca nè mè ch'i m'à davènti?
ch'i m pò tuchè s'na mèna?

dopo ho fatto il manovale in ferrovia, / e quella domenica, stai buono, a
Villagrande, / o è stato al Ponte dell'Uso? non mi ricordo più, / che ho tirato
su un cavedano / più grosso di questo braccio, / un animale di quella fatta non
l'ho mai visto, / tirava come un bue, / hai capito? poi, hai voglia, ce ne
sarebbero, / ma da far che, sono tutti discorsi di troppo, / cos'hanno bisogno,
più che me che m'hanno davanti? / che mi possono toccare con una mano?

221

The Fitting

She was tiny, with a pug nose,
mean as a snake,
her hair always uncombed, with that caved-in mouth
those two gold teeth, but since she was a seamstress
you had to leave her alone.

She was always in a foul mood,
when one day the girl,
who was doing a blind stitch,
in turning around, she didn't mean to, she tipped over the iron
with her arm,
and already that morning ironing
she had scorched a blouse,
and she just snapped, she had a pair of scissors
in her hand, they cut,
she pulled them away from her,
the girl could have lost an eye, it was a miracle,
it was nothing, she'd gotten a scrape, a cut that amounted to
                                                    [nothing,
a scratch, but still, a scare.

Al miséuri

La era znina, sgnaflèda,
catéiva cumè e' vlén,
sémpra scavcèda, sa cla bòcca spéinza
e chi du dént a d'ór, mo cmè sartòura
bsugnéa lasèla stè.

La éva sémpra e' garbéin,
un dè che la burdèla
ch' la era dri a fè un sotpéunt,
te vultès, non volénd, la à 'rbórt e' fèr
sa tótt' la brèsa,
e zà che la matéina te stiré
la i aveva vampè una camisètta,
li ció u i è vnú un rafètt, la aveva al fórbsi
tal mèni, ch' la taiéva,
la l gli à tiràti còuntra,
robi ch' la i chèva un òc, l'è stè un mirècal,
gnént, la la à ciapa ad sbréss, un tai da gnént,
un rasp, però un spavént.

Le misure. Era piccola, col naso rincagnato, / cattiva come il veleno, / sempre
spettinata, con quella bocca in dentro / e quei due denti d'oro, ma come sarta
/ bisognava lasciarla stare. // Era sempre di malumore, / un giorno che la
ragazzina / che stava facendo un sottopunto, / nel voltarsi, non volendo, ha
rovesciato il ferro / con tutta la brace, / e già che la mattina nello stirare / le
aveva strinato una camicetta, / lei le è venuto uno scatto, aveva le forbici / in
mano, che tagliava, / gliele ha tirate contro, / che poteva cavarle un occhio, è
stato un miracolo, / niente, l'ha presa di striscio, un taglio da niente, / un
graffio, però uno spavento. //

But when Fausta came in for the fitting,
gorgeous, when she passed by the cafe,
silence,
she was seventeen years old, a girl,
but she carried herself like a countess,
go figure how she turned out like that,
she was Canzio's daughter, Canzio, the charcoal maker,
she was a picture, beautiful all over,
even her ears were pretty,
like lacework,
and breasts like two little swallows,
which in a hand were hot and trembled,
enough, when Fausta arrived in the workroom,
she had her undress
and had her stand still there, in the middle, standing,
she wanted to get an idea of her shape,
she looked at her in silence,
with a pained expression, she studied her,
but the other one, after awhile of standing there not moving,

Mo quant l'avnéa la Fausta pr'al miséuri,
bèla, che te cafè quant la paséva
i stéa zétt tótt,
la aveva disèt an, una burdèla,
mo un purtamént, ch' pareva una cuntèssa,
va pò a capéi d' ch' la era scapa fura,
l'era la fióla ad Canzio e' carbunèr,
una pitéura, bèla dimpartótt,
ènca agli urècci la gli aveva bèli,
un richèm,
e cal titíni cmè du pasarótt
che tal mèni i è chèld e i trema tótt,
basta, quante la Fausta la arivéva
te camaròun, li la la féa spuiè
e ch' la stéss férma alè, te mèz, d'impí,
la s vléva fè un'idea dla fighéura,
la la guardéa da zétt,
s'un'aria da instizéida,
mo no un minéut,
la stéva alè disdài s' che canapè,
la tnéva al gambi lèrghi
e e' metar spandléun tònda me còl,
la la guardéa si ócc strétt, la la studiéva,
mo cl'èlta dop un pó, a stè 'lè d'incécch,

Ma quando veniva la Fausta per le misure, / bella, che al caffè quando passava / stavano zitti tutti, / aveva diciassette anni, una bambina, / ma un portamento che pareva una contessa, / vai pure a capire da dove era venuta fuori, / era la figlia di Canzio il carbonaio, / una pittura, bella dappertutto, / anche le orecchie le aveva belle, / un ricamo, / e quelle tettine come due passerotti / che in mano sono caldi e tremano tutti, / basta, quando la Fausta arrivava / nel camerone, lei la faceva spogliare / e che stesse ferma lí, nel mezzo, in piedi, / voleva farsi un'idea della figura, / la guardava in silenzio, / con un'aria crucciata, / ma non un minuto, / stava seduta lí su quel canapè, / teneva le gambe larghe / e il metro penzoloni attorno al collo, / la guardava con gli occhi socchiusi, la studiava, / ma l'altra dopo un po', a stare lí impalata, /

225

got bored, shook her head: "Come on now!"
and the other one hadn't given any sign that she'd heard,
so she turned around, she whined, "Is that enough?"
and she stood up, she was holding the tape measure
pulled taut between her two hands,
she said with that hoarse voice of hers,
"It's not enough. It's never enough."

la s stuféva,
li la scruléa la testa: "Mo sta bóna!"
cl'èlta la n tnéva bota,
la s'arvultéva, la sprignléva: "U n basta?",
e li la stéva sò, la tnéva e' metar
tiràt sa tutt' do al mèni,
la géva sa cla vòusa
sémpra runchèda: "U n basta, u n basta mai".

si stufava, / lei scrollava la testa: "Ma stai buona!" / l'altra non teneva botta, / si voltava, piagnucolava: "Non basta?", / e lei si alzava, teneva il metro / tirato con tutt'e due le mani, / diceva con quella voce / sempre rauca: "Non basta, non basta mai".

July

The ninth of July, a Sunday,
it must have been about five in the afternoon,
in Ciola, right up there at the top,
at Baròus' house,
but in the back there, in the shade,
between the hedge, which from there went straight down
straight down to Lasagna, and the wall,
which was a garden in itself,
with a little breeze that every so often,
did a little rummaging around in the reeds,
they were playing tressette at a small table,
and they put stones on the cards
so they wouldn't fly off.
And when, on a particular hand,
he got a slew of hearts,
and three threes, not including diamonds,
he puffed up a little bit, but quietly, so you couldn't tell,
he settled comfortably into his chair,
then he drew the ace, and he still didn't say anything,
but in his contentment
he bumped the leg of the table,
so that the wine in the glasses was all jostled,

Lói

E' nóv ad lói, 'na dmènga,
e' gév'ès vérs al zéinch de dopmezdè,
a Zula, própia in zéima,
ma la chèsa ad Baròus,
mo di dri, tl'òmbra,
tra la siva, che adlà e' cala zò drétt
ad quèll 'd Lasagna,
e e' méur, che l'era tótta una vardéura,
s'un vangín che faséva d'ogni tènt
un pó 'd smasír tra 'l cani,
m'un tavuléin i zughéva a trisétt
e i tnéva i sas al chèrti
pòsta ch'a n vuléss véa.
E quante ma quèll 'd mèna
u i è vnú la crécca ad còppi
e tri tré fal denèri,
l'à gunfiè un pó, mo zétt, u n s'è fat cnòss,
u s'è cònd sla scaràna,
pu l'è scap sl'as, e u n géva ancòura gnént,
mo da la cuntantèzza
l'à dè una bota se lègn
che ti bicír e' véin l'à tremè tótt,

Luglio. Il nove luglio, una domenica / dovevano essere le cinque del pomeriggio, / a Ciola, proprio in cima, / alla casa di Baròus, / ma di dietro, nell'ombra, / tra la siepe, che di là cala giú dritto / nel fondo di Lasagna, / e il muro, che era tutta una verdura, / con un venticello che faceva ogni tanto / un po' di tramestío fra le canne, / a un tavolino giocavano a tressette / e tenevano i sassi sulle carte / perché non volassero via. / E quando a quello di mano / gli è venuta la cricca di coppe / e tre tre senza danari, / s'è gonfiato un po', ma zitto, non s'è fatto capire, / s'è accomodato sulla sedia, / poi è uscito con l'asso, e non diceva ancora niente, / ma dalla contentezza / ha dato una botta sul legno / che nei bicchieri il vino ha tremato tutto, /

229

and the cicada in the cherry tree
out of fear was suddenly silent.
The air got so light
you could hear, at the crossroads, the chirping
of a rusty bicycle bell,
and way down below, far off,
an airplane flying over the sea.

e la zghéla se zris
la è stèda zétta ad bot da la paéura.
L'aria alòura la è dvénta acsè lizíra
che se crusèri u s'è sintí springnlé
e' campanèl ruznéid d'na biciclètta,
e alazò, mo dalòngh,
vulè un areoplano sòura e' mèr.

e la cicala sul ciliegio / ha taciuto di botto dalla paura. / L'aria allora è diventata cosí leggera / che sul crocicchio s'è sentito pigolare / il campanello arruginito di una bicicletta, / e laggiú, ma lontano, / volare un aeroplano sopra il mare.

Love

I'd like to kiss you on the mouth,
but I have a fever, and it will make my blood pressure go up.
Even just talking hurts. My lower lip.
I'd like to caress you, then undo your hair,
to see it falling down
on your shoulders, but I have chilblains, look,
they've all popped open, see how the skin is throbbing.
Just let me take hold of your hands,
easy now, if not it'll hurt,
and hold them here against my face.
What were you doing? the wash? I know it too,
they're still wet, and then in the air,
can't you see? they're blue
all covered with little ridges, they're rough
like sandpaper.
Don't cry now, what did I say? here, forget it,
because afterwards you'll ruin your face and if your skin gets all
                                          [irritated,
you'll keep pulling at it.
Don't cry, I'm right, right? your eyes are tearing up from the
                                          [cold?

L'amòur

A t vrébb dè un bès ad bòcca,
mo a i ò una févra, o dop s'u m vén e' sangh,
ch'a m faz mèl ènca a zcòrr, te labar sòtta.
A t vrébb fè una carèzza,
pu guastèt e' ciucòun,
avdài tótt i cavéll ch'i t casca zò
sal spali, mo a iò la méughi,
vèrda, a m s'è vérti, u s vaid la chèrna véiva.
Lasa ch'a t ciapa al mèni,
pianín, se no a m faz mèl,
e ch'a li ténga aquè còuntra la faza.
Mo cs'ét fat? la bughéda? a l so ènca mè,
ta li tén sémpra a mòl e pu ma l'aria,
ta n vaid? agli è murèli
e pini ad crétt, al raspa
cmè la chèrta vedrèda.
E adès nu pianz, cs'òi détt? zò, lasa andè,
che dop ta t sfraigh la faza e s' t'é al vulàdghi
u t téira tótt' la pèla.
Ta n pianz, dabón? u t còula i ócc pr'e' frèdd?

L'amore. Ti vorrei dare un bacio in bocca, / ma ho una febbre, e dopo se mi viene il sangue, / che mi faccio male anche a parlare, nel labbro sotto. / Ti vorrei fare una carezza, / poi guastarti la crocchia, / vedere tutti i capelli che ti cascano giú / sulle spalle, ma ho i geloni, / guarda, mi si sono aperti, si vede la carne viva. / Lasica che ti prenda le mani, / pianino, se no mi faccio male, / e che le tenga qui contro la faccia. / Ma cos'hai fatto? il bucato? / lo so anch'io / le tieni sempre a mollo e poi all'aria / non vedi? sono viola / e piene di cretti, raspano / come la carta vetrata. / E adesso non piangere, cos'ho detto? su, lascia andare, / che dopo ti sfreghi la faccia e se hai le volatiche / ti tira tutta la pelle. / Non piangi, davvero? ti colano gli occhi per il freddo? /

I know, I've made a big mistake, I have,
I know, believe me,
here in this nook, it'll be dark soon,
since the streetlight's burned out,
plus, no one passes through here at this hour,
but there's a little opening to stand straight against.
Let's try a little higher up, here, lean against me,
against the little doorway.
But it's worse here, can't you tell, it's all crumbling,
that way must be Muntagnúl's vegetable garden,
the wind's coming from below, feel it, it's hitting
the ankles. It's better down below, come with me,
behind the cornice, it's a little corner there,
then there are the beams, it's more protected.
wait there, it's narrow, I'll go through first.
No, come on now, it's like ice,
you can't be on it, it's like a windmill here,
on the ground? what are you thinking? it's all mud,
it's dripping, there must be pipe from a sink.
Look, it's better where we were first,
you go before me.
Let's just stay here.
See how I'm right? it's a little more protected.
Smelling like what? you're smelling stink
with this Arctic wind?

A l so, quèst l'è stè un sbai ch'a l'ò fat mè,
mè, ció, a m cridéva,
aquè, sòtta è' vultòun, fra un pó l'è nòta,
sicómm ch'u s'e' brusé la lampadéina,
pu da stagli òuri u n pasa piò niseun,
però u i è un sbòcc ch'u i è d'arvanzè téinch.
Pruvémma un pó piò in zò, ècco, puzésmi
còuntra sté purtunzéin.
Mo aquè l'è pézz, ta n vaid? l'è tótt sguardlèd,
adlà u i à da ès l'órt ad Muntagnúl,
e' pasa e' vént da sòtta, sint, e' taia
própia te còl de pi.
L'è mèi alazò 'd sòtta, vén sa mè,
di dri de curnisòun, quèll l'è un cugóll,
pu u i è chi trèv, l'arvènza, piò ciutèd.
Aspétta alè, ch' l'è strètt, préima a pas mè.
No, mo va là, l'è un séidar,
u n s'i pò stè, aquè e' fa e' pidriúl,
pu par tèra, mo cs'èll? l'è tótta mèlta,
da sòura e' sgòzzla, e' sarà un téub da scàfa.
Vèrda, l'è mèi duvò ch'a sérmi préima,
tè va 'vènti ch'a véngh. Farmésmi aquè.
Vitt ch'ò rasòun? l'è un pó pió riparèd.
Pózza ad chè? t sint la pózza? sa sta bura?

Io so, questo è stato uno sbaglio che ho fatto io, / io, sai, mi credevo, / qui,
sotto il voltone, fra un po' è notte, / siccome s'è bruciata la lampadina, / poi a
queste ore non passa piú nessuno, / però c'è uno sbocco da rimanere stecchiti.
/ Proviamo un po' piú in su, ecco, appoggiamoci / contro questo portoncino.
/ Ma qui è peggio, non vedi? è tutto sfasciato, / di là ci dev'essere l'orto di
Muntagnúl, / passa il vento da sotto, senti, taglia / proprio nel collo del piede.
/ È meglio laggiú di sotto, vieni con me, / dietro il cornicione, quello è un
angolino, / poi ci sono le travi, resta piú protetto. / Aspetta lí, che è stretto,
prima passo io. / No, ma va' là, è un gelo, / non ci si può stare, qui fa il
mulinello, / poi per terra, ma cos'è? è tutto fango, / da sopra gocciola, sarà un
tubo di lavandino. / Guarda, è meglio dove eravamo prima, / tu vai avanti che
vengo. Fermiamoci qui. / Vedi che ho ragione? è un po' piú riparato. / Puzza
di che? senti la puzza? con questa bora?

You're right, those would be Esterina's chickens,
she keeps them down below here. I don't hear a thing.
Especially with that shawl, why are you wearing that thing?
can't you see how you've tied it all up?
I'll really reach you trying to undo it, keep still,
that's it, then turn the collar around,
there, it's even tighter now,
and now there's even a knot for me to get out,
no, a knot, I'll keep it here on the stomach,
and both of us will be covered.
What are you doing? we're separating?
come here, stay close, closer.
What have you put into your hair?
a few drops of vinegar?
for what? to untangle it? then cologne?
no, I'm just asking, no of course not,
you can only smell the perfume.
And this bunch of string? did you come with a whole magic show
under your coat? did you come out in disguise?
and now where are you going? be good now,
you're pulling at it too, aren't you tightening it?
feel how warm you can stay,
it's just that you're already there with your hands,
and me with my itching
all over my body since this morning,

Mo sè, e' sarà al galéini dla Sterina,
ch' la li tén alè sòtta. Mè a n sint gnént.
Piotòst sa cla scialètta, cmè t la pórt?
ta n vaid ch' la t fa la córda?
u t tucarà pò vérzla, ténla stàisa,
acsè, pu ta t la invrócc tònda me còl,
ècco, bén strètta,
e magari una péunta ènca par mè,
no una péunta, a la téngh aquè se stòngh,
e a stémm gupléd tutt déu,
'Sa fét? al luntanèzi?
vén aquè, sta tachèda, piò tachèda.
Mo cs'èll che ta t si dèda t cavéll?
un gòzzal 'd sàida?
da fè chè par sgatiéi? pu la cologna?
no, ò dmand acsè, mo no, u s sint sno l'udòur.
E sté rudal? t si vnú sla paranènza
sòtta e' capòt? t si scapa d'amasèd?
e adès du vét? sta bóna,
strènz ènca tè, ta n strènz? sint cm'u s sta chèld.
E zà ch' t si 'lè sal mèni,
mè l'è da stamatéina
ch'u m'à ciap un scadòur par tótt la véita,

Ma sí, saranno le galline dell'Esterina, / che le tiene lí sotto. Io non sento niente. / Piuttosto con quello scialle, come lo porti? / non vedi che ti fa la corda? / ti toccherà pure aprirlo, tienilo steso, / cosí, poi te l'avvolgi intorno al collo, / ecco, ben stretto, / e magari una punta anche per me, / un una punta, la tengo qui sullo stomaco, / e stiamo coperti tutt'e due. / Cosa fai? le lontananze? / vieni qui, stai vicina, piú vicina. / Ma cos'è che ti sei data nei capelli? / un goccio d'aceto? / da far che? per scioglierli? poi la colonia? / no, t'ho chiesto cosí, ma no, si sente solo il profumo. / E questo rotolo? sei venuta con la parananza / sotto il cappotto? sei uscita di nascosto? / e adesso dove vai? stai buona, / stringi anche tu, non stringi? / senti come si sta caldi. / E già che sei lí con le mani, / io è da stamattina / che m'ha preso un prurito per tutto il corpo, /

if you could just scratch me a little, a little higher, that's enough,
[it's too much,
itch, itch it, wherever, with both hands,
keep scratching, oh, what relief, don't ever stop,
yes, there too, it feels good all over,
a little harder, what are you afraid of, hurting me?
now a little over there,
not there, you're tickling there,
up higher, in the middle, there, I can never reach there,
oh, wonderful, keep going,
I feel like I'm reborn again,
there, just like that, good girl, a little more,
are you getting tired?
of course, that's enough, do you know that I'm all heated up
[again,
and don't pull down your hands, stay hugging,
leaning against the wall, that way you'll feel less air,
What are you doing?
I want to warm you up a little too,
be a sport, come on, be a sport now,
I know, I have cold hands, but I'll go slowly,
and plus, it's starting out,
you have goose bumps? it'll pass later,
I'll hold close now, are you pressing tight against me?
not too much, it hurts,
are you imprisoning me? or do you want me to warm you up?

se ta m gratéss un pó,
énch' da sòura, tè basta t faza fórza,
grata, grata, purséa, sa tutt' do al mèni,
grata sémpra, oh pu bén, nu t straca mai,
sè, ènca 'lè, e' va bén indimpartótt,
dài piò fórt, 's'ét paéura, da fèm mèl?
adès un pó piò in là,
no alè, ch' ta m fé i sanguéttal,
piò in sò, te mèz, alè, ch'a n gn'aréiv mai,
oh, che belèzza, nu t'aférma, dài,
ch'u m pèr d'arnàs,
ècco, acsè, brèva, un èlt pó, ta t si straca?
mo sè, basta ta l sé ch'a m so arscaldè?
e nu téira zò al mèni, sta brazèda,
pòzti me mèur, acsè, che t ciap mènch' aria.
Mo cs'èll ch'a t faz?
a t ví sno scaldè un pó, ènca ma tè,
sta bóna, zò, sta bóna,
a l so, a iò mèni giazi, mo a faz pièn,
e pu l'è e' préim mumént,
u t vén la chèrna pléina? dop e' pasa,
adés a la téngh férma, ta m la strènz?
no trop che ta m fé mèl,
ta m'imparsòun? o ta m la vu arscaldè?

se mi grattassi un po', / anche da sopra, tu basta che faccia forza, / gratta, gratta, purchessia, con tutt'e due le mani, / gratta sempre, oh, che sollievo, non ti stancare mai, / sí, anche lí, va bene dappertutto, / dai piú forte, cos'hai paura, di farmi male? / adesso un po' piú in là, / no lí, che mi fai il solletico, / piú in su, nel mezzo, lí, che non ci arrivo mai, / oh, che bellezza, dai, / che mi pare di rinascere, / ecco, cosí, brava, un altro po', ti sei stancata? / ma sí, basta, lo sai che mi sono riscaldato? / e non tirare giú le mani, stai abbracciata, / appòggiati al muro, cosí, che prendi meno aria. / Ma cosa ti faccio? / ti voglio solo scaldare un po' anche a te, / stai buona, su, stai buona, / lo so, ho le mani fredde, ma faccio piano, / e poi è il primo momento, / ti viene la pelle d'oca? dopo passa, / adesso la tengo ferma, me la stringi? / non troppo che mi fai male, / m'imprigioni? o me la vuoi riscaldare? /

you're not saying anything? are you afraid?
of what? here, it's warm, and you came come in again,
the skin is smoother,
and I'll cup my hand,
what is it with all these buttons, I was almost flayed alive,
or is it a safety pin? it got me right along the knuckles,
me with my skin already falling apart.
It doesn't matter, it's nothing, I'm just saying,
don't you worry about it, be good now,
and stop looking down there, there's no one coming,
don't be so tense,
why would someone be coming into this darkness?
plus there are some sewer rats, but aren't I here?
lean your head here, don't you know I like you?
I mean a lot,
that I've always liked you?
you're so tender, I just want to eat you up,
Geez, this elastic's tight, doesn't it cut off the blood?
leave it be, don't say a thing, keep your eyes closed,
like in a dream,
come a little closer, am I hurting you?
I'm going easy, very easy, like this, okay?
there, we're two kids on a teeter-totter,
you go up and down on the see-saw too,
don't you like to play?

ta n dí gnént? t'é paéura?
mo 'd chè? ecco, la è chèlda, e tè t'arvén,
la pèla la è piò dòulza,
e mè a chèv la mi mèna,
azidént i butéun, a m so pò scòurgh,
o una spélla da bèglia? a i ò ciap dréinta
sal nusèli, zà ch'ò la pèla guasta.
L'è l'istèss, u n'è gnént, ò détt acsè,
tè nu bèdi, sta bóna,
a nu guèrda alazò ch'u n gn'è niseun,
nu sta tirata,
chi vut ch' vénga at sté schéur?
pu u i è di sórgh da ciàvga,
'sa trémti, par i sórgh? mo a n'i so mè?
pòza la testa aquè, ta l sé ta m pis?
mo una masa,
ch' ta m si sémpra pieséuda?
cómm t si tèndra, ò vòia ad dèt ad mórs,
orca ad elàstich strètt, mo u n t férma e' sangh?
lasa fè, nu dí gnént, tè tén i ócc céus,
cmè t'un insógni,
vén un pó pió tachèda, a t'ò fat mèl?
a vagh pianín pianín, acsè, e' va bén?
ècco, a sémm du burdéll ch'i zuga a blènza,
fa la blènza ènca tè, u n t pis d' zughé?

non dici niente? hai paura? ma di che? ecco, è calda, e tu rinvieni, / la pelle è piú
dolce, / e io cavo la mia mano, / accidenti ai bottoni, mi sono pur scorticato, /
o una spilla da balia? ci ho preso dentro / con le nocche, già che ho la pelle
guasta. / È lo stesso, non è niente, ho detto cosí, / tu non badarci, stai buona, /
e non guardare laggiú che non c'è nessuno, / non stare tirata, / chi vuoi che
venga in questo buio? / poi ci sono dei topi di chiavica, / cosa tremi? per i topi?
ma non ci sono io? / appoggia la testa qui, lo sai che mi piaci? / ma molto, /
che mi sei sempre piaciuta? / come sei tenera, ho voglia di morderti, / orca, che
elastico stretto, ma non ferma il sangue? / lascia fare, non dire niente, tieni gli
occhi chiusi, / come in un sogno, / vieni un po' piú attaccata, t'ho fatto male? /
vado pianino pianino, cosí, va bene? / ecco, siamo due bambini che giocano a
bilancia, / fai la bilancia anche tu, non ti piace giocare?

The Cap

It was a cap the color of ashes
that I'd found under the bench one morning.
I looked inside, there was the name of a hat maker
in Forlí written there.
It was soft, you could ball it up into your fist,
it had a button in the middle, and the visor
didn't extend, it just barely jutted out.
I unbuttoned it
then I buttoned it.
I put it on my head, it fit me.
It wasn't mine.
When I came back, I stopped all of a sudden,
my rubber soles skidded in the pebbles,
a big dust burst.
She was on the terrace. She laughed:
"I bet you forgot the cigarettes!"
I thought of things my mother goes on and on about,
in my opinion she's somewhat jealous,
she takes me to task: "Always with those short skirts,
always out dancing, and you can't say anything?"
what am I supposed to say?

È brètt

L'è stè un brètt culòur zèndra
ch'ò tróv sòtta e' sedéili una matéina.
A l'ò guèrs dréinta, u i era scrétt e' nóm
d'un caplèr ad Furlè.
L'era mórbi, u s putéva strènz t'un pógn,
l'éva un butòun te mèz e la visira
senz'anma, mo se scròch.
A la ò sbutunèda
e pu a la ò 'rbutunèda.
A m'e' so mèss tla testa, a m'e' so cònd.
U n'era e' méi.
Quant a so tòurn ò frenè un pó da sècch,
al gòmmi agli à sbriscé sòura e' giaréin,
ò fat un gran purbiòun.
Li la era se teràz e la rideva:
"A scumètt ta t si zcórd dal zigarètti!"

Mè a penséva ma zért zchéurs dla mi mà,
che sgnònd mè la è un pó zlòusa,
la m ragna: "Sémpra s' cal sutèni chéurti,
sémpra a balè, tè ta n si bón 'd dí gnént?"

Il berretto. È stato un berretto color cenere / che ho trovato sotto il sedile una mattina. / L'ho guardato dentro, c'era scritto il nome / di un cappellaio di Forlí. / Era morbido, si poteva stringere in un pugno, / aveva un bottone nel mezzo e la visiera / senz'anma, ma con lo scrocco. / L'ho sbottonata / e poi l'ho riabbottonata. / Me lo sono messo in testa, me lo sono accomodato. / Non era il mio. / Quando sono tornato, ho frenato un po' di colpo, / le gomme sono slittate sul ghiaino, / ho fattto un gran polverone. / Lei era sul terrazzo e rideva: / "Scommetto che ti sei dimenticato le sigarette!" // Io pensavo a certi discorsi di mia madre, / che secondo me è un po' gelosa, / mi sgrida: "Sempre con quelle gonne corte, sempre a ballare, tu non sei capace di dir niente?" /

243

I go out dancing myself,
"And always tooling around in the car,"
then she,
Luciana, sometimes does it on purpose,
and I don't say a thing,
when you get down to it, I like it this way,
with that short hair, with those white flecks on her fingernails,
that she doesn't always say yes, that she doesn't always
do what I say, did I make a mistake? am I completely wrong?

I went back to the store,
I went to get gas up beyond the Big Curve,
I stopped at Aurelio's
for that front tire
that's not working right,
and after that stop, I started driving uphill,
I got to Trebbio, and then at the bridge
I got out and started looking down below.

The running water
mesmerized me, I could have stayed there for hours
watching it running, never stopping,
it's always moving and always there,
water, more water,
gurgling, making foam,

cs'òi da déi? a balè a vagh ènca mè,
"E sempra in zéir in machina", li pu,
la Luciana, dal vólti la l fa pòsta,
e mè a stagh zétt, in fònd la m pis acsè,
s' chi cavéll chéurt, sa chi técc bièch tagli óngi,
ch' la n degga sémpra ad sè, ch' la n dégga sémpra
quèll ch'a déggh mè, a sbai? ò sbaiè tótt?

A so tòuran te spazi,
a so 'ndè fè benzina dop la Curva,
a m so férum da Vréglio
par cla gòmma davènti
ch' la n mu n lavòura bén,
e, zà ch'a séra alè, ò ciap vérs d'insò,
a so rivàt a Trèbbi, pu me pòunt,
a so smòunt e am so mèss a guardè 'd sòtta.

Mè l'aqua ch' la caméina
la m fa l'inchènt, a starébb òuri e òuri
a guardèla ch' la córr, ch' la n s férma mai,
ch' la va e la è sémpra alè,
aqua e pu aqua,
la gargòia si sas, la fa la sciómma,

cosa devo dire? a ballare vado anch'io, "E sempre in giro in macchina", lei poi,
la Luciana, delle volte lo fa apposta, / e io sto zitto, in fondo mi piace cosí, /
con quei capelli corti, con quelle macchioline bianche nelle unghie, / che non
dica sempre di sí, che non dica sempre / quello che dico io, sbaglio? ho
sbagliato tutto? // Sono tornato allo spaccio, sono andato a far benzina dopo
la Curva, / mi sono fermato da Aurelio / per quella gomma davanti / che non
mi lavora bene, / e, già che ero lí, ho preso in su, / sono arrivato a Trebbio e
poi al ponte, / sono sceso e mi sono messo a guardare di sotto. // A me
l'acqua che cammina / mi fa l'incanto, starei ore e ore / a guardarla, che corre,
che non si ferma mai, / che va ed è sempre lí, / acqua e poi acqua, / gorgoglia
sui sassi, fa la schiuma, /

245

it's glistening,
you're looking at it, you're staring at it,
it looks as if something's about to happen,
you feel it, you feel it in the air,
you count to ten, there, done, now, nothing,
what were you expecting to happen?
the water's flowing downstream, and you, you idiot,
are standing there watching.

That morning at the bridge it was foggy,
and the water was oppressive,
impressed with its own power
not glistening at all, I looked at it a long time,
then I heard a bang coming from the direction of the quarry,
the wind started up, a plume of smoke rising.
I'd thrown the cap in the backseat, I picked it up,
I put it back on my head, I bent over
to see myself in the mirror, it was tight, but
it didn't look bad, except that I looked like someone else.
I held it in my hands,
I twirled it around on one finger,
and then I threw it underhanded
so it would fly, and it took off,

la léus, tè ta la guèrd, ta la guèrd féss,
u t pèr cmè ch' l'apa da suzéd qualquèl,
ta te sint, ta l sint tl'aria,
t còunt fina dis, ècco, a i sémm, adès, gnént,
mo cs'àl mai da suzéd?
l'aqua la va d'inzò, e tè pataca
a stè d'avdài.

Cla matéina me pòunt l'era nuvléd,
e l'aqua la era griva,
la avnéva ad prepotenza,
la n féva lómm, a la ò guèrsa pr'un pèz,
pu vérs la chèva u s'è sintí una bota,
e' tiréva un pó 'd vént, u s'è 'lzè un fómm.
E' brètt a l'éva bótt
se sedéili di dri, a l'ò tólt sò,
a m'e' so 'rmèss tla testa, a m so cuvè
pr'avdàim te spèc, u m'era strètt, però
a n stéva mèl, sno ch'a pareva un èlt.
A l'ò tnú 'lè tal mèni,
a l'ò fat prilé un pó tònda m'un daid,
e pu a l'ò tiràt véa ad sottabràz,
par fèl vulè, e léu l'à ciap e' zéir,

riluce, tu la guardi, la guardi fisso, / ti pare come se debba succedere qualcosa, / te lo senti, lo senti nell'aria / conti fino a dieci, ecco, ci siamo, addesso, niente, / ma cosa deve mai succedere? / l'acqua va in giú, e tu coglione / a star a vedere. // Quella mattina al ponte era annuvolato, / e l'acqua era greve, / veniva di prepotenza, / non luccicava per niente, l'ho guardata a lungo, / poi s'è sentito un botto verso la cava, / tirava un po' di vento, s'è alzato un fumo. / Il berretto l'avevo buttato / sul sedile di dietro, l'ho preso su, / me lo sono rimesso in testa, mi sono chinato / per vedermi nello specchio, mi era stretto, però / non stavo male, solo che parevo un altro. / L'ho tenuto lí nelle mani, / l'ho fatto prillare un po' attorno a un dito, / e poi l'ho tirato via di sottobraccio, / per farlo volare, e lui ha preso il giro, /

it took off better than an airplane,
then it fell headlong into the water,
it tripped along awhile, and then I never saw it again.

l'è 'ndè d'insò méi d'un areoplano,
pu l'è casch 'd spuntéun tl'aqua,
l'à chéurs un pó da zòp, e a n l'ò vést piò.

/ è andato su meglio d'un aeroplano, poi è caduto a capofitto nell'acqua, / ha
corso un po' da zoppo, e non l'ho visto piú.

Noise

There's got to be a place
where all the noises in the world end up,
in the sky, way up, who knows, or down towards the bottom,
but it's got to be far, so far no one can get there,
a basin, or a pond, but immense, a sea,
which from far off you can't see a thing, but getting closer,
if you could,
the first thing you'd hear would be rumbling
like when they were bombing near the coast,
then it shifting down lower, right at the shore,
I'm saying, there's got to be a crashing,
a din, so that in order not to go deaf,
you've got to stick your fingers, tight, into your ears,
but then you get all jittery,
every so often you pull them out, a little, you try, the tiniest bit,
it's all such a hubbub outside that it scares you,
it seems like it could just carry it all away,
but nothing happens, it's a big racket, without any substance,
you've got to stay calm, keep following it,
and then you realize it's not just a ruckus,
it's like in sleep, when you're feverish,

E' malàn

a Dante Isella

U i à da ès un pòst
dvò ch'e va réss tótt e' malàn de mònd,
pr'aria, d'in èlt, chi sa, o alazò, in fònd,
mo dalòngh, ch'u n'i pò rivé niseun,
una gònga, cmè un gòurgh, mo svérs, un mèr,
che da 'd fura u n s vaid gnént, però avsinés,
s'u putéss,
te préim u s sintirébb un sbruntlamént
cmè quant i bumbardéva vérs maréina,
pu a fès piò sòtta, sl'òural,
mè a dèggh ch' l'à d'avnì fura un batibói,
un diavuléri, che par no inzurléis
éun u s chin mètt al dàidi tagli urècci,
però pu u i vén che bséi,
d'ogni tènt u li slénta, e' próva, un féil,
ad fura l'è un gluriòun ch'e' fa paéura,
e' pèr ch'u l pórta véa,
mo u n suzéd gnént, l'è cias, senza sustènza,
bsògna stè bón, andèi dri,
e alòura ta t'incórz ch'u n'è sno boba,
l'è cmè quant che te sònn, che t'é la févra

Il rumore. Ci dev'essere un posto / dove va a finire tutto il rumore del mondo, / per aria, in alto, chi sa, o laggiú in fondo, / ma lontano, che non ci può arrivare nessuno, / una conca, come una gora, ma immensa, un mare, / che da fuori non si vede niente, però ad avvicinarsi, / se si potesse, / dapprincipio si sentirebbe un brontolamento / come quando bombardavano verso marina, / poi, a farsi piú sotto, sull'orlo, / io dico che deve venir fuori un fracasso, / un diavolerio, che per non assordarsi / uno è costretto a mettersi le dita nelle orecchie, / però poi gli viene quella smania, / ogni tanto le allenta, prova, un filo / fuori è un putiferio che fa paura, / pare che lo porti via, / ma non succede niente, è chiasso, senza sostanza, / bisogna star buoni, andargli dietro, / e allora t'accorgi che non è solo baccano, / è come quando nel sonno, che hai la febbre/

in the bed upstairs,
you're hearing those women downstairs chatting away,
you don't understand a thing, but you recognize the voices,
it's the same thing there,
it's pandemonium, it seems like they're all mixed up in it,
a brouhaha, a street-bazaar,
but then instead you start to hear something,
a door that's slamming, an outburst of laughter,
a flock of pigeons taking off,
a woman in house-shoes
who's running down a staircase,
it seems like nothing at all,
but being right there gives you goose bumps,
and you start enjoying it, you close your eyes,
you play with the finger
in each ear, it's like an instrument,
you start hearing everything,
keys being fumbled into the keyhole,
Santina's gate
that creaks whenever Luisín visits,
someone who's winding the clock sitting on a bed,
Malvina
who's fiddling with the rosary in her pocket,
and Giulia who's furiously knitting away,
and then whatever's going to happen, happens,

te lèt ad sòura,
t sint ad sòtta cal dòni ch'al ciacàra,
ta n capéss gnént, però t'arcnòss al vòusi,
e ènca alè cumpàgn,
l'è un buliròun, e e' pèr ch'i i daga dréinta,
un bottasò, una fira,
e invíci pu t ravéi a sintí quèl,
una pórta ch' la sbat, 'na sbacarèda,
una masa ad pizéun ch'i vòula véa,
una dòna sal s-ciafli
ch' la córr ad scaranèda zò mal schèli,
e' pèr roba da gnént,
mo, ès alè, l'à d'avnéi la chèrna pléina,
e ta i ciap góst, t céud i ócc, t fé, zugh sal dàidi
tagli urècci, cumè t'un istrumént,
t'aréiv t sint iniquèl,
al cèvi ch'al sfurgàta tal sradéuri,
e' canzèl dla Santina
ch'e' céula ad nòta quant u i va Luisín,
éun ch'e' carga l'arlózz disdài se lèt,
la Malvina
ch' la zuga tla bascòza sla curòuna,
adiritéura la Géuglia a fè d'agócc,
e pu quèll ch' vén e' vén,

nel letto di sopra, / senti di sotto quelle donne che chiacchierano, / non capisci niente, / però riconosci le voci, / e anche lí lo stesso, / è un pandemonio, e pare che lo rimescolino, / una baraonda, una fiera, / e invece poi cominici a sentire qualcosa, / una porta che sbatte, una risata, / uno stormo di piccioni che volano via, / una donna con le ciabatte / che scende giú di corsa dalle scale, / pare roba da niente, / ma essere lí, a uno gli deve venire la pelle d'oca, / e ci prendi gusto, chiudi gli occhi, fai gioco con le dita / nelle orecchie, come in uno strumento, / arrivi a sentire tutto, / le chiavi che frugano nelle serrature, / il cancello della Santina / che cigola di notte quando ci va Luisín, / uno che carica l'orologio seduto sul letto, / la Malvina / che gioca nella tasca con la corona, / addirittura la Giulia che sferruzza, / e poi quello che viene viene, /

a stone in a well, the water's deep, splashing,
the music of the carousel with its signal
just before it starts to turn,
the bus at Borghi
wheezing under the Arch like a human being,
all that discoursing in the piazza,
the spitting, the yawning, the cursing,
Caléccia's hogs when they're being slaughtered
who screech like a tool being sharpened on the grinding stone,
and underneath the bucket for blood,
the filth that came out of Minerva's mouth,
which afterwards she'd be ashamed of,
when she made love to Doctor Tosi,
a doorbell that rings and no one's there,
two who are running, one right after the other,
they're here, they're past, they're far away,
the thud Tisbe heard
that night passing by the fish market,
it was Vincenzo who had thrown himself
off the town wall,
the holy-hell Ruggero whose mother limps let loose
when he lost his van playing cocincina,
and the guns at the time of the Front, in the field for the fair,
and way up as far as Poggio, it was like a string of rosary beads
which when they were hitting us, we'd, terrified,

un sas t'un pòzz, l'aqua la è fònda, i squézz,
la musica dal giòstri, se segnèl
che sta par cminzé e' zéir,
la curíra di Béurgh
ch' la lènsa sòtta l'Èrch cumè un cris-cèn,
zchéurs in piaza, saràc, sbadài, biastéimi,
i baghéin da Caléccia quant i i scana,
ch'i rógg cmè un fèr ch'i l róda sla smeréglia,
e sòtta u i è la caplètta par e' sangh,
al purchèri ch' la géva la Minerva,
che dop la s vargugnéva,
quant la féva l'amòur se dutòur Tosi,
un campanèl ch'e' sòuna e u n gn'è niseun,
déu ch'i córr, i s dà dri, i è 'lè, i s sluntèna,
la bota sòurda ch' la à sintéi la Tisbe
cla sàira te pasè da la pscaréa,
l'era Vizénz ch'u s'era bótt alòura
zò da al Méura,
i santéssum ch' l'à détt Gero dla Zòpa
quant l'à pérs e' furgòun a cocincina,
i canéun, témp de fròunt, te canfiré
e sò sò fina e' Pózz, l'era un rusèri,
che quant i i déva, néun da la paéura

un sasso in un pozzo, l'acqua è fonda, gli spruzzi, / la musica delle giostre, col
segnale, / che sta per cominciare il giro, / la corriere di Borghi / che ansima
sotto l'Arco come un cristiano, / chiacchiere in piazza, scaracchi, sbadigli,
bestemmie, / i maiali da Caléccia quando li scannano, / che urlano come un
ferro arrotato sulla smeriglia, / e sotto c'è il secchio per il sangue, / le porcherie
che diceva la Minerva, / che dopo si vergognava, / quando faceva l'amore col
dottor Tosi, / un campanello che suona e non c'è nessuno, / due che corrono,
s'inseguono, sono lí, si allontanano, / la botta sorda che ha sentito la Tisbe /
quella sera nel passare dalla pescheria, / era Vincenzo che s'era buttato allora
/ giú dalla Mura, / le imprecazioni che ha detto Ruggero della Zoppa / quando
ha perso il furgone a cocincina, / i cannoni, al tempo del fronte, nel campo
della fiera, / e su su fino al Poggio, era un rosario, / che quando ci davano, noi,
dalla paura /

start laughing,
someone chomping on a celery stalk
with his front teeth, Baghego's finch whistling
that sounds like an aria,
a woman's voice:
"not there, the mark will show there,"
the money Primo threw out the window
when he went bankrupt,
and his wife in the hallway, sobbing,
it was all just loose change, bouncing,
altogether there was five thousand lire,
the lightening crack that Sunday on the town hall
which set the archives on fire,
people arguing, the insults, the name-calling,
and others talking in low voices, spying on everyone else,
a boy kicking a can,
a ripe watermelon being cut, the crunch,
the words she said that you couldn't understand,
Teresa in the hospital before she died,
her people all around her,
with those hands and veins in her neck,
her breathing slowing down,

u s'avnéva da réid,
éun ch'e' biasa da fétt si dént davénti
un gamb ad sèral, e' franguéll ad Baghego
ch'e' cantéva ch'e' féva dal rumanzi,
la vòusa d'una dòna:
"No alè che ta m fé e' sègn",
i baócch ch' l'à tiràt da la finestra
Primo quant l'à faléi,
e la su mòi te curidéur a pianz,
mo l'era spiciulàia, la saltéva,
in tótt e' sarà stè zincmélla frènch,
la saètta cla dmènga se Cuméun,
ch'u s'è brusé l'archéivi,
dla zénta ch'i s'aràgna, i vitupéri,
i numàz,
e d'ilt ch'i zcòrr da bas, ch'i fa la spéa,
un burdèl ch'e' dà 'd chélz m'un busilòt,
un còmbar ch' l'è te fiòur, i l taia, e' scrécca,
al paróli ch' la à détt, ch'u n s'è capéi,
la Teresa te bsdèl préima 'd muréi,
che i sóvv i i stéva tótt alè datònda,
e li s' cal mèni e sal véini me còl,
pu u i è vnú mènch' e' fiè,

ci veniva da ridere, / uno che mastica fitto con i denti davanti / un gambo di sedano, il fringuello di Baghego / che cantava che faceva delle romanze, / la voce di una donna: "No lí che mi fai il segno", / i soldi che ha tirato dalla finestra / Primo quando è fallito, / e sua moglie nel corridoio a piangere, / ma erano spiccioli, saltavano, in tutto saranno stato cinquemila lire, / il fulmine quella domenica sul Comune, / che s'è bruciato l'archivio, / gente che litiga, i vitupèri, / i nomacci, / e altri che parlano a bassa voce, che fanno la spia, / un bambino che dà calci a un barattolo, / un cocomero che è nel fiore, lo tagliano, scricchia, / le parole che ha detto, che non s'è capito, / la Teresa nell'ospedale prima di morire, / che i suoi le stavano tutti intorno, / e lei con quelle mani e con le vene al collo, / poi lei è venuto meno il respiro, /

the storm at Bellaria when the sea
washed away the entire beach in one night,
and the morning after, the first houses
with the boarded-up windows drenched,
a fly batting against the glass,
a waltz, at the end, hands clapping,
"That's enough for me," but with such a voice,
oh my gosh, you come to mind, it's you, that time
you were afraid and the others didn't say anything,
they just went on ahead,
and this one is Emilia, there's no mistaking her,
confessing for Carlone too,
poor guy, who's not all there upstairs,
and now listen to Father Gaetano behind the screen
giving her penance,
and then another confession,
who can it be?
then some others,
you get tired out waiting behind all of them,
still others, what is it? are they just confessions?
how could it have all come down to this?
they talk, they talk, they're making such a din,
and it's that, right here, nothing gets lost,
it's all the sins of the world,
and they step forward to make a confession,

la burasca a Belaria quante e' mèr
t'na nòta u s'è magnè tótta la spiagia,
a la matéina dop al préima vélli
sagli asi mal finestri agli era a mòl,
una mòsca ch' la cóssa còuntra i véidar,
un valzer se finéi, di batimèni,
éun ch'e' déi: "A m férm aquè", mo s'una vòusa,
orca, u t vén in amént, t si tè, cla vólta
ch' t'é vú paéura e ch'ilt i n'à détt gnént,
mo i è 'ndè 'vènti,
e quèsta l'è la Miglia, u n pò sbaiè,
la s'andéva a cunsè 'nca par Carlòun,
purètt, ch'u s'i era inaquaréi e' zarvél,
e adès sint don Gaitèn spèsa la grèta
ch'u i dà la penitenza,
e pu un'èlta cunsiòun, mo chi sarà?
pu dagli èlti, l'è fadéiga stèi dri,
dagli èlti ancòura, cs'èll, l'è sno cunsiòun?
cmè ch'i avrà fat a 'rdéus-si tótt insén?
i zcórr, i zcórr, i fa una baganèra,
e l'è che què dabón u n va pérs gnént,

la burrasca a Bellaria quando il mare / in una notte s'è mangiato tutta la
spaiaggia, / e la mattina dopo le prime ville / con le assi alle finestre erano a
mollo, / una mosca che sbatte contro i vetri, / un valzer sul finire, dei
battimani, / uno che dice: "Mi fermo qui", ma con una voce, / orca, ti viene
in mente, sei tu, quella volta / che hai avuto paura e gli altri non hanno detto
niente, / ma sono andati avanti, e questa è l'Emilia, non si può sbagliare, /
andava a confessarsi anche per Carlone, / poveretto, che il cervello gli era
andato in acqua, / e adesso senti don Gaetano dietro la grata / che le dà la
penitenza, / e poi un'altra confessione, ma chi sarà? / poi delle altre, è fatica
starci dietro, / delle altre ancora, che cos'è, sono solo confessioni? / come
avranno fatto a ridursi tutti insieme? parlano, parlano, fanno una cagnara, / ed
è che qui davvero non va perduto niente, /

259

how many do they have?
listen to this stuff, that's enough isn't it?
there are more?
and they just can't keep quiet, they can't stand it anymore,
someone to forgive them, isn't there anyone?

l'è tótt pchè de mònd,
e i va 'vènti a cunsès, quant ch'i n n'à fat?
sint che robi, mo un basta? u n gne n'è d'ilt?
e i n'è bón da stè zétt, u n s nu n pò piò,
qualcadéun ch'u i pardòuna, u n gn'è niséun?

sono tutti i peccati del mondo, / e vanno avanti a confessarsi, quanti ne hanno
fatti? / senti che robe, ma non basta? ce ne sono altri? / e non sono capaci di
star zitti, non se ne può piú, / qualcuno che li perdoni, non c'è nessuno?

Night

All night long they've been knocking,
but when I went down, no one was there.
It's got to be those kids who make me so mad,
it's two o'clock now, they got me all flustered.
You shouldn't get up, just let them knock,
but I, if I hear that there's someone downstairs,
I can't just roll back over,
I go and see, if I don't go, either way,
I'm there worrying, I'm not going to fall asleep.
But then, come on now, who's talking about sleeping,
they knock, they just knock, it doesn't matter when,
for me nights, it's been years, there's just no way
I can rest, there I am keeping watch,
sitting on the bed, hearing the train passing.
I just can't take it anymore, sleeping, every second
my sleep gets broken, and what good is it lying there tormenting
[yourself,
I put on my slippers, I go downstairs,
I turn on the light, walk back and forth,
drink a glass of water, I'll even eat if there's something left,

La nòta

L'è tótt' la nòta ch'i bóssa,
mo quant ch'a vagh ad sòtta u n gn'è niseun.
L'à da ès chi burdlézz ch'i m fa rabiè,
l'è bèla ad do, i m'à sgumbuié tótt.
Bsugnarébb no stè sò, lasè ch'i bóssa,
mo mè, s'a sint che ad sòtta u i è qualcadéun,
a n so bón d'arvultèm da cl'èlta pèrta,
a vagh avdài, s'a n vagh intinimódi
a stagh sa che pensír, a n m'indurmént.
Mo pu, va là, 's'ut zcòrr d'indurmantès,
ch'i bóssa quant ch'i vó, la n bat da 'lè,
mè la nòta, lè di an, u n gn'è piò mèzi
d'arpunsèm, a so 'lè ch'a faz la vèggia,
disdài se lèt, a sintí ch' pasa e' treno.
A n gne la faz a durméi, tótt i mumént
u m s ròmp e' sònn, e 's'ut stè 'lè a sisméi,
a m mètt al mi pupózzi, a vagh ad sòtta,
a zènd la luce, a zéir d'in quà e d'in là,
a bèggh un bicír d'aqua,
a magn ènca qualcósa s'u i è 'rvènz,

La notte. È tutta la notte che bussano, / ma quando vado di sotto non c'è nessuno. / Devono essere quei ragazzacci che mi fanno arrabbiare, / sono ormai le due, mi hanno scombuiato tutto. / Bisognerebbe non alzarsi, lasciare che bussino, / ma io se sento che di sotto c'è qualcuno, / non sono capace di voltarmi dall'altra parte, / vado a vedere, se non vado ad ogni modo / sto con quel pensiero, non m'addormento. / Ma poi, va' là, cosa vuoi parlare d'addormentarsi, / bussino quanto vogliono, non dipende di lí. / io la notte, sono anni, non c'è piú mezzo / di riposarmi, sono lí che faccio la veglia, / seduto sul letto, a sentire che passa il treno. / Non ce la faccio a dormire, tutti i momenti / mi si rompe il sonno, e cosa vuoi stare lí a tormentarti, / mi metto le mie babbucce, vado di sotto, / accendo la luce, giro di qua e di là, / bevo un bicchier d'acqua, / mangio anche qualcosa se è rimasto, /

a slice of cheese, a bunch of grapes,
I straighten things, oh, in the night
I've got plenty to do,
then when I'm a little tired I go back upstairs,
I lie down in bed and I wait
to see if sleep is going to come, you bet I wait,
it seems like I'm still awake, or am I dreaming it,
if only I were really dreaming it, but there's the clock
on the night stand, and there's the Campanone,
I don't only hear the hour, I hear the half-hour too,
but then later I get all riled up,
I go downstairs,
slip out the door, go as far as the street,
then come back inside, but I'm not at ease anywhere,
I'm grumbling, I'm protesting, I'm walking with my head down,
I'm opening up drawers, enough's enough, I'm tired,
sleep, time,
there's not a single thing you can do about it,
I go and sit down on the step outside,
to get some fresh air, which is better than lying in bed,
I look at that oleander which is sick,
it's losing its leaves,

una fètta ad furmài, un grapal d'óvva,
a mètt a pòst dal robi, mè la nòta
ò sémpra un gran dafè,
pu quant a so un pó strach a tòurn ad sòura,
a m bótt te lèt e a stagh d'aspitè 'lè
s'e' vén e' sònn, mo t'é vòia d' spitè,
mè u m pèr sémpra d'ès svégg, o ch'a m l'insógni?
s'a m l'insugnéss dabón, mo a iò l'arlózz
se cumudéin, e pu u i è e' Campanòun,
a n sint sno agli òuri, a sint i tócch dal mèzi,
alòura dop un pó u m vén e' furbsòun,
a vagh ad sòtta,
a scap sla pórta, aréiv fina sla strèda,
pu a tòuran dréinta, mo a n stagh bén invéll,
a sóffi, a ragn, a caméin ad spuntéun,
a éiruv di casétt, pu basta, a m stóff,
e' sònn, agli òuri, un azidént ch'u t spaca,
a m vagh a mètt disdài se scaléin 'd fura,
a ciapè e' frèsch, ch' l'è mèi ca nè te lèt,
a guèrd ma che leàndar, ch' l'è malèd,
e' pérd al fòi,
a sint alazò in fònd, ma la furnèsa,

una fetta di formaggio, un grappolo d'uva, / metto a posto delle cose, io la notte / ho sempre un gran da fare, / poi quando sono un po' stanco torno di sopra, / mi butto nel letto e sto ad aspettre lí / se viene il sonno, ma hai voglia d'aspettre, / a me mi pare sempre d'essere sveglio, o che me lo sogno? / se me lo sognassi davvero, ma ho l'orologio / sul comodino, e poi c'è il Campanone, / non sento solo le ore, sento i tocchi delle mezze, / allora dopo un po' mi viene la stizza, / vado di sotto, / esco sulla porta, arrivo fin sulla strada, / poi torno dentro, ma non sto bene in nessun posto, / sbuffo, protesto, cammino a testa bassa, / apro dei cassetti, poi basta, mi stufo, / il sonno, le ore, un accidente che ti pigli, / vado a mettermi a sedere sullo scalino di fuori, / a prendere il fresco, che è meglio che nel letto, / guardo quell'oleandro che è malato, / perde le foglie, /sento laggiú in fondo, alla fornace, /

down over there I hear, at the brickworks,
the ones working the night shift with their motorbikes,
in the Borgo I see a light in a window,
who can it be? I'm there thinking this over,
the wheels turn however they want to,
things like this just pop into my mind,
and I have great deliberations about them.
I wouldn't even mind talking to someone else,
if an outsider passes by, a traveler,
but there's not a soul in sight.
Even tonight,
I must have gone down six or seven times,
it seemed absolutely like they were knocking.

quéi de téuran ad nòta se mutòur,
a vèggh te Bòurgh una finestra zàisa,
mo chi pò ès? a stagh alè a pansè,
la testa la lavòura par còunt sóvv,
u m vén in mént 'd cal robi,
e a i faz sòura di gran ragiunamént.
U m pisarébb ènch' d' zcòrr sa qualcadéun,
s' paséss un furistír, un viazadòur,
mo u n s vaid un'anma.
Ènca stanòta
a sarò andè zò 'd sòtta si sèt vólti,
u m paréa 'diritéura ch'i buséss.

quelli del turno di notte con la moto, / vedo nel Borgo una finestra accesa, /
ma chi può essere? sto lí a pensare, / la testa lavora per conto suo, / mi
vengono in mente di quelle cose, / e ci faccio sopra dei gran raggionamenti. /
Mi piacerebbe anche parlare con qualcuno, se passasse un forestiero, un
viaggiatore, / ma non si vede un'anima. / Anche stanotte / sarò andato di sotto
sei sette volte, / mi pareva addirittura che bussassero.

Liqueur

He goes where he wants to,
he never says a thing,
and I'm the one who's stuck in the shop.
So every once in awhile I go upstairs
and I have quick shot.
It does me good, I go back down, I feel tip-top,
and if someone mouthy comes in
and gives me some crap
I'll say whatever comes to mind,
it's better to laugh than to cry,
and he comes in whenever he feels like coming in,
and on top if it he's always exhausted,
and at night he throws himself down in bed
like an old sack of potatoes, opens the paper, tries to read,
but falls asleep with his mouth open,
he snores, and I stretch out,
reach my arm over him and turn out the light.

China

Léu e' va dvò ch'u i pèr,
u n déi mai gnént,
e tla butàiga u m tòcca stèi mu mè.
Alòura d'ogni tènt a vagh ad sòura
e a bèggh do dàidi ad china.
La m fa bén, a véngh zò ch'a m sint in èsar,
e s'e' vén dréinta qualche squaiunèd
e mè u m scapa da déi do tre buièdi,
a n mu n dagh 'd mórs tla lèngua,
l'è mèi réid ca nè pianz,
e léu ch'e' vénga quant ch'u i pèr d'avnéi,
che pu l'è sémpra starch,
e la sàira te lèt u s bótta zò
cmè un sach, l'irva e' girunèl, e' próva 'd lèz,
mo u s'indurménta ad bot sla bòcca vérta,
e' surnèccia, e mè a m slòngh,
a i pas sòura se braz e a i smórt la luce.

China. Lui va dove gli pare, / non dice mai niente, / e nella bottega mi tocca starci io. / Allora ogni tanto vado di sopra / e bevo due dita di china. / Mi fa bene, vengo giú che mi sento in forma, / e se viene dentro qualche spiritoso, / e a me mi scappano dette due tre boiate, / non mi mordo la lingua, / è meglio ridere che piangere, / e lui che venga quando gli pare di venire, / che poi è sempre stanco, / e la sera nel letto si butta giú / come un sacco, apre il giornale, prova a leggere, / ma s'addormenta di botto a bocca aperta, / russa, e io mi allungo, / gli passo sopra col braccio e gli spengo la luce.

Snow

First, the northeast wind blew in and there was snow,
it started out with flakes like shreds
of rags, wet ones, limp ones,
hitting the ground
they changed color, it turned to water.
But after awhile
the puddles were solid,
like glass,
the benches in the piazza,
the blue letters of the Cassa di Risparmio,
Bigia's trestle-table, all started turning white at the edges,
Nello slipped on his way to the bakery.
It stuck, if only it hadn't,
people came out without umbrellas.
Then about four the air shifted,
you heard a clicking at the windows, by then it was already hail,
it came down hard, you had to close your eyes,
it was dry, not wet, it scraped,
it got inside your scarf, under your collar,
it worked its way down the back.

La nàiva

Pu l'à vólt carnaséin, e l'è stè nàiva,
te préim dal fróffli grandi
cmè di straz, mòli fràidi, sbandunèdi,
agli arivéa ma tèra
e al cambiéva culòur, l'era tótt'aqua.
Mo dop un pó al piscòlli era férmi,
smerigliédi,
i sedéili dla piaza,
al lèttri bló dla Casa de Rispèrmi,
i cavalétt dla Bigia
ma i éural i raviéva a dvantè biènch,
Nello pr'andè te fòuran l'à sguilé.
La tachéva, mo cmè che la n nu n vléss,
la zénte la scapéva senza umbrèla.
Pu vérs al quatar l'aria la s'è mosa,
ti véidar u s sintéa un furmigadézz,
u n'era fróffli, ormai l'era garlétt.
La avnéva zò, m fétta, da céud i ócc,
la era sótta sbrulèda, la raspéva,
la s'instichéa tal schèrpi, te cupètt,
la s'infiléa ti póst dri ma la zénta.

La neve. Poi ha girato grecale, ed è stata neve, / dapprincipio dei fiocchi grandi / come stracci, molli fradici, dinoccolati, / arrivavano a terra / e cambiavano colore, erano tutt'acqua. / Ma dopo un po´ le pozzanghere erano ferme, / smerigliate, / le panchine delle piazza, / le lettere blu delle Cassa Risparmio, / i cavalletti della Bigia / agli orli cominciavano a diventare bianchi, / Nello per andare al forno è scivolato. / Attaccava, ma come non volesse, / la gente usciva senza ombrello. / Poi verso le quattro l'aria s'è mossa, / ai vetri si sentiva un formicolio, / non erano fiocchi, ormai erano chichi. / Veniva giú, ma fitta, da chiudere gli occhi, / era asciutta, secca, raspava, / si ficcava nelle scarpe, nel collo, / s'infilava nei posti dietro la gente. /

At Ganasa's grocery store, they all hunched over, heads bent,
sacks over their heads, they looked like monks.
In the neighborhood by the Scaletta, Elletra was shouting:
this time we're really going to get hit.

Around midnight, coming out of the movies,
people could hardly manage to walk.
Those kids came into the café, leaving the door open,
they looked like drowned rats, letting in Siberia,
What do you think this is, the fairgrounds?
close that door,
they shook out their coats, asked for hot rum drinks,
and glass in hand each one stood there
watching two guys playing an open-hand game of briscola.
Then when they left and went out in the street,
the streetlights were all swirly.

And the next morning, it was still coming down.
At the hospital windows
you could see faces peering through the windows,
they came out from the shops to shovel,
the people under the arcades kicked their shoes against the wall.
It was a light snowfall, like a piece of gauze,
it reached the steps of the Monument,

Da Ganasa i scarghéa testa 'd spuntéun
s'una bala a capócc cumpàgn di frè.
Mal Scàletti la Létra la rugéva:
stavólta mò u n fa un créin!

Vérs mezanòta, quant i è scap de cino,
u n s'è sintí caminé. Chi burdéll
i è rivàt te cafè, a bóssla vérta,
tótt arnèd, l'è vnú dréinta la Sibéria,
mo cs'èll ch' l'è, e' canfiré? ciudí cla pórta,
i s'è scrulé i capótt, i à tólt un póng,
e si bicír tal mèni i è stè 'lè
a vdai déu ch'i zughéva a bréscla zcvérta,
pu i è scap, par al strédi
i lampiéun e' paréa di dvanadéur.

E la matéina dop u i déva ancòura.
Mal finestri de bsdèl
u s'avdéva dal fazi dri di véidar.
Dal butàighi i scapéva a sbadilé,
la zénta sòtta i pórtich
i batéva sal schèrpi còuntra e' méur.
La caléva lizíra, cmé una ghèrza,
la parzéva i scaléin de Monumént,

Da Ganasa scaricavano a testa bassa / con un sacco a cappuccio come i frati. / Alle Scalette l'Elettra urlava: / stavolta davvero ne fa una cesta! // Verso mezzanotte, quando sono usciti dal cinema, / non s'è sentito camminare. Quei ragazzi / sono arrivati al caffè, a porta aperta, / tutti conciati, è venuta dentro la Siberia, / ma cos'è, il campo della fiera? chiudete quella porta, / si sono scrollati i cappotti, hanno preso un punch, / e con i bicchieri in mano sono stati lí / a vedere due che giocavano a briscola scoperta, / poi sono usciti, per le strade / i lampioni parevano dipanatoi. // E la mattina dopo ci dava ancora. / Alle finestre dell'ospedale / si vedevano delle facce dietro i vetri. / Dalle botteghe uscivano a spalare, / la gente sotto i portici / battavano con le scarpe contro il muro. / Calava leggera, come una garza, / pareggiava gli scalini del Monumento, /

it covered the chain that goes around the Arch,
at Medardo's corner,
near the door, it piled into a snow drift
that nearly went up to the transom.
On Irma's balcony
the clothes were stiff on the clothesline,
every once in awhile, they'd swing all together.
A car in the Borgo groaned,
it just didn't want to start.
Over in the Baròun neighborhood, some little boys
in rubber boots
were walking across the piazza,
others were playing pissing games,
making yellow holes,
and the snow looked worm-eaten.

And it just kept coming down all night. In the morning
that snowdrift at Medardo's was gone.
At the market, a kilo of apples
was up to nine hundred lire, two artichokes were going for a
                                           [hundred scudi,
and they were cleaned out.
Those broken-down bikes
that nobody claimed leaning against the passageway Cíocchi
were still there, the seats were visible.
The lights were still on
at Lino's,

la cruvéva al cadéini tònda l'Èrch,
me cantòun ad Medardo,
tachèd la pórta, u s'era fat un réifal
ch' l'arivéa guèsi fina e' luminèl.
Se teràz dl'Irma i pan stéis i era téinch,
d'ogni tènt i dindléva tótt insén.
Una machina te Bòurgh la gnuléva,
la n s vléva invié.
In piaza qualch' burdèl si stivèl 'd gòmma
e' travarséva,
d'ilt te Baròun i zughéva a pisé,
i féva di béus zal,
e la nàiva l'era cmè ch' la tarléss.

U i à dè tótt' la nòta, la matéina
e' réifal ad Medardo u n gn'era piò.
Se marchè un chéll ad màili l'è rivàt
ma novzént frènch, du scarcióffal zént schéud,
e i à puléi.
Che struncòun 'd biciclètta
puzèda vsina e' Ciócch, senza padròun,
la era ancòura alè, u s'i avdéa la sèla.
Da Lino i tnéva sémpra

/ copriva le catene attorno all'Arco, / alla cantonata di Medardo, / vicino alla
porta, s'era fatto un refolo / che arrivava quasi fino alla lunetta. / Sulla terrazza
della Irma i panni stesi erano stecchiti, / ogni tanto dondolavano tutti assieme.
/ Una macchina nel Borgo mugolava, / non si volveva avviare. / In piazza
qualche ragazzino con gli stivali di gomma / attraversava, / altri nel Baròun
giocavano a pisciare, / facevano dei buchi gialli, / e la neve era come se
tarlasse. // Ci ha dato tutta la notte, la mattina / il refolo di Medardo non c'era
piú. / Sul mercato un chilo di mele è arrivato / a novecento lire, due carciofi
cento scudi, / e hanno pulito. / Quello sganghero di bicicletta / appoggiata
vicino al Ciócch, senza padrone, / era ancora lí, le si vedeva la sella. / Da Lino
tenevano sempre /

it was smoke-filled,
condensation was trickling down the windows.
At one in the afternoon
in the big field
a linden tree just split apart like a clam,
the clock on town hall said eleven,
the hands were jammed.

And there was still more snow,
the walls of the houses were made of hoarfrost,
chirping was coming from the fish market,
it was all these little sparrows that had decided to stay put inside,
there must have been a hundred,
every once in awhile one of them would fall
and, underneath, the cats would fight over them.
For awhile, the drinking fountain at the Voltone
kept sputtering,
then nothing came out.
Late in the afternoon, the group decorating
the public hall for the big hunting dance,
just left, without a word, went home.
The next day, the newspapers didn't arrive.

la luce zàisa,
l'era pin 'd fómm, i véidar i culéva.
Un'òura pasmezdè
te Prè un tiglio u s'è sbrènch, cmè una puràza,
mo l'arlózz de Cuméun e' féva agli óngg,
u s'i era inciudè al sféri.

E l'era sémpra nàiva,
i méur dal chèsi i s'era fat canéud,
da la pscaréa l'avnéva un rugiadézz,
l'era tótt pasaròtt, i aveva tróv
da stè alè dréinta, i gev'ès dal zantnèra,
d'ogni tènt u n caschéva qualcadéun
e sòtta u i era i gat ch'i s'i aragnéva.
La pòumpa de Vultòun
pur'un pèz la è 'ndèda avènti a tartaiè,
pu u n'è vnú zò piò gnént.
Se tèrd la squèdra ch'i era dri a dubè
la Sèla pr'e' vegliòun di cazadéur
i à las alè, da zétt, e i è 'ndè chèsa.
E' dè dop i giurnèl i n'è rivàt.

/ la luce accesa, / era pieno di fumo, i vetri colavano. / All'una del pomeriggio
/ nel Prato un tiglio s'è sbrancato, come una vongola, / ma l'orologio del
Comune faceva le undici, / gli si erano inchiodate le sfere. // Ed era sempre
neve, / i muri delle case s'erano fatti canuti, / dalle pescheria veniva uno
schiamazzo, / erano tutti passerotti, avevano trovato / da stare lí dentro,
dovevano essere delle centinaia, / ogni tanto ne cadeva qualcuno / e sotto
c'erano i gatti che se li litigavano. / La fontanella del Voltone / per un pezzo
è andata avanti a tartagliare, / poi non è venuto giú piú niente. / Sul tardi la
squadra che stavano addobbando / la Sala per il veglione dei cacciatore /
hanno lasciato lí, senza parlare, e sono andati a casa. / Il giorno dopo i giornali
non sono arrivati. //

It didn't clear up anywhere.
Inside the houses, you could hear people hacking,
walking upstairs, downstairs,
someone would light a match
and stick an arm outside to see
if it was still coming down.
But by this point to see anything you needed to go up a flight.

Plédga Senior was quite content in his big armchair
at the window, still awake
from the evening before, but then he nodded off,
he didn't know if it was daytime,
he heard it strike eight, it was completely dark,
he got afraid,
slowly, he went upstairs, slowly, to look
out the girls' bedroom window,
it was night there too,
he felt along the wall with his hand
he tried to flick on the light,
he tried it two or three times,
nothing came on,
he tried to call out, he stood there open-mouthed.

E u n'arluséva invéll.
Dréinta al chèsi u s sintéva scatarè,
caminé 'd sòtta e 'd sòura,
mal finestri, la nòta,
qualcadéun e' zandéva un furminènt
e e' slughéva e' braz 'd fura par avdai
s'u déva ancòura.
Mo ormai pr'avdài bsugnéva fè un rèm 'd schèli.

Pledga e' vèc l'è stè bón te scaranòun
davènti la finestra, sémpra svégg,
da la sàira, mo pu u i è vnú un parlózz,
u n s n'è incórt ch' l'era d' dè,
l'à sintí sunè agli òt, l'era tótt schéur,
l'à vú paéura,
pianín pianín l'è 'ndè 'd sòura a guardè
me finistréin dla cambra dal burdèli,
l'era nòta ènca 'lè,
l'à strisé un pó sla mèna còuntra e' méur,
l'à tróv e' scròch dla luce,
u i à dè do tre vólti, u n s'è zais gnént,
l'à próv 'd ciamè, l'è 'rvènz a bòcca vérta.

E non schiariva da nessuna parte. / Dentro le case si sentiva scatarrare, / camminare di sopra e di sotto, / alle finestre, la notte, / qualcuno accendeva un fiammifero / e allungava il braccio fuori per vedere / se ci dava ancora. / Ma ormai per vedere bisognava fare un ramo di scale. // Plédga il vecchio è stato buono nel seggiolone, / davanti alla finestra, sempre sveglio, / dalla sera, ma poi s'è appisolato, / non s'è accorto che era giorno, / ha sentito suonare le otto, / era tutto buio, / ha avuto paura, pianino, pianino è andato di sopra a guardare / al finestrino della camera delle bambine, / era notte anche lí, / ha strisciato un po' con la mano contro il muro, / ha trovato lo scrocco della luce, / ci ha dato due tre volte, non s'è acceso niente, / ha provato a chiamare, è rimasto a bocca aperta. //

And outside it was a beast,
the air was just snow, thick, like smoke,
and at night, if you were quiet,
in the dark, you could hear it settling.
Wednesday morning, the roof of the wine bar
made a creak
then it gave way all at once
with a crash like an earthquake.
Then we heard that the Suffraggio
had collapsed too, and that underneath the portico
the main door had been thrown open,
so it looked just like a Sunday morning.
And certain nights, when the wind picked up,
the rafters in houses would creak,
people didn't dare breathe,
they were wide awake listening.

You could hear the creaking Friday night too
at the Brucòuna passageway, then all along from there to the
                              [slaughterhouse
the snow rose up in a huge whirlwind,
and black smoke all over,
filthy, you couldn't even catch your breath,
and then you could see the blaze,
flames and smoke, the snow was hissing,

E 'd fura e' féva e' dièval,
pr'aria l'era sno nàiva, una fumíra,
e la nòta, a stè zétt,
u s sintéva te schéur che la s punséva.
Mircal matéina e' tètt de Cantinòun
te préim l'à fat un gnécch,
pu tótt t'un bot l'à zdéu
s'un malàn cmè ch'e' déss e' taremòt.
E dop u s'è savéu ch'ènca e' Sufràz
u s'era insachè tótt, e sòtta e' pórtich
e' purtòun da la bota u s'era vért
ch'e' pareva la dmènga.
E zérti nòti, quant la avnéva ad vént
e tal chèsi e' scrichéva tótt i trèv,
la zénta i n'arfiadéva,
mo i era svégg, i stéva da sintéi.

U s'è sintí scriché 'nca vèndar nòta
ma la Brucòuna, pu dlà de pladéur
la nàiva la è 'ndè sò t'un gran sfunézz,
e dimpartótt un fómm
nir, impstèd, ch'u n s putéva tiré e' fiè,
e pu u s'è vést e' fugh,
fiambi e nàiva, la nàiva la frizéva,

E fuori faceva il diavolo, / per aria era solo neve, una fumiera, / e la notte, a
star zitti, / si sentiva nel buio che si posava. / Mercoledí mattina il tetto del
Cantinone / prima ha fatto uno scricchio, / poi tutt'in un botto ha ceduto /
con un fracasso come fosse il terremoto. / E dopo s'è saputo che anche il
Suffragio / s'era insaccato tutto, e sotto il portico / il portone dalla botta s'era
aperto / che pareva la domenica. / E certe notti, quando veniva di vento / e
nelle case scricchiolavano tutte le travi, / la gente non fiatava, / ma erano
svegli, stavano a sentire. // S'è sentito scricchiolare anche venerdí notte / alle
Brucòuna, poi di là dal mattatoio / la neve è andata su in gran turbine, / e
dappertutto un fumo / nero, impestato, che non si poteva tirare il fiato, / e poi
s'è visto il fuoco, / fiamme e neve, la neve friggeva, /

281

but the flames had no strength,
they were tumbling into the smoke,
at times it seemed like they were falling headlong,
but then later, they took off,
lifted up, it all opened up, they wrapped around,
higher, the top was dense with cinders,
and people just stood there looking, their faces scorched.

The lumberyard caught fire,
a horrible accident, or set on purpose,
or some crazy person who wanted to get in out of the weather,
it wasn't clear, it was never determined.
For one whole day, it was a terrifying thing,
the flames spread from there,
they devoured the Ravaglia's house,
Velia's shop, the tobacco-drying shed,
and for hours on end
the overwhelming smell of cigars,
Fasúl's shed
caught fire,
three hundred chickens died in their coops,
a thousand kilos of cheese turned into sludge.
From on the streets, the Roccolo was all lit up
like there was a game of bocce going on,

mo al fiambi al n'éva fórza,
agli andéva rugléun te mèz de fómm,
di mumént e' paréa ch'al déss e' còl,
pu invíci agli à ciap vàila,
agli è 'ndè sò, al s'è vérti, al s'invrucéva
sémpra piò in èlt, e in zéima pini ad lózzli.
I véidar mal finestri i era róss,
e la zénta ch'i stéva da guardè
u i scutéva la faza.

L'éva ciap fugh e' magazéin de lègn,
una sgrèzia o un dispèt
o un mat ch'e' vléva andè còuntra me témp,
u n s'è putú capéi, u n s'è mai savéu.
Pr'un dè l'è stè e' spavént,
al fiambi agli è 'ndè dlà,
al s'è magnè la chèsa di Ravàia,
la butàiga dla Vèglia, e' sicatòio,
e tl'aria par dagli òuri u s'è sintéi
un gran udòur ad zigar,
e' capanòun 'd Fasúl
l'à ciap 'na brustighéda
che tal ghèbi l'è mórt trezént galéini
e dis quintèl 'd furmài l'è dvént 'na lèca.

ma le fiamme non avevano forza, / andavano ruzzoloni in mezzo al fumo, /
a momenti pareva che dessero il collo, / poi invece hanno preso velo, / sono
andate su, si sono aperte, si avviluppavano, / sempre piú in alto, e in cima piene
di scintille. / I vetri alle finestre erano rossi, / e la gente che stavano a guardare
/ gli scottava la faccia. // Aveva preso fuoco il magazzino del legno, / una disgrazia o un dispetto / o un matto che voleva andare contro il tempo, / non s'è
potuto capire, non s'è mai saputo. / Per un giorno è stato lo spavento, / le
fiamme sono andate di là, / si sono mangiate la casa dei Ravaglia, / la bottega
della Velia, l'essiccatoio, / e nell'aria per delle ore s'è sentito / un gran odore
di sigari, / il capannone di Fasúl / ha preso una scottata / che nelle gabbia sono
morte trecento galline / e dieci quintali di formaggio sono diventati una
melma./

that Japanese loquart tree in Gualtiero's garden was lit up,
the blasts of heat made their way
even farther down,
as far as the post office, and there, right below the main entrance,
Baravelli's dog came walking out.

And up above it was endless,
it came down like it was having a good laugh,
on the Piazza, down toward the Borgo, even along the Costa,
the houses were low, like they were kneeling,
along the Big Curve, the street disappeared,
from there to the Fabbricone, the river was gone,
water, fields, you couldn't recognize a thing,
the chestnut trees at the Passeggio were turned into
a hedge that looked heads of lettuce.
And then night came,
and the next morning, looking outside,
it was another world.

How much more of this can we take?
it started on a Wednesday afternoon,
or was it a Thursday? it didn't matter,
it seemed to everyone

e' nèspal de Giapòun tl'órt ad Gualtiero,
pu al vampèdi de chèld agli éva zcvért
ènca piò in sò,
fina la Posta, e alè sòtta e' purtòun
l'era vnú fura e' chèn ad Baravèl.

E d'in èlt l'era sfònd,
la avnéva ch'e' pareva ch' la ridéss,
sla piazza, zò me Bòurgh, ènch' ma la Costa
al chèsi agli era basi, cmè d'inznòc,
ma la Curva la strèda la s pardéva,
dlà de Fabrécch e' fiómm u s'era férum,
aqua, campagna, u n s cnunséva piò gnént,
i castàgn de Pasègg i s'era ardótt
di cacétt, una siva.
E pu e' vnéva la nòta,
e la matéina dop, a guardè 'd fura,
l'era tótt un èlt mond.

Mo da quante ch'u i déva?
l'aveva ravié un mircal dopmezdè,
o la zóbia? mo pu l'era l'istèss,
ma la zénta u i pareva

Di là, sulla strada, il Roccolo era lustro, / si vedeva il gioco delle bocce, / il nespolo del Giappone nell'orto di Gualtiero, / poi le vampate del caldo avevano scoperto / anche piú in su, / fino alla Posta, e lí sotto il portone / era venuto fuori il cane di Baravelli. // E in alto era senza fondo, / veniva giú che pareva che ridesse, /sulla piazza, giú per il Borgo, anche alla Costa / le case erano basse, come in ginocchio, / alla Curva la strada si perdeva, / di là dal Fabbricone il fiume si era fermato, / acqua, campagna, non si conosceva piú niente, / i castagni del Passeggio s'erano ridotti / dei cespi, una siepe. / E poi veniva la notte, / e la mattina dopo, a guardare di fuori, / era tutto un altro mondo. // Ma da quanto ci dava? / aveva cominciato un mercolodí pomeriggio, / o il giovedí? ma poi era lo stesso, / alla gente gli pareva /

285

that there had always been snow,
they wandered around in their houses all wrapped up
in blankets, like bishops,
but the old people by this point just stayed in bed.
At Viuléina's restaurant, they laid boards
from one window to another building across the street,
farther down, they dug a tunnel,
between Gaboùn's and Baruzett's front steps,
they opened up the Co-op,
keeping candles lit on the counter,
the shutters rolled halfway down, you entered all hunched over,
it was like they were continuously closing up for the night.

And there was no break from above,
in the bedrooms, even in the ones upstairs, it was dark.
The Arch looked like a bridge,
down low toward Savignano, the chimney
at the brickyard was sticking out, all by itself,
the rest of it, you have to understand this, it wears me out
                                          [thinking of it,
with snow all the way up to the top, it confuses you,
that dip down there must be the Piazza Grande,
farther in the same direction, the Vecchioni, Canapa, then the
                                          [Consortium,

ch' l'éss sémpra fat la nàiva,
i ziréva tal chèsi tótt gupléd
tal cvérti, cmè di véscuv,
mo i vécc ormai i arvanzéva te lèt.
Tla Viuléina i aveva bótt dagli asi
da una finestra a cl'èlta dirimpèt,
da bas i éva sbusé
tra i pórtich ad Gabòun e Baruzètt,
un èlt budèl i era dri a fèl piò in zò,
ma la coperatéiva i éva vért,
i tnéva dal candàili se bancòun
e al serandi a mità, u s'antréa cuvéun,
cmè ch'e' fóss sémpra al sèt e mèz sunèdi.

E sòura u n'éva òsi,
tal cambri, ènca d'in èlt, u s féva nòta,
l'Èrch e' pareva un pòunt,
tla basa, vérs Savgnèn, l'avnéva fura
e' caméin dla furnèsa, da par léu,
e' rèst, va pò a capéi, zà ch' l'è fadéiga,
sla nàiva ènca da sòura, ch' la t'imbròia,
cla gònga l'à da ès la Piaza Granda,
piò in quà u i è i Vcéun, Canapa, pu e' Consórzi,

che avesse sempre fatto la neve, / giravano nelle case tutti avvolti / nelle
coperte, come dei vescovi, / ma i vecchi ormai rimanevano a letto. / Nella
Viuléina avevano buttato delle assi / da una finestra all'altra dirimpetto, / da
basso avevano bucato / tra i portici di Gabòun e Baruzètt, / un altro budello
stavano facendolo piú in giú, / alla cooperativa avevano aperto, / tenevano
delle candele sul bancone / e le serrande a metà, si entrava chinati, / come se
fossero sempre le sette e mezzo suonate. // E sopra non dava tregua, / nelle
camere, anche in alto, si faceva notte, / l'Arco pareva un ponte, / nella bassa,
verso Savignano, veniva fuori, / il camino della fornace, da solo, / il resto, vai
pura a capire, già che è fatica, / con la neve anche da sopra, che t'imbroglia, /
quella conca dev'essere la Piazza Grande,/ piú in qua ci sono i Vecchioni,
Canapa, poi il Consorzio, /

the only thing still visible in the Borgo was the Credit Union
[building
and Liverani's house,
but what's that going on down there? at the chapel of the Cella,
in a high window someone's giving a sign
to someone, now, from San Giovanello
someone else is waving a rag,
he's making other signs, and towards the Suore Nere,
then at the Pieve, you can hear bells ringing,
at San Rocco too, at the schools
they're ringing everywhere, to break up time,
a cloud of snow fell
from the dome of the Collegiata's belltower,
then more came down,
and I knew it too, they were shaking,
even the air was vibrating,
they'll have to keep going like that if they hope to break it up,
the Campanone, instead, was pounding so fast,
less noise, but it just kept hitting, hitting, hitting,
it grated on your nerves,
the Suore Bianche with its chirping, same with the Cappuccini,
but you need them too, it's like hearing it ring at noon.

zò me Bòurgh l'è 'rvènz fura sno e' palàz
de Crèdit e la chèsa ad Liverani,
mo alazò csà suzédal? da la Zèla
m'un finistréin d'in èlt éun e' fa un sègn
ma qualcadéun, adès da San Zvanèl
un èlt e' sbat un straz,
e' fa d'ilt ségn, mo vérs al Sóri Niri,
pu ma la Piva u s sint sunè al campèni,
ènch' ma San Roch, mal scóli,
i sòuna dimpartótt, par ròmp e' témp,
di cópp de campanéil dla Colegèta
l'è casch un patòun 'd nàiva, u n va zò dl'èlta,
e a l so ènca mè, i sbatòca
ch'e' trema ènch' l'aria,
i à d'andè 'vènti acsè s'i vó sbranchè,
e' Campanòun invíci u i dà a martèl,
mènca boba, mo e' péccia sémpra alè,
quèll l'è una léima sòurda, e' pèr cmè gnént,
e magari l'è léu che pu e' sfuràcia,
al Sóri Biènchi al fa che sprignlamént,
i Capuzéin l'istèss,
mo i i vó ènca lòu, l'è cmè sintí mezdè.

lungo il Borgo è rimasto fuori solo il palazzo / del Credito e la casa di Liverani,
/ ma laggiú cosa succede? dalla Cella / a un finestrino in alto uno fa un segno
/ a qualcuno, adesso da San Giovannello / un altro sbatte uno straccio, / fa
altri segni, / ma verso le Suore Nere, / poi alla Pieve si sentono suonare le
campane, / anche a San Rocco, alle scuole, / suonano dappertutto, per
rompere il tempo, / dai coppi del campanile della Collegiata / è caduto un
cumulo di neve, ne va giú dell'altra, / e lo so anch'io, sbatacchiano / che trema
anche l'aria, / devono andare avanti cosí se vogliono squarciare, / il Campanone invece ci dà a martello, / meno chiasso, ma piacchia sempre lí, / quello
è una lima sorda, pare niente, / e magari è lui che poi sforacchia, / le Suore
Bianche fanno quel pigolio, / i Cappuccini lo stesso, / ma ci vogliono anche
loro, è come sentire mezzogiorno. //

My God, with all of them ringing, it's unworldly.
At this point it's dark and it's louder,
they're really going at it now,
and what's that up there, they've come up with something else?
from the castle, they're firing flares,
to see what the weather's doing,
streaks, like flames, that fall open like an umbrella,
they make it daytime, and each time, a color,
yellow, then red, this one's green,
and just look up in the air,
it's not snow anymore,
it looks like parsley coming down.

And the others are ringing too,
their hands must be raw by now, all night long,
it's finally morning, and what's coming down at this point
is absolutely
thicker, the air is a cloud of dust,
and below it's flowing like spilled milk,
you can't even see the edges of the buildings,
it's covering, it's hiding, everything,
that spur sticking out, what is it? the Mulini or the Ròst?
you're lost,
because the bells aren't ringing anymore,

Orca, fra tótt cm'i sòuna, ach diavuléri,
l'è bèla schéur e i i dà sémpra piò fórt,
i i à ciap góst,
e adès cs'èll alasò, i n n'à strulghè un'èlta?
i spèra da la Roca, l'è di raz
pr'avdài quèll ch'e' fa e' témp,
dal stréssi, cumè i fugh, pu al s'éirva a umbrèla,
al fa e' dè, e ogni vólta d'un culòur,
zal, pu ròss, quèst l'è vaird, e guèrd pr'aria,
u n'è mègga piò nàiva,
e' pèr ch'e' vénga zò tótt pandarséul.

E ch'ilt intènt i sòuna,
i i dà da splès al mèni, tótt la nòta,
l'è bèla e' dè, mo quèll ch'e' vén zò adès,
la s'è infitéida
adiritéura, l'aria l'è un purbiòun,
e sòtta la va sò cmè e' lat ch'e' vòunta,
u n s vaid piò un spéigal,
la cvérz, la mèsa tótt,
che spròun alà cs'èll ch' l'è, i Muléin? o e' Ròst?
aquè éun l'è pérs,
ènch' parchè ormai 'l campèni a n sòuna piò,

Orca, fra tutti come suonano, che diavolerio, / è ormai buio e ci danno sempre
piú forte, / ci hanno preso gusto, / e adesso cos'è lassú, ne hanno inventata
un'altra? / sparano dalla Rocca, sono razzi, / per vedere quello che fa il tempo,
/ delle strisce, come i fuochi, poi s'aprono a ombrello, / fanno il giorno, e ogni
volta d'un colore, / giallo, poi rosso, questo è verde, e guarda per aria, / non
è mica piú neve, / pare che venga giú tutto prezzemolo. // E gli altri intanto
suonano, / ci danno da spellarsi le mani, tutta la notte, / ormai è giorno, ma
quello che viene giú adesso, / s'è infittita / addirittura, l'aria è un polverone, /
e sotto va su come il latte che trabocca, / non si vede piú uno spigolo, / copre,
nasconde tutto, / quello sperone là cos'è, i Mulini? o il Ròst? / qui uno è perso,
/ anche perché ormai le campane non suonano piú,

they're not out there,
look at San Rocco, the church of the Pieve, there's nothing
[anymore,
the Campanone is almost completely covered,
town hall is a staircase and the roof
is full of dead pigeons,
the Borgo is gone, that knot there in the middle
is the coat of arms with the crown on top of the Arch,
that clump up there is the Castle.
And way down there is the train station.

And gusts and still more gusts. There, that's it,
the Arch is gone,
and now it's covered over the Castle too,
everything's the same now, what an endless expanse.
And it's still coming, where will it end?
it's coming from all directions, it's a blanket,
it's all riled up, it's making a whirlwind,
it just won't quit.

But come on, buck up now, it's been awhile since the last burst,
it's not coming down as hard, or am I imagining it?
no, it's falling, look at those flakes,
it's coming down here and there like confetti,
there's even less now, you can count them,

i n gn'à riséu,
vèrda San Roch, la Piva, u n gn'è piò gnént,
me Campanòun, e' sta par ciutè tótt,
e' Cuméun l'è un scaléin e tal sufétti
l'è pin ad pizéun mórt,
e' Bòurgh l'è 'ndèd, che gnòch alè te mèz
l'è e' stèmma sla curòuna in zéima a l'Èrch,
dla Roca u s vaid la póppla.
E alazò in chèva u i era la staziòun.

E e' bóffa, e' bóffa sémpra. Ècco, la è fata,
l'Èrch u n gn'è piò,
e adès u i è mòunt sòura ènch' ma la Roca,
l'à parzè tótt, ach stàisa!
E u i dà 'ncòura, mo dvò ch'e' vó rivé?
la vén da tótt' al pèrti, a sbutazèdi,
la s'aragna, la fa di mulinéll,
la n s férma piò.

Però, 'ta bón, l'è un pó ch' l'à un'èlta mnèda,
la vén zò mènca fétta, o u m pèr mu mè?
no, la cala, vè al fróffli,
al va d'in quà e d'in là cmè di curiàndal,
agli è sémpra piò póchi, al s pò cuntè,

non ci sono stati dietro, / guarda San Rocco, la Pieve, non c'è piú niente, / al
Campanone sta per coprire tutto, / il Comune è uno scaline e nelle soffitte /
è pieno di piccioni morti, / il Borgo è andato, quel gnocco lí in mezzo / è lo
stemma con la corona in cima all'Arco, / della Rocca si vede il ciuffo. / E
laggiú in fondo c'era la stazione. // E bufa, bufa sempre. Ecco, è fatta, /
l'Arco non c'è piú, / e adesso è montato sopra anche alla Rocca, / ha
pareggiato tutto, che distesa! / E ci dà ancora, ma dove vuol arrivare? / viene
da tutte le parti, a rovesci, / s'infuria, fa dei mulinelli, / non si ferma piú. //
Però, stai buono, è un po' che ha un'altra andata, / viene giú meno fitta, o pare
a me? / no, cala, ve' i fiocchi, / vanno in qua e in là come coriandoli, / sono
sempre piú pochi, si possono contare, /

a minute, five, almost fifteen,
that I'm here with my hand open,
and nothing has fallen, it's dry,
can it really be done?
over there, it's shifting,
it's clearing up, it's breaking up, you see it there,
there's a nice break down there too,
it's opening up everywhere,
the clouds are pulling apart, they're fraying, they're moving fast,
it looks like they're being lit up at the edges,
look, the moon, such light,
and the snow from down below, how it's giving off light,
and nothing's moving, there's a silence, hours pass,
the moon's getting dim, the sun's coming up.
Oh my, it hurts, there's such reflection
that it blinds you, you can't even keep your eyes open,
you've got to put two hands
against your face and look between your fingers.
But what are you looking at anyway? this is the end of the world.

l'è un minéut, zéinch minéut, l'è bèla un quèrt
ch'a stagh sla mèna vérta,
e u n gn'è casch gnént, la è sótta,
dabón ch' la séa finéida?
alè u s'armóv,
u s fa piò cièr, e' ròmp, u s vaid adlà,
u s'è fat un bel sbrènch ènca 'lazò,
u s'éirva dimpartótt,
al nóvli al s s-cènta, al fa i sfilàz, al córr,
e' pèr che tònda i éural al s'azènda,
vèrda, la léuna, ach lómm,
e la nàiva da sòtta cmè ch' la léus,
l'è fadéiga vdai 'l stèli,
e u n s móv gnént, u i è un zétt, e' pasa agli òuri,
la léuna la s sbiavéss, e' vén sò e' sòul,
azidénti cm'e' bréusa, u i è un sulóstar
ch'u t'inzíga, u n s pò mègga tnai vért i ócc,
bsògna mèttsi al do mèni
còuntra la faza e guardè da tra 'l dàidi.
Mo 's'ut guardè, quèst' l'è la féin de mònd.

è un minuto, cinque minuti, è quasi un quarto / che sto con la mano aperta, /
e non c'è caduto niente, è asciutta, / che sia davvero finita? / lí si smuove, /
si fa piú chiaro, rompe, si vede di là, / s'è fatto un bello squarcio anche laggiú, /
si apre dappertutto, / le nuvole si stracciano, fanno sfilacci, corrono, / pare che
attorno agli orli s'accendano, / guarda, la lune, che lume, / e la neve da sotto
come riluce, / è fatica vedere le stelle, / e non si muove niente, c'è un silenzio,
passano le ore, / la luna sbiadisce, viene su il sole, / accidenti come brucia, c'è
un riflesso / che ti acceca, non si può mica tenere aperti gli occhi, / bisogna
mettersi le due mani / contro la faccia e guardare di tra le dita. / Ma cosa vuoi
guardare, questa è la fine del mondo.

OUTSIDER

FURISTÍR

Let's Just Say

Let's just say that the end of the world comes, tomorrow,
the day after tomorrow and we all die, let's say that the earth
falls apart, that it's blown to smithereens,
that it's reduced to a cloud of dust, that it gets lost in the air,
the same thing with the moon, the sun goes out,
the stars, a darkness comes,
there's nothing anymore, and in all of this darkness will time
keep marching onwards? on its own two feet?
and just exactly where does it march to?

Mètt

Mètt ch'e' vénga la féin de mònd, admèn,
pasdmèn, e a murémm tótt, mètt che la tèra
la s'infràida, la s sfrangla,
ch' la s'ardéusa un purbiòun, ch' la s pérda tl' aria,
e la léuna l'istèss, u s smórta e' sòul,
al stèli, e' vén un schéur,
u n gn'è piò gnént, e at tótt che schéur e' témp
l'andarà ancòura avènti? da par léu?
e dò ch' l'andrà?

Metti. Metti che venga la fine del mondo, domani, / dopodomani, e
moriamo tutti, metti che la terra / s'infradici, si sbricioli, / che si riduca un
polverone, che si perda nell'aria, / e la luna lo stesso, si spegne il sole, / le
stelle, viene un buio, / non c'è piú niente, e in tutto quel buio il tempo /
andrà ancora avanti? da solo? / e dove andrà?

Outsider

With all these engines it's one big racket,
it's packed
at Baruzètt's corner,
at certain times of the day, you can't even get through,
there they are,
all of them, bickering, eating ice cream,
coming, going, the other night, if I hadn't been alert,
brakes screeching, Hey! you want to run me over?
I just stood there staring at him, this one I know,
you're Vittorio's son,
pay attention when you're driving, and that one there,
with the red sweater, come over here, he's a Broggi,
he's Oreste's grandson, right? isn't your grandfather
Oreste? aren't you Ugo's son? Who are you?
and he told me a name, which I don't remember anymore.
Cavalli? Marietti? no, a name like that,
which I'd never heard before, Barbieri, it's not that either,
he says his father works for Fisi,
they come here from outside,
you can tell it's a nice life here,
they come and never leave, so I, on Sundays,
in the piazza, when I go to buy the paper,
you see all these faces,

Furistír

S' chi mutéur, una boba, mo l'è pin,
me cantòun, 'd Baruzètt
a una zért'òura ta n'i pas, i è 'lè,
tótt, ch'i bacàia, i magna di gelè,
i va, i vén, l'altrasàira s'a n so svélt,
una frenèda, ció, ta m vén madòs?
pu a so stè 'lè a guardèl, mè quèst a l cnòss,
tè t si e' fiúl ad Vitorio, mo sté 'ténti
quant andé par la strèda, e quèll che là,
sla maia ròssa, vén aquè, l'è un BRògi,
l'è l'anvòud ad Ristín, no? u n'è e' tu nòn
Ristín, ta n si e' fiúl d'Ugo? mo chi sit?
e léu u m'à détt un nóm, ch'a n m'arcórd piò,
Cavalli? no, Marietti? un nóm acsè,
ch'a n l'éva mai sintéi, Barbieri? gnénca,
dis che e' su bà e' lavòura ma la Fisi,
i vén da fura, aquè u s vaid ch'u s sta bén,
i aréiva e i n va véa piò, ch mè la dmènga
in piaza quant a pas a tó e' giurnèl,
u s vaid 'd cal fazi,

Forestiero. Con quei motori, un chiasso, ma è pieno, / all'angolo di Baruzètt / a una cert'ora non ci passi, sono lí, / tutti, che baccagliano, / mangiano dei gelati, / vanno, vengono, l'altra sera se non sono svelto, / una frenata, ehi, mi vieni addosso? / poi sono stato lí a guardarlo, io questo lo conosco, / tu sei il figlio di Vittorio, ma state attenti/ quando andate per la strada, e quello là, / con la maglia rossa, vieni qui, è un Broggi, / è il nipote di Oreste, no? non è tuo nonno / Oreste? non sei il figlio di Ugo? ma chi sei? / e lui mi ha detto un nome, che non mi ricordo piú, / Cavalli? no, Marietti? un nome cosí, / che non l'avevo mai sentito, Barbieri? nemmeno, / dice che suo padre lavora alla Fisi, / vengono da fuori, qui si vede che si sta bene, / arrivano e non vanno via piú, che io la domenica / in piazza quando passo a prendere il giornale, / si vedono di quelle facce, /

I mean everywhere, in the bank, the Consortium,
the post office, which every so often, and that one, who's he?
new people, never seen before, which at times
I say: around here the foreigner
is me, I don't know anyone anymore,
even the ones from here, who were born here, I don't know,
don't they have their rights too, or doesn't that count for
                                                    [anything?
and at the town hall, it's the same thing with the examinations,
the others win out, are all of ours stupid?
it's better to shut up, come on now, with Bonini
a few days ago, we argued,
he says: you think the world belongs to you? what are you
                                                    [talking about?
this is our home, and the others are running things,
they come from outside and tell us what to do,
he said I was selfish, do you understand what I'm saying?
that I was taking it all wrong, come off it, if there's someone,
I say it all the time, I do,
everyone in the world has to scrape by, everyone wants to be
                                                    [rich,
I don't have a drop of envy in me, I have my work,
it's that Bonini when he wants to talk,
I'm the one who's got to listen to him,
even yesterday, I just happened to run into him,

mo dimpartótt, tla bènca, te consórzi,
tal pòsti, d'ogni tènt, e quèll chi èll?
zénta nóva, mai vésta, che dal vólti
a déggh: e' furistír
aquè a so mè, a n cnòss bèla piò niseun,
mo quéi de pòst, ch'i è nèd aquè, a n'e' so,
i avrà pò i su dirétt, o u n vó dí gnént?
e te Cuméun, zà che par fè un cuncòurs,
e pu i l véinz ch'ilt, i nóst i è tótt pataca?
l'è mèi stè zétt, va là, che sa Bonini
ir un èlt pó a ragnémm,
dis: mo quèst l'è egoéisum, cum sarébal?
a sémm ad chèsa nòsta, e' cmanda ch'ilt,
i vén da fura e i cmanda,
u m'à dè dl'egoésta, t'é capéi?
ch'a so 'rvènz mèl, fighéurt, ch s'u i è éun,
a l déggh sémpra, mè, i à da campè tótt
te mònd, la zénta a vrébb ch'i fóss tótt sgnéur,
a n'ò nisuna invéidia, ò e' mi lavòur,
l'è che Bonini quant l'à vòia ad zcòrr,
e mè a i casch sémpra,
ènca ir, a m'i so imbatú par chès,

ma dappertutto, nella banca nel consorzio, / alle poste, ogni tanto, e quello
chi è? / gente nuova, mai vista, che delle volte / dico: il forestiero / qui sono
io, non conosco ormai piú nessuno, / ma quelli del posto, che sono nati qui,
non lo so, / avranno pure i loro diritti, o non vuol dir niente? / e nel
Comune, già che per fare un concorso, / e poi lo vincono gli altri, i nostri
sono tutti cretini? / è meglio star zitti, va' là, che con Bonini / ieri un altro
po' litighiamo, / dice: ma questo è egoismo, come sarebbe? / siamo in casa
nostra, comandano gli altri, / vengono da fuori e comandano, / m'ha dato
dell'egoista, hai capito? / che sono rimasto male, figurati, che se c'è uno, /
lo dico sempre, io devono campare tutti / nel mondo, la gente vorrei che
fossero tutti ricchi, / non ho nessuna invidia, ho il mio lavoro, / è che Bonini
quando ha voglia di parlare, / e io ci casco sempre, / anche ieri, mi ci sono
imbattuto per caso, /

I was coming back from the cemetery,
I go there every year,
to see my wife, it's not that I don't keep it up,
every year, every two years, I go when I feel like it,
I just pick up and go, by myself, a stroll,
I get there, clear everything away, it's covered with weeds,
I clean her picture, then, going back, I wander around
                                                    [wherever,
it's a long walk there, I'm always at work,
it's gotten bigger, they're as far as
the street now, and they're always new ones,
they just jump out at you, there, look, Guaza,
and this one's Diego, it looks like he's talking,
that one's Santarelli, he already had one foot in the grave,
then Canzio, Nando Ricci, and here, this is Sghètta,
they're doing Garattoni's right now, I didn't even know it,
this one's just arriving, there's just a number,
it's got to be Cambéin, they took him away
the other day, and this is Ottavio, who always just had to brag:
I've got a doctor in the house,
and that one there laughing, that's Battistini,
look at Emilio, Emilio Bréina, what trumps we played,
Mosca, Dirani, it's one big hello,
here, it's like being in the piazza,
I know everyone.

avnéva da e' campsènt, a i vagh tótt i an,
da la mi mòi, mo u n'è ch'a i ténga e' còunt,
un an, du an, a vagh quant a me sint,
a ciap sò da par mè, una pasagèda,
aréiv alè, a téir véa, ch' l'è pin 'd graménga,
a i pulses e' ritràt, pu, a turnè indrí,
a zéir un pó purséa,
mo u i è da caminé, i è sémpra dri
ch'i lavòura, i ingrandéss, i è rivàt
bèla sla strèda, e u i n'è sémpra di nóv,
i scap fura ad bot, alè, vè, Guàza,
e quèst l'è Diego, l'è parlènt, e quèll
l'è Santarèli, l'è vlú 'ndè tla tèra,
pu Canzio, Nando Ricci, e aquè u i è Sghètta,
e' féva Garatoni, a n'e' savéva,
quèst l'è rivàt adès, u i è sno un nómar,
l'à da ès Carabéin, i l'à pórt véa
l'altredè, e quèst l'è Otavio, ch'u s stimèva:
a iò e' dutòur ad chèsa:
e quèll che 'lè ch'e' réid l'è Batistini,
vè Miglio 'd Bréina, al scòppi ch'avémm fat,
Mòsca, Dirani, mo l'è tótt' 'n'avdéuda
aquè, l'è cmè ès in piaza, a i cnòss ma tótt.

venivo dal cimitero, ci vado tutti gli anni, / da mi moglie, ma non è che tenga il conto, / un anno, due anni, vado quando me la sento, / prendo su da solo, una passeggiata, / arrivo lí, tiro via, che è piano di gramigna, / le pulisco il ritratto, poi, a tornare indietro / giro un po' purchessia, / ma c'è da camminare, sono sempre dietro / a lavorare, ingrandiscono, sono arrivati, / ormai sulla strada, e ce n'è sempre di nuovi, / scapano fuori di botto, lí, ve', Guaza, / e questo è Diego, sembra che parli, e quello / è Santarelli, è voluto andare nella terra, / poi Canzio, Nando Ricci, e qui c'è Sghètta, / faceva Garattoni, non lo sapevo, / questo è arrivato adesso, c'è solo un numero, / dev'essere Carabéin, l'hanno portato via / questo è Ottavio, che si vantava: ho il dottore in casa, / e quello lí che ride è Battistini, / ve' Emilio 'd Bréina, le scope che abbiamo fatto, / Mosca, Dirani, ma è tutto un salutare / qui, è come essere in piazza, li conosco tutti.

Enough

Enough already, I'm tired of it all.
Every day the same.
I can't take it anymore.
I think
I'll grow a mustache.

Basta !

E pu basta, a m so stóff,
l'è tótt i dè cumpàgn, u n s nu n pò piò.
A m ví fè crèss i bafi!

Basta! E poi basta, mi sono stufato, / è tutti i giorni uguale, non se ne può
piú. / Mi voglio far crescere i baffi!

Dough

I made money? I made money. So what?
I'm set up nicely, so long as there are fools in this world,
you're getting angry. Now. Why? to play the gentlemen
don't you have to get rich? you're saying I robbed them?
but not you, Mr. Clever One who never had a cent,
oh calm down, why are you raising your voice,
plus it'll make you thirsty,
Peppina, is the coffee ever going to get here?
make it two, come on now, let me pay, no, for this fellow here,
better bring him a chamomile, to calm his delicate nerves,
I'm not going to let you get under my skin, see, I'm laughing
                                                    [about it,
it hurts I'm laughing so hard, what do you expect anyway,
the world's turned upside down,
but let's talk about you, you haven't done so bad for yourself
                                                    [either,
shuffle around a few papers at city hall, off at two,
you've even got new shoes, a real gentleman,
and you're still not happy?

I bócch

Ò fat i bócch? ò fat i bócch, e alòura?
a m so ragnè, fintènt ch'u i'è di pataca,
ta t'incapèl? cumè? ch'ès galantóman
u n s dvénta sgnéur? alòura a i ò rubé?
no ma tè, tè t si féurb, t n'é mai vú un frènch,
mo sta bón, 's'ut ragnè, che pu n t vén sàida,
Pepina, sté cafè u n'aréiva piò?
déu, va là, ch'a pègh, mè, no, léu, l'è mèi,
pórti una capumélla ch' l'à e' nervòus,
ta n t la si da ciapè, mè, vè, a i réid sòura,
tanimódi, zò, e' mònd e' va a l'arvérsa,
mo tè pu la n t'è gnénca andè malàz,
te Cuméun ta n fé póca, al do t si lébar,
t'é ènca al schèrpi nóvi, e galantòm.
ta n si cuntént?

I soldi. Ho fatto i soldi? ho fatto i soldi, e allora? / mi sono arrangiato, finché ci sono dei coglioni, / t'arrabbi? come? che a essere galantuomini / non si diventa ricchi? allora li ho rubati? / non a te, tu sei furbo, non hai mai avuto una lira, / ma sta' calmo, cosa gridi, che poi ti viene sete, / Peppina, questo caffè non arriva piú / due, va' là , che pago io, no, lui, è meglio, / portagli una camomilla che ha il nervoso, / non te la devi prendere, io ve', ci rido sopra, / tanto, cosa vuoi, il mondo va alla rovescia, / ma poi a te non t'è neanche andata malaccio, / nel Comune ne fai poca, alle due sei libero, / hai anche le scarpe nuove, e galantuomo, / non sei contento?

Beautiful

She comes back every so often, to see her mother,
she doesn't stay long, she never goes out.
I on the other hand am always out.
I ran into her, at the pharmacy.
"How long has it been since we've seen each other?"
she seemed smaller,
"You have short hair," because she used to wear it long, to her
                                                    [shoulders,
she closed her eyes: "You remember my hair?"

Vincio had it bad for her.
And her, nothing. With those green eyes and a yellow sweater.
Lele Guarnieri tried to woo her too.
On Sundays he'd come up from Cesena
to dance, a blond guy with a red Alfa Sprint,
I, she was too beautiful, I didn't even try.

After I walked her back to the house,
she opened up, I said: "What I would have given
to have not been wearing glasses!" she laughed: "We'll see each
                                                    [other again
in another twenty years,"

310

Bèla

La tòurna d'ogni tènt, par la su mà,
la sta póch, du tri dè, la n scapa mai,
mè pu a so sémpra fura.
A la ò incòuntra par chès, tla farmacéa,
"Mo quant'èll ch'a n s'avdémm?",
la m'è pèrsa piò znina,
"T'é i cavéll chéurt", ch' la i éva lóngh, sal spali,
la à céus i ócc: "Ta t'arcórd di mi cavéll?"

Vinicio u i éva fat una pasiòun.
E li gnént. Sa chi ócc véird e e' maiòun zal.
U i era ènca andè dri Lele Guarnieri,
e la dmènga l'avnéva da Ceséina
a balè un biònd s'una Giulietta sprint.
Mè, la era tròpa bèla, a n m'arisghéva.

Dop a la ò cumpagnèda fina chèsa,
la à vért, ò détt: "Cs'èll ch'avrébb paghè 'lòura
par no purtè i ucèl!",
la à ridéu: "A s'avdémm fr'agli èlt vint'an,"

Bella. Torna ogni tanto, per sua madre, / sta poco, due tre giorni, non esce mai, / io poi sono sempre fuori. / L'ho incontrata per caso, in farmacia, / "Ma quant'è che non ci vediamo?", / mi è sembrata piú piccola, / "Hai i capelli corti", che li aveva lunghi, sulle spalle, / ha chiuso gli occhi: "Ti ricordi dei miei capelli?" // Vinicio ci aveva fatto una passione. / E lei niente. Con quegli occhi verdi e il maglione giallo. / Le aveva fatto la corte anche Lele Guarnieri, / e la domenica veniva da Cesena / a ballare un biondo con una Giulietta sprint. / Io, era troppo bella, non m'arrischiavo. // Dopo l'ho accompagnata fino a casa, / ha aperto, ho detto: "Cosa avrei pagato allora / per non portare gli occhiali!", / ha riso: "Ci vediamo fra altri vent'anni", /

311

then from the door which was still ajar, right before closing it,
she looked at me and said: "I liked you,"
and without laughing, "I dreamed of you how many nights?"

pu da e' purtòun custèd, préima da céud,
la m'à guèrs: "Ta m pisévi",
senza réid, "Quanti nòti a t'ò insugné!"

poi dal portone accostato, prima di chiudere, m'ha guardato: "Mi piacevi," /
senza ridere, "quante notti t'ho sognato!"

The Bishop

I was on the run, my father was looking for me,
they'd seen me smoking behind the Wall,
he was going to wring my neck.
I made a big loop, I was crunching a mint,
I was a little drunk on top of it, where do I go now?
I saw the front door open, it was usually kept closed,
I slipped in, I was panting,
a cold, a darkness, my eyes adjusted, what's all this?
on the floor, a St. Anthony without a nose,
pews, candlesticks, an open tabernacle,
I heard them talking farther down, the floor
was a wreck, and down there in a hole,
standing, was Doctor Zanzi, the engineer,
and three or four outsiders, one with a beard,
and in the middle of it all was some holy thing, some workers
were underneath a big stone,
they called out, "All set? Go now!" they were breathing hard,
they loosened it, some plaster debris showered,
they pulled it out a couple more inches, "Come on now!"

E' vèscuv

Andéva ad chéursa, u m zarchéva e' mi bà,
i m'éva vést fumé spèsa la Méura,
ch' s'u m'inguantéva e ch'u m sintéva e' fiè,
ò fat un zéir, a biaséva una menta,
e un pó imbariégh, adès dú vaghi? ò vést
e' purtòun vért, ch' l'era sémpra tótt céus,
a m so infilé, a lanséva,
un frèdd, un schéur, pu a i ò fat l'òc, e quèll?
ma tèra, un Sant'Antóni senza nès,
bènchi, candlír, un tabarnècal vért,
ò sintí zcòrr in fònd, e' pavimént,
i éva guàst tótt, e alazò, t'una béusa,
d'impí u i era l'inznír, e' dutòur Zanzi,
tri quatar furistír, éun s'una bèrba,
e te mèz un santéssum, di operai
i s'era ciap da sòtta m'una péidria,
i s déva vòusa: "A i sémm? forza!", i sufiéva,
i la à smòsa, l'è casch de calzinàz,
i la à tiràta sò 'd do dàida, "Dài!",

Il vescovo. Andavo di corsa, mi cercava mio padre, / m'avevano visto fumare dietro la Mura, / che se m'agguanatava e mi sentiva il fiato, / ho fatto un giro, masticavo una menta, / e un po' ubriaco, adesso dove vado? / ho visto / il portone aperto, che era sempre tutto chiuso, / mi sono infilato, ansavo, / un freddo, un buio, poi ci ho fatto l'occhio, e quello? / per terra, un Sant'Antonio senza naso, / panche, candelieri, un tabernacolo aperto, / ho sentito parlare in fondo, il pavimento, / avevano guastato tutto, e laggiú, in una buca, / in piedi c'erano l'ingegnere, il dottor Zanzi, / tre quattro forestieri, uno con una barba, / e in mezzo un sacramento, degli operai / s'erano attacati da sotto a un pietrone, / si davano voce: "Ci siamo? forza!", soffiavano, / l'hanno smosso, è caduto del calcinaccio, / l'hanno tirato su di due dita, "Dai!", /

they put a crowbar underneath, "Rotate it! Easy!
Slow!" the others got closer,
they craned their necks, the one with the beard
pointed with the flashlight, and I slipped in among them,
below the jackets, the marble
got as high as my chin, and little by little
I saw someone emerge from inside,
it was beautiful, all dressed in red, horrifying,
with velvet slippers, and gloves,
and so very much of that gold, a bishop?
it was like a dream, they all said: oh!
and he turned into dust, in a heartbeat,
like he'd been made of powder, there was nothing left.

i i à mèss sòtta un fèr, "Ruglèla, adèsi!
andé 'dèsi!", ch'ilt i s'è fat daprèsa,
i à basè e' còl, quèll sla bèrba e' puntéva
la lampadéina, mè a m so instècch te mèz,
da sòtta al sèrghi, e' mèrum
u m'arivéva me barbètt, e dréinta
pianín pianín ò vést vní fura éun,
bèl, tótt vistéid ad ròss, una paéura!
sa dal pupózzi ad vléut, ènca si guènt,
e tènt ad cl'ór, un vèscuv?
mo l'è stè cmè un insógni, i à fat: oh!
e léu u s'è sfariné,
t'un sóffi,
cmè ch'e' fóss fat ad cipria, u n gn'è 'rvènz gnént.

ci hanno messo sotto un ferro, "Ruzzolatelo, adagio! / andate adagio!", gli
altri si sono accostati, / hanno abbassato il collo, quello con la barba puntava
/ la lampadina, io mi sono infilato in mezzo, / da sotto le giacche, il marmo
/ m'arrivava al mento, e dentro / piano piano ho visto venir fuori uno, /
bello, tutto vestito di rosso, una paura! / con delle babbucce di velluto, anche
coi guanti, / e tanto di quell'oro, un vescovo? / ma è stato come un sogno,
hanno fatto: oh! / e lui è sfarinato, / in un soffio, / come fosse fatto di
cipria, non c'è rimasto niente.

317

The Shop

This odor, I don't get it, it's been two or three days,
it's not the sewer, which, when the wind's coming from the
                                                    [southwest,
there's a bone-chilling wind, it's like food that's gone bad,
then it passes, for awhile,
it could be that window, I keep it open sometimes
to get fresh air, and a cat,
it wouldn't take much, a jump up, a quick piss,
but I've never seen one, plus this isn't piss,
it permeates everything, you can imagine, what could this be?
and it's not coming from far,
it's that here, by myself, keeping up with everything,
this and that, this and the other, it is what I've chosen,
always keeping an eye out,
because someone might come in, even if it's been,
could be someone from the countryside,
then they're bent out of shape, but it's not my fault
if they didn't know, it's been over a year
since I put up the posters
in Poggio Berni,
in Ciola,
in San Martino, for ten days,

La butàiga

Sta pózza, mè a n capéss, l'è du tri dè,
u n'è la ciavga, che quant l'è garbéin,
mo e' téira un vént giazéd, l'è cmè ch'e' fóss
andè da mèl dla roba da magnè,
pu la pasa, pr'un pó,
e' putrébb ès, cla finestra, dal vólti
a la téngh vérta par dè aria, e un gat,
u n'i vó gnént, un sèlt, una piséda,
mo a n n'ò mai vést, e pu quèst u n'è péss,
ch'u s'instècca, fighéurt, cs'èll ch'e' sarà?
e la n vén da dalòngh,
l'è che què, da par sè, stè dri ma tótt,
d'in quà, d'in là, la strèda ch'a faz mè,
e buté sémpra l'òc,
ch'e' pò vní qualcadéun, ènca se ormai,
però da la campagna,
e dop i arvènza mèl, mo mè a n n'ò còulpa
s'i n l'à savéu, pu l'è pas piò d'un an,
ch'éva fat mètt i manifést me Pózz,
a Zula, a San Martéin, l'è stè dis dè,

La bottega. Questa puzza, non capisco, sono due tre giorni, / non è la fogna, che quand'è libeccio, / ma tira un vento ghiacciato, è come fosse / andata a male della roba mangiare, / poi passa, per un po', / potrebbe essere, quella finestra, delle volte / la tengo aperta per dare aria, e un gatto, / non ci vuol niente, un salto, una pisciata, / ma non ne ho mai visti, e poi questo non è piscio, / che s'infiltra, figurarsi, cosa sarà? / e non viene da lontano, / è che qui, da solo, star dietro a tutto, / di qua, di là, la strada che faccio io, / e buttar sempre l'occhio, / che può venire qualcuno, anche se ormai, / però dalla campagna, / e dopo rimangono male, ma io non ne ho colpa / se non l'hanno saputo, poi è passato piú d'un anno, / che avevo fatto mettere i manifesti a Poggio Berni, / a Ciola, a San Martino, sono stati dieci giorni, /

they were swarming, bigger than any fair,
I should have taken out the buzzer,
it drilled in your head, all of them hovering
over the counter, shoving,
tussling, ripping
things out of each other's hands, please,
please, let's settle down,
do you want to come to blows?
let me check the size, there's enough for everyone,
plenty more, but you couldn't control them,
ah, a close-out,
all first class stuff, pure wool,
full-length dresses, I was selling them
for fifty thousand lire,
I was ashamed of myself, I gave away
designer jackets,
Facis, thirty thousand,
blouses, fifteen thousand,
pure Egyptian cotton, long sleeved, and then,
at a certain point I just went crazy, go ahead,
ten thousand, it was no holds barred,
there wasn't a scrap left,
they didn't leave so much as a lining, a thread
to donate to the old people's home, they cleaned me out,
and those first days in the shop, by myself,
it was like vultures circling, it's empty,
it's time to rent it out, a hundred people had asked me,

i s muntéva madòs, èlt che la fira,
e' campanèl dla bóssla ò cnú cavèl,
u t tuléva la testa, e tótt alè
me bancòun, al spatàsi,
i s'aragnéva al pèzi, i si li rubéva
dal mèni, mo sté bón, a vlí fè al boti?
zò, lasém misuré, ch'u i n'è par tótt,
adlà l'è pin, mo ta n'i févi faza,
amo cumè, mo una liquidaziòun,
tótt' roba ad préima scelta, lana pura,
di vstéi, tri metr'e véint, a so rivàt
ch'a i ò vandú zinquentamélla frènch,
ch'a m vargugnéva mè, ò dè véa dal sèrghi
marchèdi, Facis, trentamélla frènch,
al caméisi quengmélla,
puro makò, sal manghi lònghi, e pu
a un zért mumént u m'è vnú e' mat, alè,
dismélla frènch e e' pasa la paéura,
e u n gn'è 'rvènz gnént, gnénca una fódra, un schèmpal
da regalè mi Vcéun, i a pulí l'èra,
e i préim dè tla butàiga, da par mè,
l'era una piaza d'èrmi, ció, tótt sgòmbar,
e adès fité, ch'i m la éva dmanda in zént,

si montavano addosso, altro che la fiera, / il campanello della porta ho
dovuto levarlo, / ti andava in testa, e tutti lí / al bancone, le spinte, / si
litigavano le pezze, se le rubavano dalle mani, ma state buoni, volete fare a
botte? / su, lasciatemi misurare, che ce n'è per tutti, / di là è pieno, ma non
gli facevi fronte, / e beh, una liquidazione, / tutta roba di prima scelta, lana
pura, / dei vestiti, tre metri e venti, sono arrivato, / che li ho venduti
cinquantamila lire, / che mi vergognavo io, ho dato via delle giacche /
marcate, Facis, trentamila lire, / le camicie quindicimila, / puro makò, con
le maniche lunghe, e poi / a un certo momento m'è venuto il matto, alè, /
diecimila lire e passa la paura, / e non c'è rimasto niente, neanche una fodera,
uno scampolo / da regalare ai Vecchioni, hanno pulito l'aia, / e i primi giorni
nella bottega, da solo, / era una piazza d'armi, tutto vuoto, / e adesso
affittare, che me l'avevano chiesto in cento, /

321

I was worn out, really, why should I ask for trouble,
at home we're a couple of lovebirds, but even Norina
was saying it to me: sell it all, but then afterwards,
back inside, I started putting things back in place,
one day, two days, a week, no rush,
someone every once in awhile: you, with this shop,
are you making love to it, and well, a place
you've been in for years,
to just one day leave it all,
I said: let's just wait a while, no one's after me,
I've got some money salted away,
you bet I waited, I'm still going at it,
things you'd never have to do in a shop,
which you'd say, but now instead it's worse,
the dust alone,
before there were those girls, they did it,
they didn't do a thing, but it's best not to go into it, let it go,
the things I found that would be right there under their noses,
if you don't check the corners,
that's where it really collects, if you don't move things around,
and climb on a chair, up high
is where you get the dust balls,
then with all of these shelves,
it's a huge job, I used snuff, the coughing,
you never see the end of it, you could wash it down all you
                                                      [want,

a m séra stóff, dabón, 's'ut bazilé,
ma chèsa a sémm dú cócch, ènch' la Norina
la m'e' géva: vènd tótt, però pu dop,
alè dréinta, a m so mèss a radanè,
un dè, du dè, un stmèna, senza préssia,
qualcadéun d'ogni tènt: tè sta butàiga
ta i fé l'amòur, ciò, un pòst ch'u si è stè di an,
da un dè a cl'èlt lasè tótt,
e ò détt: spitémma, u n mu n dà dri niseun,
a iò da pèrta qualche baiuchètt,
e spétta pò, a so 'ncòura què ch'a i dagh,
quèll ch'u i è mai da fè t'una butàiga,
ch'éun e' girébb, invíci adès l'è pézz,
mo sno la pòrbia, préima
u i era cal burdèli, al féva lòu,
ch'a n féva gnént, l'è mèi no zcòrr, va là,
quèll ch'ò tróv, a l'i déva drétt me nès,
mo s' t n'aréiv ti cantéun,
ch' la s' t'ardéus própia alè, s' ta n squèns al robi,
e muntè s'na scaràna, che alasò
u s fa i rózzal, pus a tótt' stal scanzéi,
l'è stè un lavòur, ò tabachè, la tòsa,

m'ero stufato, davvero, cosa vuoi tribolare, / a casa siamo due cocchi, anche
la Norina / me lo diceva: vendi tutto, però poi dopo, / lí dentro, mi sono
messo a riordinare, / un giorno, due giorni, una settimana, senza fretta, /
qualcuno ogni tanto: tu, questa bottega / ci fai l'amore, e beh, un posto che
ci s'è stati degli anni, / da un giorno all'altro lasciar tutto, / e ho detto:
aspettiamo, non m'insegue nessuno, / ho da parte qualche soldarello, / e
aspetta pure, sono ancora qui che ci do, / quel che non c'è mai da fare in una
bottega, / che uno direbbe, invece adesso è peggio, / ma solo la polvere,
prima / c'erano quelle ragazze, facevano loro, / che non facevano niente,
meglio non parlarne, va' là, / quel che ho trovato ci davano dritto al naso, /
ma se non arrivi negli angoli, / che si raccoglie proprio lí, se non sposti le
cose, / e salire su una sedia, che lassú / si fanno i bioccoli, poi con tutte
queste scansie, / è stato un lavoro, ho tabaccato, la tosse, /

there'd still be dust,
go at it with a wet rag,
what's the point?
where does it come from? "Good morning, I'd wanted to see,
you don't have it, but. . ."
"You're not from here?"
"No, I was passing through, I thought,"
"And you weren't mistaken, this shop, I dressed everyone
for more than thirty years," "And now?"
"And now this, which is a long story, but you've got things to do,
and I've got even more to do than you, it'll have to keep for
another time,
and them: "Yes, yes," then once they're outside they turn around
and look,
I feel sorry for them, I know, but if you had to listen every time,
when there's a thousand things to get done,
because nothing's hidden anymore,
whatever's here shows. I've got an electrical system,
all on the same switchbox, the outlets don't always work,
the letters in the sign flicker, plus the cost of using it,
I got along fine for years with this little hole in the wall,
they're just going to stay burnt out,
calm down, because when I think about it,
I did the right thing doing what I did, go ahead, let them talk,
I wouldn't go back, and do what?
all day long behind the counter, and when night came,
the taking out, putting away, on top, underneath,

e u n s vaid la féin, daqua quant t vu, u i n'è sémpra,
dài se straz mòl, mo cmè ch' la s fa? da gnént,
da dò ch' la nas? "Bongiorno, a vléva vdai,
a n'aví mégga, mo. . .", "Vò a n si d'aquè?",
"No, a paséva, ò cridéu", "E a n'i sbaiè,
sta butàiga, mè a i ò vistí ma tótt
par piò 'd trent'an", "E adès?", "Adès acsè,
ch'e' sarébb un zcòurs lòngh, mo vò 'i da fè,
mè piò ch' nè vò, e' sarà pr'un'èlta vólta",
e lòu: "Sè sè", pu ad fura i s vólta indrí,
purétt, a l so, mo dè rèta ma tótt,
ch'u i n'è mélla da fè,
parchè aquè 'dès u n vén piò masèd gnént,
quèll ch' l'è scap fura, a iò un impiènt elèctrich,
tótt un contàt, al pràisi a n tén, al lèttri
dla luminòusa al bala, pu e' consómm,
a so 'ndè 'vènti di an s'una baràca,
ch'u i era d'arvanzè ènca fulminéd,
'ta bón, che quant a i péns,
ò fat bén quèll ch'ò fat, las' pò ch'i dégga,
e a n turnarébb indrí, mo da fè chè?
tótt e' dè me bancòun, quant l'era nòta,
chèva, mètt, sòura, sòtta,

e non si vede la fine, innaffia quanto vuoi, ce n'è sempre, / dacci con lo
straccio bagnato, ma come si fa? da niente, / da dove nasce? "Buongiorno,
volevo vedere, / non avete mica, ma. . .", "Voi non siete di qui?", / No,
passavo, ho creduto,", "E non avete sbagliato," / "E non avete sbagliato,
/ questa bottega, io li ho vestiti tutti / per piú di trent'anni," "E adesso?",
"Adesso cosí, / che sarebbe un discorso lungo, ma voi avete da fare, / io
piú di voi, sarà per un'altra volta", / e loro: "Sí, sí", poi di fuori si voltano
indietro, / poveretti, lo so, ma dar retta a tutti, / che ce n'è mille da fare, /
perché qui adesso noviene piú nascosto niente, / quel che è venuto fuori,
ho un impianto elettrico, / tutto un contatto, le prese non tengono, le
lettere / della luminosa ballano, poi il consumo, / sono andato avanti degli
anni con una baracca, / che c'era da rimanere anche fulminati, / sta'
buono, che quando ci penso, / ho fatto bene quel che ho fatto, lascia pur
che dicano, / e non tornerei indietro, ma da far che? / tutto il giorno al
bancone, quand'era notte, / cava, metti, sopra, sotto, /

with people who talk at you, but then won't listen,
this one doesn't fit, this one doesn't either,
don't you have something else?
what else do you want there to be?
you're not understanding a thing, you're looking only at the
                                                    [colors,
and then they'd complain, even now
they come in, they look around, with a superior attitude:
"There's nothing here,"
"So?" "There's not much here." "Even this is too much for
                                                    [me."
then they leave, they're criticizing me outside, I can hear them,
there's even some who object:
"If you're not selling anything, close up, put up a sign,
otherwise you're just making fools of them,
"What did I do? aren't you the one who invited yourself in?
I was here working, this morning
I didn't even have time to get a coffee," someone else
passed by the other day: "shops like this one,
plenty more like this in Crazytown," I laugh,
now they're saying I'm nuts, first they were saying
I was a lazy bum, no, lots of them were saying it,
go ahead and let them, it's high season right now,
and I've got lots, I do, to consider,
I see what's happening, even in town,
insofar as tourism goes, the outsiders coming in,

sla zénta ch'i t fa zcòrr, pu i n t sta a sintéi,
quèst u n va bén, quèst gnénca,
u n gn'è qualchecos'èlt? csa i àl da ès,
ch'a n capí gnént, a guardé sno i culéur,
e dop i s lamantéva, mo ènca adès,
i éintra, i guèrda, s'un'aria: "Mo u n gn'è gnént",
"E alòura?", "L'è un pó póch", "Mè, l'è ènca trop",
pu i scapa, e ad fura i crética, ch'a i sint,
'u i n'è 'nca 'd quéi ch'i ragna:
"S'a n vandí gnént, ciudéi, mití un cartèl,
se no acsè u s cèma tó pr'e' chéul la zénta",
"Csa fazi mè? mo vò chi ch' v'à ciamè?
ch'a so què ch'a lavòur, che stamatéina
a n'ò vù témp gnénch' d'andè a tó un cafè",
éun l'altredè l'è pas: "Ad stal butàighi
u i n'è dagli èlti a Imola", mè a réid,
i m dà de mat adès, che préima i géva
ch'a séra un vagabònd, mo i n n'à détt tènti,
ch'i faza lòu, adès sla stasòun bona
a i n'ò, mè, da pensè,
parchè a li vèggh al robi, ènch' pr'e' paàis,
pr'e' turéisum, l'aréiva i furistír,

con la gente che ti fa parlare, poi non ti sta a sentire / questo non va bene,
questo nemmeno, / non c'è qualchecos'altro? cosa ci dev'essere, / che non
capite niente, guardate solo i colori, / e dopo si lamentavano, ma anche adesso,
/ entrano, guardano, con un'aria: "Ma non c'è niente", / "E allora?", "È un po'
poco", "Per me è anche troppo", / poi escono, e di fuori criticano, che li sento,
/ e ce n'è anche di quelli che protestano: / "Se non vendete niente, chiudete,
mettete un cartello, / se no cosí si chiama prendere per il culo la gente". / Cosa
faccio io? ma voi chi v'ha chiamato? / che sono qui che lavoro, che stamattina
/ non ho avuto tempo neanche d'andare a prendere un caffè", / uno l'altro
giorno è passato: "Di queste botteghe / ce ne sono altre a Imola", io rido, / mi
danno del matto adesso, che prima dicevano / che ero un vagabondo, ma ne
hanno dette tante, / che facciano loro, adesso con la stagione buona, / ne ho,
io, da pensare, / perché le vedo le cose, anche per il paese, / per il turismo,
arrivano i forestieri, /

a place like this, right on the piazza, those windows,
they won't do, really, a good dusting's not going to be enough,
and you can't just send them back, Sormani said:
"It's your calling card,"
and I know too how they're supposed to enter,
I've seen them,
in Rimini, near Guidi, plus this door's
got to be enlarged, these racks, no way, gone,
a mirror, full-length, the ideas
come to me, and the work, there's just not enough time
to keep up, it's just that I, with all this,
I don't have time to think, because first of all,
the taxes, the bills, insurance payments, the accountant,
wrangling with the tourists, the banks, the interest, all eating
                                    [you alive,
for goodness sakes, no, now it's a whole different ball of wax,
Ugo the fishmonger's always telling me, "You, you know,
you saw it coming," And what did you expect?"
it's just one more step, they're afraid,
it's like respect for humanity, which if they only had,
I sometimes, in the evening, I close up from inside
and just sit here,
with all the lights on, everything's in order,

un pòst cmè quèst, in piaza, cal vedréini,
a n'i sémm, zò, alè, u n basta una spurbièda,
e la n s pò 'rmandè piò, Sormani e' géva:
è il biglietto da visita, e mè a l so
ènca cm'a gli à d'avnéi, a gli ò zà vésti
a Rémin, tachèd Guidi, pu sta pórta
bsògna slarghè, che tacapàn, gnént, via,
un spèc, fighéura intíra, mo gli idéi
mè u n mu n vén, e i lavéur putài stèi dri
e' témp ch'u i vó, tanimódi mè què
pensír a n n'ò, che préima,
tasi, chéunt, contribéut, e' ragiunír,
ragnè si viazadéur,
al bènchi, i interéss, ch'i t magna véiv,
par carità! no, adès l'è un èlt campè,
u m'e' dí sémpra Ugo de pèss: "Tè, vitt,
ta la é indvinéda", "E tè cs'èll t sté spitè?",
sno ch' l'è un pas, i à paéura,
l'è cmè un rispèt umèn, ch s'i savéss,
mè dal vólti, la sàira, a m céud da dréinta
e a stagh aquè disdài,
sa tòtt' al luci zàisi, mo sno l'òurdin,

un posto come questo, in piazza, quelle vetrine, / non ci siamo, dai, lí non basta una spolverata, / e non si può piú rimandare, Sormani diceva: / è il biglietto da visita, e io lo so / anche come devono venire, le ho già viste / a Rimini, vicino a Guidi, poi questa porta / bisogna allargare, quell'attaccapanni, niente, via, / uno specchio, figura intera, ma le idee / me ne vengono a me, e i lavori poterci star dietro / il tempo che ci vuole, tanto io qui / pensieri non ne ho, che prima, / tasse, conti, contributi, il ragioniere, / litigare coi viaggiatori, / le banche, gli interessi, che ti mangiano vivo, / per carità! no, adesso è un altro campare, / me lo dice sempre Ugo del pesce: "Tu, vedi! / l'hai indovinata", "E tu cosa stai ad aspettare?", / solo che è un passo, hanno paura, / è come un rispetto umano, che se sapessero, / io delle volte, la sera, mi chiudo da dentro / e sto qui seduto, / con tutte le luci accese, ma solo l'ordine, /

the yardstick, the scissors, each in its place,
the wrapping paper, the string, the drawers, that never used
                                        [to open right,
and now, with just one finger, it's a tidy little garden inside,
and myself as well, I feel light,
every so often a thought, I put it out of my head, I lose it,
it's nothing, all things, quiet, one, two, three, four,
seven, eight, and continuing on, and now they're doing it
it's no work for them, on account of the quartz,
they're not off so much as a minute,
and putting a barometer here,
right in front, for symmetry,
that's all, I, these, wait I'm going to turn off the lights
that's better, in the dark, there are certain moments,
outside, people are going about their business,
and I'm here in my little,
I'm master of the world, what am I lacking?
I get up, walk around, touch, "It's closed, come back
tomorrow, no, I can't, if the police come by
they'll write me up," then such faces,
they want to chitchat, they make you lose time,
and I, on the other hand, I must really be out of my mind,
five minutes ago, I was looking, it came in a flash,

e' metr, al fórbsi, sémpra te su pòst,
la chèrta, e' spègh, e i casétt, ch'i n s'arvéva,
adès, s'un daid, e dréinta un zardinètt,
e ènca mè, a m sint lizír,
d'ogni tènt un pensír, a i vagh dri, a l pérd,
mo gnént, tott' robi, zétt, éun, déu, tréi, quatar,
. . . sèt, òt, l'è sémpra 'vènti, e adès i i fa
ch'i n s carga, al quarzo, e i n sbaia d'un minéut,
e ad quà mètt un barometro,
própia in faza, da fè la simetréa,
ecco, mè, quést, spétta ch'a smórt, l'è mèi,
te schéur, l'è di mumént,
'd fura la zénta i va par la su strèda,
e mè què, te mi péccal,
a so e' padròun de mònd, cs'èll ch'u m'amènca?
a stagh sò, a zéir, a tòcch, "L'è céus, turné
admatéina, no, a n pòs, se pasa al guèrdi
a m fa contravenziòun", pu l'è dal fazi,
i à vòia ad ciacri, i t fa sno pérd de témp,
che invíci mè, a sarò pò mat dabón,
zéinch minéut fa, a guardéva, l'è stè un lèmp:
e' bancòun l'è a l'arvérsa, e' va pr'e' lòngh,

il metro, le forbici, sempre al loro posto, / la carta, lo spago, e i cassetti, che non s'aprivano, / adesso con un dito, e dentro un giardinetto, / e anch'io, mi sento leggero, / ogni tanto un pensiero, ci vado dietro, lo perdo, / ma niente, tutte cose, zitto, uno, due, tre, quattro, / . . . sette, otto, è sempre avanti, e adesso li fanno / che non si caricano, al quarzo, e non sbagliano d'un minuto, / e di qua mettere un barometro, / proprio di fronte, da fare la simmetria, / ecco, io questi, aspetta che spengo, è meglio, / nel buio, sono dei momenti, / fuori la gente va per la sua strada, / e io qui, nel mio piccolo, / sono il padrone del mondo, cosa mi manca? / mi alzo, giro, tocco, "È chiuso, tornate / domattina, no, non posso, se passano i vigili / mi fanno contravvenzione", poi sono facce, / hanno voglia di chiacchierare, ti fanno solo perdere tempo, / che invece io, sarò pur matto davvero, / cinque minuti fa, guardavo, è stato un lampo: / il bancone è alla rovescia, va per il lungo, /

the counter is backwards, it's been like this forever,
I never even noticed it,
it's because things, that's how it is, when you're in the middle
                                                    [of them,
and standing in the corner, right here nothing, open,
a sitting area, and two nice display lights on the wall,
I'll break it all down, they won't have a clue, they,
I'll start right here right now,
this is a place, if up until now I sold cloth,
but it could work perfectly well as a café,
a furniture store, a supermarket,
with the stockroom in back, you'd enter from the piazza
and exit in the Borgo, why not a bank?
there are days when I'm in the right mood,
with eyes closed, I feel like an architect, knock down,
put up, I'm always changing it around, right here, my friends,
all things are possible, a driving school,
a hardware store, the only other one is Rumblaza,
it would do really well, there's access, or if not, offices,
you could put two or three professionals together,
no big deal, they're here again?
what do they want now, "What do you want?" "Nothing,"
they're poking each other with their elbows,
it's night already, why are they yanking my chain,
"Don't you have anything?" they've started in with the laughing,

ch'a n gn'éva mai fat chès,
l'è che al robi, l'è 'csè, quant ta i si dréinta,
e me cantòun farmès, adquà gnént, vért,
un salòt, e te méur du béi farétt,
a i faz s-ciupè ma tótt, pu i n'e' sa, lòu,
mè aquè a ravéi adès,
quèst l'è un pòst, se finòura ò vandú e' pan,
mo e' pò dvantè benéssum un cafè,
una mòstra ad mobéglia, un supermarket,
se magazéin di dri, ch' t'éintar in piaza
e t scap te Bòurgh, parchè e una bènca no?
e u i è di dè, quant a so in véina, a ócc céus,
u m pèr d'ès un geometra, a bótt zò,
a téir sò, a cambi sèmpra, aquè, burdéll,
e' pò vní l'univérs, 'na scuola guida,
'na ferarèccia, ch'u i è sno Rumblàza,
ch' la farébb, quèst l'è un sbòcch, o se no uféizi,
i s mètt insén du tri profesionesta,
ch'u n gn'è al schèli da fè, i è què d'arnóv?
csa vói adès, "Csa vléiv?", "Gnént", i s dà 'd gòmat,
ch' l'è bèla nòta, cs'èll ch'i ròmp e' caz,
"A n'aví gnént?"

che non ci avevo mai fatto caso, / è che le cose, è cosí, quando ci sei dentro, / e all'angolo fermarsi, di qua niente, aperto, / un salotto, e al muro due bei faretti, / li faccio schiattare tutti, poi non lo sanno, loro, / io qui comincio adesso, / questo è un posto, se finora ho venduto stoffa, / ma può diventare benissimo un caffè, / una mostra di mobili, un supermarket, / col magazzino di dietro, che entri in piazza / e esci nel Borgo, perché e una banca no? / e ci sono dei giorni, quando sono in vena, a occhi chiusi, mi par d'essere un geometra, butto giú, / tiro su, cambio sempre, qui, ragazzi, / può venire l'universo, una scuola guida, / una ferramenta, che c'è solo Rumblaza, / che farebbe molto, questo è uno sbocco, o se no uffici, / si mettono insieme due tre professionisti, / che non c'è da fare le scale, sono qui di nuovo? / cosa vogliono adesso, "Cosa volete?", "Niente", si danno di gomito, / che è ormai notte, cosa rompono i coglioni, / "Non avete niente?", gli viene da ridere, credono /

they think they're making fun of me, "Hey, answer us,"
                              [they're hitting the windows,
imbeciles, "Don't you have anything?" they're yelling, one's
                              [giving the high sign,
quiet, all together: "Don't you have anything?" I look at
                              [them, in a quiet voice,
quietly, still more quiet, a whisper, I say: "I've got everything."

i rógg, éun e' fa sègn, zétt, tótt insén:
"A n'aví gnént?", a i guèrd, a mèza vòusa,
pièn, piò pièn, un susórr, a déggh: "Ò tótt".

di prendermi in giro, "Allora?", battono nei vetri, / imbecilli, "Non avete
niente?" / urlano, uno fa segno, zitti, tutti insieme: / "Non avete niente?",
li guardo, a mezza voce, / piano, piú piano, un sussurro, dico: "Ho tutto".

Petrangola

"Three, four and five, what are you looking at? don't touch it!
well what do you know, two of them, I had no idea,"
he cheated at petrangola, with those queens,
"What are you laughing about? you, Sauro, don't pay any
                                        [attention to him,"
he had quick hands, "It's my turn? pass, I'm good, Sauro,
                                        [you add up the points,
twenty-six, good man, who's the master? Fabbri?
very good, but the best classroom
remember this now, is life," he had run off
to Milan as a boy,
and for thirty years he wasn't heard of again,
fenced stuff, they said,
that he'd stumbled upon,
gold watches, suede shoes.
then there was other talk,
talk of stolen stuff
some talk even about counterfeit money.

One day they saw him in the piazza, he was fat,
with a short beard, they say it was to hide a scar,
he started coming into Augusto's, a coffee with a shot,

Petrangla

"Tre, quatr'e zéinch, csa guèrdti? lasa stè!
orca, agli è do, a n mu an séra mégga incórt",
e' rubéva, a petrangla, sa cal dòni,
"Cs'avéiv da réid? tè, Sauro, nu dài rèta",
l'èva dal mèni féini, "U m sta mu mè?
non prendo, chiuso, Sauro, còunta tè,
vintsí, bravo, chi èll e' tu mèstar? Fabbri?
benissimo, però la vera scuola,
ricordati, è la vita", l'era scap
da burdlàz a Milèn,
e par trent'an u n s'è savú piò gnént,
i géva contrabànd, chi ch' l'éva incòuntrar,
arlózz a d'ór, schèrpi ad camoscio, anéll,
pu u i è stè dagli èlt' ciacri,
i à zcòurs 'd roba rubéda,
e qualcadéun ènca ad munàida fèlsa.

Un dè i l'à vést in piaza, l'era gras,
s'na barbètta, dis par masè un castròun,
l'à tach a vní da Gusto, un cafè lòngh,

Petrangola. "Tre, quattro e cinque, cosa guardi? lascia stare! / orca, sono due, non me n'ero mica accorto", / rubava, a petrangola, con quelle donne, / "Cos'avete da ridere? tu, Sauro, non dargli retta", / aveva delle mani fini, "Sta a me? / non prendo, chiuso, Sauro, conta tu, / ventisei, bravo, chi è il tuo maestro? Fabbri? / benissimo, però la vera scuola, / ricordati, è la vita", era scappato / da ragazzo a Milano, / e per trent'anni non s'è saputo piú niente , / dicevano contrabando, chi l'aveva incontrato, / orologio d'oro, scarpe di camoscio, anelli, / poi ci sono state delle altre chiacchiere, / hanno parlato di roba rubata, / e qualcuno anche di moneta falsa. // Un giorno l'hanno visto in piazza, era grasso, / con una barbetta, dice per nascondere un cicatrice, / ha cominciato a venire da Augusto, un caffè lungo, /

his half-smoked cigar, sometimes when he was in the mood
he'd read your palm, a little performance,
and he was excellent at checkers, the moves, he trapped you,
click click clack, but if it was one of his bad days,
he had a lap dog, one evening, it was barking at him
and he walloped it so hard with his cane
that Zelmira told him he should be ashamed of himself.

Then, as he got old, arthritis,
his nose dripped,
those kids would jeer at him
and one Sunday he had nodded off
right next to the heater with the newspaper in his hands,
Sergio di Galòun lit the bottom,
which if it hadn't been for Nenè, who batted it away with a
                                                    [dishrag
and put it out, it didn't do him any harm, a little of his beard
                                                    [is all,
but he had such a scare, no one saw him for two or three days,
then he came back, but he wasn't himself anymore,
always quiet, in a corner, with that vest
all dirty with ashes,
his glasses that were missing a sidepiece,
and every so often, all of a sudden, an enormous hack and a
                                                    [gob of spit,

e' mèz tuschèn, dal vólti ch' l'era in véina
u t lizéva la mèna, un cumédia,
e a dèma brèv, dal mòsi, u t'intrapléva,
tac tac tac tac, mo s'u n'era in zurnèda,
m'un cagnuléin, 'na sàira, ch'u i baiéva,
u i à dè una scaviéda se bastòun
che la Zelmira la i à détt vargògna.

Pu, si an, l'artrite, la gòzzla me nès,
chi burdéll dal sgrignédi,
e una dmènga ch'u s'era imparluzéi
vsina la stóvva se giurnèl tal mèni,
Sergio ad Galòun u i à dè fugh da sòtta,
che s'u n'era Nenè, u s'i è bótt, s'un straz,
l'à smórt, léu u n s'è fat gnént, sno un pó la bèrba,
mo un spavént, u n s'è vést par du tri dè,
pu l'è tòuran, però u n'è stè piò léu,
sémpra zétt, t'un cantòun, sa che panciòt
tótt spórch ad zèndra,
i ucèl ch'u amanchéva una stanghètta,
e d'ogni tènt, da sècch, un gran saràc.

il mezzo toscano, certe volte che era in vena / ti leggeva la mano, una
commedia, / e a dama bravo, delle mosse, t'intrappolava, / tac tac tac tac, ma
se non era in giornata, / a un cagnolino, una sera, che gli abbaiava / gli ha dato
una randellata col bastone / che la Zelmira gli ha detto vergogna. // Poi, con
gli anni, l'artrite, la goccia al naso, / quei ragazzi delle sghignazzate, / e una
domenica che s'era appisolato / vicino alla stufa col giornale nelle mani, /
Sergio di Galòun gli ha dato fuoco da sotto, / che se non c'era Nenè, ci s'è
buttato, con uno straccio, ha spento, lui non s'è fatto niente, solo un po' la
barba, / ma uno spavento, non s'è visto per due tre giorni, / poi è tornato, ma
non è stato piú lui, / sempre zitto, in un angolo, con quel panciotto / tutto
sporco di cenere, / gli occhiali che gli mancava una stanghetta, / e ogni tanto,
di colpo, un gran scaracchio. //

Then he became incontinent,
and sitting there, wet, with Augusto grumbling.
So then his sister filled out the paperwork,
and Christmas Eve they brought him down,
without saying anything, to the old people's home, he thought
he was back in school: "Where are we going?"
Edoardo was there too: "Let's go in where it's warm,"
he stopped all of a sudden, near the main door,
"Give me your arm, are you afraid?"
"Get away from me!" cursing,
screams, "Have you all gone crazy?"
and coughing fits enough to suffocate, he'd turned purple,
a crowd was gathering,
"Well let's just go home then," "Don't touch me!"
drenched in sweat, drool from his mouth,"
"You can all rot in hell! his knees buckled,
he fell into the wall, a heap, he let out a fart,
he didn't move again.

Dop l'à pérs un pó e' tnai,
e alè, disdài, bagnèd, Gusto e' sbruntléva.
La su surèla alòura la à fat dmanda
e la vzéiglia 'd Nadèl la l'à pórt zò,
senza dí gnént, ti Vcéun, léu l'à capéi
ch' l'era ancòura mal scóli: "Dò ch'andémm?",
u i era ènca Dovardo: "Andémm me chèld",
u s'è férum ad bot vsina e' purtòun,
"Dém e' braz, cs'iv paérua", "Stam dalòngh!",
dal biastéimi, di rógg, "A si dvént mat?",
e tòsa, d'afughès, nir cmè un capèl,
u s'era ardótt la zènta,
"Turnémma a chèsa, alòura", "Nu tuchém!",
tótt sudéd, un féil 'd bèva da la bòcca,
"Andé su l'òs-cia tótt!", l'à pighé al znòci,
l'è calè zò me méur, u s'è insachè,
l'à fat una scurèzza, e u n s'è mòs pió.

Dopo ha perso un po' la ritenzione, e lí, seduto, bagnato, Augusto brontolava. / Sua sorella allora ha fatto domanda, / e la vigilia di Natale l'ha portato giú, / senza dir niente, nei Vecchioni, lui ha capito / che era ancora alle scuole: "Dove andiamo?", / c'era anche Edoardo: "Andiamo al caldo", / s'è fermato di botto, vicino al portone, / "Datemi il braccio, cos'avete paura?, " "Stammi lontano!", / delle bestemmie, degli urli, "Siete diventato matto?", / e tosse, da soffocare, nero come un cappello, / s'era raccolta della gente, / "Torniamo a casa, allora", "Non toccatemi!", / tutto sudato, un filo di bava dalla bocca, / "Andate sull'ostia tutti!", ha piegato le ginocchia, / è calato giú al muro, s'è insaccato, / ha fatto una scorreggia, e non s'è mosso piú.

Traveling

You go ahead, you travel, I'm fine where I am.
They all come here from outside anyway. Plus we've got
                                        [Sogliano,
Verucchio, Perticara, which I've never even been to,
Perticara. Not you either? what's with all this traipsing around?
for me, even my bed,
a strange one, the pillow, if I don't have my own,
plus leave in sun, arrive in rain,
you don't know anyone, you've always got to ask,
and at night your legs, see the world?
then you're a bigger galoot than before,
I remember Curio, with that trip of his to London,
big deal, he came back, and the next day
we were playing billiards just like he'd made a trip to San Vito,
and now he says he's going to Kenya?
you've got to want it pretty bad,
and you, where are you going?
Montecarlo and Nice? I see, and the whole coast, too,
I see, how long will you be away,
ten days? and I would get what out of it? I know how it works,
let me finish, you pack your bags,
you lug them around, for me, it's even too much of a pain in the
                                        [neck
lugging the Sunday paper around the piazza, then the food,

Viazè

Mo viaza tè, mè a stagh bén dò ch'a so,
ch'i vén da fura, aquè pu u i è Suièn,
Vrócc, la Pargàia, ch'a n'i so mai stè,
ma la Pargàia, gnénca tè? mo 'lòura
csa vét zarchè vaiéun, che mè sno e' lèt
furistír, e' cuscéin, che s'a n'ò e' méi,
pu tótt, t vé véa se sòul, t'aréiv ch'e' pióv,
ta n cnòss niseun, u t tòcca dmandè sémpra,
e al gambi quant l'è nòta,
                                        vdai e' mònd?
che dop t si piò pataca ca nà préima,
a m'arcórd Curio, sa che viàz a Lòndra,
'na boba, pu l'è tòuran, e e' dè dop
a zughémmi a bucètti, ch'e' pareva
ch' fóss stè a San Véid, e adès dis ch'e' va in Kenia,
u i vó una bèla vòia, e tè dú vét?
a Montecarlo e a Nizza? t'è capéi,
e tótt la Costa Azzurra, quant t sté fura?
dis dè? mo 's'ut ch'a próva, ch'a l so zà,
'ta bón, fè la valéisa,
purtèsla dri, che mà la dmènga in piaza

Viaggiare. Ma viaggia tu, io sto bene dove sono, /che vengono da fuori, qui, poi c'è Sogliano, / Verucchio, Perticara, che non ci sono mai stato / a Perticara, neanche tu? ma allora / cosa vai a cercare in giro, che io, solo il letto / forestiero, il cuscino, che se non ho il mio, / poi tutto, vai via col sole, arrivi che piove, / non conosci nessuno, devi sempre chiedere, / e le gambe quand'è notte, — vedere il mondo? / che dopo sei piú coglione di prima, / mi ricordo Curio, con quel viaggio a Londra, / una cagnara, poi è tornato, e il giorno dopo / giocavamo a boccette, che pareva / fosse stato a San Vito, e adesso dice che va in Kenia, / ci vuole una bella voglia, e tu dove vai? / Montecarlo e a Nizza? hai capito, / e tutta la Costa Azzurra, quanto stai fuori, / dieci giorni? ma cosa vuoi che provi, lo so già, / sta' buono, fare la valigia, / portarsela dietro, che io la domenica in piazza, /

everything fried, Curio told me,
disgusting, lamb with jelly,
they eat spaghetti at the same time they drink their coffee,
can you imagine me, who likes everything just so? don't even
                                        [mention it,
I'll stay in my own house, is there anything better?

plus I do travel some, I'm going to Carghín's
to play bocce,
which no one plays anymore, it's all covered with leaves,
but I like the places where nothing happens, too,
you can hear a pinball machine inside,
the sparrows that had gone away are coming back,
that same poster still hanging on Canzola's wall,
"Live!" What do you mean Live?
and he's laughing, what are you laughing about? plus in
                                        [summer
when I see all those fools, at the Rocca, at the Arch,
in the Pieve, all sweaty, I just want to stop them,
follow me up to the Cappuccini, then walk along
the Wall, we'll go slow, through the grass,
stop to catch our breath, it's somewhat of a climb,
all you have to do is reach out a hand for plums

344

u m dà dan e' giurnèl, e pu e' magnè,
u m géva Curio, tótta roba frétta,
una pozza, l'agnèl sla marmelèda,
i spaghétt ch'i bai dri e' cafelàt,
e mè ch'a so un viziéd, no, gnénca zcòrrni,
a stagh ma chèsa méa, piò bén che mai,

che pu a viàz ènca mè, aréiv da Carghín,
a vagh me zugh dal bòci,
ch'i n zuga piò niseun, l'è tótt pin 'd fòi,
mo mè u m pis ènca i póst ch'u n suzéd gnént,
dréinta u s sint sunè un flipper,
i pasaròtt ch'i era scap véa i artòurna,
u i è che mainifèst sémpra spandléun
me mèur 'd Canzola, "Viva. . .", viva chè?
e léu e' réid, csa réidti? che d'instèda
quant a vèggh chi sgraziéd, la Roca, l'Èrch,
la Piva, tótt sudéd, mè 'lè avrébb vòia
da farmèi, vní sa mè, mi Capuzéin,
e' zéir dla méura, pièn, tramèza l'erba,
e d'ogni tènt punsès, u i è un rapètt,
basta slunghè una mèna, dal suséini

mi dà fastidio il giornale, e poi il mangiare, / mi diceva Curio, tutta roba fritta,/ una puzza, l'agnello con la marmellata, / gli spaghetti che ci bevono dietro il caffelatte, / e io che sono un viziato, no, neanche parlarne, / sto a casa mia, meglio di qui? // che poi viaggio anch'io, arrivo da Carghín, / vado al gioco delle bocce, / che non gioca piú nessuno, è tutto pieno di foglie, / ma a me piacciono anche i posti dove non succede niente, / dentro si sente suonare un flipper, / i passerotti che erano scappati via ritornano, / c'è quel manifesto sempre penzoloni / al muro di Canzola, "Viva. . .", viva che? / e lui ride, cosa ridi? che d'estate / quando vedo quei disgraziati, la Rocca, l'Arco, / la Pieve, tutti sudati, io lí avrei voglia / di fermarli, venite con me, ai Cappuccini, / il giro delle mura, piano, in mezzo all'erba, / e ogni tanto una sosta, c'è una salitella, / basta allungare una mano, delle susine, /

345

that are sweeter than honey, the monks never pick them,
then, towards Savignano, the lane,
with the cypresses, a scent, and lower down below nothing,
you come out into the alfalfa, which sometimes,
from here, here we are, the fields lead straight down
to the Marecchia, a widening, whichever way you want, and
                                        [all these stones,
look at all those colors, they're reflecting under the water,
these are the cities.
am I the hick? and farther up two girls
with a big bunch of yellow flowers, they're laughing, they're
                                        [running,
barefoot, over the stones, how do they do it?

piò dòulzi ca nè e' mél, i frè n li còi,
pu, vérs Savgnèn, e' vièl,
di arzipréss, un udòur, e in chèva gnént,
u s scapa tla spagnèra, che d'alè,
dal vólti, zà ch'a i so, travérs cantír,
a cal zò te Marèccia,
un slèrgh, t vé dò ch'u t pèr, e tótt chi sas,
mo u i n'è ch'i à di culéur,
i léus, sòtt'aqua, quèsti l'è al zità!
o a so balèngh? e piò in là do burdèli
s'un gran maz ad fiéur zal, al réid, al córr,
a pi néud, sòura i sas, mo cmè ch'al fa?

piú dolci del miele, i frati non le raccolgono, / poi, verso Savignano, il viale,
/ dei cipressi, un odore, e in fondo niente, / si esce nell'erba spagna, che di
lí / delle volte, già che ci sono, per i campi / calo giú nel Marecchia, / uno
slargo, vai dove ti pare, e tutti quei sassi, / ma ce n'è che hanno dei colori, /
rilucono, sott'acqua, queste sono le città! / o sono balengo? e piú in là due
bambine / con un gran mazzo di fiori gialli, ridono, corrono, / a piedi nudi,
sui sassi, ma come fanno?

Cognac

"Argentinean dance, tango, this one I know.
The father of the gods," Jupiter. Doesn't fit,
Four letters. . ." These flies are ruthless.
Martina gives it a good wipe down, puts the billiard cues back
[in place,
refills the shot glass with cognac. The lawyer, Grilli, hacks,
drinks. By the door they're playing low stakes,
they laugh, they argue over low stakes that are getting too high.
"You seen Paglierani?" a guy comes in. Looks around. Leaves.

Martina comes by again. Bertino shouts, "It was a sure goal,
come on now, it's the whole strategy
that's not working."
Nino, nonchalantly, slips in the door near the coat rack,
upstairs they're playing poker.
Tomorrow, the people in Verucchio are saying
they want fourteen million,
they'll get six or seven and that's it.

Cognac

"Ballo argentino, tango, quèst a lo so.
Il padre degli dei". "Giove", "U n'i sta,
l'è quatar lèttri. . .", al mòschi agli è rabièdi,
la Martina la dà bota ad straz,
la mètt a pòst al stècchi de biglièrd,
e la i rimpéss e' biciaréin 'd cognac.
L'avuchèd Grilli e scatàra, pu e' bai.
Vsina la bóssla i zuga a no ciapè,
i réid, i ragna, i ciapa sémpra trop.
"U n s'è vést Paiarèn?", éun e' vén dréinta,
e' dà un'ucèda in zéir e pu e' va véa.

La Martina la pasa un'èlta vólta.
Bertino e' rógg: "L'era un gol fat, cumè!
l'è ch'a n'i sémm, l'è tótt l'atàch ch'u n va".
Nino, cmè gnént, u s'inféila t'na pórta,
dri e è tacapàn, ad sòura i zuga a poker.
Admèn l'à d'andè a Vrócc,
quéi che là i zcòrr ch'i vó quatórg migliéun,
u i n'avnirà si sèt, e pu a dí bén.

Cognac. "Ballo argentino, tango, questo lo so. / Il padre degli dei," "Giove", "Non ci sta, / sono quattro lettere. . ." le mosche sono rabbiose, / la Martina dà un colpo di straccio, / mette a posto le stecche del bigliardo, / e gli riempie il bicchierino di cognac. / L'avvocato Grilli scattara, poi beve. / Vicino alla porta giocano a non prendere, / ridono, litigano, prendono sempre troppo. / "Non s'è visto Paglierani?" uno viene dentro," / dà un'occhiata in giro e poi va via.// La Martina passa un'altra volta. / Bertino urla: "Era un gol fatto, come! / è che non ci siamo, è tutto l'attacco che non va". / Nino, come niente, s'infila in una porta, / vicino all'attaccapanni, di sopra giocano a poker. / Domani deve andare a Verucchio, / quelli là dicono che vogliono quattordici millioni, / gliene verranno sei o sette, e a dir bene./

349

Muzio waltzes in, eats two chocolate-covered cherries,
goes to the mirror, combs his hair nice.

Martina comes over, bottle raised,
another shot?
Hey, too much. She even makes it overflow. Oh sure, she can
afford to be all cheery,
they're calling her: "A lemon soda!"
she's fanning herself with a piece of cardboard
finally, she comes back,
"This one's uncorked now."
"No, leave it here."

It's late. Outside the post office walls are still giving off heat,
a car, where you going? where does this fool think he's going?
and how long are they going to keep this torn up? dammit,
little slip here, he's going to lean here just a second
against a pillar, Renzi passes by,
he pretends he doesn't even see him, lamp posts, the drinking
                                                           [fountain,

ah, he goes in, flings himself down
on the sofa,
and those two up there are still shooting, Is that Glenn Ford?
on the table, on a tablecloth, folded in half, water, bread, the
                                                           [covered plate,
these cigarettes are unsmokeable, they're all crumpled up,
son of a bitch, he was supposed to go see Quinto,
he'll go in the morning,

L'aréiva Muzio, u s magna du boeri,
e' va me spèc, u s pètna.

La Martina la vén sla bòcia alzèda,
u i n'è un èlt biciaréin?
ènch' trop, la l fa vuntè, mo sè alegria,
i la cèma da dlà: "Una limunèda!",
la s fa vént s'un cartòun, ecco, la tòurna,
"Quèst l'è stapèd adès", "No, lasl'aquè".

L'è tèrd, ad fura i méur dla Posta i scòta,
te travarsè un machina, dú val?
mo dú val sté sgraziéd?
e aquè, ch'u i vénga un còulp, quant'èll ch'i sbéusa?
e' sguélla, e' sta un minéut
puzéd m'una culònna, e' pasa Renzi,
e' fa féinta 'd no vdail, i pèl, la pòumpa,
l'éintra, u s bótta d'indrí se canapè,
quéi che là i spèra sémpra, l'è Glenn Ford?
sla tèvla u i è mèza tvàia, l'aqua e' pèn,
un piàt cvért,
stal Nazionèli a n so pò fumé, agli è zèppi,
porca putèna, l'éva d'avdài Quinto,
e' pasarà 'dmatéina,

Arriva Muzio, si mangia due boeri, / va allo specchio, si pettina.// La
Martina viene con la bottiglia alzata, / ce n'è un altro bicchierino? / anche
troppo, lo fa traboccare, ma sí, allegria, / la chiamano da di là: "Una
limonata!", / si fa vento con un cartone, ecco torna, / "Questo è stappato
adesso", "No, lascialo qui". // È tardi, fuori i muri della Posta scottano, /
nell'attraversare, una macchina, dove va? ma dove va questo disgraziato? /
e qui, gli venga un colpo, quant'è che scavano?" / scivola, sta un minuto /
appoggiato a una colonna, passa Renzi / fa finta di non vederlo, i pali, la
fontanella, / entra, si butta all'indietro sul canapè, / quelli là sparano sempre,
è Glenn Ford? / sulla tavola c'è mezza tovaglia, l'acqua, il pane, / un piatto
coperto, / queste Nazionali non si possono fumare, sono zeppe, / porca
putana, doveva vedere Quinto, / passerà domattina, /

351

in the afternoon, Gnoli, who's still wavering,
and the other one who still hasn't been convinced of it, and
                                              [then Ada,
which as far as that goes, her brothers hadn't even
                                              [badmouthed him
and she's turned against selling, what's the use of arguing,
they're all out of their stinking minds, it was better with the
                                              [canaries,
when he was a boy, in the morning, coming into the Big
                                    Hall, big goings-on,
excitement, there'd be thirty cages, then he got tired of it all,
sold everything. The two of them riding off on their horses.
                                    ["THE END."
And she gets up. Switches the light off. Goes to bed.
Even this watch is off kilter, it says two-thirty.
And these papers, what's all this? a lottery ticket,
a light bill, a bus ticket, a little money, she would have found
                                              [it all in his pocket,
all these receipts, Valium,
which he hasn't taken yet, two tokens, Merry Christmas!
see, he keeps track of his affairs, there's a remedy though,
here's how, turn it all into confetti.
And this button that's about to fall off,
dangling, twirling,
he pinches it, tugs it, carefully,
it gives, it's off, he opens his hand,
and it's there in the middle not moving, looking like a dead man.

dopmezdè Gnóla, ch'e' va 'ncòura zòp,
e cl'èlt ch'u n'era sicuréd, pu l'Ada,
che alé u n dí u n gnénca mèl i su fradéll,
e' tòurna còunt a vènd, 's'ut questionè,
l'è ch'i è tótt mat, l'era mèi si canèri,
da burdlàz, ch' l'arivéva la matéina
te camaròun, al fèsti, un rugiadézz,
e' gev'ès trenta ghèbi, pu u s'è stóff,
l'à vandú tótt.
                                    Ma la televisiòun
u s vaid déu a cavàl e sòura "Fine".
Li la sta sò, la smórta, la va a lèt.
L'è mat ènca st'arlózz, e' fa al do e mèz.
E alè cal chèrti, cs'èll? una schedéina,
'na bulètta dla luce, un bigliètt dll'Atam,
méll frènch, la gli avrà tróvi t'na bascòza,
sti chéunt, boh, una rizèta, Trifanil,
che pu u n l'à tnú dacòunt, mo u i è e' rimédi,
acsè, fè tótt curiàndal.
E sté butòun e' va a finéi ch'u l pérd,
e' sta spandléun, e' bala,
u l ciapa tra do dàidi, e' téira, pièn,

nel pomeriggio Gnoli, che va ancora zoppo, / e l'altro che non era assicurato,
poi l'Ada, / che lí non dicono neanche male i suoi fratelli, / torna conto
vendere, cosa vuoi questionare, / è che sono tutti matti, era meglio coi
canarini, / da ragazzo, che arrivava la mattina, / nel camerone, le feste, uno
schiamazzo, / saranno state trenta gabbie, poi s'è stufato, / ha venduto tutto.
– Alla televisione / si vedono due a cavallo e sopra "Fine". / Lei si alza,
spegne, va a letto. / È matto anche quest'orologio, fa le due e mezzo. / E lí
quelle carte, cosa sono? una schedina, / una bolletta della luce, un biglietto
dell'Atam, / mille lire, le avrà trovate in una tasca, / questi conti, boh, una
ricetta, Trifanil, / che poi non l'ha preso, due marche, Buon Natale, / ve'
quel che ha tenuto a conto, ma c'è il rimedio, / cosí, far tutti coriandoli. / E
questo bottone va finire che lo perde, / sta penzoloni, balla, / lo prende tra
due dita, tira piano, /

And now what? eat? he's not hungry, he's not tired either,
he goes outside, go down to Rimini? but first
a good piss under the stars,
and he's on his way, flooring it because the world is huge,
taking the curves, screeching, the Bridge,
here we are, it's daytime now,
here they're singing everywhere, lights, women,
who's thinking about canaries now, and he's never been here
                                     [before,
idiot, lots have made this trip,
back and forth to the Grand Hotel,
maybe, later on, maybe even, a couple of dances,
this newspaper, who left it here?
let me see,
what is it, German? Swedish?
he's walking, he's holding it open like he's reading it,
in Bar Mocambo, he sits down,
"Ice cream?"
"Nix"
"Coca Cola?
"Nix."
"Beer?"
"Nix. Cognac."

e' sint ch'e' zéd, l'è vnéu, l'éirva la ména,
l'è 'lè, férum, te mèz, e' pèr un mórt.
E adès? magnè, u n'à fèma, durméi gnénca,
e' scapa, e andè zò a Rémin? però préima
una bèla piséda sòtta al stèli,
e via pò, dài de gas, che e' mònd l'è grand,
e tal curvi se scrécch, e' pòunt, a i sémm,
u s fa e' dè 'dès aquè,
i sòuna dimpartótt, al luci, al dòni,
èlt che i canèri, e léu ch'u n'i vén mai,
pataca, quést i à fat tènt' ad cla strèda
pr'andè sò e zò davènti e' Grand Hotel,
e magari, piò tèrd, ènca du bal,
sté giurnèl, chi ch' l'à las aquè? ch'a vègga,
cs'èll ch' l'è, tedèsch? svedàis?
e' caméina, u l tén vért, cmè ch'e' lizéss,
Mocambo, u s mètt disdài, "Gelato", "Nix",
"Coca Cola?", "Nix", "Birra?", "Nix. Cognac".

sente che cede, è venuto, apre la mano, / è lí fermo, nel mezzo, pare un morto. // E adesso? mangiare, non ha fame, dormire nemmeno, / esce, e andar giú a Rimini? però prima / una prima pisciata sotto le stelle, / e via pure, dai del gas che il mondo è grande, / e nelle curve con lo scricchio, il ponte, ci siamo, / si fa giorno adesso, qui, / suonano dappertutto, le luci, le donne, / altro che i canarini, e lui che non ci viene mai, / coglione, questi hanno fatto tanta di quella strada / per andare su e giú davanti al Grand Hotel, / e magari, piú tardi, anche due balli, / 'sto giornale, chi l'ha lasicato qui? fammi vedere, / cos'è tedesco? svedese? / cammina, lo tiene aperto, come se leggesse, / Mocambo, si siede, "Gelato?", "Nix, / "Coca Cola?", "Nix", "Birra", "Nix. Cognac".

Windowless Room

But then, it hardly ever happens, and no one hears it,
in the room without a window, downstairs, among all the
                                                [dirty clothes.
I close the door, and I just howl. Then I feel better.

La cambra schéura

Che pu u m suzéd da rèd, e u n sint niseun,
tla cambra schéura, ad sòtta, tra i pan spórch,
a céud la pórta, e a rógg. Dop a stagh mèi.

La camera cieca. Che poi mi succede di rado, e non sente nessuno, / nella
camera cieca, di sotto, tra i panni sporchi, / chiudo la porta, e urlo. Dopo sto
meglio.

Picking

Go ahead, you pick, it makes absolutely no difference to me,
they should too, I'm not just saying it,
go ahead and pick, for me any of them are just fine.
You like this one? take it then.
Or this one? you're not sure? you like both?
take them both, there's plenty.
Only one? whatever you want, think about it, no rush, this one?
me? what do you want me to say, you're the one who's got to
[like it,
my opinion is that I think it looks good, you think so too?
so take it then.
And the rest of you, don't just stand there frozen in place,
first you're laughing, and now you're all stressed out?
pick whichever one you want, I haven't even given it a thought,
they're all the same to me, do I have to draw you a picture?
But you, we're not settled anymore? I can see it in your face,
you're having second thoughts? you want to make a change?
what are you looking at? show me, you want that one?
go on, put back the other one, you know you've really got a good
[eye,
So now, everyone's picked?
And this one's left for me, well just look what's inside,
I hadn't even given it a second thought,
you know what I've got to say to all of you?

Capè

Dài, capa tè, che par mè l'è l'istèss.
Enca lòu, a n'e' faz par cumplimént,
capé, mè u m va bén tótt.
U t pis quèll? e tól sò.
O st'èlt? ta n si sichéur? i t pis tutt déu?
pórti véa, u i n'è tint.
Éun sno? cmè t vu, pénsi, u n gn'è préssia, quèst?
mè, 's'ut ch'a t dégga, u t'à da pis ma tè?
e alòura tól.
E vuílt, nu sté 'lè cmè di candléun,
préima a ridévi, adès aví paéura?
tulí sò quèll ch'a vléi, a n gn'ò gnénch' chéunt,
i è tótt cumpàgn par mè, cm'a v l'òi da déi?
Mo tè, a n'i sémm ancòura, a t vèggh tla faza,
ta i é 'rpéns? t vu cambiè?
dò che t guèrd? fam avdài, t vu quèll che 'lè?
tò, mètt zò cl'èlt, però ta l sé ch' t'é òc?
Alòura, 'iv capè tótt?
E mu mè u m'è 'rvènz quèst, mo guèrda dréinta,
a n gn'éva méggh' badè,

Scegliere. Dai, scegli tu, che per me è lo stesso. / Anche loro, non lo faccio per complimento, / scegliete, a me mi va bene tutto. / Ti piace quello? e prendilo. / O quest'altro? non sei sicuro? ti piacciono tutt'e due? / portali via, ce ne sono tanti. / Uno solo? come vuoi, pensaci, non c'è fretta, questo? / io, cosa vuoi che ti dica, deve piacere a te, / per me è molto bello, anche per te? / e allora prendilo. / E voi, non state lí come dei boccaloni, / prima ridevate, adesso avete paura? / prendete quel che volete, non li ho nemmeno contati, / sono tutti uguali per me, come ve lo devo dire? / Ma tu, non ci siamo ancora, ti vedo in faccia, / ci hai ripensato? vuoi cambiare? / dove guardi? fammi vedere, vuoi quello lí / to', metti giú l'altro, però lo sai che hai occhio? / Allora, avete scelto tutti? / E a me m'è rimasto questo, ma guarda dentro, / non ci avevo mica badato, /

359

that if I'd been the one with first choice this is the one I'd
[have picked.
But then again, really, they're all nice.
At any rate, we're all even, one for everyone,
no bickering, you're looking at me, you're not happy?
you want this one?

ció, a savéi quèll ch'a v déggh?
s'avéss capè par préim avrébb tólt quèst.
Mo pu, zò, i è béll tótt.
Insòmma, adès a sémm a pòst, éun pr'ón,
senza ragnè, ta m guèrd, ta n si cuntént?
t vu quèst che què?

beh, sapete quel che vi dico? / se avessi scelto per primo avrei preso questo.
/ Ma poi, dai, sono belli tutti. / Insomma, adesso siamo a posto, uno per
uno, / senza litigare, mi guardi, non sei contento? / vuoi questo qui?

Traviata

If at noon they'd said to me: tonight
you're not going anywhere, I would have laughed in their faces.
Just the tickets alone, enough now, are you crazy,
you can't get your hands on them,
and Rinaldo in the café:
"I'll never see a Traviata like this again,"
to make us mad, then later, there was a bunch of us,
we got ourselves organized, two cars, leave
at five, starts at nine,
fine, they come pick me up, I'll be standing on the street,
I was ready, blue suit, black shoes,
no tie, open neck, it's August,
I heard them shouting from below: "Bruno!"
and inside myself, a split-second: I'm not going,
"Bruno, where are you? answer!" I didn't say anything,
"Where'd he go, the idiot, he's making us late,"
they started honking, I didn't say a word,
"People, it's five-thirty," my mother
came out from the kitchen: "Bruno, they're talking to you,
and you're not budging? are you sick?" "No,"
"All right, answer them then,
because if you wait any longer,"
"Don't say anything, let them go,"

Traviata

Che se a mezdè mè i m'avéss détt: stasàira
ta n vé invéll, a i avrébb ridú sla faza,
sno pr'i biglétt, 'ta bón, da dvantè mat,
ch'i n s truvéva, e Rinaldo te cafè:
"Una Traviata acsè e n la avdirò piò",
per fès rabiè, dop, a sérmi una squèdra,
émm cumbiné, do machini, u s partéss
al zéinch, al nóv i taca,
basta, i m'è pas a tó, mè a stagh sla strèda,
a séra pròunt, e' vstí bló, al schèrpi niri,
gravata gnént, a l'aperto, d'agòst,
a i ò sintí ciamè da 'd sòtta: "Bruno!"
e dréinta ad mè, l'è stè un mumént: a n vagh,
"Bruno, dú sit? arspòndl!", a so stè zétt,
"Mo dò ch' l'è 'ndè st' pataca, aquè u s fa tèrd",
i à ravié a strumbitè, mè sémpra zétt,
"Burdéll, l'è al zéinch e mèz", da la cuséina
l'è vnú la mi mà: "Bruno, i dí sa tè,
ta n t móv? t sté mèl?", "No", "Alòura, mo dài vòusa,
s' t'aspèt 'n'èlt pó", "Sta què, lasa ch'i vaga",

Traviata. Che se a mezzogiorno a me m'avessero detto: stasera / non vai da nessuna parte, gli avrei riso in faccia, / solo per i biglietti, sta' zitto, da diventar matti, / che non si trovavano, e Rinaldo al caffè: / "Una Traviata cosí non la vedrò piú", / per farci arrabbiare, dopo, eravamo un gruppo, / abbiamo combinato, due macchine, si parte / alle cinque, alle nove cominciano, / basta, sono passati a prendermi, io sto sulla strada, / ero pronto, vestito blu, scarpe nere, / cravatta niente, all'aperto, d'agosto, / li ho sentiti chiamare da sotto: "Bruno!" / e dentro di me, è stato un attimo: non vado, / "Bruno, dove sei? rispondi!", sono stato zitto, / "Ma dov'è andato 'sto coglione, qui si fa tardi", / hanno cominciato a strombettare, io sempre zitto, / "Ragazzi, sono le cinque e mezzo", dalla cucina / è venuta mia madre: "Bruno, dicono a te, / non ti muovi? stai male?", "No", "Allora, ma dagli voce, / se aspetti un altro po'", "Stai qui, lascia che vadano", /

"What's wrong, did you argue with someone?"
"A fight? with who?" she looked at me: "What's going on?
first you're frantic to go, and now, who can understand you,
do you hear? they're leaving, that's right, run to the window,"
I stood there awhile, pressed against the glass,
pleased, I flopped down on the bed, my shoes
were pinching a little, I changed them,
a sweater, jeans, "Don't wait for me tonight,"

is the wind picking up? not at all, a light breeze,
you can hear leaves
skittering across the pavement,
near the wall,
Vignali's lighting up a cigar, a stump,
he's cupping his hands, he gives me the long face,
Santín's coming up slowly,
what's he picking up from the ground?
what could he have found?
Alma goes by with paper bag full of eggplants,
you can see a television on through a window that's flung
wide open
and this guy, with the straw hat, let me see, is painting,
painting, look what's appearing,
the Suore Bianche, the Rocca, he's making flecks, but in this part
he's doing whatever he feels like,

"Cs'èll ch'u i è? t'é ragnè se qualcadéun?",
"Ragnè? sa chéi?", la m guardéva: "Cs'èll t'é?"
préima una préssia, e adès, capéit ma tè,
sint, i va véa, sè, córr ma la finestra",
a so stè un pèz alè, tachèd mi véidar,
cuntént, a m so bótt zò se lèt, al schèrpi
al m'era ènca un pó strètti, a m so cambiè,
maiètta, jeans, "Stasàira nu spitém",

u s'è 'lzè e' vént? gnént, un fiè, u s sint al fòi
ch'al s dà dri se saighè, tachèd me mèur
Vignali e' zènd un zigar, un mucòun,
e' tén al mèni céusi, e' fa un méus lòngh,
Santín e' vén sò pièn,
cs'èll ch'e' tó sò ma tèra? cs'avràl tróv?
e' pasa l'Alma s'un scartòz 'd manzèni,
da una finestra, l'è tótt vért, u s vaid
la televisiòun zàisa,
e quèst che què e' pitéura, fam avdài,
se su capèl ad paia,
vè quèll ch'e' scapa fura, al Sóri Biènchi,
la Roca, sa che pnèl
u i dà dal boti sècchi, però alè

"Cosa c'è? hai litigato con qualcuno?", / Litigato? con chi?", mi guardava:
"Cos'hai?/ prima una fretta, e adesso, capirti a te, / senti, vanno via, sí, corri
alla finestra", / sono stato lí un pezzo, incollato ai vetri, / contento, mi sono
buttato sul letto, le scarpe, / mi erano anche un po' strette, mi sono
cambiato, / maglietta, jeans, "Stasera non aspettatemi", // s'è alzato il vento?
niente, un soffio, si sentono le foglie / che s'inseguono sul selciato, vicino al
muro / Vignali accende il sigaro, un mozzicone, / tiene le mani chiuse, fa un
muso lungo, / Santín viene su piano, / cosa raccoglie da terra? cos'avrà
trovato? / passa l'Alma con un cartoccio di melanzane, / da una finestra, è
tutto aperto, si vede / la televisione accesa, / e questo qui dipinge, fammi
vedere, / col suo cappello di paglia, / ve' quel che vien fuori, le Suore
Bianche, / la Rocca, con quel pennello / dà dei colpi secchi, però lí /

365

he didn't put in Balughèn's house
Sirena's trees, he didn't put those in either,
he's got a flag on the Campanone now,
a piazza which isn't there,
with people at the windows, fancy covers draped over,
like it's some kind of procession, all these colors,
where there's nothing there, but for him it is, but he's good,
and the thing about the world is this, we're all out of our minds,
oh no, it's seven
I want to stop in, see if he's made tripe, Gioti,
or maybe even involtini, there's fish soup?
I'll sit here, give me a different fork,
this one's got no heft, no soup,
no, you don't have the tagliatelle either,
red, a half,
if I say no, oh all right, a little of the angel hair pasta then,
in butter, and a little grated cheese, not too much,
but I want them cooked in broth!
                        – this fish soup, from the smell of it
it's not half bad, a prawn, it's got the roe,
redfish, eel,
this is a calamari, some clams,
you've even put in a crab? wait, afterwards,

e' fa cm'u i pèr, la chèsa ad Balughèn
u n la mètt, gnénca i èlbar dla Sirena,
adès se Campanòun una bandira,
una piaza, ch' la n gn'è,
sla zénta mal finestri, al cvérti stàisi
cmè pr'una purcisiòun, tènt 'd chi culéur,
ch'u n gn'è gnént, mo léu sè, però l'è brèv,
pu e' mònd, a sémm tótt mat, ció, mo l'è al sèt,
a ví pasè, s' l'éss fat la tréppa, Gioti,
o ènca do tre invultéini,

                    u i è e' brudètt?
a m mètt aquè, ta m cambi la furzéina,
quèsta la n pàisa gnént, senza minestra,
no, gnénca al taiadèli, nir, un mèz,
s'a déggh ad no, va bén, du taiuléin
se butír, e un pó 'd fòurma, una sfurznéda,
e cótt te bród!
                    sté brudètt, da l'udòur
u n gn'è mèl, 'na canòcia, la à la zira,
rusúl, inguélla,
quèst l'è un calamaròun, un pó 'd puràzi,
t'i é mèss ènch' 'na granzèla? spétta, dop

fa come gli pare, la casa di Balughèn / non la mette, neanche gli alberi della
Sirena, / adesso sul Campanone una bandiera, / una piazza, che non c'è, /
con la gente alle finestre, le coperte stese / come per una processione, tanti
di quei colori, / che non c'è niente, ma lui sí, però è bravo, / poi il mondo,
siamo tutti matti, ehi, ma sono le sette, / voglio passare, se avesse fatto la
trippa, Gioti, / o anche due tre involtini, – c'è il brodetto? / mi metto qui,
cambiami la forchetta, / questa non pesa niente, senza minestra, / no, neanche le tagliatelle, rosso, un mezzo, / se dico di no, va bene, due tagliolini /
col burro, e un po' di grana, una forchettata, / e cotti nel brodo! – questo
brodetto, dall'odore / non c'è male, una canocchia, ha la cera, / triglie, an-
guilla, / questo è un calamaro, un po' di vongole, / ci hai messo anche un
granchio? aspetta, dopo /

if there's a little bowl of
radicchio, if it's tender, if not, forget it,

and don't be stingy with the vinegar,
a little more, I like how it smells,
where did this arugula come from? above the river?
I know the place too, where the pebbles are,
what've you got there? green beans? just a spoonful,
oh make it two, and cut them up for me,
it gives them such a good scent,
one or two really, really thin slices of onion, salt and pepper,
a dash of oil, that's it, enough, otherwise it's gluttony,

and now, how about a nice peach, I'll take this one,
white, see how it comes apart, and inside it's red
cut into little pieces, right into the glass, and use the good wine,
and then, every once in awhile, don't forget to push it down
with your fingers,
it's got to get a good soaking,
you can't rush it, believe me, it's so much better than ice cream,
can you give me a light? you stopped smoking? good for you,
I on the other hand,
I know it, it's not good for you, but,
at times like this, a cigarette after eating,
did you used to smoke in bed? for me that's the ultimate,
in the dark, lighting up, the two of us together,
what are they having
over there? what's the big fuss about? "A cantaloupe."

s'u i fóss 'na supirína
ad radécc, ch'i séa, téndar, se no gnént,
dài, sla sàida, un èlt pó, ch'u m pis ch' la s sinta,
addò ch' la vén star róccla? sò me fiómm?
a l so ènca mè, tla gèra,
cs'èll che t'é 'lè? fasúl? un cucèr sno,
fèmma déu, e ta m tai, par dèi l'udòur,
mo do fitíni 'd zvòlla, pàivr' e sèl,
un gòzz d'óli, acsè, basta, una luvéria,

e adès 'na bèla pésga, a ví tó quèsta,
biènca, vè cmè ch' la s spécca, e dréinta ròssa,
a tuchétt, te bicír, e pu e' su véin,
e s'un daid ogni tènt 'na calcadína,
i à da stè sòtta, lòu, i à da imbumbès,
u n'i vó préssia, sint, mèi d'un gelè,

ta m fé zènd? ta n fómm piò? bravo, mè invíci,
a l so, e' fa mèl, però,
cmè 'dès, 'na zigarètta dop magnè,
tè t fumévi te lèt? par mè l'è e' masum,
te schéur, a zènd e a sémm in déu, csa fai
adlà, sta boba, cs'èll suzèst? "Un mlòun",

se ci fosse una zuppierina / di radicchio, che sia tenero, se no niente, // dai
con l'aceto, un altro po', che mi piace si senta, / da dove viene questa rucola?
su al fiume? / lo so anch'io, nella ghiaia, / cos'hai lí? fagioli? solo un cucchiaio, / facciamo due, e mi tagli, per dargli l'odore, / un due fettine di
cipolla, pepe e sale, / un goccio d'olio, cosí, basta, una golosità, // e adesso
una bella pesca, voglio prendere questa, / bianca, ve' come si stacca e dentro
rossa, / a tocchetti, nel bicchiere, e poi il suo vino, / e con un dito ogno tanto una calcatina, / devono star sotto, loro, devono inzupparsi, / non ci vuol
fretta, senti, meglio d'un gelato, // mi fai accendere? non fumi piú? bravo,
io invece, / lo so, fa male, però / come adesso, una sigaretta dopo mangiato,
/ tu fumavi nel letto? per me è il massimo, / nel buio, accendo e siamo in
due, cosa fanno / di là? questo baccano, cos'è successo?" "Un melone", /

369

"Where is it?" "Too late, all gone."
"Was it good?" "Good? you couldn't ask for better."
"You're all a bunch of hogs." "You were too busy talking."
"Gioti, I've only got big bills, we'll settle up later."

I want to walk up there a little ways, as far as the Wall,
I'll stop at Rico's, what's going on?
Everything On Sale, Join the Navy Today!
Public health guidelines for the control
of flies, The Great Orfei Circus is Coming to Town,
they're screaming at the tamburello court,
                              "And now where would this
                                    [young lady be going
all by herself?" "Nowhere in particular," "I'll go with you,"
"Weren't you supposed to be at the opera tonight?"
"Come over here and watch Piero play. Come on, don't run
                                                    [away,"
"It's late," "Aren't I here?"
"Why didn't you go to the opera?"
"I don't know, but isn't it nice being here too?"
"Why don't you want to tell me why you didn't go?"
"No big reason, sometimes I like not being there,"
"Where?"
"Some places; I like for others to go there,"
"And what about you?" "For me it's being here,
having a stroll, talking to you,"
"Aren't you always here?"
"And the next day too, in the café,
when they'll be telling me all about it,
and me asking, and me saying: come on, really?"

"Duv'èll?", "I s l'è slampè", "Bón", "Bón? specèl",
"A si di sgulmanéd", "Mo tè t ciacàr",
"Gioti, a n gn'ò spécch, a fémm",

a ví 'ndè un pó d'insò, fina la Méura,
a m'aféurum da Rico, csa i èll 'd nóv?
Liquido tutto, Arruòlati in Marina,
Disposizioni per la lotta contro
le mosche, Circo Orfei, sint cmè ch'i rógg
me tamburèl,
                          "Dú vala sta ragaza
da par li?", "Invéll", "A t'acumpàgn", "Mo tè
ta n'évi d'ès a l'ópera stasàira?",
"T vlévi vdai zughé Piero? zò, nu scapa",
"L'è tèrd", "A n'i so mè?",
"Parchè ta n si 'n si 'ndè a l'ópera?" "A n'e' so,
mo u n s sta bén ènca què?", "Ta n m'e' vu déi?"
"Mo gnént, acsè, dal vólti u m pis 'd no èsi",
"Duvò?", "Ti póst, u m pis ch'i i vaga ch'ilt",
"E tè?", "Mè què, andè a spas, a zcòrr sa tè",
"Mo aquè ta n'i si sémpra",
"E e' dè dop, te cafè, ch'i m la racòunta,
e mè ch'a i dmand, ch'a déggh: va là, dabón?",

Dov'è, "Se lo sono pappato", "Buono?", "Buono? speciale", / "Siete degli
screanzati", "Ma tu chiacchieri", / "Gioti, non li ho spicci, faremo", //
voglio andare un po' in su, fino alla Mura, / mi fermo da Rico, cosa c'è di
nuovo? / Liquido tutto, Arruòlati in Marina, / Disposizioni per la lotta contro / le mosche, / Circo Orfei, senti come urlano, — "Dove
va questa ragazza / da sola?", "Da nessuna parte", "Ti accompagno", "Ma
tu / non dovevi essere all'opera stasera?", / "Volevi veder giocare Piero? su,
non scapare", / È tardi", "Non ci sono io", / "Perché non sei andato
all'opera?", / "Non lo so, / ma non si sta bene anche qui?", "Non me lo vuoi
dire?", / "Ma niente, cosí, delle volte mi piace non esserci", / "Dove?", "Nei
posti, mi piace che ci vadano gli altri", / "E tu?," "Io, andare a spasso,
parlare cono te", / "Ma qui non ci sei sempre?" / "E il giorno dopo, al caffè,
che me la raccontano, / e io che domando, che dico: va' là, davvero?", /

371

"It's already eleven thirty,"
"But you don't understand, don't you feel it in the air
that this is an evening, look, fireworks,
down there, it must be over there by the river,
four pinwheels, and a fountain
and the sparks look like water, a flower, a rose,
it's changing colors, red, white, yellow,
you can see it even better from here than you can close up,
on top of it I, I'm crazy for fireworks,
and you don't like them at all?
Giorgia! you're not talking? Giorgia?
where are you going?"

"L'è bèla agli óngg e mèz", "Mo ta n capéss,
ta n'e' sint tl'aria,
che quèsta l'è una sàira, orca, vè i fugh,
alazò, l'à da ès adlà de fiómm,
quatar zirandli, adès una funtèna
e al lózzli ch'e' pèr aqua, un fiòur, 'na rósa,
la cambia culòur, ròssa, biènca, zala,
da què u s vaid ènca mèi ch' nè da davséin,
pu mè, i fugh, a dvént mat, tè i n t pis? t sté zétta?
dù sit? mo dò t si 'ndèda? Giorgia! Giorgia!"

"Sono ormai le undici e mezzo", "Ma non capisci, / non senti nell'aria / che
questa è una sera, orca, ve', i fuochi, / laggiú, dev'essere di là dal fiume, /
quattro girandole, adesso una fontana / e le scintille che sembrano acqua, un
fiore, una rosa, / cambia colore, rossa, bianca, gialla, / da qui si vede anche
meglio che da vicino, / poi io, i fuochi, divento matto, a te non ti piacciono?
stai zitta? / dove sei? ma dove sei andata? Giorgia! Giorgia!"

Just For Laughs

They're pulling my leg, they do it to me,
when they start up with it,
because I trick easy,
I don't get certain things, and they laugh,
but they're not mean,
sometimes I start laughing myself.
And when it's over they buy me a glass of wine.

Par réid

I m tó in zéir, i m nu n fa, quant i s'i mètt,
parchè mè a n'ò maléizia,
zérti robi a n gn'aréiv, e lòu i réid,
mo i n'è catéiv,
dal vólti u m vén da réid ènca mu mè.
E pu tl'éultum i m pèga un bicír 'd véin.

Per ridere. Mi prendono in giro, me ne fanno, quando ci si mettono, / perché io non ho malizia, / certe cose non ci arrivo, e loro ridono, / ma non sono cattivi, / delle volte mi viene da ridere anche a me. / E poi alla fine mi pagano un bicchiere di vino.

Permit

Because with all those leaves,
you didn't get any light even at noon, and in the evening,
you couldn't take it, the birds, all roosting up there,
and the mornings even worse,
it was like having the bell tower right over my head,
a walnut, it must have been a hundred years old,
you couldn't get your arms around it,
branches that went out, almost, far enough
to block Otilla's windows,
and down below, a garden, a big thick wall, enclosed,
no one can see you,
but, then again, you can't see in if something were to happen,
only above, star-filled, when it's night,
a prison, where my wife keeps
five or six pots of geraniums, some basil,
and that's it, near the walnut tree, the well
where the water's no good,
and inside it's covered with flowers, it's all mallow,
down in the corner, a pomegranate,
a snakes' nest, and farther on a ticket of an overgrown lilac,
then, on this other wall, ivy,

E' permèss

Parchè ènca tótt cla frònda,
t' n'avdévi lómm gnénca a mezdè, e la sàira
u n s campéva, i gazótt, l'apularèda,
e la matéina pézz,
zà ch'a iò e' Campanòun sòura la testa,
ció, mo un anéus, e' géve 'vài zént'an,
ta n l'abrazévi,
dal rèmi ch' l'arivéva guési a cruv
al finestri dla Tilla,
e sòtta l'órt, tótt' 'na muràia, céus,
ch'u n t'avidrà niseun,
mo ènca tè pu ta n vaid un azidént,
sno d'in èlt, dal gran stèli, quant l'è nòta,
un'imparsòun, che la mi mòi la i tén
zéinch si vès ad gerèni, un pó 'd basélgh,
e pu piò gnént, vsina l'anéus e' pòzz,
che l'aqua la n'è bóna,
e dréinta l'à fiuréi, l'è tótta malva,
te cantòun alazò un melingarnèd,
un bisèr, e piò in là un maciòun 'd siréni,
dop, sa st'èlt méur, un'edera,

Il permesso. Perché anche tutto quel fogliame, / non vedevi lume neanche a mezzogiorno, e la sera / non si campava, gli uccelli, l'appollaiata, / e la mattina peggio, / già che ho il Campanone sopra la testa, / e beh, un noce, avrà avuto cent'anni, / non l'abbracciavi, / dei rami che arrivavano quasi a coprire / le finestre dell'Otilla, / e sotto l'orto, tutt'una muraglia, chiuso, / che non ti vedrà nessuno, / ma anche tu poi non vedi un accidente, / solo in alto, delle gran stelle, quand'è notte, / una prigione, che mia moglie ci tiene / cinque sei vasi di gerani, un po' di basilico, / e poi piú niente, vicino al noce il pozzo, / che l'acqua non è buona, / e dentro è fiorito, tutta malva, / nell'angolo laggiú un melograno, / un bisciaio, e piú in là un macchione di sirenelle, / dopo, su quest'altro muro, un'edera, /

377

but it's so vigorous, it goes all the way over, it's falling over,
in the middle there's that stone, it's huge, like a millstone,
you can go and sit on it,
but what's the use, it's crawling with ants,
with lizards, old houses, it would be better
just to tear them down and start all over again,
there's always something to keep up with, I sent Cardamoni
to fix the roof three or four times already, when it rains,
if it's a rain with wind, in the kid's room
you've got to keep a washbasin underneath, the kitchen's
got the same stains, I can't get rid of them,
then the staircase has got to be redone, which will be quite an
                                           [expense,
with what you've got to pay masons these days,
if you could even get them to come,
if you could just open it up on the side where the Little
                                           [Chapel is,
there's a hidden door, that would do it,
put it back how it was originally, a place to park,
install a rolldown shutter,
since, at any rate,
the well, with all that the debris, then it got cleared out,
I cut down the walnut tree, what could you do?
but our thinking was,
you've got to, because I was having to throw away good,

mo s'un vigòur, la è pasa dlà, spandléun,
te mèz u i è che sas, gròs, cmè un mèsna,
ch' ta t'i pò mètt disdài,
mo 's'ut, l'è pin 'd furméighi,
'd lusérti, al chèsi vèci vèci, e' sarébb mèi
buté zò e arfè tótt nóv,
mè alè a i so sémpra dri, ò mand Cardamòun
si cópp tre quatar vólti, quant e' pióv,
s' la vén ad vént, tla cambra di burdéll
u i vó la caldarètta, la cuséina
sémpra cal maci, ch'a n li pòs dumè,
pu u i è d'arfè la schèla, ch'andrò a spènd,
sa quèll ch'e' gòsta adès i muradéur,
e zà ch'i i è.
s'a putéss ènca arvéi còuntra la Zèla,
ch'u i è una pórta ziga, bastarébb,
u s fa cmè ch' l'era préima,
passo carraio, t mètt la su seranda,
sicómm che tanimódi
e' pòzz, se rimpidéur, dop u n gn'è piò.
l'anéus a l'ò taiè, cs'èll ch'e' sarébb?
mo ragiunémma, zò, parchè i baócch
mè a i ò da buté véa, che la mi Ritmo,

ma con un vigore, è passata di là, penzoloni, / in mezzo c'è quel sasso, grosso, come una macina, / che ti ci puoi mettere a sedere, / ma cosa vuoi è pieno di formiche, / di lucertole, le case vecchie, sarebbe meglio / buttar giú e rifare tutto nuovo, / io lí ci sono sempre dietro, ho mandato Cardamoni / sui coppi tre quattro volte, quando piove, / se piove di vento, nella camera dei bambini / ci vuole la bacinella, la cucina / sempre quelle macchie, che non riesco a domarle, / poi c'è da rifare la scala, che andrò a spendere, / con quel che costano adesso i muratori, / e già che ci sono, / se potessi anche aprire contro la Cella, / che c'è una porta cieca, basterebbe, / si fa com'era prima, / passo carraio, metti la sua serranda, / siccome, tanto, / il pozzo, coi detriti, dopo non c'è piú, / il noce l'ho tagliato, cosa sarebbe? / ma ragioniamo, su, perché i soldi / io devo buttarli via, che la mia Ritmo, /

because the Fiat sedan, money, which was money that,
I got it in '80, it's acting like it's ten years old,
this is '83, it's that a car,
keeping it outside all the time, summer and winter,
it would be better if instead, if I, it would have been
something done right, even insofar as the placement,
but just from the standpoint of public health concerns,
what do you expect,
if you don't do anything about it, I don't have time,
it's all covered with weeds,
nettles, it's awful, you call this a garden?
I can't say what it is for you but for me it's a trash heap,
there are some days, I better be quiet , but come on now,
the stuff they throw down from up there,
calm down now, I have absolutely no desire to get into an
argument,
they'll do whatever it is they want to do, which as far as
sanitation goes,
that would be a whole different discussion,
because with just one bathroom, there's five of us, and the girl,
sleeping with two boys, when gets to be
sixteen or seventeen you think that's going to work? you tell me,
and the solution would be, it wouldn't do anyone
any harm, on the via Dolci side, to pull it down,
no big deal, downstairs a bath, upstairs a small bedroom,
let's get this straight, certain things, it wears you out,

amo l'è sóld, a la ò tólta dl'utènta,
e' pèr ch' la apa dis an,
a sémm dl'utentatrè, l'è che una machina,
a tnàila sémpra fura, instèda e invéran,
invíci, s'a putéss, mè, l'avnirébb
una roba bén fata, ènca pr'e' pòst.
mo sno l'igiene, cs'ut, a no fèi gnént,
mè a n'ò témp, e' vén sò tótt arbazéun,
urtéighi, una schivèra, l'è un órt quèll?
par tè a n'e' so, par mè l'è una mundèzza,
ch'u i è di dè, l'è mèi stè zétt, va là,
da 'd sòura quèll ch'i bótta zò, 'ta bón,
mè a n n'ò vòia ad ragnè,
ch'i faza quèll ch'i vó, ch' pu par l'igiene
u i sarébb ènch' da fè tótt un èlt zcòurs,
parchè un bagn sno, a sémm zéinch, e la burdèla,
a durméi sa du mas-ci, quant la avrà
ségg disèt an, e' va bén? arspònd tè,
e e' rimédi u i sarébb, senza dè dan
ma niseun, vérs via Dolci, tiré sò,
gnént, sòtta un bagn, sòura una cambarètta,
intendéssum, zért' robi, l'è fadéiga,

sono soldi, quelli, l'ho presa nell'ottanta, / pare che abbia dieci anni, / siamo
nell'ottantatre, è che una macchina, / a tenerla sempre fuori, estate e inverno,
/ invece, se potessi, io, verrebbe / una cosa ben fatta, anche per il posto, /
ma solo l'igiene, cosa vuoi, a non farci niente, / io non ho tempo, vengono
su tutte erbacce, / ortiche, uno schifo, è un orto quello? / per te non lo so,
per me è un immondezzaio, / che ci sono dei giorni, è meglio star zitti, va'
la, / da sopra quel che buttano giú, sta' buono, / io non ne ho voglia di
litigare, / facciano quel che vogliono, che poi per l'igiene / ci sarebbe anche
da fare tutt'un altro discorso, / perché un bagno soltanto, simao cinque, e la
bambina, / a dormire con due maschi, quando avrà / sedici diciassette anni,
va bene? rispondi tu, / e il rimedio ci sarebbe, senza far danno / a nessuno,
verso via Dolci, tirare su, niente, sotto un bagno, sopra una cameretta, /
intendiamoci, certe cose, è fatica, /

you think I don't understand these things,
you can't rush them, the bathroom,
we've gotten along until this point, we can go along
a little longer, as for the bedroom,
they still want to be in the same room,
what I have to say, a car, it's not as if it were a truck,
parked in that itty-bitty spot, it's a big undertaking, it is,
you could have it all finished in a month, it's just that here
it's one big bureaucracy, you,
how does this involve you?
you can only do what falls into your area of responsibility,
I'm just saying, there's a piece of land, it's vacant,
say it's yours, I'm talking to you here
in general terms, because leaving it as it is,
it's better not to think about it, it does no one any good,
only the worms,
smack-dab in the middle of town, let me finish,
which you couldn't even see it, it'd be like nothing's there,
I'd cover it with three or four meters of, all right, five,
roof tiles, rustic style,
what's going to be lost?
and I, on the other hand, I've got a shelter,
I explained it all to them in the application,
with all the plans, in detail, the whole project,
which one day this whole thing's really going to wear me out,
I'll get the masons to start work and then they can just make me
tear it down if they have the guts to, this is what we've come to,

382

t vu ch'a n'e' sapa, u n'i vó préssia, e' bagn,
avémm fat fina adès, andrémm avènti
un èlt pó, par la cambra,
i vó stè 'ncòura tótt insén, no, mè,
quèll ch' déggh mè, una Ritmo, fóss un camion,
la i sta t'un fazulètt, l'è un lavòur, quèll,
t'un màis u s fa iniquèl, sno che què ormai
l'è tótt una burocrazéa, mo tè
cs'èll ta i éintar? tè t'é da fè e' tu dvàir,
io dico solo, u i è un pèz 'd tèra, un zcvért,
e' putrébb ès e' tóvv, io qui ti parlo
in generale, che a lasèl acsè
u n vó dí gnént, u n sarvéss ma niseun,
sno ma i imbréisal,
nel mezzo del paese, fam finéi,
ch'u n s vaid, l'è cm'u n'i fóss, s'a n cruv tri quatar
metar, zéinch, tò, si cópp, in stile rustico,
cs'èll ch'e' va pérs? e mè invíci ò un ripèr,
agli ò spieghè tla dmanda,
si su diségn, precéis, tótt e' progèt,
che un dè s'a m stóff dabón
a i mètt i muradéur e dop ch'i m faza
buté zò s'i à e' curàg, ch'a s sémm ardótt,

vuoi che non lo sappia, non ci vuol fretta, il bagno, / abbiamo fatto fino adesso, andremo avanti, / un altro po', per la camera, / vogliono stare ancora tutti insieme, no, io, / quello che dico io, una Ritmo, fosse un camion, / sta in un fazzoletto, è un lavoro, quello, / in un mese si fa tutto, solo che qui ormai / è tutt'una burocrazia, ma tu / cosa c'entri? tu devi fare il tuo dovere, / io dico solo, c'è un pezzo di terra, uno scoperto, / potrebbe essere il tuo, io qui ti parlo / in generale, che a lasciarlo cosí / non vuol dir niente, non serve a nessuno, / solo ai lombrichi, / nel mezzo del paese, fammi finire, / che non si vede, è come non ci fosse, se ne copro tre quattro / metri, cinque, to', coi coppi, in stile rustico, / cosa va perso? e io invece ho un riparo, / glel'ho spiegato nella domanda, / coi suoi disegni, precisi, tutto il progetto, / che un giorno se mi stufo davvero / ci metto i muratori e dopo che mi facciano / buttar giú se hanno il coraggio, ci siamo ridotti, /

all these permits, how is it, it belongs to me,
I have a wife and kids, and other people
can tell me what do to with what's mine?
you couldn't have invented a better screw-up, we've got laws,
it's late? you've got to go home, sorry for what?
it's me here apologizing to you, when I get started,
that's enough, I'll be seeing you, I'm leaving too,
same thing with me, they're waiting for me, it's just that
these are discussions, which when you have them,
your blood pressure goes up,
but Gino di Magnózz, this much I must say,
because for me, hypocrites, who whenever they see me,
they give me these big smiles, even yesterday in the piazza,
and then in the committee meeting it's even nastier,
and Adelmo, who's afraid of compromising himself,
on account of we're related,
and what I'm asking of him, I wouldn't ask him for beans,
oh come on now, being the assessor, the airs he puts on,
and his wife's the same, my cousin,
but these are things, forget about it, in a small town,
which everyone knows, but it's not done with yet,
I wrote, to someone, in a high place, what,
I'm supposed to pay the taxes, I'm, and then just shut up?

tótt sti perméss, cumè, l'è roba méa,
ò mòi e fiúl, u m l'à d'avní a dí ch'ilt
quèll ch'ò da fè te méi?
ch'a faséss un caséin, avémm dal lèzi,
l'è tèrd? t'é d'andè chèsa? schéusa ad chè?
a so mè ch'a t dmand schéusa, quant a tach,
basta a s'avdémm, a vagh
ènca mè, ch'i m'aspétta, tanimódi
l'è tótt zchéurs, da fè chè, ta t guast e' sangh,
però Gino ad Magnózz, quèst a l ví déi,
parchè mè i impustéur, che quant u m vaid
u m fa bòcca da réid, ènca ir in piaza,
e pu tla Comisiòun l'è e' piò 'canéid,
e Delmo, ch' l'à paéura 'd compromèttsi,
sicómm ch'a sémm parént,
che mè da léu, mo a n vrébb gnénca un luvéin,
t si mat, ès asesòur, e' pais ch'u s dà,
e la su mòi precéis, la mi cuséina,
però l'è robi, andémma, t'un paàis
ch'a s cnunsémm tótt, mo la n'è méggh' finéida,
ò scrétt, ma qualcadéun, d'in èlt, cumè,
ò sno da paghè al tasi, mè, e stè zétt?

tutti questi permissi, come, è roba mia, / ho moglie e figli, me lo devono
venir a dire gli altri / quel che devo fare nel mio? / facessi un casino,
abbiamo delle leggi, / è tardi? devi andare a casa? scusa di che? / sono io che
ti domando scusa, quando attacco, / basta, ci vediamo, vado / anch'io, che
m'aspettano, tanto / sono tutti discorsi, da far che, ti guasti il sangue, / però
Gino di Magnózz, questo lo voglio dire, / perché io gli impostori, che
quando mi vede / mi fa dei gran sorrisi, anche ieri in piazza, / e poi nella
Commissione è il piú accanito, / e Adelmo, che ha paura di compromettersi,
/ siccome siamo parenti, / che io da lui, ma non vorrei neanche un lupino,
/ figurarsi, essere assessore, le arie che si dà, / e la sua moglie uguale, mia
cugina, / però sono cose, andiamo, in un paese che ci conosciamo tutti, ma
non è mica finita, / ho scritto, a qualcuno, in alto, come, / devo solo pagar
le tasse, io, e star zitto? /

it's that I will not stop,
and then all this crap for one permit,
to pull one permit, which doesn't affect them at all in the least,
no one at all, do I hear them complaining, do I, in my shop?
and so, what is it they want?
I've always worked, I've never asked anybody for anything,
I care for this town more than they do,
and you, I know, you've got to go, but just one minute,
I just wanted to tell you this, because at this point I've
been at this a year-and-a-half, and I've still got the same
problem,
and there are days, you've got to believe me, that I feel
as if they've beaten me over the head, for me the thing is this,
we've known each other since we were kids, we, you're a friend,
if you could just put in a word, that doesn't mean if,
you're in a different department, I know that, but
you they'd listen to,
no, wait, no, you don't have to take my side,
just to let them know, don't laugh now, I haven't lost my mind,
if they would just give me this permit,
that would be the end of, I wouldn't do a thing,
I'm serious here, they have to give it to me, I have the right,
stamped, signed, then I don't touch so much as a brick,
it's not about my kids anymore,

l'è ch'a n m'aférum,
mo pu tótt' stal pugnètti, pr'un permèss,
par tiré sò, ch'u n gn'arimpórta gnént
ma niseun, a n'i sint, mè, tla butàiga?
e alòura? cs'èll ch'i vó?
ch'ò sémpra lavurè, a n'ò mai dmand gnént,
ma sté paàis a i ví piò bén ch' nè lòu,
a tè, a l so, t'é d'andè, mo l'è un minéut,
a t vléva sno déi, parchè mè, l'è bèla
un an e mèz, sémpra sa sté pensìr,
e u i è di dè, te m'é da craid, ch'a m sint
cmè ch'i m'éss bastunè, mè, l'è una roba,
ch'a s cnunsémm da burdéll, néun, t si un améigh,
s't putéss spènd 'na paróla, mo u n vó déi
se t si t'un èlt uféizi, a l so, però
ma tè i t sta da sintéi,
no, spétta, no, t n'é da ciapè al mi pèrti,
sno fèi savài, nu réid, a n so dvént mat,
s'i m'e' dà sté permèss, basta, a n faz gnént,
a déggh dabón, mo i m l'à da dè, ò dirétt,
témbar, firmi, pu a n móv gnénca un madòun,
ch'a n vègga piò i mi fiúl,

è che non mi fermo, / ma poi tutte 'ste menate per un permesso, / per tirar
su, che non gliene importa niente / a nessuno, non li sento, io, in negozio?
/ e allora? cosa vogliono? / che ho sempre lavorato, non ho mai chiesto
niente, / a questo paese gli voglio piú bene di loro, / e tu, lo so, devi andare,
ma è un minuto, / ti volevo solo dire, perché io è ormai / un anno e mezzo,
sempre con questo pensiero, / e ci sono dei giorni, mi devi credere, che mi
sento / come se mi avessero bastonato, per me è una cosa, / che ci
conosciamo fin da bambini, noi, sei un amico, / se potessi spendere una
parola, ma non vuol dire / se sei in un altro ufficio, lo so, però, / a te ti
stanno a sentire, / no, aspetta, no, non devi prendere le mie parti, / solo
fargli sapere, non ridere, non sono diventato matto, / se me lo danno questo
permesso, basta, non faccio niente, / dico sul serio, ma me lo devono dare,
ho diritto, / timbri, firme, poi non tocco neanche un mattone, / che non
veda piú i miei figli, /

it's just for myself, do you understand? I have to have it,
and if they don't have enough trust
I'll put it down in writing for them,
we could get it notarized, they can't say no,
I'm doing everything they want,
it's enough that they just give it to me,
I won't say a word to anyone, not even to my family,
I'll keep it in my wallet, I have lots of these pieces of paper,
folded up inside there, like nothing,
and sometimes, when I'm alone,
pull it out, look at it, what would it cost them?

l'è sno par mè, t capéss? a l'ò d'avài,
e s'i n s'aféida a i e' mètt par iscrétt,
andémm ènch da un nutèri, i n pò dí 'd no,
a faz tótt quèll ch'i vó, bast', ch'i, m'e' daga,
a n'e' déggh ma niseun, gnénca mi méi,
a l téngh te partafòi, ch'ò tènt' 'd cal chèrti,
pighéd alè, cmè gnént,
e dal vólti, quant a so da par mè,
tirél fura, guardèl, cs'èll ch' l'è par lòu?

è solo per me, capisci? devo averlo, / e se non si fidano glielo metto per
iscritto, / andiamo anche da un notaio, non possono dire di no, / faccio tutto
quello che vogliono, basta che me lo diano, / non lo dico a nessuno, neanche
ai miei, / lo tengo nel portafoglio, che ho tante di quelle carte, / piegato lí,
come niente, / e delle volte, quando sono solo, / tirarlo fuori, guardarlo,
cos'è per loro?

Summer

Then it'll turn into summer,
when it's never night, and inside the houses, in the dark
the wardrobes are like ghosts,
keys jingling in pockets, the spiders
with such patience, water getting covered with scum,
a boy on a step cracking hazelnuts
with a nutcracker, in the morning, in the garden, the streaks
left by snails glisten,
what are they burning down there?
just look where those swallows have built their nest,
what nice geraniums, Barócc's kid is going at it
with his violin, the cats' backs
razor thin, at the Arch
an outsider in a white cap
asks how to get to San Leo,
                                    at the café they're discussing
Alvaro's situation:
"It must have been the left." "At any rate,
now he'll get a nice pension." "But without an arm."
"Better an arm than a leg." "I'm not so sure."

L'instèda

Pu l'avnirà l'instèda,
ch'u n s fa mai nòta, e dréinta al chèsi, tl'òmbra,
i armèri e' pèr fantèsum,
al cèvi al bala tal bascòzi, i ragn
i à una pazinzia, l'aqua la fa e' tès,
un burdèl s'un scaléin e' zaca i óss
par e' cruchènt, tl'órt la matéina e' léus
al stréssi dal luméghi,
cs'èll ch'i bréusa alazò?
mo vè cla rònda dò ch' la à fat e' néid,
che bèi gerèni, e' fiúl 'd Barócc u i dà
sa che viuléin, i gat i à al schéini stili
cmè di curtéll, ma l'Èrch
un furistír s'un britín biènch e' dmanda
pr'andè a San Li,
         te cafè i zcòrr d'Alvaro,
"Fóss stè e' manzéin", "Par quant adès u i vén
una bèla pensiòun", "Mo senza un braz",
"Mèi un braz ch' nè una gamba", "A n'e' so mégga",

L'estate. Poi verrà l'estate, / che non si fa mai notte, e dentro le case, nell'ombra, / gli armadi sembrano fantasmi, / le chiavi ballano nelle tasche, i ragni / hanno una pazienza, l'acqua fa il taso, / un bambino su uno scalino schiaccia i noccioli / per il croccante, nell'orto la mattina luccicano / le strisce delle lumache, / che cosa bruciano laggiú? / ma guarda quella rondine dove ha fatto il nido, / che bei gerani, il figlio di Barócc ci dà / con quel violino, i gatti hanno le schiene sottili / come coltelli, all'Arco / un forestiero con un berrettino bianco domanda / per andare a San Leo, – al caffè parlano di Alvaro, / "Fosse stato il sinistro", "Per quanto adesso gli viene / una bella pensione", "Ma senza un braccio", / "Meglio un braccio che una gamba", "Non lo so mica", /

391

"Come on, two good legs." "If you've got to run,
but to swim, hammer a nail, to shoot a shotgun."
"Why, did he hunt?" "I'm saying,
even to wipe your ass."
                              the two Bagiagia girls
strolling up the Passeggio to get an ice cream,
"I'm sending the bunch of you to jail," what?
are they arguing now in the piazza?
no, listen, they're laughing,
and Zanini and His Honor the Gentleman
are walking back and forth, hands behind back, conferring,
the night is a theater, from the Rocca you can see the world,
Rimini, Cesenatico, Cervia, then back home, with just the sheet,
and her, she's even naked, it seems like she's asleep,
but slowly, with a foot, she gives you a sign.

"Va là, do gambi bóni", "S' t'é da córr,
mo nudé, piantè un ciód, tiré sla s-ciòpa",
"Parchè, l'andéva a caza?", "U s fa par déi,
ènca puléis e' chéul",
                        al do Bagiagia
al va sò me Pasègg a tó e' gelè,
"A v mand tótt in galera!", i ragna in piaza?
no, sint, i réid,
sòtta i pórtich Zanini e e' cavalír
i va sò e zò, mèni di dri, i zcòrr fétt,
la nòta l'è un teètar, da la Roca
u s vaid e' mònd, Rémin, Eznàitch, Ziria,
pu a chèsa, a lèt, sno se lanzúl, e li,
néuda ènca li, ch'e' pèr ch' la dórma, invíci,
pièn, s'un pi, la t fa sègn.

"Va' là , due gambe buone", "Se devi correre, / ma nuotare, piantare un
chiodo, tirare con la doppietta," / "Perché, andava a caccia?", "Si fa per dire,
/ anche pulirsi il sedere", – le due Bagiagia / vanno su al Passeggio a
prendere il gelato, / "Vi mando tutti in galera!", litigano in piazza? / no,
senti, ridono, / sotto i portici Zanini e il cavaliere / vanno su e giú, mani di
dietro, parlano fitto, / la notte è un teatro, dalla Rocca / si vede il mondo,
Rimini, Cesanatico, Cervia, / poi a casa, a letto, solo col lenzuolo, e lei, /
nuda anche lei, che pare dorma, invece, / piano, con un piede, ti fa segno.

Handkerchief

The fears I've got, I'm the only one who knows,
it seems like I hear movement, like they're walking around
upstairs, could it be mice? coming downstairs,
fiddling around with the door, but these?
standing there listening hard,
not just at night, it's all day long,
and when I saw myself in the mirror, gaunt, with my eyes,
at the end of my rope, in my own house,
I said, enough is enough, this can't go on, I'm going crazy here,
I'm losing my grip,
I called Bruni, do it, he came with a lock,
a whole big rigamarole, drilled metal into the wall,
the other one with the latch and two bolts,
bars covering the windows,
he did some brickwork at the garden gate, and imbedded
four cramps in certain places, two bars going across,
from outside, you'd really have to work to get in,
it wasn't on account of the money, there's, in the dresser I've got,
at the most,
I keep, in the top drawer, a twenty,

E' fazulètt

Amo ò vú dal paéuri, a l so sno mè,
u m paréa 'd sintí móv, ch'i caminéss
ad sòura, e' sarà sórgh? vní zò mal schèli,
sfurgatè ma la pórta, quést però,
e a stéva alè in urèccia,
mo mégga sno la nòta, tótta e' dè,
ch'a m'avdéva te spèc, spartéd, sa di ócc,
a séra cmè sla frasca, ad chèsa méa,
e pu ò détt basta,
quèst che què u n'è campè, mè aquè a dvént mat,
éva ciap di aretrati, ò ciamè Bréun,
fa tè, léu l'è vnú sò s'una sradéura,
un santéssum, di férr ch'i éintra te méur,
pu u i è cl'èlta se scròch e du carnàz,
mal finestri tótt frèdi,
la pórta dl'órt u i à muré 'd quà e dlà
quatar grapi, e ad travérs u i è du murèl
ch da 'd fura i à vòia lòu 'd calchè,
u n'è megga pr'i bócch, mè te cumò
u i sarà, a dí una masa,
a i téngh te préim casètt, vintmélla frènch,

Il fazzoletto. Le paure che ho preso, lo so soltanto io, / mi pareva di sentir muovere, che camminassero / di sopra, saranno topi? scendere le scale, / armeggiare alla porta, questi però, / e stavo lí in orecchi, / ma mica solo la notte, tutto il giorno, / che mi vedevo nello specchio, sparuto, con degli occhi, / ero come sulla frasca, in casa mia, / e poi ho detto basta, / questo non è campare, io qui divento matto, / avevo preso degli arretrati, ho chiamato Bruni, / fa tu, lui è venuto su con una serratura, / un sacramento, dei ferri che entrano nel muro, / poi c'è l'altra con lo scrocco e due catenacci, / alle finestre tutte inferriate, / alla porta dell'orto ha murato di qua e di là / quattro grappe, e di traverso ci sono due travi / che da fuori hanno voglia loro a spingere, / non è mica per i soldi, io nel comò /ci saranno, a dire molto, / li tengo nel primo cassetto, ventimile lire, /

395

that's what they'd find in the house, the ones trying to get in,
and if you don't have money it's worse, they get infuriated,
they're capable of beating you up even,
and I haven't got anything else, no gold, no rings, if they want it,
there's the passbook, even there, I'm sure
they'd start swearing, but what am I supposed to do?
I have the pension, it's just that,
Lucio goes and takes out some for me each month,
because, going out, if there's good weather,
but going down the Scalette, with this weather,
Palmina goes shopping for me,
I eat like a canary,
I've got to go to the doctor, but I can never make up my mind,
Edmondo comes to visit me every so often,
he's the nurse at the hospital, we're first cousins,
otherwise if someone rings it's by mistake,
which I'm not going to answer anyway,
the mailman slips the bills under the door, at Christmas
there's a card from Seconda,
she always remembers,
beautiful Madonnas, they paint them with their feet,
the ones that don't have hands,
then what else is there? nothing, yesterday I pricked a finger,

l'è che truvèsi ad chèsa, quéi ch'i à próv,
e s' ta n'é i bócch l'è pézz, i s'incapèla,
i è capèzi magari ch'i t bastòuna,
e mè a n'ò èlt, nè ór nè anéll, s'i l vó,
u i è e' librètt, ènca 'lè, a so sichéur,
i tacarà a biastmé, mo cs'òi da fè?
ò cla pensiòun, mè, sno,
ch'u m la va a tiré Lucio tótt i méis,
parchè scapè, s'e' vén la stasòun bóna,
mo adès zò mal Scalètti, sa sté témp,
la spàisa la m la va a fè la Palmina,
mè a magn cumè un canèri,
ò d'andè de dutòur, mo a n m'ardéus mai,
u m vén a truvè Mondo d'ogni tènt,
léu l'è infermír te bsdèl, a sémm cusbréin,
se no aquè, quant i sòuna l'è par sbai,
ch'a n'arspònd gnénca, e' pustéin al bulètti
u m li inféila da sòtta, par Nadèl
u i è una cartuléina dla Secònda,
li la s'arcórda sémpra,
dal piò bèli Madòni, i li pitéura
si pi, quéi ch' n'à 'l mèni,
pu csa i èll? gnént, ir a m so furè un daid,

è che trovarseli in casa quelli che hanno provato, /e se non hai i soldi è
peggio, s'arrabbiano, / sono capaci magari di bastonarti, / e io non ho altro,
né oro né anelli, se lo vogliono / c'è il libretto, che anche lí, sono sicuro, /
cominceranno a bestemmiare, ma cosa devo fare? / ho quella pensione, io
soltanto, / che me la va a ritirare Lucio tutti i mesi, / perché uscire, se viene
la buona stagione, / ma adesso giú per le Scalette, con questo tempo, / la
spesa me la va a fare la Palmina, io mangio come un canarino, / devo andare
dal dottore, ma non mi decido mai, / viene a trovarmi Edmondo ogni tanto,
/ lui è infermiere all'ospedale, siamo procugini, / se no qui, quando suonano
è per sbaglio, / che non rispondono nemmeno, il postino le bollette / me le
infila da sotto, per Natale / c'è una cartolina della Seconda, / lei si ricorda
sempre, / delle Madonne bellissime, le dipingono / coi piedi, quelli che non
hanno le mani, / poi cosa c'è? niente, ieri mi sono punto un dito, /

it swelled up a little bit,
with those leaves, what do you call it? with the thorns?
Gemma left me some: put it right here,
then she didn't come back to get them,
pretty, she said they bloom every hundred years,
and I waited, I'm not in a hurry, when evening comes,
even just to move around a little,
I go around checking on things, for a change of pace,
I give the bolts a good hard turn,
then, if it's Thursday, I watch the Cesena channel,
where they do all these games, you can't imagine the things
they come up with,
and I laugh, there all by myself,
which if they heard me they'd think I've gone out of my mind,
seeing all these ridiculous, yesterday one of them had to swim
in sawdust, there was so much dust, he started coughing,
he was spitting, he was hacking, and I started laughing so hard
even now, which when he stood up, when he got there,
he was completely coated, scratching himself furiously,
I couldn't do anything else but laugh, then with the sawdust
in his underwear, behind, all poofed out,
it looked like he'd gone in his pants,
my stomach hurt, it made me wet my pants,
I'm not kidding, I had little drips, where did I put

u m s'è un pó gòunfi,
s' cal fòi, cmè ch'al s cèma? agli à di spéin,
la m li à lasi la Gemma: ténli aquè,
pu la n li è vnú a tó piò,
bèli, dis ch'al fiuréss ogni zént an,
e mè aspèt, a n'ò préssia, quant l'è sàira,
ènca par móvmi, a vagh a dè un'ucèda
in zéir, a cambi l'aria,
a dagh 'na rincalchèda mi carnàz,
pu, s' l'è la zóbia, a guèrd Tele-Cesena,
ch'i fa tènt ad chi zugh, mo i n stròlga 'd quèlli,
e mè a réid, da par mè,
che s'i m sint i girà ch'a so dvént mat,
vdai sti pataca, ir éun l'à cnú nudé
te sgadézz, un purbiòun, l'à tach a tòs,
e' spudéva, e' ras-céva, u m vén da réid
ènca adès, ch' l'è stè sò, quant l'è rivàt,
impanèd, u s gratéva s'una tégna,
a n nu n pòs piò da e' réid, pu se sgadézz
ti mudandéin, di dri, mo una malètta
ch' pareva ch'u s la fóss fata madòs,
u m dól la pènza, aquè a m la faz madòs
dabón, a i ò i guzlótt, duv'è ch'ò mèss

mi s'è un po' gonfiato, / con quelle foglie, come si chiamano? hanno delle
spine, / me le ha lasciate la Gemma: tienile qui, / poi non è piú venuta a
prenderle, / belle, dice che fioriscono ogni cent'anni, / e io aspetto, non ho
fretta, quand'è sera, / anche per muovermi, vado a dare un'occhiata / in
giro, cambio l'aria, / do una stretta ai catenacci, / poi, se è giovedí, guardo Tele-
Cesena, / che fanno tanti di quei giochi, ma ne inventano di quelle, / e io
rido, da solo, / che se mi sentono diranno che sono diventato matto, /
vedere 'sti minchioni, ieri uno ha dovuto nuotare / nella segatura, un
polverone, ha cominciato a tossire, / sputava, raschiava, mi viene da ridere
/ anche adesso, che s'è alzato, quando è arrivato, / impanato, si grattava con
una stizza, / non ne posso piú dal ridere, poi con la segatura / nei mutandini,
di dietro, uno sgonfio / che pareva se la fosse fatta addosso, / mi duole la
pancia, / qui me la faccio addosso / davvero, ho i goccioloni, dove ho
messo/

the handkerchief? which I should have left right there,
no, it's not there, or did I put it on the nightstand?
it's always like this, with stuff, I
use it, then I leave it somewhere, this house,
it piles up, it piles up, and what it comes down to
is I can't find anything anymore,
and now it's the handkerchief,
which I must have blown my nose with five minutes ago,
this one here is a sock, look here are the gloves, both of them,
which this morning it was so cold, my hands were ice,
but I've got six or seven handkerchiefs, just one, that's right,
one of them has to be here someplace, I remember now,
I had a seismic sneeze, or was it the day before yesterday?
wait, here, in the glass cabinet, oh come on now,
and not among all these papers either,
because I was laughing, I was so happy,
oh for the love of Pete, all for one handkerchief,
which I always see floating around the house,
it's that things, when you're looking for them,
okay even a napkin would do,
a rag, which this is how it all starts out,
then you end up,
the other day I was hacking into a towel,
which I won't do again, no, no this you just can't do,
even if no one sees me, but, me, who am I anyway?
I'm not nothing, am I? and now these others,

400

e' fazulètt? ch'a l'apa las adlà?
no, u n gh'è, o ch'a l'ò pòuns se cumudéin?
sémpra acsè, mè sal robi,
a li dróv, pu a li las alè, sta chèsa,
móccia, móccia, u s'è 'rdótt, a n tróv più gnént,
adès, e' fazulètt,
ch'a m sarò sufié e' nès zinch minéut fa,
quèst che què l'è un calzètt, vè i guènt, tutt déu,
che stamatéina un frèdd, dal mèni giazi,
mo i fazulétt a n n'ò si sèt, éun, zò,
e' scaparà pò fura, ch'a m'arcórd,
ò fat un gran starnéud, o l'è stè ir?
spétta, aquè, tla vedréina, mo va là,
e gnénca tra stal chèrti,
ch'a ridéva, ch'a séra più cuntént,
mo vèrda alè, pr'un fazulètt, ch'a n vèggh
sémpra in zéir, l'è che al robi, quant ti li zirch,
mo ènca un tvaiúl, un stràz, che però acsè,
u s ravéa cumè gnént, pu e' va a finéi,
l'altredè ò scatarè t'un sugamèn,
ch'a n e' faz più, no, u n s pò,
ènch' s'u mu n vaid niseun, mo e mè, chi sòi?
a n so gnént, mè? e adès quèsti,

il fazzoletto? che l'abbia lasciato di là? / no, non c'è, o l'ho posato sul comodino? / sempre cosí, io, con le cose, / le adopero, poi le lascio lí, questa casa, / ammucchia ammucchia, s'è ridotta, non trovo piú niente, / adessso, il fazzoletto, / che mi sarò soffiato il naso cinque minuti fa, / questa qui è una calza, ve' i guanti, tutt'e due, / che stamattina un freddo, delle mani ghiacce, / ma di fazzoletti ne ho sei sette, uno, dai, / verrà pur fuori, che mi ricordo, / ho fatto un gran starnuto, o è stato ieri? / aspetta, qui nella vetrina, macché, / e neanche fra queste carte, / che ridevo, ero cosí contento, / ma guarda lí, per un fazzoletto, che ne vedo / sempre in giro, è che le cose, quando le cerchi, / ma anche un tovagliolo, uno straccio, che però cosí, / si cominicia come niente, poi va a finire, / l'altro giorno ho scatarrato in un asciugamano, / che non lo faccio piú, no, non si può, / anche se non mi vede nessuno, ma, e io chi sono? / non sono niente, io? e adesso queste, /

which are all in the wash, so I'll just use my hands instead,
like kids do, sooner or later I'll find
a handkerchief, it's all the same difference,
but that's as far as it goes, I'm in charge here,
no, and no again, I will not wipe my glasses,
this I will not do, with a pair of underpants.

ch'agli è 'd bughéda, mo piotòst a faz
sal mèni, cmè i burdéll, un fazulètt
préima o dop a l'atróv, pu l'è l'istèss,
mo quèsti no, mè a so e' padròun aquè,
no e pu no, a n m'aséugh i ócc, mè, sal mudandi!

che sono di bucato, ma piuttosto facccio / con le mani, come i bambini, un
fazzoletto / prima o dopo lo trovo, poi è lo stesso, / ma questo no, io sono
il padrone qui, / no e poi no, non mi asciugo gli occhi, io, con le mutande!

The Weather's Changing

You can really hear the train, oh my, the weather's changing,
it must be an express, it's running with such fury,
like it's chasing after someone, there must be a big storm coming,
today was so hot, just how many cars does that thing have?
and inside they're all sleeping with those blue lights on, how nice
to be going faraway, but it's not bad either in your own house,
here, at the window, alone, with the sliver of a moon and a starry
sky, is that lightning down there?
and getting that perfume from the mock orange
in the nuns' garden.

E' cambia e' témp

Orca, cm'u s sint e' treno, e' cambia e' témp.
L'à da ès un dirèt, e córr s'na ténga,
e' pèr ch'e' daga dri ma qualcadéun.
Ch' féss dabón 'na buràsca, òz l'è stè un chèld.
Mo quant vaghéun àl mai?
e dréinta i dórma, s' chi lómm bló, pu bén
andè dalòngh, mo u n s sta mèl gnénch' ma chèsa,
aquè, ma la finestra, da par mè,
ch'u i è un féil 'd léuna, u s vaid una starlèda,
e' baléina, alazò?
e da e' zardéin dal sóri e' vén l'udòur
dla filadelfia.

Cambia il tempo. Orca, come si sente il treno, cambia il tempo. / Dev'essere
un diretto, corre con una rabbia, / pare che insegua qualcuno. / Facesse
davvero una burrasca, oggi è stato un caldo. / Ma quanti vagoni ha mai? /
e dentro dormono, con quei lumi blue, che bello / andare lontano, ma non
si sta male neanche a casa, / qui, alla finestra, da solo, / che c'è un filo di
luna, si vede uno stellato, / balena, laggiú? / e dal giardino delle suore viene
il profumo / della filadelfia.

405

Understanding

Yes, I understand, but the thing of it is, so many,
whatever you do you're wrong,
I see it with my own, and you, has yours
already finished? a surveyor? no kidding?
and you're not happy? with an uncle, have you talked to him?
sure, he'll take him, plus just one son, why wouldn't it work out?
as for me, I've got three, and they're all students, the oldest,
Gianluca, wants to be an electrical engineer, we'll see,
it's a long time in school, and the other two, the girl,
okay, a teacher, then she'll get married,
and Massimo, that one, he's a worry, a little,
because, I understand, studying, I was the first
to want them to go to school, if you don't know things,
the ignoramuses in this world today, but at a certain point,
I've got a thriving business, I'm capitalized,
that's the university, how can you learn
any better than that? it's that young people today,
I try to drop hints, if it comes up in the conversation,
they don't understand a thing, they study,
they study, but in practical life,
and Liliana doesn't want to understand this, either,

Capèi

Sè, ò capéi, mo l'è zchéurs che, tanimódi,
cmè t fé t fé mèl, a l vèggh si méi, tè, e' tóvv
l'à zà finéi? geometra? dabón?
ta n si cuntént? s'un zéi che, ta i é zcòurs?
mo sè ch'u l tó, pu un fiúl sno, 's'ut che séa,
e mè ch'i è tréi? e i stéudia tótt, e' grand,
Gianluca, lui vuol fare
l'ingegnere elettronico, avdirémm,
l'è stéudi lóngh, e ch'ilt déu, la burdèla,
li, va bén, mèstra, pu la s spusarà,
e Massimo, quèll, mè, l'è un pó un pensír,
parchè, a capéss, studié, mo a so e' préim mè
ch'a ví ch'i vaga a scóla, s' ta n sé al robi,
òz te mònd i ignurènt, però a un zért péunt,
ò un esercéizi inviéd, mè, un capitèl,
quèlla l'è l'università, cumè,
mo mèi d'alè? l'è che i zóvan adès,
mè a próv da buté i lèmp, s'e' vén e' zcòurs,
i n capéss mégga gnént, i stéudia, i stéudia,
mo nella vita pratica,
e la Liliana ch' la n la vó capéi

Capire. Sí, ho capito, ma sono discorsi che, tanto, / come fai fai male, lo vedo
coi miei, tu, il tuo / ha già finito? geometra? davvero? / non sei contento?
con uno zio che, gli hai parlato? / ma sí che lo prende, poi un figlio solo,
cosa vuoi che sia, / e io, che sono tre, e studiano tutti, il grande, / Gianluca,
lui vuol fare l'ingegnere elettronico, vedremo, / sono studi lunghi, e gli altri
due, la bambina, / lei, va bene, maestra, poi si sposerà, / e Massimo, quello,
io è un pó un pensiero, / perché, capisco, studiare, ma sono il primo io / che
voglio che vadano a scuola, se non sai le cose, / oggi nel mondo gli ignoranti,
però a un certo punto, / ho un esercizio avviato, io, un capitale, / quella è
l'università, come, / ma meglio di lí? è che i giovani adesso, / io provo a far
qualche accenno, se viene il discorso, / non capiscono mica niente, studiano,
studiano, / ma nella vita pratica, / e la Liliana che non la vuol capire /

she says that if Massimo doesn't want
to become a butcher, you know I'd like to go
dancing too, if only you could do whatever
you wanted in this world,
but, there, she was in agreement,
every once in awhile, no big deal, send him down
to give me a hand, he's fifteen years old, I slip him
a few bucks, a few more, and after awhile,
he sees the money flowing, he gets the feel of it,
what's it take to understand this?
these walls are bought and paid for,
it's a kind of work where no one bosses you around,
you're in charge, they're all yours,
it's that even with Liliana, last year, with that motorcycle,
which I didn't want, but she said: they've all got them, Gianluca
can't be inferior to them, and so I had to buy him one,
which he never uses,
even him, I don't know, I, I don't understand him,
always with the long face, he can only say I'm wrong,
everything is one big mistake, now he's saying
they want to put cars in the Piazza Grande,
they're thinking about
doing it at night, and putting a parking lot there by the Mulini,
which who's going to come up here afterwards to go shopping?
they must be imbeciles, but you can't tell him that,
"Dad, you're not getting it,"
it seems like I'm hearing him,
but what is there to understand?
they're all riding around in Mercedes
even to go take a piss,
and those other two always telling him he's right,
two snot-nosed brats, what do you expect me to say?

gnénca li, dis se Massimo u n'i pis
da fè e' mazlèr, mo ènca mu mè u m pieséva
d'andè a balè, se te mònd u s putéss
fè sémpra quèll ch'e' pis,
che invíci, alè, se li la fóss d'acórd,
d'ogni tènt, cumè gnént, la l manda ad sòtta
a dèm 'na mèna, l'à quéngg an, mè a i slòngh
dismélla frènch, vintmélla, e dop un pó,
e' vaid ch'e' córr e' bòch, u i ciapa góst,
mo cs'èll ch'u i vó a capéila? i méur l'è i méi,
l'è un lavòur quèll che sòura
ta n'é niseun, t cmand tè, l'è tótt i tóvv,
l'è che ènca la Liliana, an, s' che mutòur,
che mè a n vléva, mo li: i l'à tótt, Gianluca
u n'à da stè da mènch, e agli ò cnú tó,
ch'u n'i va mai,
ènca léu, a n'e' so, mè, a n'e' capéss,
l'à sémpra un méus, l'è sno bón 'd dí ch'a sbai,
l'è tótt un sbai, mè, adès in Piaza Granda
dis ch'i vó cavè al màchini, i li pensa
la nòta, e fè un parchègg dlà di Muléin,
che quasò dop chi ch' vén a fè la spàisa?
i sarà pò imbezéll, mo a n'e' pòs déi,

nemmeno lei, dice se Massimo non gli piace / fare il macellaio, ma anche a me mi piaceva / andare a ballare, se nel mondo si potesse, / far sempre quel che piace, / che invece, lí, se fosse d'accordo, / ogni tanto, come niente, lo manda di sotto / a darmi una mano, ha quindici anni, io gli allungo / diecimila lire, ventimila, e dopo un po', / vede che corre il soldo, ci prende gusto, / ma cosa ci vuole a capirla? i muri sono i miei, / è un lavoro quello che sopra / non hai nessuno, commandi tu, sono tutti i tuoi, / è che anche la Liliana, l'anno scorso, con quella moto, / che io non volevo, ma lei: l'hanno tutti, Gianluca / non deve star da meno, e gliel'ho dovuta comprare, / che non ci va mai, / anche lui, non lo so, io, non lo capisco, / ha sempre un muso, è solo capace di dire che sbaglio, / io, è tutto uno sbaglio, adesso in Piazza Grande / dice che vogliono cavare le machine, le pensano / di notte, e fare un parcheggio di là dai Mulini, / che quassú dopo chi viene a fare la spesa? / saranno pure imbecilli, ma non lo posso dire, /

that you don't know anything,
what are they teaching you at school with all those books,
that your father's an idiot? and they laugh,
and their mother: why are you getting upset?
I'm supposed to laugh along with them? the day's going to come
when I'm going to lose my patience,
and then, I know it, I'll be sorry,
because on top of it this boy, the teachers,
the commendations, he's in the top, he's got a passion for it,
but if he can contradict me,
he's angry with me, what did I do to him?
there are days when he wanders around the house
like a soul in torment,
his mother, we'll talk about it later, he confides in her:
I feel all alone, a boy seventeen years old,
well go out where there are people!
and it's exhausting even to talk, we don't see each other much,
I've got to be in the shop, if we're all together
at the table, of course, there's no way of it happening,
they wolf it down, where do you have to be going off to?
and there's always the radio, they keep it loud,
it's a zoo, then that's not enough,
one of them gets up, turns on the television,

"Tu, babbo, non capisci", u m pèr 'd sintéil,
mo csa i èll da capèi? ch'i va in Mercedes
ènca a pisé, e ch'ilt déu ch'i i dà rasòun,
du murgantéun, csa vliv savài vuílt,
ch'a n savì gnént,
csa v'inségni tal scóli, tótt chi léibar,
che è vòst bà l'è un pataca? e lòu i réid,
e la su mà: mo cs'èll che ta t a la aciàp?
ò da réid ènca mè? che un dè o ch'èlt
e' va a finéi ch'u m scapa la pazinzia,
e dop, a l so, u m dispís,
parchè pu sté burdèl, i profeséur,
i elogi, l'è tra i préim, mo una pasiòun,
però s'u m pò dè còuntra,
u la à sa mè, che mè, cs'èll ch'a i ò fat?
u i è di dè ch'e' zéira par la chèsa
cmè un'anma in pena,
la su mà, pu a zcurémm, sa li u s cunféida:
mi sento solo, un ragàz 'd dissèt an,
mo va dò ch'u i è la zénta!
l'è ch' l'è fadéiga ènca' zcòrr, a s'avdémm póch,
mè a chin stè tla butàiga, ma la tèvla,
ch'u s'è 'lè tótt insén, mo u n gn'è mai mèzi,

"Tu, babbo, non capisci," mi par di sentirlo, / ma cosa c'è da capire? che
vanno in Mercedes / anche a pisciare, e quegli altri due che gli danno
ragione, / due mocciosi, cosa volete sapere voialtri, / che non sapete niente,
/ cosa v'insegnano a scuola, tutti quei libri, / che vostro padre è un coglione?
e loro ridono, / e la loro mamma: ma cosa te la prendi? / devo ridere
anch'io? che un giorno o l'altro / va a finire che mi scappa la pazienza, / e
dopo, lo so, mi dispiace, / perché poi 'sto ragazzo, i professori, / gli elogi, è
tra i primi, ma una passione, / però se mi può contraddire, / ce l'ha con me,
che io, cosa gli ho fatto? / ci sono dei giorni che gira per la casa / come
un'anima in pena, / sua madre, poi parliamo, con lei si confida: mi sento
solo, un ragazzo di diciassette anni, / ma vai dove c'è la gente! / è che è
fatica anche parlare, ci vediamo poco, / io devo stare in bottega, a tavola, /
che si è lí tutti assieme, ma non c'è mai modo, /

411

turn it off! no, you turn it off! could you please just knock if off?
you can't take it anymore, and on top of it, this
is a good corner, but for living,
the trucks, the off-ramp, and now just listen to these people,
a wedding, you'll go deaf, oh go jump in the lake
and blow your horns there, it's bad enough
it's so blasted hot,
windows open, of course, it makes me raise my voice,
and she's looking at me: "Are you angry?" "No, I was just

[saying,"
"I didn't understand, what?" "Nothing, it doesn't matter,"
"You see, you are angry, whatever you say you are,"
"I am not angry!"
"But you're yelling," "I am not yelling!
All I'm saying is that no one around here understands anything
about anything."

i magna a pidriúl, duv'ív d'andè?
e u i è sémpra cla radio, i la tén èlta,
una boba, pu u n basta,
éun e' sta sò, e' zènd la televisiòun,
smórta! no, smórta tè! vliv lasè è 'ndè?
ch'u n s chèmpa, tra che què,
e' sarà un bèl cantòun, mo avaii la chèsa,
i camion, s' che rapètt, e adès sint quést,
un spusaléizi, i t'inzurléss, mo andé
te fiómm a strumbitè, zà ch' l'è ènca un chèld,
finestri vérti, u m tòcca alzè la vòusa,
che li la m guèrda: "T si incaplèd?", "No a géva",
"A n'ò capéi, cumè?", "Gnént, l'è l'istèss",
"Vitt, t si incaplèd, però acsè", "A n so incaplèd!",
"Mo t fé di rógg", "A n rógg!
a déggh sno ch'u n s capéss un azidént!"

mangiamo a imbuto, dove dovete andare? / e c'è sempre quella radio, la tengono alta, / un baccano, poi non basta, / uno si alza, accende la televisione, / spegni! no, spegni tu! volete smetterla? / che non si campa, già che qui, / sarà un bell'angolo, ma averci la casa, / i camion, su quella rampa, e adesso senti questi, / un matrimonio, ti assordano, ma andate / nel fiume a strombettare, già che è anche un caldo, / finestre aperte, mi tocca alzar la voce, / che lei mi guarda: "Sei arrabbiato?", "No, dicevo", / "Non ho capito, come?", "Niente, è lo stesso", / "Vedi, sei arrabbiato, però così"," "Non sono arrabbiato!" / "Ma fai degli urli", "Non urlo!" dico solo che non si capisce un accidente!"

413

Putting on Airs

Tell me he wasn't putting on airs, Libero, the teacher's son,
even the way he'd blow his nose,
you'd have to have seen it, with that handkerchief he kept
in his back pocket, he'd open it, linen,
white, he'd shake it out, spread out his hands underneath it,
balance it like a tray, then all of a sudden,
throw his head way back,
still with both hands, all right all ready just do it,
as if he's got all the time in the world,
and all of us watching intently,
it's not for nothing that they called him, "King,"
then with a finger, a sputtering, then he's perfectly still,
a movement? a thought?
all you could see were his eyes, then down slowly,
hands together,
it looked like he'd just taken communion,
he'd open his eyes, just a slit, a quick look,
he'd get it perfectly set up again, two or three wipes
between mouth and nose, nothing, just a dab,
over and done, put it back in his pocket,
pat it with his hand ever so gently,
like a compress. Then, he'd light up a menthol.

Pacòun

S'u n'era pacòun Libero dla mèstra,
sno cm'u s sufiéva e' nès,
bsugnéva vdai, s' che fazulètt, u l tnéva
tla bascòza di dri, u l'arvéva, ad léin,
biènch, u l féva balè sal mèni sòtta,
cmè un gabarè, pu ad scat, testa d'indrí,
sémpra sa tutt' do al mèni, strènz e mòla,
al canèli al sunéva, e néun tótt séri,
amo i l ciaméva "e' rè",
e pu sal dàidi, un s-ciuptadézz, pu férum,
un mumént, un pensír?
u s'i avdéva sno i ócc, pu zò pianín,
a mèni unéidi,
e' pareva ch' l'éss fat la cumagnòun,
l'arvéva, una fiséura, sno un'ucèda,
u l radanéva, u s déva do tre boti
tra bòcca e nès, gnént, un'incipriéda,
finito, u s l'armitéva tla bascòza,
u l palpéva sla mèna, mo lizír,
cmè un impàch. Pu e' zandéva una Mentola.

Arie. Se non si dava delle arie Libero della maestra, / solo come si soffiava il naso, / bisognava vedere, con quel fazzoletto, lo teneva / nella tasca di dietro, lo apriva, di lino, / bianco, lo faceva ballare con le mani sotto, / come un vassoio, poi di scatto, testa all'indietro, / sempre con tutt' e due le mani, stringi e molla, / le canne suonavano, e noi tutti seri, non per niente lo chiamavano "il re", / e poi con le dita, uno scoppiettio, poi fermo, / un momento, un pensiero? / gli si vedevano solo gli occhi, poi giú piano, / a mani unite, / pareva che avesse fatto la comunione, / apriva, uno spiraglio, solo un'occhiata, / lo riordinava, si dava due tre colpetti / tra bocca e naso, niente, un'incipriata, / finito, se lo rimetteva in tasca, / lo palpava con la mano, ma leggero, / come un impacco. Poi accendeva una Mentola.

Drenched

for Fabien Giraud

Somewhere along the way it got cloudy.
At San Bartolo, it started to rain. I was pedaling hard.
My pants had motor oil on them, I didn't even consider
it might be from the chain. I was a mess, and soaked
to the bone. My hair. I felt it rolling down my neck. My shirt
was stuck to my skin. Sleet. At Pozzo Lungo, I got off.
I walked uphill, hunched over, gripping the handlebars.
Through puddles. It was all mud. Every so often one of the tires
flicked a piece of gravel. I cursed. I looked up. And there
on Nina di Scòccia's outcrop, I saw standing, all nestled in together,
some sheep, in grass, in the middle of the downpour,
completely still, like stones.

Mòl

E par la strèda u s'è nuvlé, a San Bèrtal
l'à tach a pióv, pedèla pò, i calzéun,
ch'u n gn'éva péns, sl'untómm, ma la cadéina,
a m séra sasiné,
e mòl pléin, i cavéll, a la sintéva
culè zò ma la còppa, e la caméisa
sla pèla, giaza,
me Pòzza Lòngh a so smòunt, andéva sò,
a testa basa, agrapèd me manubrio,
tra 'l piscòlli, e una mèlta,
mo butéi un pó 'd brèssa d'ogni tènt!
a biastméva, ò alzè i ócc, e ò vést se grèpp
dla Nina ad Scòcia, sòtta l'aqua, al stéva
alè arguglédi,
dal pigri, tl'érba, férmi, cmè di sas.

Bagnato. E per la strada s'è annuvolato, a San Bartolo / ha cominciato a
piovere, pedala pure, i calzoni, / che non ci avevo pensato, con l'unto, alla
catena, / mi ero rovinato, / e mollo fradicio, i capelli, la sentivo / colar giú
alla nuca, e la camicia / sulla pelle, ghiaccia, / al Pozzo Lungo sono sceso,
andavo su / a testa bassa, aggrappato al manubrio, / tra le pozzanghere, e un
fango, / ma buttateci un po' di ghiaia ogni tanto! / bestemmiavo, ho alzato
gli occhi, e ho visto sul greppo / della Nina di Scòcia, sotto l'acqua, stavano
/ lí accoccolate, / delle peccore, nell'erba, ferme, come dei sassi.

417

Driver's License

"Who's that they're carrying away?
with the town banner? Gianín Padoia?"
"Gianín died? I just saw him, when did this happen?
What was he sick with?" "Nothing, he was shaving,
Wednesday morning, and in two minutes,"
"But even going like that," "It's better isn't? without
suffering,"
"Poor Gianín, he wasn't working on all cylinders,"
"No people, no flowers, and now there's just three,
and that's without counting him."
"He did have those periods when he came out of it, every
once in a while,"
"It depended on the moon,"   "Do you remember when he
tried
the grape-cure, they said a monk from Casale gave it to him,
he ate them, then a lot of lemonade,
can you imagine, grapes, his wife ended up
having to call the doctor."
"He was a good guy, but he drove her crazy."
"It's not having kids."
"Should we walk down that way too?"
"As far as the Mulini."
"And that time he got it into his head
to get a license?

La patenta

"Chi ch' l'è ch'i pórta véa
se stendèrd de Cuméun? Gianín 'd Padòia",
"L'è mort Gianín? ch'a l'ò vést, quant l'è stè?",
"Cs'èll ch' l'éva?", "Gnént, l'era dri a fès la bèrba,
mircal matéina, e in du minéut", "Però
ènca acsè", "Mo u n'è mèi? senza patéi",
"Póri Gianín, léu fura 'd che gabiòt",
"Zénta póca, fiéur gnént, che adès i è in tréi
e i n fa mènca ch' nè léu",
"L'éva ènca all su scapèdi, d'ogni tènt",
"Sgònd la léuna", "Ta t'arcórd quant l'à fat
la chéura dl'óvva, dis ch'u gli éva détt
un frè 'd Casèl,
mo u n n'à magnè, dop dal gran limunèdi,
t si mat, l'óvva, e pu tl'éultum la su mòi
la à cnú ciamè e' dutòur",
"L'era bón, mo u la à fata dvantè mata",
"L'è che quant u n gn'è i fiúl",
"Andémm zò un pó ènca néun?", "Fina i Muléin",
"Mo e cla vólta ch'u s'era mèss tla testa
da ciapè la patenta?

La patente. "Chi portano via / con lo stendardo del Comune? Giannino di Padoia?", / "E morto Giannino? che l'ho visto, quand'è stato?", / "Cos'aveva?", "Niente, si stava facendo la barba, / mercoledí mattina, e in due minuti", "Però / anche cosí", "Ma non è meglio? senza patire", / "Povero Giannino, lui fuori di quel gabbiotto", / "Gente poca, fiori niente, che adesso sono in tre / e ne fanno meno di lui", / "Aveva anche le sue uscite, ogni tanto", / "Secondo la luna", "Ti ricordi quando ha fatto / la cura dell'uva, dice che gliel'aveva detto / un frate di Casale, / ma ne ha mangiata, dopo delle gran limonate, / te l'immagini, l'uva, e poi alla fine sua moglie / ha dovuto chiamare il dottore", / "Era buono, ma l'ha fatta diventar matta", / "È che quando non ci sono figli", / "Andiamo giú un pó anche noi?", "Fino ai Mulini", / "Ma, e quella volta anche s'era messo in testa / di prendere la patente?

419

he was over fifty, then with that bad leg,
he hadn't even served in the military,"
"And without saying anything," "It was a little that he was
[ashamed,"
"But with me, who knows, I never asked him anything,"
and one evening at Gioti's
it was him who jumped into the conversation: I want to
[travel,
he was laughing, I want to go see Marsilio,
my brother-in-law, I'll just show up at his door,"
"Hey, is it raining?" "It's nothing, just a few drops,"
"That must have been a real blow,"
"Even there, when you've taken the test three times,
after the fourth, people are going to start to laugh,"
"Just putting yourself through it,"
come on, with all the driving rules,
if you're not a kid is there any way you're going to know them?
"But he never knew anything, did he, poor guy,"
"That you can get around just as well on foot, why make
[yourself miserable?"
"Well now he knows everything."
"Should we turn around?"

a zinquènt'an sunèd, pu sa cla gamba
ch'u n'éva fat gnénca, e' suldè, mè a déggh-che",
"E tótt da zétt", "Amo un pó u s vargugnéva",
"Però sa me, chi sa, a n gn'ò mai dmand gnént,
e una sàira da Gioti
l'è stè léu ch' l'è vnú in zcòurs: a ví viazè,
e' ridéva, a ví 'ndè truvè Marsiglio,
e' mi cugnèd, i a faz 'n'improvisèda",
"Ció, e' pióv?", "Mo gnént, du gózzal",
"Zért che quèll l'è stè un smach",
"Ench 'lè, quant t'é dè l'esèm tre vólti,
a la quèrta la zénta dop i réid",
"Mo gnènca mèttsi, dài, sa tótt chi cmand,
s' ta n si un burdlàz, u n l'éva da savài?"
"Mo u n'à mai savú gnént, léu, zò, purètt",
"Ch'u s va piò bén a pi, 's'ut bazilé",
"E adès e' sa iniquèl",
                                        "Turnémma indri?"

a cinquant'anni suonati, poi con quella gamba, / che non aveva fatto neanche
il miltare, io dico che", / "E tutto in silenzio", "Ma un po' si vergognava",
/ "Però con me, chi sa, non gli ho mai domandato niente, / e una sera da
Gioti / è stato lui che è venuto in discorso: voglio viaggiare, / rideva, voglio
andare a trovare Marsilio, mio cognato, gli faccio un'improvvisata", / "Ehi,
piove? "Ma niente, due gocce", / "Certo che quello è stato uno smacco", /
"Anche lí, quando ha dato l'esame tre volte, / alla quarta la gente dopo ride",
/ "Ma neanche mettercisi, dai, con tutti quei comandi, / se non se un
ragazzo, non doveva saperlo?", / "Ma non ha mai saputo, lui, poveretto,"/
"Che si va cosí bene a piedi, cosa vuoi tribolare", / "E adesso sa tutto", –
"Beh, torniamo?"

Sick Bed

This cough, this cough, come here,
come here, do you see? gunk,
in bed, now, I'll make you something hot,
then a good sweat.
Fine, in bed, good, look at your knees,
get under, come on now, quick, I need
to get
over there. What's going on here,
how sick do you have to be before you go to bed,
do I have to climb in there too? look, bare feet,
on the floor, what are you looking for?
I'll get it, I'll get it for you, licorice,
it's going to make you thirsty, get in bed,
feel your feet, the blood's not circulating,
and your teeth are chattering, do you want to get really sick?
the milk's boiling over now, my gosh, all because I've got to be
two places at once
with you, who never obeys, it's because I've had enough,
I'm coming right now, don't move, all because you can't behave
for one minute. Here, it's hot, where are you,
even his head's under now, come out, don't make me stand
                                                    here,
it'll get cold, sit up, I put in honey,
taste it and see if it isn't good, this is better than medicine,

E' litòun

L'è una tòsa, mè, quèsta, vén aquè,
vén aquè, vitt, e' scòta,
a lèt, svélti, ch'a t faz 'na roba chèlda,
pu una bèla sudéda.
E va bén, te litòun, vèrda ch znòci,
va sòtta, dài, fa prèst, ch'ò d'andè dlà.
Mo cs'èll ch'e' fa, quant u i vól andè lèt,
ò d'avní mè? vèrdal, alè, a pi néud
se sulèr, cs'èll ch t zirch?
a t la dagh mè, a t la dagh, la riguléizia,
che dop la t fa vní sàida, va te lèt,
sint chi pi, i taia,
e e' bat i dent, ta t vu malè dabón?
orca, e adlà e' lat e' vòunta, par stè què,
sa tè ch' ta n fé mai mód, l'è che s'a m stóff,
a véngh sóbit, nu t móv, ch' ta n pòsa stè
bón un minéut. Ecco, l'è chèld, dú sit?
l'è 'ndè sòtta ènch' sla testa,
vén fura, dài, nu fam stè què d'impí,
ch'u s'agiàza, zò, ch'a i ò mèss e' mél,
sint pu bón, quèst l'è mèi d'na midizéina,

Il lettone. È una tosse questa io, vieni qui, / vieni qui, vedi? scotta, / a letto,
presto, che ti faccio una cosa calda, / poi una bella sudata. / E va bene, nel
lettone, guarda che ginocchi, / va' sotto, dai, fa' svelto, che devo andare di
là. / Ma cosa fa, quanto ci vuole ad andare a letto, / devo venire io?
guardalo, a piedi nudi, / sul pavimento, cosa cerchi? / te la do io, la
liquerizia, che dopo ti fa venir sete, vai a letto, / senti che piedi, tagliano, /
e batte i denti, ti vuoi ammalare sul serio? / orca, di là il latte trabocca, per
star qui, / con te che non obbedisci mai, è che se mi stufo, / vengo subito,
non ti muovere, che tu non possa star / buono un minuto. Ecco è caldo,
dove sei? / è andato sotto anche con la testa, / vieni fuori, dai, non farmi
stare in piede, / che si fredda, su, che ci ho messo il miele, / senti che buono,
questo è meglio di una medicina, /

oh I am trying to be patient,
are you trying to suffocate there underneath?
that's enough now,
get under these covers, and sit still, listen to me right now,
I'm telling you, thirty-nine years old, look at those
eyes, what are you laughing about? you're happy now aren't you?

oh, che pazínzia!
ta t tu fughè alè sòtta? adès e' basta,
zò stal cvérti, e sta férum, fam sintéi,
mè a déggh ch' l'à trentanóv, vè ch du ócc
da birichéin, csa réidti, t si cuntént?

oh, che pazienza! / vuoi soffocarti lí sotto? adesso basta, / giú queste
coperte, e sta' fermo, fammi sentire, / io dico che ha trentanove, ve' che due
occhi / da birichino, cosa ridi, sei contento?

The Saint

So. I believe, I believe in it, in a something,
and I'm not ashamed, but I'm not at all claiming,
I, people, as far as I'm concerned, each one has got to do
however one feels about it, according to one's conscience,
we're not living in the old days anymore, I'm just saying
when I hear certain discussions, arguing otherwise,
what's there to discuss, it's merely one opinion,
I don't agree, then let it rest, have respect,
that it is a mystery as well, if you ask me
what I feel, I don't know,
but when I'm in church, the priests
have got nothing to do with it,
how can I put it? it is our common religion,
but I'm not some bigot, I go there,
you're not going to believe me but six days ago,
one afternoon, I passed by, I say, I'm going to stop,
in the Collegiata, and inside it was cool,
Peppino was in there sweeping, I was standing,
quiet, in that half-light,
and the thought came to me there,
I know it's present in every place,
but in church, and you, you really have it in for the priests,
of course they make mistakes too,
they're human just like the rest of us,

E' sènt

Ció, mè a i craid, io ci credo, in un qualcosa,
e a n mu n vargògn, mo non pretendo mica,
mè, la zénta, par mè, i à da fè ognéun
come si sente, sgònd la su coscienza,
a n sémm piò témp d'na vólta, mè a déggh sno,
quant a sint zért dischéurs fat a l'arvérsa,
mo 's'ut dischéut, è un sentimento quello,
ta n'e' cnòss, lasa stè, pórta rispèt,
ch'è anche un mistero, s' ta m'e' dmand mu mè,
quèll ch'a sint, a n'e' so,
mè quant a so tla cisa, u n gn'éintra i prit,
csa vól déi, è la nòstra religione,
mo a n so bigòt, mè, a i vagh,
te ta n mu n cridaré, si sèt dè fa,
un dopmezdè, a paséva, ò détt: a m férum,
tla Colegèta, e dréinta un frèsch, Pepino
l'era dri ch'e' spazéva, mè d'impí,
da zétt, at cla penòmbra,
e lí il pensiero, a l so ch'è in ogni luogo,
mo però in chiesa, e tè dàila si prit,
zért ch'i sbàia ènca lòu,

Il santo. Insomma, io ci credo, in un qualcosa, / e non mi vergogno, ma non pretendo mica, / io, la gente, per me, devono fare ognuno / come si sente, secondo la sua coscienza, / non siamo piú ai tempi d'una volta, io dico solo, / quando sento certi discorsi fatti alla rovescia, / ma cosa vuoi discutere, è un sentimento quello, / non lo conosci, lasica stare, porta rispetto, / che è anche un mistero, se me lo domandi a me / quello che sento, non lo so, / io quando sono in chiesa, non c'entrano i preti, / cosa vuol dire? è la nostra religione, / ma non sono un bigotto, io, ci vado, / tu non mi crederai, sei sette giorni fa, / un pomeriggio, passavo, ho detto: mi fermo, / nella Collegiata, e dentro un fresco, Peppino / stava spazzando, io in piedi, / zitto, in quella penombra, / e lí il pensiero, lo so ch'è in ogni luogo, / ma però in chiesa, e tu dagliela coi preti, / certo che sbagliano anche loro, /

why? you think we never make mistakes? this is a world
where we should all be brothers, love one another,
as one's self, but
don't you see the injustice, the egotism,
the cruelty, we are never content,
which makes me think sometimes,
if you're right
that it all ends here, how can that be, so then
the ones with power always win?
robbing, killing, it's bad enough they never get caught,
if up above us there is no one,
haven't you ever looked up there?
all those stars, millions,
these infinite worlds, come on, up there,
a supreme being, there's got to be,
who created them, it's not just me who believes in it,
there's lots, professors, important scientists,
you know more than they do? prove it,
stand there with one hand open, stay put for years,
hand still open, what will grow there, two balls, that's what,
nothing plus nothing still makes nothing, one needs a God,
just one breath, and life is born,
and here we are, trials and tribulations, for me,

sono esseri umani come noi,
parchè, néun a n sbaiémm? che quèst l'è un mònd
ch'a duvrésmi ès fradéll, volerci bene
uno con l'altro, invíci,
non vedi l'inguistizia, l'egoéisum,
la cativéria, ch'a n sémm mai cuntént,
che mè dal vólti a i péns, s' t'éss rasòun tè
ch'e' finéss tótt aquè, cumè, mo 'lòura
i à d'avài rasòun sémpra i prepotent?
rubé, mazè, basta sno no fès zcruv,
se al di sopra di noi non c'è nessuno,
mo tè la nòta ta n guèrd mai d'insò?
tótt' cal stèli, migliéun,
questi mondi infiniti, andémma, zò,
un essere supremo u i à da ès,
che li ha creati, a n so sno mè ch'a i craid,
u i n'è tint, profeséur, grandi scienzati,
ta n sé piò tè ch' nè lòu? mo fa la próva,
sta s'una mèna vérta, sta 'lè di an,
sémpra vérta, csa crèssal? du quaiéun,
gnént piò gnént e' dà gnént, ci vuole un Dio,
che basta un sóffi, ed è nata la vita,
e a sémm aquè ch'à bazilémm, che mè,

sono esseri umani come noi, / perché, noi non sbagliamo? che questo è un mondo / che dovremmo essere fratelli, volerci bene / l'uno con l'altro, invece, / non vedi l'ingiustizia, l'egoismo, / la cattiveria, che non siamo mai contenti, / che io delle volte ci penso, se avessi ragione tu / che finisce tutto qui, come, ma allora / devono aver ragione sempre i prepotenti? / rubare, ammazzare, basta solo non farsi scoprire, / se al di sopra di noi non c'è nessuno, / ma tu la notte non guardi mai in alto? / tutte quelle stelle, milioni, / questi mondi infiniti, andiamo, su, / un essere supreme ci dev'essere, / che li ha creati, non sono solo io che ci credo, / ce n'è tanti, professori, grandi scienzati, / ne sai piú tu di loro? ma fai la prova, / stai con una mano aperta, stai lí degli anni, / sempre aperta, cosa cresce? due coglioni, / niente piú niente dà niente, ci vuole un Dio, / che basta un soffio, ed è nata la vita, / e siamo qui che triboliamo, che io, /

just listen to this, come on now,
there's a new one every day,
the tax guy came to see me yesterday, they were there
flipping through pages for hours on end,
they made a big Statement,
all over two Invoices,
and he says they were missing the required stamps as well,
try to talk with these people,
you know they have to find something,
all over a couple of bucks, but see,
yesterday evening, I was so wound up,
at home, I was by myself, no, I sent Jolanda
up to the mountains, with Silvana, to Madonna di Campiglio,
she needed to relax, after what had happened,
and well, you know, four hours under the knife,
because that night, there was no sign, we'd eaten
spaghetti in a white sauce,
clams, some pickled mackerel,
we'd watched television too, then bed,
and at a certain point I hear: "Carlo, I'm sick."
"Indigestion?" "There's a stabbing. Here."
"Do you have to go to the bathroom?" what else could you say,
at eleven she was fine, then I turned on the light
and I understood immediately, I called Giunchi,
straight to the hospital, one hour later

'ta bón, va là, u i n'è óna tótt i dè,
u m'è vnéu la finènza ir, i è stè 'lè
a scartablè dagli òuri,
i à fat un gran verbèl, par do fatéuri,
e dis ch'u i amanchéva ènca dal bòlli,
va a zcòrr sa lòu,
tanimódi qualquèl i à da truvè,
u s buscarà du bòch, mo t'avdiré-che,
e irisàira un nervòus,
ma chèsa, da par mè, no, la Jolanda
a la ò manda in muntagna,
sla Silvana, a Madonna di Campiglio,
la s'à da divaghè, dop quèll ch' la à pas,
amo cumè, quatr'òuri sotto i férr,
che cla sàira, mo gnént, émmi magnè,
spaghétt in biènch,
puràzi, du tri sgómbar marinéd,
émm guèrs ènch' la televisiòun, pu a lèt,
e a una zért'òura a sint: "Carlo, a stagh mèl",
"T n'é digeréi", "L'è dal curtlèdi, aquè",
"T'é bsògn d'andè de córp?", ció, 's'ut ch'a géss,
agli óngg la stéva bén, pu ò zais la luce,
e ò capí tótt, ò ciamè Giunchi, via
te bsdèl, e un'òura dop la antréva zà

sta' buono, va' là, ce n'è una tutti i giorni, / m'è venuta la finanza ieri, sono
stati lí / a scartabellare delle ore, / hanno fatto un gran verbale, per due
fatture, / e dice che ci mancavano anche delle bolle, / va' a parlare con loro,
/ tanto qualcosa devono trovare, / si guadagneranno quattro soldi, ma vedrai
che, / e ieri sera un nervoso, / in casa, da solo, no, la Jolanda / l'ho mandata
in montagna, / con la Silvana, a Madonna di Campiglio, / deve svagarsi,
dopo quel che ha passato, / e beh, sai, quattro ore sotto i ferri, / che quella
sera, ma niente, avevamo mangiato / spaghetti in bianco, / vongole, due tre
sgombri marinati, / abbiamo anche guardato la televisione, poi a letto, / e a
una cert'ora sento: "Carlo, sto male", / "Non hai digerito?", "Sono delle
coltellate, qui", / "Hai bisogno d'andare di corpo?", cosa vuoi che dicessi, /
alle undici stava bene, poi ho acceso la luce / e ho capito tutto, ho chiamato
Giunchi, via / all'ospedale, e un'ora dopo entrava già /

431

she was already in the operating room, then Silvana
arrived, crying, it's her mother,
you can imagine, and the two of us, in the hallway,
waiting, how long will it be? what are they doing to her in there?
to my wife? by this time it was morning,
My Lord! Mother of God! in these moments
I don't know how those who don't believe get through it,
it is a need, to address someone,
that you are in his hands, he can help you out,
because Alessandri, I can't say enough good things about him,
but his words, when he came out, he said:
"This is a miracle, if the delay
had been three minutes longer," and I started crying,
right there, and laughing,
if it hadn't burst, but I understood a lot after those things,
that this mortal life, when it's all said and done, nothing's ever
[enough,
and we, whatever it is we believe in,
all our ambitions, for what?
we are holding on by a thread.

because in the hospital I saw Nandi, I didn't recognize him,
he'd gone down to have X-rays taken, we talked and then
saying goodbye he squeezed my hand,

tla sèla operatória, ch' l'è rivàt'
la Silvana, t'un piènt, li la su mà,
t si mat, e alè nun déu, 't che curidéur,
a spitè, quant u i vó? csa i fai adlà
ma la mi mòi? l'era bèla matéina,
Madòna! Signuréin! at chi mumént,
mè a n'e' so cmè ch'i fa quéi ch'i n'i craid,
è un bisogno, rivolgersi a qualcuno,
che sei nelle sue mani, u t pò 'iuté,
parchè Alesandri, brèv e sol che brèv,
mo al su paróli, quant l'è scap, l'à détt:
"Questo è stato un miracolo, che se
tardava tre minuti", e mè alè ò tach
a piànz, a réid, una nòta cmè quèlla,
s'a n so s-ciòp, mo ò capéi tènt' ad cal robi,
che questa vita, in fondo e' basta gnént,
e néun ch'a s cridémm d'ès,
tótt' la nòsta imbiziòun, mo da fè chè?
siamo tacati a un filo,

che te bsdèl ò vést Nandi, a n l'ò 'rcunséu,
l'andéva zò a fè i raggi, émm zcòurs, e pu
te salutém u m'à tnú strètt' la mèna,

in sala operatoria, che è arrivata / la Silvana, in un pianto, lei sua madre, / figurarsi, e lí noi due, in quel corridoio, / ad aspettare, quanto ci vuole? cosa le fanno di là / a mia moglie? era ormai mattina, / Signore! Madonnina! in quei momenti, / non lo so come fanno quelli che non ci credono, / è un bisogno, rivolgersi a qualcuno, / che se nelle sue mani, ti può aiutare, / perché Alessandri, bravo e piú che bravo, / ma le sue parole, quando è uscito, ha detto: / "Questo è stato un miracolo, che se / tardava tre minuti", e io lí ho cominciato / a piangere, a ridere, una notte come quella, / se non sono scoppiato, ma ho capito tante di quelle cose, / che questa vita, in fondo, basta niente, / e noi che ci crediamo d'essere, / tutta la nostra ambizione, ma da far che? / siamo attaccati a un filo, // che nell'ospedale ho visto Nandi, non l'ho riconosciuto, / andava giú a fare i raggi, abbiamo parlato, e poi / nel salutarmi m'ha tenuta stretta la mano, /

without looking at me: "But fifty's
a little early," and he went away with the nurse,
I didn't know how to answer him, and then during the night,
those words, I thought about them,
because he, yeah, a real wheeler-dealer, true, but everyone
likes money, let's be honest, plus with deals,
if you don't do it someone else will,
he'd bought out Cecchi months ago,
and now even Armanda, alone,
a woman, we were talking the other day
about Paolino Campidelli, he goes strictly by the books,
and he ends up in that living hell, in that case instead,
but this is not the time, with that boy,
who he bragged about, think about that, then try to
understand,
it's that they have too much, but it's not all their fault either,
his mother, all he had to do was ask her,
and his head, or was it someone he associated with,
one year? it must be two by now,
and he doesn't write, nothing,
they don't hear a single thing,
it's as if he's dead,
and I know him well, Paolino, when I needed some help,
he always worked hard, he never screwed
anyone, why then is he castigated
in this way? I don't know, but even yesterday evening,

senza guardèm: "Però a zinquètun'an
l'è un pó prèst", e l'è 'ndè véa sl'infermír,
che mè a n gn'ò savú 'rspònd, e dop la nòta,
cal paróli, a i ò péns,
parchè léu, sè, afarésta, mo i baócch
i i pis ma tótt, andémma, pu i afèri
s' ta n'i fé tè u i fa un èlt,
ch' l'éva còmpar da Cecchi si méis fa,
e adès ènca l'Armanda, da par li,
'na dòna, ch'a zcurémmi l'altredè
ad Palín Campidèli, léu l'è strètt,
e pu alazò a l'inféran, alè invíci,
mo adès u n'è e' mumént, sa che burdèl,
ch'u s stiméva, fighéurt, pu, va a capéi,
l'è ch'i à trop, u n'è gnénca còulpa sóvva,
la su mà, léu bastéva ch'e' dmandéss,
e tla su testa, o l'è stè qualch' cumpàgn,
un an? i è bèla déu,
e u n scréiv, gnént, u n s sa gnént, è come morto,
ch'a l cnòss bén, mè, Palín, quant ò vú bsògn,
l'à sémpra lavurè, u n'à mai freghè
niseun, e parchè 'lòura castighél
at sté módi? a n'e' so, mo ènca irisàira,

senza guardarmi: "Però a cinquantun anni / è un po' presto", ed è andato via
con l'infermiere, / che io non ho saputo rispondergli, e dopo, la notte, /
quelle parole, ci ho pensato, / perché lui, sí, affarista, ma i soldi / piacciono
a tutti, andiamo, poi gli affari / se non li fai tu li fa un altro, / che aveva
comprato da Cecchi sei mesi fa, / e adesso anche l'Armanda, da sola / una
donna, che parlavamo l'altro giorno / di Paolino Campidelli, lui è stretto, /
e poi laggiú all'inferno, lí invece, / ma adesso non è il momento, con quel
ragazzo, / che si vantava, figurarsi, poi va' a capire, / è che hanno troppo,
non è nemmeno colpa loro, / sua madre, lui bastava che chiedesse, / e nella
sua testa, o è stato qualche compagno, / un anno? sono ormai due, / e non
scrive, niente, non si sa niente, è come morto, / che lo conosco bene, io,
Paolino, quando ho avuto bisogno, / ha sempre lavorato, non ha mai fregato
/ nessuno, e perché allora castigarlo / in questo modo? non lo so, ma anche
ieri sera, /

435

that girl, who I'd passed
just five minutes before,
they went right up on the sidewalk, killed instantly,
what wrong could she have done?
I know, they're questions,
but I see certain things,
which is a sin, I know, but if there is a God,
which even if there isn't, all of my masses, communions,
but it's not just me, all those who go to church,
all those lit candles,
all the churches, how many of them are there in this world?
beautiful, enormous buildings, for nothing? I, at St. Peter's,
I remember, I got goose bumps,
no, you need a faith,
what are we, animals? are we donkeys?
we each have a brain, we make use of it,
there's got to be a reason, a basis,
which we don't get right now,
but one day
everything will be understood,
there's got to be a purpose, because if not,
if it doesn't matter,
if this world is just an Instant Lottery,
where if your number comes up you don't even know
if you've won or if you've lost

cla burdèla, ch'a séra pas d'alè
zéinch minéut préima, i la è 'ndèda a tó sò
se marciapí, dis an, mórta se còulp,
che mèl pòla avài fat? a l so, l'è dmandi,
mo mè vdai zérti robi,
che è peccato, lo so, mo se c'è un Dio,
però ènch s'u n gn'è, al mi mèssi, al cumagnòun,
mo no sno mè, tótt quéi ch'i va tla cisa,
tótt cal candàili zàisi,
tótt al cisi quant u i n'è mai te mònd,
bèli, grandi, par gnént? che mè a San Pitar,
a m'arcórd, u m'è vnú la chèrna pléina,
no, una feda ci vuole,
cs'èll ch'a sémm, di animèli? a sémm di brécch?
émm e' zarvèl, druvémmal,
ci sarà una ragione, un fundamént,
che adès a n gn'arivémm, mo però un giorno
u s capirà iniquèl,
u i à da ès un vérs, parchè se no,
s' l'è tótt cumpàgn,
se aquè sté mònd l'è sno una loteréa,
che s'e' vén e' tu nómar ta n sé gnénca
se t'é véint, se t'é pérs. . .

quella bambina, che ero passato di lí / cinque minuti prima, sono andati a prenderla su / sul marciapiede, dieci anni, morta sul colpo, / che male può aver fatto? lo so, sono domande, / ma io a vedere certe cose, / che è peccato, lo so, ma se c'è un Dio, / però anche se non c'è, le mie messe, le comunioni, / ma non solo io, tutti quelli che vanno in chiesa, / tutte quelle candele accese, / tutte le chiese, quante ce ne sono mai nel mondo, / belle, grandi, per niente? che io in San Pietro, / mi ricordo, m'è venuta la pelle d'oca, / no, una fede ci vuole, / cosa siamo, degli animali? siamo dei somari? / abbiamo il cervello, adoperiamolo, / ci sarà una ragione, un fondamento, / che adesso non ci arriviamo, ma però un giorno / si capirà ogni cosa, / ci dev'essere un verso, perché se no, / se è tutto uguale, / se qui questo mondo è solo una lotteria, / che se viene il tuo numero non sai nemmeno / se hai vinto, se hai perso. . . /

437

                    these are discussions, these are,
afterwards, the inside of my head is roiling, I can't stand it,
but I think about this every so often,
you have to,
today people don't want to think about anything,
having fun,
and they mock you, a girl on the train,
last year, with her friends, I'd said: We are smaller
because everyone does whatever he feels like doing, the world
isn't right, and from here it will only get worse,
and she said, "From where?" they all laughed, what did I say
                                    [that was hilarious,
"We're not going to wait our turns in line, there's too many
                                              [of us,"
and I wanted to answer her, but I kept quiet,
then I got off, I don't understand,
how they think in a certain way,

        sometimes in Rimini, on the street,
I'm standing there for a minute, there are a lot of them, I
                                    [mean lots,
where are they all going? what are they all doing?
in summer, in the Piazza Tripoli, at the beach,
speaking different languages, what are they saying?
then the thoughts, sometimes I watch them for a half-hour,
another half-hour,
and at night I dream of ants,

l'è zchéurs, mè, quést,
che la testa, a m'imbròi, dop, a n gn'aréss,
però a i faz d'ogni tènt, bsògn fèi, òz
la zénta invíci i n vó pensè ma gnént,
sno divertéis,
e i t tó ènca in zéir, una ragaza in treno,
an, si su améigh, mè a géva: a s sémm ardótt,
tótt i fa quèll ch'u i pèr, e dop e' mònd
u n pò andè bén, e adlà e' sarà ènca pézz,
e li: "Di là?", i ridéva tótt, cs'òi détt?
"Non ci stanno più dietro, siamo troppi",
e mè alè a i vléva arspònd, pu a so stè zétt,
dop a so smòunt, sti zóvan, a n'e' so,
i ragiòuna t'un módi,

però dal vólti, a Rémin, par la strèda,
ch'a m'aférum un mumént, i è tint, dabón,
dò ch'i va? boh, csa fai?
e d'instèda, a maréina, in piazza Tripoli,
ch'i zcòrr at tótt' al lèngui, csa girài?
pu i pensír, che dal vólti
a stagh alè a guardèi par dal mèz'òuri,
e la nòta a m'insógni tótt' furméighi,

— sono discorsi, questi, che io, / la testa, dopo, m'imbroglio, non ci sto
dietro, / però li faccio ogni tango, bisogna farli, oggi / la gente invece non
vuol pensare a niente, / solo divertirsi, / e ti prendono anche in giro, una
ragazza in treno, / l'anno scorso, coi suoi amici, io dicevo: ci siamo ridotti,
/ tutti fanno quel che gli pare, e dopo il mondo / non può andar bene, e di
là sarà anche peggio, / e lei: "Di là?", ridevano tutti, cos'ho detto? / "Non
ci stanno piú dietro, siamo troppi", / e io lí le volevo rispondere, ma sono
stato zitto, / dopo sono sceso, questi giovani, non lo so, / ragionano in un
modo, // però delle volte a Rimini, per la strada, / che mi fermo un
momento, sono tanti, davvero, / dove vanno? boh! cosa fanno? / e d'estate,
al mare, in piazza Tripoli, / che parlano in tutte le lingue, cosa diranno? / poi
i pensieri, che delle volte / sto lí a guardarli per delle mezz'ore, / e la notte
sogno tutte formiche, /

439

the pavement's covered, even the stairs, they're black,
some fly, they're walking over my feet, they crunch,
they form little mounds around me,
and I say: standing here, for them,
I am the Lord, wherever I am is war,
I can do anything, make rivers flood, earthquakes,
still in the dream, I get afraid,
I wake up wide awake, I walk to the window,
lights out there, people, on that highway,
they never stop, and I'm here facing the window,
bare feet, in my underwear,
and I pray, I find a saint on the calendar,
I don't want to say his name, but it's one I've never heard
                                                 [mentioned,
I'm sure I'm the only one who knows that one,
Jolanda's complaining, "It's four in the morning,
What are you doing?" I don't ask him for anything.
I don't want any grace. It's good enough
that he'll do what he can. But it doesn't matter.
Even if he can't do anything. I know he's there.
That I pray. That he hears me.

e' sulèr bróst, ènca i scaléin, i è nir,
u i n'è ch'al vòula, a i caméin sòura, al scrécca,
u m s fa i patéun, e a déggh: mè què par lòu
a so e' Signòur, dò ch'a pas l'è la guèra,
a pòs fè tótt, fiumèna, taremòt,
sémpra tl'insógni, e u m ciapa una paéura,
a m svégg ad bot, a vagh ma la finestra,
i lómm ch'u i è, la zénta, sl'autostrèda
i n s férma mai, e mè aquè spèsa i véidar,
a pi néud, sal mudàndi,
e a pràigh, ò tróv un sènt te calendèri,
ch'a n faz e' nóm, mo a n l'ò mai sintí déi,
quèll che 'lè, a so sichéur, a l cnòss sno mè,
la Jolanda la sbròuntla: "Mo l'è al quatar,
csa fét?", e a n'i dmand gnént,
a n ví nisuna grèzia, tanimódi
quèll ch'e' pò fè léu u l fa, mo u n m'arimpórta,
ènca s'u n pò fè gnént, mè a so ch' l'è 'lè,
che mè a pràigh e che léu u m sta da sintéi.

il pavimento, coperto, anche gli scalini, sono neri, / ce n'è che volano, ci cammino sopra, scricchiano, / mi si fanno i grumi, e dico: io qui per loro / sono il Signore, dove passo è la guerra, / posso fare tutto, fiumi in piena, terremoto, / sempre nel sogno, e mi prende una paura, / mi sveglio di botto, vado alla finestra, / le luci che ci sono, la gente, sull'autostrada / non si fermano mai, e io qui dietro i vetri, / a piedi nudi, in mutande, / e prego, ho trovato un santo nel calendario, / che non faccio il nome, ma non l'ho mai sentito dire, / quello lí, sono sicuro, lo conosco solo io, / la Jolanda brontola: "Ma sono le quattro, / cosa fai?", e non gli domanda niente, / non voglio nessuna grazia, tanto / quel che può fare lui lo fa, ma non m'importa, / anche se non può far niente, io so che è lí, / che io prego e che lui mi sta a sentire.

441

The Villa

Later, when the front moved, there was a German command,
the English bombed it, there was nothing left of it,
it was such a villa, a monument, I mean gorgeous,
set among trees, it emerged all of a sudden,
with columns, everything picture-perfect, white,
the walls ash grey, and all those steps,
and being under them, if it was foggy,
I would sometimes would get scared. They'd come up in the
[summer.
They were never seen again, they sold everything, they had a
[Lancia, a convertible,
that went from here to there,
I'd look inside it, the scent of leather,
It could go a hundred and fifty, I tried steering it
with one hand and the wheels turned.
There was a clock too. And grand tours,
with two German shepherds that were always jumping up on
[him,
white clothes, silk scarves,
in the ashtray there were half-smoked cigarettes
with gold cigarette holders, the big party at the end of July,
lights until morning.
But there was one thing, at that time, I couldn't understand,
[he didn't want kids,

La vélla

Dop, pr'e' fròunt, i tedésch, u i era un cmand,
i ingléis i à bumbardè, u n gn'è 'rvènz piò gnént,
ch' l'era una vélla, un monumént, mo bèla,
tra i èlbar, la scapéva fura ad bot,
sa dal culònni, di santéssum, biènchi,
i méur zèndra, mo e tènt ad chi scalèin,
ch'èsi sòtta, se e' témp l'era nuvléd,
mè, dal vólti, la m féva ènca paéura.
Lòu i avnéva d'instèda, i n s'è vést piò,
i à vandú tótt, i éva una Lancia zcvérta
lònga da què e là,
mè a la guardéva dréinta, un udòur 'd pèla,
la féva i zentzinquènta, s'una mèna
a pruvéva ad guidé, u s muvéva al ródi,
u i era ènca l'arlózz. E di gran viàz,
s' chi du chèn lópp ch'i i saltéva madòs,
vstí biènch, scialètti ad sàida,
ti portazèndra mèzi zigarètti
se buchéin d'ór, la fèsta a la fin 'd lói,
tótt al finestri zàisi fina e' dè.
Mo u i era un chè, mè 'lòura

La villa. Dopo, al passaggio del fronte, i tedeschi, c'era un commando, / gli inglesi hanno bombardato, non c'è rimasto piú niente, / che era una villa, un monumento, ma bella, / tra gli alberi, veniva fuori all'improvviso, / con delle colonne, dei sacramenti, bianche, / i muri color cenere, ma tanti di quei gradini, / che esserci sotto, se il tempo era annuvolato, / io, delle volte, mi faceva anche paura. / Loro venivano d'estate, non si sono visti piú, / hanno venduto tutto, avevano una Lancia scoperta / lunga da qui a là, / io la guardavo dentro, un odore di pelle, / faceva i centocinquanta, con una mano / provavo a guidare, si muovevano le ruote, / c'era anche l'orologio. E dei gran viaggi, / con quei due cani lupo che gli saltavano addosso, / abiti bianchi, scialli di seta, / nei portacenere mezze sigarette / col bocchino d'oro, la festa di fine luglio, / tutte le finestre accese fino a giorno. / Ma c'era un che, io allora /

he'd play the piano in the evenings, and I'd be
down below, nose pointing upwards, listening,
she would look at me, an exquisite woman,
she'd give me candy every once in a while,
I'd run all the way home,
I'd count them,
My father: "Too much,"
He'd shake his head no,
"And then later you'll have a stomach ache,"
and my mother, under her breath,
"They might be upper class,
but even she goes around without underwear."

a n putéva capéi, léu u n vléva i fiúl,
e' sunéva e' pienfórt la sàira, e mè
ad sòtta, se nès pr'aria, a stè sintéi,
li la m guardéva, una piò bèla dòna,
la m déva d'ogni tènt dal caramèli,
mè ad chéursa fina chèsa, a li cuntéva,
e' mi bà: "Tropi", e' féva ad no sla testa,
"Pu u t dól la pènza",
e la mi mà tra i dint: "I sarà sgnéur,
mo ènca li, sémpra in zéir senza mudandi. . ."

/ non potevo capire, lui non voleva figli, / suonava il pianoforte la sera, e io
/ di sotto, naso all'aria, ad ascoltare, / lei mi guardava, una donna bellissima,
/ mi dava ogni tanto delle caramelle, / io di corsa fino a casa, le contavo, /
mio padre: "Troppe", faceva di no con la testa, / "Poi ti duole la pancia", /
e mia madre tra i denti: "Saranno signori, / ma anche lei, sempre in giro
senza mutande. . ."

Crank

see that sneer? you know him?
Migani? from Stradone? he's a good man. really.
no, it just seems like that. but he's not pissed off.
                                        he's just deaf.

Incaplèd

U t guèrda sémpra tórt? chéi? mo ta l cnòss?
Mighèni de Stradòun? ch' l'è un piò bón òm,
no, e' pèr acsè, mo u n'è incaplèd,
                              l'è sòurd.

Arrabbiato? Ti guarda sempre storto? chi? ma lo consocsi? / Migani dello
Stradone? che è tanto un buon uomo, / no, pare cosí, ma non è arrabbiato,
– è sordo.

Misplay

Briscola, scopone, tressette,
he was king of the piazza, in all games,
nothing ever got by him,
always level-headed, after five or six plays
he knew what you had in your hand.
And brilliant even when he lost,
when the cards weren't falling his way,
he'd never shuffle them either,
he'd clean his pipe,
shake his head yes, he'd say: fine.
On Sundays he'd go with friends
to the rectory for a snack. He was over sixty,
you'd have thought he was fifty.

Then a little pain, he didn't think anything of it,
when he went to the doctor, his weight was down a little,
he'd lost his appetite,
he had X-rays taken,
Alessandri did the operation,
everything went well, but as part of the recuperation he had to
                                                                    [start,
it was partly the treatment, and partly only eating small portions,
and having to eat often, tea with cookies, broth,
he wasn't used to it, soft vegetables,

Capòt

Bréscla, scupòun, trisétt,
l'era e' padròun dla piaza, ad tótt i zugh,
u n'i scapéva gnént,
'na quadradéura, léu dop zéinch si dèdi
u t lizéva tal mèni quèll t'avévi.
E brilènt ènch' te pérd, quant a n li avnéva,
u n'i déva gnénch' dréinta,
e' puléva la péppa,
e' féva ad sè sla testa, e' géva: bóni.
E la dmènga si améigh ma la Calònga
a fè un'imbrènda. L'éva piò 'd sènt' an,
ta n gnu n dévi zinquènta.

Pu u i'è vnú un dulurtéin, u n gn'à dè pais,
quant l'è 'ndè de dutòur l'era un pó zò,
l'éva ènca pérs la ptéita,
l'à fat i raggi, u l'à operè Alesandri,
l'è 'ndè tótt bén, mo arciapès u i mitéva,
un pó al chéuri, un pó ènca magnè póch
e spèss, tè si biscótt, 'na ministréina,
ch'u n gn'era abituèd, vardéura còta,

Cappotto. Briscola, scopone, tressette, / era il padrone della piazza, in tutti i giochi, / non gli scappava niente, / una quadratura, lui dopo cinque sei giri / ti leggeva nelle mani quello che avevi. / E brillante anche nel perdere, quando non gli venivano, / non le mescolava nemmeno, / puliva la pipa, / faceva di sí con la testa, diceva: buone. / E la domenica con gli amici alla Canonica / a fare una merenda. Aveva piú di sessant'anni, / gliene davi cinquanta. // Poi gli è venuto un dolorino, non gli ha dato importanza, / quando è andato dal dottore era un po' giú, / aveva perso l'appetito, / ha fatto i raggi, l'ha operato Alessandri, / è andato tutto bene, ma a riprendersi ci metteva, / un po' le cure, un po' anche mangiar poco / e spesso, tè coi biscotti, una minestrina, / che non c'era abituato, verdura cotta, /

449

an egg yoke, a spoonful of jam,
he felt better if he didn't eat any bread.
Seeing him from behind
he was all ears.
He'd stay at the café until late,
but when he stood up, his mouth would form a grimace,
then one night, he started not leaving,
still playing with deliberation, except that at certain moments
in dealing, he'd stop,
his eyes were dull, he was there
but far away, one afternoon he forgot
about the king of spades he'd already discarded,
another time he went down with a six of diamonds
and the seven still hadn't been played.

The next day, he went up to town hall
to fill out a form,
he got up as far as the archives,
and he collapsed, paper in hand.

un tòural d'óv, un cucèr 'd marmelèda,
e' pèn mèi gnént, l'èva fat dagli urècci
a guardèl da di dri.
Te cafè l'arvanzéva ènch' fina tèrd,
mo a stè sò, dop, e' sturzéva la bòcca.
Pu l'à tach qualche sàira ch'u n scapéva.
Però sémpra un argòi, sno ch' di mumént
te dè al chèrti u s farméva,
pu s' chi ócc panèd, l'era alè mo e' pareva
cm'e' fóss dalòngh, un dopmezdè u s'è zcórd
un rè 'd spèdi ch'i l'éva schèrt ad mèna,
un'èlta vólta l'à sbaiè un capòt,
l'è vnú zò s'un si 'd còppi
ch'u i era ancòura e' sèt.

E e' dè dop l'è 'ndè 'd sòura te Cuméun
e fè un certifichèd,
l'è mòunt fina l'archéivi,
e se su fòi tal mèni u s'è bótt zò.

un tuorlo d'uovo, un cucchiaio di marmellata, / il pane meglio niente, aveva fatto delle orecchie / a guardarlo da dietro. / Al caffè rimaneva anche fino a tardi, / ma ad alzarsi, dopo, torceva la bocca. / Poi ha cominciato qualche sera a non uscire. / Però sempre una grinta, solo che dei momenti / nel dare le carte si fermava, / poi con quegli occhi appannati, era lí ma pareva / come fosse lontano, un pomeriggio s'è dimenticato / un re di spade che l'avevano scartato di mano, / un'altra volta ha sbagliato un cappotto, / è venuto giú con un sei di coppe / che c'era ancora il sette. // E il giorno dopo è andato di sopra in Comune / a fare un certificato, / è salito fino all'archivio, / e col suo foglio in mano s'è buttato giú.

451

Turn it off

You can't see a thing, who turned on the light?
I tell you, they're all out of their minds, turn it off,
it's enough to make someone blind,
what are they thinking now, come on,
when I object if they so much as light a match,
are they outsiders? who are they? and they never get turned off,
there's a burning, it penetrates into my eyes,
am I supposed to follow the wall? groping with my hands,
feeling my way, that's right, this is how to do it,
slowly, very slowly, because it's not like I have anywhere to go.

Smurté

U n s vaid piò gnént, mo chi è ch' l'à la zais la luce?
mè a déggh ch'i è mat, smurté, ch'u i è da inzghéis!
csa i èll avnú in amént adès, fighéurt
che mè a ragn quant i zènd un furminènt,
l'è furistír? chi séiv? e i n smórta mégga,
ò un brusòur ti ócc, i m còula,
e caminé tachèd me méur? sal mèni,
a tast, mo sè, u s va pò,
pianín, pianín, che pu a n'ò d'andè invèll.

Spegnete! Non si vede piú niente, ma chi è che ha acceso la luce? / io dico che sono matti, spegnete, che c'è da accecarsi! / cosa gli è venuto in mente adesso, figurarsi / che io protesto quando accendono un fiammifero, / sono forestieri? chi siete? e non spengono mica, / ho un bruciore agli occhi, mi colano, / e camminare lungo il muro? con le mani, / a tastoni, ma sí, si va pure, / piano piano, che poi non devo andare da nessuna parte.

The Fair

Why's that little girl crying? What happened?
are you all by yourself? did you lose your mommy? don't cry,
we'll find her, it's all right, don't cry, what's your name?
come with me, give me your hand,
on fair day children should stay
close to their mothers,
so what's your name? you can't talk?
now stop crying, and those hands,
look how dirty you are, oh, and such an ugly little girl,
I don't know if
your mother's going to want you anymore,
are you afraid of the beard? look at what I have
in my pocket, here take one, they're lozenges,
mint, they're sweet, it's not medicine,
where's that you're looking? I get it, come on let's go,
Novario, give this little girl
a cone, chocolate and vanilla,
or would your rather have the chocolate chip?
and she's not saying anything,
how old are you? use your fingers, come on, so I can see,
four years old? oh, Marianna,
you're already a big girl! and don't let it drip

La fira

Csa piànzla cla burdèla? cs'èll suzèst?
ti si da par tè? t'é pérs la mà? nu piànz
ch'a la truvémm, zò, nu piànz, cmè ta t cèm?
vén sa mè, dam la mèna,
e' dè dla fira i burdéll i à da stè
tachèd ma la su mà,
alòura cmè ta t cèm? ta n'é la lèngua?
e lasa andè da piànz, e pu s' cal mèni
vè cmè ta t si bafèda, amo acsè brótta
a n'e' so mégga
la tu mà s' la t vó piò,
t'è paéura dla bèrba? vè cs'èll ch'ò
tla bascòza, tón óna, l'è pastéini
ad menta, dòulzi, u n'è una midizéina,
mo dò che t guèrd? ò capí tótt, andémma,
Novario, dài un cono
ma sta burdèla, crema e cecolèta,
o t vu la straciatella? e la n dí gnént,
quant'an t'é? fa sal dàidi, zò, ch'a vègga,
quatr'an? mo la Mariana,
t si bèla una ragaza! e nu te fa

La fiera. Perché piange quella bambina? cos'è successo? / sei da sola? hai
perso la mamma? non piangere, che la troviamo, su, non piangere, come ti
chiami? / vieni con me, dammi la mano, / il giorno della fiera i bambini
devono stare / attaccati alla mamma, / allora come ti chiami? non hai la
lingua? / e smettila di piangere, e poi con quelle mani / ve' come ti sei
conciata, ah, ma cosí brutta / non lo so mica / se la tua mamma ti vuole piú,
/ hai paura della barba? ve' quel che ho / in tasca, prendine una, sono
pastigle / di mente, dolci, non è una medicine, / ma dove guardi? ho capito
tutto, andiamo, / Novario, dalle un cono / a questa bambina, crema e
cioccolato, / o vuoi la straciatella? e non dice niente, / quanti anni hai? fa'
con le dita, su, che veda, / quattro anni? oh la Marianna, / sei ormai una
ragazza! e non te lo far /

on your dress, look at this mess! wait till your mother sees it!
wait right here, where are you going? did you see her?
come on, she's running too,
you see how we found her? you're welcome, nothing, it was
                                        [nothing at all,
she cried a little bit, she was upset,
then we got an ice cream,
but she didn't want to tell me her name,
Sandra? oh, your name is Sandra? a beautiful name,
bye now, goodbye now, give your hand
to your mother, bye-bye.

And you, where did you come from?
would it have been better if she'd lost her mother?
I know that, but what are you supposed to do? I'm here,
watching, these people, where are they all going?
what's the big rush, are they afraid they're not going to get there?
I'm sick and tired of them, really,
it's nothing but a big pain in the ass,
you call this a festival? if it's a zoo, and you can't even tell?
you call this a good time? and you want to talk,
ticked off? who says I'm ticked off? if you like all this racket,
listen to how those people are singing? Go ahead and climb
                                        [up there with them,
you're tone deaf too, keep singing with them until nightfall,
I'll see you later, why do need to know where I'm going?
I'll tell you tonight at the café,

culè se stéi, vè ch' roba, adès la mama!
sta bóna aquè, du vét? ah, ta la é vésta?
dài, ch' la córr ènca li,
vitt ch'a la émm tróva? prego, gnént, mo gnént,
la à pianzú un pó, la s'era spavantèda,
pu avémm tólt un gelè,
mo la n m'à vlú dí mégga cmè ch' la s cèma,
Sandra? ah, ta t cèm Sandra? l'è un bèl nóm,
e adès ciao, a t saléut, e dà la mèna
ma la tu mà, ciao, ciao.

E tè da dò t scap fura?
l'era mèi s'u s pardéva la su mà?
a l so ènca mè, 's'ut ch'a faza, a so què
ch'a stagh d'avdài, sta zénta, mo dú vai?
s'na préssia, i à paéura 'd no rivé,
e pu a m so stóff, dài, tuléssmi de caz,
cumè, una festa? s' l'è un caséin, ta n vaid?
mo che 'legréa, t'avré vòia 'd zcòrr,
rabièd ad chè? s'u t pis da stè in baraca,
sint quéi che là cm'i chènta, mòunta sò,
che tè t si ènca intunèd, t vé fina nòta,
a s'avdémm, 's'ut ch'a sapa dò ch'a vagh,
a t'e' girò stasàira te cafè,

colare sul vestito, ve' che roba, adesso la mamma! / stai buona qui, dove vai?
ah, l'hai vista? / dai, che corre anche lei, / vedi che l'abbiamo trovata? prego,
niente, ma niente, / ha pianto un po', s'era spaventata, / poi abbiamo preso
un gelato, / ma non mi ha mica voluto dire come si chiama, / Sandra? ah, ti
chaimi Sandra? è un bel nome, / e adesso ciao, ti saluto, e da' la mano / alla
tua mamma, ciao, ciao. // E tu da dove vieni fuori? / era meglio se si
perdeva la sua mamma? / lo so anch'io, cosa vuoi che faccia, sono qui / che
sto a guardare, questa gente, ma dove vanno? / con una fretta, hanno paura
di non arrivare? / e poi mi sono stufato, dai, togliamoci dai coglioni, / come,
una festa? se è un casino, non vedi? / ma che allegria, avrai voglia di parlare,
/ arrabbiaito perché? se ti piace far baldoria, / senti quelli come cantano,
monta su, / tu sei anche intonato, vai fino a notte, / ci vediamo, cosa vuoi
che sappia dove vado, / te lo dirò stasera al caffè, /

I don't know, a little walk up to the Fossa,
to Casale? and do what? no, I just don't want to,
and what's going on at the Villa that's so important?
then plus I'll be sleepy, I'd be better off going to bed,
I ate too much today, I did, proscuitto with figs,
forget about the tagliatelle, and then, what a thirst,
to Ganghèn's? for one beer?
where did you leave the car? look at all these license plates,
from Pesaro, from Ravenna,
and this one? let's make it quick,
I'm not supposed to comment? what am I supposed to say?
hey, where are you turning?
to Montalbano? go wherever you want,
it's because there's fresh air, I'm not sure about beer though,
what's called for is a good Sangiovese,
how long has it been since I've been on it this road,
that's Gèpi's old house over there,
what a palace he built himself,
would you please take the curves a little easier?
and here are chairs, tables, right in the shade,
all right then, what are we drinking?

So what if it's half an hour since I've said anything,
what is there to say? the wine's good,
we're outside, look at all the boats down there,

mo a n'e' so, a fè du pas sò ma la Fosa,
a Casèl? a fè chè? no, ch'a n n'ò vòia,
e csa i èll ma la Vélla?
pu ò sònn, e' sarébb mèi ch'andéss a lèt,
ò magnè trop òz, mè, e' parsótt si féigh,
a las al taiadèli, e dop 'na sàira,
da Ganghèn, una bérra? guèsi guèsi,
dò t la é mèssa la machina? vè al tèrghi,
i vén fina da Pàisar, da Ravènna,
l'è quèsta? fémma prèst,
a n déggh gnént? cs'òi da déi? ció, dò che t volt?
a Muntalbèn? mo sè, va dò ch'u t pèr,
l'è che alasò u i è un'aria, mè a n'e' so,
la bérra, u i vrà e' sanzvàis,
sta strèda, quant l'è mai ch'a n'i paséva,
e quèll l'è Gèpi,
s' che barachéin, ach palàz ch'u s'è fat,
t vu 'ndè piò pièn tal curvi?
e aquè scaràni, tavuléin, ma l'òmbra,
alòura csa bivémmi?

E dàila, l'è mez'òura ch'a n déggh gnént?
mo cs'èll ch'u i è da déi? e' véin l'è bón,
a stémm me frèsch, alazò vèrda al bèrchi,

ma non lo so, a far due passi su alla Fossa, / a Casale? a far che? no, che non
ne ho voglia, / e cosa c'è alla Villa? / poi ho sonno, sarebbe meglio che
andassi a letto, / ho mangiato troppo oggi, io, il proscuitto coi fichi, / lasio
le tagliatelle, e dopo una sete, / da Ganghèn? una birra? quasi quasi, / dove
l'hai messa la macchina? ve' le targhe, / vengono fino da Pesaro, da Ravenna,
/ è questa? facciamo presto, / non dico niente? cosa devo dire? ehi, dove
volti? / a Montalbano? ma sí, va' dove ti pare, / è che lassú c'è un'aria, non
lo so / la birra, ci vorrà il sangiovese, / questa strada, quant'è mai che non
ci passavo, / e quello è Gèpi, / col suo baracchino, che palazzo s'è fatto, /
vuoi andare piú piano nelle curve? / e qui sedie, tavolini, all'ombra, / allora
cosa beviamo? // E dai, è mezz'ora che non dico niente? / ma cosa c'è da
dire? il vino è buono, / stiamo al fresco, laggiú guarda le barche, /

459

who knows how many tons of mullet they've caught,
what? to the coast? now? and do what?
there's not even anyone there, it's the end of September,
it's all clam shells,
all right fine, but wait a minute,
this one, with the trumpet for a beak, where's he going?
And the cardinal, who's eating a piece of lettuce,
is that a finch
or a sparrow? that girl is combing her hair
at the window, something that never happens
at Montalbano, you follow me? you lose the best ones,
look at that guy, he's fallen down, what an imbecile,
he wanted to do a wheelie, no he's not hurt,
and she's laughing, you're laughing now too,
it's a show, free admission,
you better believe it's time go, I'm crazy?
I'm aware of it, but it's the best I can do.

Just look at the all people, you predicted it,
there are even more now,
it is a good time of the day to be sitting here,
barefoot, the pontoon boats all in a line,
that guy's testing the water, too cold,
a girl's closing the beach umbrellas,
someone down there sends up a kite,
he's running, it's pointing upward,
but now he's saying no, not enough wind,

chi sa rusúl ch'i à ciap,
cumè, a maréina? adès? cs'andémmi a fè?
ch'u n gn'è niseun, a sémm la féin 'd setèmbar,
l'è tótt' còzli ad puràzi,
e' va bén, però spétta, fam avdài,
quèst, sla tromba dú val? e l'arziprít
ch'e' dà un pó d'insalèda, l'è un franguéll
o un pasaròt? cla ragaza la s pètna
ma la finestra, cs'èll ch'e' suzéd mai
a Muntalbèn, ta m guèrd? t pérd e' piò bèl,
vè quèll, ch' l'è casch, pataca,
e' vléva andè s'na róda, la i sta bén,
e li la réid, réid ènca tè, ch' l'è gratis,
e adès andémma pò, a so mat? a l so,
mo a n pòs fè mèi.

Ciò, la zénta, t i é indviné, u i n'è 'ncòura,
e l'è ènca un'òura bóna, aquè disdài,
si pi schèlz, i muschéun i è tótt in fèila,
quèll e' va sintí l'aqua, tròpa giaza,
una burdèla la céud i umbriléun,
alazò éun e' manda la cumètta,
e' córr, u s vólta, la péunta d'in èlt,
pu la dí 'd no, u n gn'è e' vént,

chissà le triglie che hanno preso, / come, a marina? adesso? cos'andiamo a
fare? / che non c'è nessuno, siamo alla fine di settembere, / son tutti gusci
di vongole, / e va bene, però aspetta, fammi vedere, / questo, con la tromba,
dove va? e l'arciprete / che dà un po' d'insalata, è un fringuello / o un
passerotto? quella ragazza si pettina / alla finestra, cosa non succede mai /
a Montalbano, mi guardi? perdi il piú bello, / ve' quello, che è caduto,
coglione, / voleva andare con una ruota, gli sta bene, / e lei ride, ridi anche
tu, che è gratis, / e adesso andiamo pure, sono matto? lo so, / ma non posso
far meglio. // Però, la gente, ci hai indovinato, ce n'è ancora, / *ed è anche*
un'ora buona, seduti qui, / *coi piedi scalzi, i mosconi sono tutti in fila,* / *quello va a*
sentire l'acqua, troppo fredda, / *una bambina chiude gli ombrelloni,* / *laggiú uno manda*
l'aquilone, / *corre, si volta, quello punta in alto,* / *poi dice di no, non c'è vento,* /

461

a dog runs by, his master gives a call,
those two lying down, she gets up, her back's
all covered with sand, the sun is low, it's reflecting,
and the waves aren't even making it to the shore, they're turning back.

That time, on a motorbike, it was raining hard,
July, and there was lightening,
so she held me tighter and shouted
in my ear, "Go fast, come on, faster!"
and then, in the dark, there was less light,
we couldn't find the door,
it's this one, I opened, "Is it you?" holy mother,
we got out of there, we had the giggles, then silence, in the hallway,
should we try this one?
and then on the bed, still whispering, Sandra said, "Now, because I'm cold,
it'll make me start crying."
Where did she ever end up?

e' pasa un chèn, e' padròun u i dà vòusa,
chi déu stuglèd, li la sta sò, la schéina
l'è tótta sabia, e' sòul l'è bas, la léus,
e agli òndi ch'a n s'aréisga, al tòurna indrí.

Cla vólta, se mutòur, un'aqua, ad lói,
e dal saètti,
ch' la m tnéva brazèd strètt e la m rugéva
tagli urècci: "Va fórt, dài, va piò fórt!"
e dop, te schéur, ch' l'era vnú mènch la luce,
a n truvémmi la pórta,
l'è quèsta, ò vért, "Sei tu?", porca masóla!
a sémm scap véa,
e una sgrégna, da zétt, te curidéur,
pruvémma quèsta? e pu
se lèt, li, sémpra sottavòusa: "Adès,
ch'ò frèdd, ch'u m vén da piànz".
La Sandra, dú saràla andè a finéi?

passa un cane, il padrone gli dà voce, / quei due sdraiati, lei si alza, la schiena / è tutta sabbia, il sole è basso, riluce, / e le onde che non s'arrischiano, tornanano indietro. // Quella volta, in moto, un'acqua, di luglio, / e delle saette, / che mi teneva abbracciato stretto e mi urlava / nelle orecchie: "Va' forte, dai, va' piú forte!" / e dopo, nel buio, che era venuta meno la luce, / non trovavamo la porta, / è questa, ho aperto, "Sei tu?", porca masóla / siamo scappati via, / e una ridarella, in silenzio, nel corridoio, / proviamo questa? e poi / sul letto, lei sempre sottovoce: "Adesso, / che ho freddo, che mi viene da piangere". / La Sandra, dove sarà andata a finire?

Shadows

Dino my oldest runs the café now,
the other one's studying
to become an accountant,
I hardly ever go down,
but I can hear everything from up here,
the market reports in the morning,
vermouth, Campari when it's eleven forty-five,
then cups, tea spoons, all the coming and going,
and towards evening people talking
at the outside tables, always about the same things,
I mean, they argue, shout, they pound their fists,
I go to the window,
but I have cataracts. I see shadows.

Òmbri

E' cafè adès u l manda avènti Dino,
e' mi grand, cl'èlta e' stéudia
da ragiunír, mè a n vgh zò guèsi mai,
mo da 'd sòura a sint tótt,
e' marchè la matéina,
vermut, Campari quant l'è agli óngg e tréi,
pu tazi, cicaréin, avènti e indrí,
e vérs sàira mi tavuléin ad fura
la zénta ch'i dizcòrr, sémpra al stèss' robi,
mo i s'aràgna, di rógg, i bat i pógn,
mè a vagh ma la finestra,
mo a iò la catarata, a vèggh dagli òmbri.

Ombre. Il caffè adesso lo manda avanti Dino, / il mio grande, l'altro studia / da ragioniere, io non vado giú quasi mai, / ma da sopra sento tutto, / il mercato la mattina, / vermut, Campari quando sono le undici e tre quarti, / poi tazze, cucchiaini, avanti e indietro, / e verso sera ai tavolini di fuori / la gente che parla, sempre le stesse cose, / ma litigano, degli urli, battono i pugni, / io vado alla finestra, / ma ho la cataratta, vedo delle ombre.

Water

It was my buddies, go on, go, you go,
for laughs, so I walked up, there were six or seven of us,
he'd set up chairs, and seeing him up close,
he was slight, with this shabby jacket,
and, man, was he was frenetic,
jabbering away, in five minutes
I was already dazed, he talked a mile a minute,
there I was, head hanging,
where have I ended up? he picked Mirko first:
"Observe all the butterflies! here is the net, now catch them!"
and Mirko, intent, with that butterfly net, is running, he's
leaping,
as if there were moths, then he stopped him,
he was pointing like a bloodhound, people were saying: "Come
                                                        [on,
it's right there," flick, swoosh, and that guy: "You caught it,"
he slapped him on the back: "Congratulations!"
next he picked Dato and Carlín di Faióun,
he positioned them in front of him: "Brrr, it's freezing!"
they began to shiver, they were stomping their feet,
they blew into their hands, "This snow
is wicked!" they turned up their collars,
both of them standing, they opened an umbrella, Dato

Aqua

Mè, l'è stè chi burdéll, va tè, va tè,
par réid, e a so 'ndè sò, a sérmi si sèt,
léu u s'à dè dal scaràni, e a vdail alè
da davséin, l'era znin, s'na sèrga léisa,
mo l'éva la tarèntla,
e s'una parlantéina, in zéinch minéut
u m'éva zà invurnéi, 'na machinètta,
mè a stéva a testa basa,
dò ch'a so capitè? l'à tach da Mirko:
"Quante farfalle! ecco il retino, prendile!",
e Mirko, séri, s' ché ridéin, córr, sèlta,
cm'u i fóss dal paviaòti, pu u s'è férum,
e' puntéva cmè un brach, la zénta: "Dài,
ch' la à 'lè", léu, tac 'na bota, e cl'èlt: "L'hai presa",
u i à batéu s'na spala, "Complimenti!",
l'è 'ndè da Dato e da Carlín 'd Faiòun,
u s'i è pustè davènti: "Brrr! che gelo!",
lòu i à tach a bublé, i batéva i pi,
i s sufiéva tal dàidi, "E questa neve!
una tormenta!", i s'è tiràt sò e' bèvar,
tutt du d'impí, i à vèrt l'umbrèla, Dato

Acqua. Io, sono stati quei ragazzi, / va' tu, va' tu, / per ridere, e sono andato
su, eravamo sei o sette, / lui ci ha dato delle sedie, e a vederlo lí, / da
vicino, era piccolo, con una giacca lisa, / ma aveva la tarantola, / e con una
parlantina, in cinque minuti / m'aveva già intontito, una macchinetta, / io
stavo a testa bassa, / dove sono capitato? ha cominciato da Mirko: /
"Quante farfalle! / ecco il retino, prendile!", / e Mirko, serio, con quel
retino, corri, salta, / come ci fossero delle farfalle, poi s'è fermato, / puntava come un bracco, la gente: "Dai, / che è lí", lui tac, una botta, e l'altro:
"L'hai presa", / gli ha battuto su una spalla: "Complimenti", / è andato da
Dato e da Carlino di Faiòun, / gli si è piazzato davanti: "Brrr, che gelo!", /
loro hanno cominciato a bubbolare, battevano i piedi, / si soffiavano nelle
dita, "E questa neve, / una tormenta!", si sono tirati su il bavero, / tutt'e
due in piedi, hanno aperto l'ombrello, Dato /

both of them standing, they opened an umbrella, Dato
pointed it down low into the wind,
Carlín, right there behind him, hunched over, his cap
jammed
down to his ears, and I sat with my arms crossed,
what is this crap?
I came here believing it was going to be games of skill,
with handkerchiefs, cards,
that they'd cut your tie in two, stuff like that,
entertainment, a top hat
and out flies a dove,
but to make people laughing-stocks,
no, no, this I won't stand for, I have a business, I
have a clientele, I have a reputation,
he's talking to someone else: "Would you like
to have a Guzzi? the California model?" I'm not familiar with
that particular model, "There it is, it's all yours,
would you like to take it for a spin?"
and this idiot takes off, vroom, vroom,
straddling a chair, don't these people get it? do people just not
[listen?

Dato has a staff position with the Province,
and Carlín, even him, with a wife and kids,
how could he have pulled this off? did he trick them?
what could he have said to them: you will not ignore me, you
will do as I command,
or maybe he promised them money? he's coming this way,
every so often, he looks at me out of the corner of his eye,

u la puntéva basa còuntra e' vént,
Carlín di dri, gubéun, se brètt calcèd
fina agli urècci, e mè disdài alè,
brazi incrusèdi, mo cs'èll ch' l'è sta roba?
mè a so vnéu concredend ch'e' fóss di zugh
d'abellità, si fazulétt, sal chèrti,
ch'i t taia la gravata, robi acsè,
da divertéis, ch'i s chèva la bumbètta
e e' vòula véa 'n pizòun, mo fè e' zimbèl,
no, no, a n'i stagh, ò un esercéizi, mè,
'na clientela, ò una riputaziòun,
e' zcòrr s'un èlt: "Ti piace
la Guzzi California?", a n'e' cnòss quèll,
"Eccola qui, è la tua, la vuoi provare?",
e st' pataca e' partéss, brrrum! brrrum!
a caval d'na scaràna,
mè a n'e' so, mo i n s n'incórz? i n sint la zénta?
che Dato l'è impieghèd ma la Pruvéinza,
e Carlín, ènca léu, l'à mòi e fiùl,
cm'àl fat? u i à intraplè?
csa i avràl détt? nu m'arviné, fé mód,
o u i à prumèss di bócch? però aquè u n vén,
u m guèrda d'ogni tènt sla còuda dl'òc,

lo puntava basso contro il vento, / Carlino, di dietro, curvo, col berretto calcato / fino alle orecchie, e io seduto lí, / braccia incrociate, ma cos'è questa roba? / io sono venuto credendo che fossero dei giochi /d'abilità, con i fazzoletti, le carte, / che ti tagliano la cravatta, cose cosí, / da divertirsi, che si tolgono la bombetta /e vola via un piccione, ma fare lo zimbello, / no, no, non ci sto, ho un esercizio, io, / una clientela, ho una reputazione, / parla con un altro: "Ti piace / la Guzzi California?", non lo conosco quello, / "Eccola qui, è la tua, la vuoi provare?" / e 'sto coglione parte, brrrum! brrrum! / a cavallo di una sedia, / io non lo so, ma non se n'accorgono? non sentono la gente? / che Dato è impiegato alla Provincia, / e Carlino, anche lui, ha moglie e figli, / come avrà fatto? li ha intrappolati? / cosa gli avrà detto? non mi rovinate, fate quel che vi dico, / o gli ha promesso dei soldi? però qui non viene, / mi guarda ogni tanto con la coda dell'occhio, /

it would be quite a feat to put me to sleep,
what if I fake it? whatever he wants, for awhile,
it would be hilarious,
then, this would be the best part: "That's enough, I'm bored,
I'm going for a cup of coffee, see you guys later,"
now that would really thwart him,
afterwards people would run him out of town,
poor guy, they'd chase him all the way to Cesena,
no way, no, I'm telling you no, you're not glomming onto me,
that's that, but what if it has consequences for him?
if I just let him say it: "This fellow is not an appropriate
subject,"
then I go back to my seat and that's it,
meanwhile my friend over there on the Guzzi is not slowing
[down,
he's leaning into all the curves, he's going to end up falling,
it's been going on for a quite some time now,
that's it, he's stopped, if I could just say something to him,
for his own good, so he could come back to his senses,
but there's no way to do it, I wave, no response,
doesn't he understand? is he afraid? come here,
you might have gotten into an accident,
he's gone over to someone else:
"*You* have a great gift,"
that fat guy, the redhead, who works at the methane gas plant,
he's zeroed in on him: "Will you grant us this honor?
We have here among us an artist of first order"

la sarà gnara indurmantèm mu mè,
o magari fè féinta,
tótt quèll ch'e' vó, pr'un pó, u i sarébb da réid,
pu te piò bèl, "Adès basta, a m so stóff,
a vagh a tó un cafè, a s'avdémm, burdéll",
che ta l'arvéin dabón, la zénta dop
i i da dri, me puràz, fina Ceséina,
no, gnént, a i déggh ad no, sa mè la n taca,
e basta, ch' pu l'è robi ch'al suzéd,
u l pò déi: "Questo qui non è il sogetto",
mè a tòuran te mi pòst e bonanòta,
e quèll dla Guzzi u n mòla,
e' pènd tal curvi, e va finéi ch'e' casca,
sno, che què la vén lònga,
no, ècco, u l férma, s'a i putéss dí quèl,
ènca par léu, ch'u s pòsa regolè,
mo u n gn'è mèzi, a i faz ségn, e léu cmè gnént,
u n capéss? l'à paéura? vén aquè,
ch'u t vénga un azidént, l'è 'ndè da un èlt:
"Lei ha avuto un gran dono",
che gròs, gag, che lavòura me metano,
u s'i è fisé: "Ci farà questo onore?
È qui con noi un artista di grido",

sarà dura addormentarmi a me, / o magari far finta, / tutto quello che vuole,
per un po', ci sarebbe da ridere, / poi sul piú bello: "Adesso basta, mi sono
stufato, / vado a prendere un caffè, ci vediamo, ragazzi", / che lo rovini
davvero, la gente dopo / lo insegue, poveraccio, fino a Cesena, / no, niente,
gli dico di no, con me non attacca, / e basta, che poi sono cose che
succedono, / lo può dire: "Questo qui non è il soggetto", / io torno al mio
posto e buonanotte, / e quello della Guzzi non molla, / pende nelle curve,
va finire che cade, / solo che qui viene lunga, / no, ecco, lo ferma, se potessi
dirgli qualcosa, / anche per lui, che si possa regolare, / ma non c'è mezzo,
gli faccio segno, e lui come niente, / non capisce? ha paura? vieni qui, / che
ti venga un accidente, è andato da un altro: / "Lei ha avuto un gran dono",
/ quel grosso, rosso di capelli, che lavora al metano, / l'ha fissato: "Ci farà
questo onore? / É qui con noi un artiste di grido",

he shouted, "Italo, you are magnificent!"
and Italo stood up, he nodded yes,
he walked to the front,
he closed his eyes, "*Una furtive lacrima,*"
he didn't hit a single note, people were shouting, Bravo!
Bravissimo!
they didn't even let him finish, they wanted an encore:
"*Che gelida manina!*" "No!" from another row
others were yelling out: "*Fin che la barca va!*" "*Mamma!*" It was a
[circus,
you couldn't understand a word anyone was saying,
one guy in the hall had flashlight, and was slashing it
around like a knife, someone else answered
with another flashlight, making lightening
bolts in the dark, there was even more of a ruckus,
so Goffredino turned on the lights, but that made it worse,
in the balcony they started stomping their feet:
"We want our money back!" it was chaos, the light bulbs were
[flickering,
some of the hotheads down in the lower sections
were coming to blows, some of the old people got up and
[scurried out,
their heads bent over, coats draped over their arms,
we were up on the stage, completely silent, watching,

472

u s'è sintí rógg: "Italo, sei grande!",
e Italo l'è stè sò, l'à fat ad sè
sla testa, l'è vnú 'vènti,
l'à tach a ócc céus "Una furtive lacrima",
u n déva invéll, la zénta: "Bravo! bravo!",
i n l'à las gnénch' finéi, i vléva e' bis:
"Che gelida manina!", "No!", da un pèlch
d'ilt i à dè sò: "Fin che la barca va!",
"Che gelida manina!", "O sole mio!",
"Fin che la barca va!", "Mamma!", un caséin,
u n s capéva piò gnént,
éun sla pila, tla sèla, cmè un curtèl,
da d'in èlt u i à 'rspòst un'èlta pila,
dal saètti te schéur,
e sémpra piò cagnèra,
alòura Gufredín l'à zais al luci,
mo l'è stè pézz, te luzòun i s'è méss
a bat i pi: "Vogliamo i soldi indietro!",
un purbiòun, e' treméva al lampadéini,
di scalmanèd ad sòtta i s'atachéva,
qualch' anzièn u s'alzéva e véa cuvéun
se capòt sottabraz,
néun tótt zétt se pelcsènic a guardè,

si è sentito urlare: "Italo, sei grande!" / e Italo s'è alzato, ha fatto di sí / con la testa, è venuto avanti, / ha attaccato a occhi chiusi "Una furtive lacrima", / non imbroccava una nota, la gente: "Bravo! bravo!", / non l'hanno lasciato neanche finire, volevano il bis: / "Che gelida manina!", "No!", da un palco / altri hanno dato su: "Fin che la barca va!", / "Che gelida manina!", "O solo mio!", / "Fin che la barca va!", "Mamma!", un casino, / non si capiva piú niente, / uno con la pila, nella sala, come un coltello, / dall'alto gli ha risposto un'altra pila, / delle saette nel buio, / e sempre piú cagnara, / allora Goffredino ha acceso le luci, / ma è stato peggio, nel loggione si sono messi / a battere i piedi: "Vogliamo i soldi indietro!", / un polverone, tremavano le lampadine, / degli scalmanti di sotto venivano alle mani, / qualche anziano si alzava e via a testa bassa, / col cappotto sottobraccio, / noi tutti zitti sul palcoscenico a guardare, /

he was watching too, then he strutted out:
"All eyes on me!" with that smirk, "Everyone stop!
Cease! This is an order!" and at that exact moment
a crash onstage, and all this splashing,
what? a bag of water,
then another, and another, I said to my pals:
Hey! what do you think you're doing?
they thought it was just fine,
water and bags, great fun,
horsing around, they started lifting the chairs
over their heads, for protection, the legs turned up,
another bag, the redhead pointed a finger:
"Giorgio! I saw you!" whistles from above:
"Referee! Are you blind? You need glasses?"
Then everything was being pelted down,
pieces of carob, apple cores, banana peels,
orange peels, a can of Fanta,
a barrage, if you were to get hit, and this? you pigs,
it's not water, and where is he? oh, there,
his ears all slick and shiny from his hair cream,
sweating, with his crooked bowtie,
"It's really coming down now, it's time to make a break for it,"
I said to him, he was looking at me: "If you can."
"If I can? me, who's going to stop me?"

e' guardéva ènca léu, pu u s'è indrizé:
"A me gli occhi!", s'na zurma, "Fermi tutti!
fermi, vi dico!", e própia at che mumént
una bota se pèlch e tènt 'd chi squézz,
cs'èll stè? i éva tiràt un sachètt d'aqua,
pu un èlt, un èlt, i mi cumpàgn, mè ò détt:
"Ció, aquè cm'a la mitémmi?", mo lòu sè,
aqua, sachétt, l'era un divertiment,
i zughéva, al scaràni, i s li era mèssi,
par arparès, gambi d'insò, sla testa,
in èlt sachètt, e' gag l'à punté un daid:
"Giorgio, a t'ò vést", da d'in èlt di gran fés–ci:
"Arbitro, occhiali!", pu l'è vnú zò e' mònd,
pézz 'd carobla, tursóll, bózzi 'd banana,
ad melarèza, un busilòt dla Fanta,
pin, ch' s'i t ciapa, mo quèsta, brutti porci,
u n'è aqua, e duv'èll léu? l'era alè,
u i luséva agli urècci ad brilantina,
sudéd, se nòtal tórt,
"Aquè u s'è smòs 'na vèggia ch' l'è mèi còisla",
a i ò détt, léu u m'à guèrs: "Se ce la fai",
"S'a gli à faz mè? mo mè chi vut ch' m'afèrma?"

guardava anche lui, poi s'è impettito: / "A me gli occhi!", con una mutria,
"Fermi tutti!" / fermi, vi dico!", e proprio in quel momento / una botta sul
palco e tanti di quegli schizzi, / cos'è stato? avevano tirato un sacchetto
d'acqua, / poi un altro, un altro, i miei compagni, io ho detto: / "Ehi, qui
come la mettiamo?", ma loro, sí, / acqua, sacchetti, era un divertimento, /
giocavano, le sedie se le erano messe, / per ripararsi, gambe in su, sulla testa,
/ un altro sacchetto, il rosso ha puntato un dito: / "Giorgio, t'ho visto!", /
dall'alto dei gran fischi: / "Arbitro, occhiali!", poi è venuto giú il mondo, /
pezzi di carruba, torsoli, bucce di banana, / d'arancia, un barattolo della
Fanta, / pieno, che se ti prendono, ma questa, brutti porchi, / non è acqua,
e dov'è lui? era lí, / le orecchie gli lucevano di brillantina, / sudato, col not-
tolino storto, / "Qui vien fuori un pieno che è meglio tagliare la corda", / gli
ho detto, lui m'ha guardato: "Se ce la fai",/ "Se ce la faccio io? ma a me chi
vuoi che mi fermi?" /

475

"I'm not talking about the people," "What then?" "The water,"
"This mess?" "Is getting bigger," "Only seven or eight bags,"
"There's something else," "Something else?"
and while we were talking I got drenched, what the hell? Soaked,
a faucet? in this mayhem?
there's got to be someone behind this,
it wouldn't take much, "It is not stopping," "But it's got to be
                                                            [stopped,
give them a yell," "It's late," I felt ice-cold, my feet were wet,
I jumped up on a chair, what's going on?
because a minute ago, it could be, Goffredino?
where is he? doesn't he realize? doesn't he see?
there's already three inches, it's filthy,
it's full of cigarette butts, matchsticks,
and I need to get back home, what am I going to do?
now this, it's not a faucet,
the water-main has burst, it's a flood,
someone go notify the police,
because if it's not cut off, be quick, it's gushing,
it's above the transoms,
the lights are reflecting down into them, I can see myself,
where are the others? my pals, him,
they're not here anymore, how did they get out? and the
                                                            [pandemonium

"Non parlo della gente", "E 'lòura?", "L'acqua",
"Sté pacéugh?", "Cresce", "Mo sèt òt sachétt",
"E un'altra cosa", "Come un'altra cose?"
e te zcòrr a m so mòs, orca, a sguazéva,
mo quèsta addò ch' la vén? ch'i apa las vért
un rubinètt, aquè, ad sta baraònda,
mo là spèsa u i sarà pò qualcadéun,
u i vó póch, "Non si ferma",
"Marà farmèla invíci, fai un rógg",
"È tardi", e ò sintí un giàz, éva i pi a bagn,
a so mòunt s'na scaràna, csa suzédal?
che un mumént fa, mo èl dóbbi, Gufredín
dò ch' l'è? u n s n'è incórt? u n vaid?
u i n'era bèla quatar dàida, spórca,
pina ad cichi, ad ziréin,
e mè ch'ò d'andé chèsa, cmè ch'a faz?
pu quèst, 's'ut rubinètt,
u s'è ròtt un cundótt, l'è un canòun d'aqua,
qualcadéun, zò, ch'e' vaga a visé al guèrdi,
s' ta n la stagn, e fè prèst, quèsta la córr,
la è zà mòunta sòura mi cavéi,
u s'i vaid dréinta i lómm, a m vèggh par mè,

"Non parlo della gente", "E allora?", "L'acqua", / "Questo paciugo?",
"Cresce", "Ma sette otto sacchetti", / "E un'altra cosa", "Come, un'altra
cosa?" / e nel parlare mi sono mosso, orca sguazzavo, / ma questa da dove
viene? che abbiano lasciato aperto / un rubinetto? qui, in questa baraonda,
/ ma là dietro ci sarà pure qualcuno, / ci vuol poco, "Non si ferma", /
"Bisognerà fermarla invece, fagli un urlo", / È tardi", e ho sentito un
ghiaccio, avevo i piedi a bagno, / sono salito su una sedia, cosa succede? /
che un momento fa, ma è possibile, Goffredino / dov'è? non se n'è accorto?
non vede? / ce n'era ormai quattro dita, sporca, / piena di chicche, di cerini,
/ e io che devo andare a casa, come faccio? / poi questo, cosa vuoi
rubinetto, / s'è rotta una conduttura, è un torrente d'acqua, / qualcuno, dai,
che vada ad avvisare i vigili, / se non la stagni, e far presto, questa corre, /
è già salita sopra le traverse, / ci si vedono dentro le luci, mi ci vedo io, / ma
e gli altri dove sono? i miei compagni, e lui,

477

ahead, it's all collapsing, no, it's the cover
of the prompt box which has given,
the water has found another route,
it's receding, listen to it rumbling below,
it's gone down, there on the wall
you can see the watermark,
or is it? it's still too soon, it was all the way up to the knees,
but it must be going down, see how much it's gone down
already,
but in case it hasn't, be on the lookout for a landmark,
plaster peeling,
that one, I saw earlier that one in the evening,
it looked like a leaf on a stem,
where is it? I don't see it anymore,
oh no, instead of going down, wait, what's all that stuff
coming this way? a loaf of bread?
completely saturated? bloated,
it's enough to turn your stomach,
and here, on the seat of this chair, is a puddle,
the other chairs are going in every direction,
knocking against each other,
what's going on down there?
a crash of windows breaking, a roar,
you can't wait here any longer, but where can you go?

mo e ch'ilt duv'èi? i mi cumpàgn, e léu,
i n gn'è piò, dò ch'i è pas? e sté malàn
alè 'vènti, e' casca tótt, no, l'à zdéu
e' cvérc dla béusa de sugeridòur,
l'aqua, u s'i è vért un pas,
la va zò, sint ad sòtta cmè ch' la arbòmba,
aquasò adès u s sgòmbra, alè te méur
u s'avdirà la réiga de bangèd,
o no? l'è prèst ancòura, u i n'era un znòc,
però la chin calè, quèll ch' va mai zò,
se no basta tní d'òc un sègn, un scòurgh,
quèll alè, ch'a l'ò vést ad préima sàira,
u m pareva una foia se gambòz,
dò ch' l'è? l'era alè dès, a n'e' vèggh piò,
ció, mo invíci 'd calé, spétta, cs'èll ch' l'è
cla roba ch' vén avènti? una pagnòta,
tótt' imbumbèda, gòunfia, la fa séns,
e sla pivira aquè u i è la piscòlla,
agli èlt scaràni al s móv,
al va d'in quà e d'in là, al sbat tra 'd lòu,
e alazò in fònd cs'èll stè?
un scatramàz ad véidar rótt, un scióun,
aquè u n s pò spitè piò, sno che dú s val?

non ci sono piú, dove sono passati? e questo fracasso / lí avanti, crolla tutto,
no, ha ceduto / il coperchio della buca del suggeritore, / l'acqua, le si è
aperto un passo, / va giú, senti di sotto come rimbomba, / adesso quassú si
svuota, lí sul muro / si vedrà la riga del bagnato, / o no? è presto ancora, ce
n'era un ginocchio, / però deve calare, quel che va mai giú, / se no basta
tener d'occhio un segno, una scrostatura, / quello lí, che l'ho visto di prima
sera, / mi pareva una foglia col gambo, / dov'è? era lí adosso? non lo vedo
piú, / ehi, ma invece di calare, aspetta, che cos'è / quella roba che viene
avanti? una pagnotta, / tutta inzuppata, gonfiia, fa senso, / e qui sull'impagliatura c'è la pozzanghera, / le altre sedie si muovano, / vanno in qua e in
là, sbattono fra loro, / e laggiú in fondo cos'è stato? / un fragore di vetri
rotti, uno scroscio, / qui non si può piú aspettare, solo che dove si va? /

enough, whatever's going to happen will happen,
that little table, I've extended my arm, come on,
come on,
if I can reach it, I'm touching the marble ledge
with my feet, I've been here for awhile straddling
between a table and chair, if I slip
I'm done for, I'm balancing, then an impulse,
I tilted my arms slightly, I've righted myself,
I've done it, steady, and then there's clapping,
which scares the living daylights out of me,
I wasn't expecting that, who's the applause for
anyway? for me? then I saw them, everyone,
tons of people, someone with gold teeth,
no, they're laughing, can't you hear? bursts
of laughter, they're slapping their thighs,
elbowing each other, doubled over, their shoulders
are quaking, they're wiping off tears with shirt sleeves,
then shrieks and catcalls, women with their heads thrown back,
even the necklaces are convulsed with laughter,
some are splayed out, completely disheveled,
they start coughing, they're choking with laughter,
a little boy standing in the aisle
was watching me, they are laughing at me,

basta, quèll ch' vén e' vén,
che tavuléin, ò slòngh 'na gamba, dài,
s'a i putéss arivé, se pi ò tòcch l'òural
de mèrum, a so stè pr'un pó a cavàl
tra la scaràna e e' tavuléin, s'a sguéll
a m sbrènch, ò fat la blènza, a m so dè e' slènz,
ò dvanè un pó sal brazi, a m so indrizé,
aglia ò fata, 'ta bón, e un batimèni,
ch'a m so ènca spavantè, a n mu n l'aspitéva,
mo sta festa ma chéi?
mu mè? pu a i ò vést, tótt,
la zénta mai ch'u i era, i dént a d'ór,
no, i réid, ta n sint? l'era una sbacarèda,
i s batéva sal còsci, i s déva ad gòmat,
i s pighéva, u s'i avdéva tremè al spali,
i s'asughéva al lègrimi se braz,
mo pu di sgréss, di céul, al dòni al stéva
testa d'indrí, u i ridéva ènca al culèni,
d'ilt i era a gambi vérti, tótt sbudléd,
u i avnéva da tòs, i s'afughéva,
un burdèl u m guardéva
d'impí te curidéur, i réid sa mè,

basta, quel che viene viene, / quel tavolino, ho allungato una gamba, dai, / se ci potessi arrivare, col piede ho toccato il bordo / del marmo, sono stato per un po' a cavallo / fra la sedia e il tavolino, se scivolo / mi squarto, ho fatto la bilancia, / mi sono dato lo slancio, / ho giostrato un po' con le braccia, mi sono raddrizzato, / ce l'ho fatta, sta' buono, e un applauso, / che mi sono anche spaventato, non me l'aspettavo, / ma questa festa a chi? / a me? poi li ho visti, tutti, / la gente che c'era mai, i denti d'oro, / no, ridono, non senti? era una risata, / si battevano sulle cosce, si davano di gomito, / si piegavano, gli si vedevano tremare le spalle, / si asciugavano le lacrime col braccio, / ma poi degli stridi, dei sibili, le donne stavano / testa all'indietro, gli ridevano anche le collane, / altri erano a gambe aperte, scamiciati, / gli veniva da tossire, soffocavano, / un bambino mi guardava / in piedi nel corridoio, ridono di me, /

I got dizzy, too much
of a din, it was all flickering, I raised my hand:
"Be quiet!" someone yelled out: "Silence in the hall!"
someone else: "Speech!" what's with them?
"Speech!" Are they all insane? "We're all waiting, Four Eyes!"
I don't dare say a word, plus, what can I tell them?
"You're the Boss, you tell *us*," all right, be quiet then,
"Here, folks, whoever is able,
should get up and go home," you could hear snickering,
"It's nothing to laugh about, you don't believe me? look,
no, look at me, up here, at me, don't you see me?"
from one row someone heckled: "Projector!
He's all out of focus!"
it was worse than before, now they were hoarse,
with flushed faces, and over there?
what's that rumbling?
like it's boiling, plus it was rising, a gush,
it was the hole that had filled up below,
it was spouting up again,
then something broke, this isn't happening,
it was like when they opened the sluice at the millstream,
it went down, but the river rose, screams,
you couldn't see a thing anymore,
a dense fog, in gusts, it forced you to close your eyes,

u m ziréva la testa, tropa boba,
avdéva imbarbaièd, o 'lzè una mèna:
sté zétt, éun l'à rugéu: "Silenzio in sala!",
un èlt: "Hai la parola", cs'ài capéi?
"Discorso!", mo i è mat? "Quattr'occhi, dài",
ch'a n m'aréisgh, pu cs'a i dégghi? "Capo, alòura?",
va bén, sté zétt: "Aquè, burdéll, chi ch' pò",
a n'éva e' spéud, "Quèst l'è un zavài ch' l'è mèi
tó sò e 'ndè chèsa", u s'è sintí sgrigné,
"La n'è da réid, a n mu n cridéi? guardé,
mo guardém, aquasò, mu mè, a n m'avdéi?"
da un pèlch i m'à 'rpòst: "Quadro!", la è stè fata,
pézz ch' nè préima, i era ormai tótt runchèd,
dal fazi lóstri, e alè cs'èll ch'e' sbarbòtla?
cmè ch' la buléss, pu la à dè sò, mo un zèt,
l'era la beusa, sòtta u s'era impéi,
u la arbutéva fura,
e pu la à ròtt, u n s'è capèi, l'è stè
cmè quante mi muléin i éirva e' butàz,
la andéva zò, mo una fiumèna, rógg,
u n s'avdéva piò gnént,
un nibiòun, a vampèdi, da srè i ócc,

mi girava la testa, troppo chiasso, / vedevo imbarbagliato, ho alzato una
mano: / state zitti, uno ha urlato: "Silenzio in sala!" / un altro: "Hai la
parola", cos'hanno capito? / "Discorso!" ma sono matti? "Quattr'occhi, dai",
/ che non m'arrischio, poi cosa gli dico? "Capo, allora?" / va bene, state zitti,
"Qui, ragazzi, chi può", non avevo la saliva, "Questo è un pasticcio che è
meglio / prender su e andare a casa", si è sentito ghignare, / "Non è da
ridere, non mi credete? guardate, / ma guardatemi, quassú, a me, non mi
vedete?", / da un palco m'hanno risposto: "Quadro!" è stata la fine, / peggio
di prima, erano ormai tutti rauchi, / delle faccie lustre, e lí cos'è che
borbotta? / come se bolisse, poi ha dato su, ma un getto, / era la buca, sotto
s'era riempito, / la ributtava fuori, / e poi ha rotto, non s'è capito, è stato /
come quando ai mulini aprono il bottaccio, / andava giú, ma un fiume in
piena, urli, / non si vedeva piú niente, / un nebbione, a vampate, da chiudere
gli occhi, /

a downpour, and below,
it was the end of the world, water, you could hear it slapping
against the walls, my face was being sloshed against,
I saw a rope, I grabbed it, up we go,
I found myself behind the wing,
there was a board, like over a war trench,
careful now, all the way to an iron door,
I pulled it open, a hallway with red carpet,
different tiers, *Level II,*
some stairs, up, *Level III,* wait a second,
that tier with the open door, let's have a look,
I went in, I looked down, oh mother,
people, seats, it was all water,
on the surface, furs,
gloves, hats,
and still rising, the first tiers already submerged,
the second tiers are under too,
so why am I standing here watching,
you need to get up higher,
come on now, this is the upper balcony, this is the snack bar,
I jumped onto the counter, I got through,
then stuff everywhere, jam-packed,
a storage area, enormous boxes,
crates, sacks, empty bottles,
if I come down wrong on my foot, watch out for my head,

la m piuvéva madòs, e ad sòtta l'era
la fèin de mònd, l'aqua, u s sintéva sbat
ti méur, u m'arivéva i squézz tla faza,
ò vést 'na córda, a l'ò ingrandfèda, sò,
a m so tróv spèsa al quéinti,
u i era un'asa, cmè um caminamént,
avènti pò, fina una pórta ad fèr,
ò vért, un curidéur se tapàid ròss,
mo quést l'è i pèlch, ò vést scrétt "II Ordine",
sò pr'al schèli, "III Ordine", un mumént,
che pèlch sla pórta vérta, fam avdài,
a so éintar, ò guèrs ad sòtta, mama,
zénta, pultròuni, gnént, l'era tótt' aqua,
sòura u i baléva plézzi, guènt, capéll,
e la crèss sémpra, i préim pèlch i è zà a bagn,
l'è sòtta ènca i sgónd pèlch, èlt che guardè,
aquè bsògna 'ndè sò.
forza, quèst l'è e' luzòun, quèst l'è e' bufè,
a so sèlt se bancòun, a so pas 'dlà,
l'era pin 'd roba, un magazéin, scatléun,
casi, sach, bòci svéiti,
s'a vagh zò mèl s'un pi, ahi, la mi testa!

mi pioveva addosso, e di sotto era / la fine del mondo, l'acqua, si sentiva
sbattere / contro i muri, m'arrivavano gli schizzi in faccia, / ho visto una
corda, l'ho aguantata, su, / mi sono trovato dietro le quinte, / c'era un asse,
come un camminamento, / avanti pure, fino a una porta di ferro, / ho
aperto, un corridoio col tappeto rosso, / ma questi sono i palchi, ho visto
scritto "II Ordine", / le scale, su, "III Ordine", un momento, / quel palco
con la porta aperta, fammi vedere, / sono entrato, ho guardato di sotto,
mamma, / gente, poltrone, niente, era tutt'acqua, / sopra ci ballavano pel-
licce, guanti, cappelli, / e cresce sempre, i primi palchi sono già a bagno, /
sono sotto anche i secondi palchi, altro che guardare, / qui bisogna salire, /
forza, questo è il loggione, questo è il buffet, / sono saltato sul banco, sono
passato di là, / era pieno di roba, un magazzino, scatoloni, / casse, sacchi,
bottiglie vuote, / se vado giú male con un piede, ahi, la mia testa! /

what did I hit it on? is it bleeding? on this iron pipe,
I work my way behind it, careful, it's the handrail
of another staircase, water, below, listen to
it rumbling, I ran as fast as I could,
two stairs at a time,
a door, the door handle
gave, it opened, all the lights were blazing,
it's town hall, the meeting chambers,
there wasn't a soul,
I passed through it, into the engineering department,
from there into the archives, another staircase, this one's stone,
narrower, Jesus, look at these pendulums,
the town clock, nothing but bricks attached to a piece of wire,
and what's happening down below?
it looks like a storm at sea, there's an opening,
three steps, a tiny gate,
what's this stuff flying around, pigeons?
underneath the roof tiles, music is coming from where?
careful walking, it's all just laths,
if I stumble, I fall down below,
you can still hear music playing,
a narrow chute, if you crawl on all fours,
and where have I been belched out?
this is the organ loft

dò ch'ò batéu? u m vén e' sangh? sté fèr,
a i so 'ndè dri, 'ta bón, l'è e' tinimèn
d'un'èlta schèla, l'aqua, sòtta, sint
cmè ch' la gargòia, andéva ad scaranèda,
du scaléin a la vólta,
una pórta, a m so ciap ma la manéglia,
la à zdéu, l'è vért, e tótt' al luci zàisi,
mo l'è e' Cuméun, la sèla de cunséi,
u n gn'era un'anma,
ò travarsè, a so 'ndè tl'uféizi tecnich,
da 'lè tl'archéivi, un'èlta schèla, ad sas,
piò strètta, orca, vè i péndal, l'è l'arlózz,
ch' pu l'era di madéun lighéd s'na spranga,
e sòtta csa suzédal? e' pareva
cumè un mèr in burasca, alè che béus,
tri scaléin, un rastèl,
e' svulaza dla roba, l'è pizéun?
a sera sòtta i cópp, mo dò ch'i sòuna?
aténti a caminé, l'è tótt sturúl,
se t sgar t vé ad sòtta, e u s sint sémpra sunè,
sté budèl, u s'i va cuvéun, e què?
dò ch'a so scap? mo quèst

dove ho battuto? mi viene il sangue? questo ferro, / gli sono andato dietro,
sta' buono, è il corrimano / di un'altra scala, l'acqua, sotto, senti / come
gorgoglia, / andavo a gambe levate, / due scalini alla volta, / una porta, mi
sono afferato alla maniglia, / ha ceduto, è aperto, e tutte le luci accese, / ma
è il Comune, la sale del consiglio, / non c'era un'anima, / ho attraversato,
sono andato nell'ufficio tecnico, / da lí nell'archivio, un'altra scala, di pietra,
/ piú stretta, orca, ve' i pendoli, è l'orologio, / che poi erano mattoni legati
con del fil di ferro, / e sotto cosa succede? pareva / come un mare in
burrasca, lí quel buco, / tre scalini, un cancelletto, / svolazza della roba, sono
piccioni? / ero sotto i coppi, ma dove suonano? / attenti a camminare, è
tutto canniccio, / se sgarri vai di sotto, e si sente sempre suonare, / questo
budello, ci si va carponi, e qui? / dove sono sbucato? ma questo /

at San Rocco, two kids, fooling around, one of them is banging
on the keyboard, helter-skelter, the other, at the bellows,
has seen me, stopped, the keys playing by themselves,
from below, I heard a hissing, the stink of wax,
it had already dripped all over the altars, a few candles
were still lit,
with sputtering flames,
then it all went out,
but over there, it looks like, maybe, that door
leads up into the bell tower, I ran to it, it's just that these stairs,
the wood's old, they're creaking,
stop, wait, this one's giving, this one's vibrating too,
it's no good, it's rotten, don't you see that fissure up there?
those hanging boards that are swaying,
it's falling, boom, so now go back the way you came,
slowly, that's right, it's angled, the wall's slanted,
what's this? I hadn't seen it at first,
this hatch, it's open, a passageway, a room,
I hold my breath, that's Father Gaetano, in the back,
in an armchair, his mouth hanging open,
without his dentures, snoring, forward I go,
on tiptoes, a step,
the laundry room, sheets hanging,
pillowcases, towels, shirts, tablecloths,

l'è e' pèlch dl'órgan 'd San Ròch, ècco chi ch' sòuna,
l'è du burdéll, i zuga, éun e' pacéuga
si tast, purséa, cl'èlt me mèng u m'à vést,
u s'è férum, i tast i à batú ciòch,
ad sòtta ò sintí frézz, 'na pózza ad zira,
la éva ancòura zàisa,
sla fiamba ch' la baléva,
pu u s'è smórt tótt, però alè u m pèr, cla pórta,
u s va se campanéil, a m'i so bótt,
sno che i scaléin, lègn vèc, un scricadézz,
alt, férma, quèst e' zéd, e' zóccla ènch' quést,
gnént, l'è tótt fraid, ta n vaid alasò ch' sbrènch?
e cagli asi spandléun, óna la déndla,
la casca, plòff, adès a turnè indri,
pianin, acsè, 'd curtèl, tachèd me méur,
e quèst? che préima a n l'éva mégga vést
sté purtunzéin, l'è vért, 'n'andit, 'na cambra,
a tnéva e' fiè, mo quèll l'è don Gaitèn,
d'indrí s'un scaranòun, a bòcca vérta
senza dantira, e' surnicéva, avénti
in pèunta 'd pi, 'na schèla,
e' cambaròun da stènd i pan, lanzúl,
fudrètti, sugamèn, caméisi, tvai,

è il palco dell'organo di San Rocco, ecco chi suona, / sono due ragazzi, giocano, uno pasticcia / coi tasti, a caso, l'altro al mantice m'ha visto, / s'è fermato, i tasti hanno battuto a vuoto, / di sotto ho sentito friggere, una puzza di cera, / aveva già coperto gli altari, qualche candela / era ancora accesa, / con la fiamma che ballava, / poi s'è spento tutto, però lí mi pare, quella porta, / si va sul campanile, mi ci sono buttato, / solo che gli scalini, legno vecchi, uno scricciolio, / alt, ferma, questo cede, traballa anche questo, / niente, è tutto fradicio, non vedi lassú che spacco? / e quelle assi penzoloni, una dondola, / cade, ploff, adesso tornare indietro, / pianino, cosí, di taglio, a ridosso del muro, / e questo? che prima non l'avevo mico visto / 'sto portoncino, è aperto, un andito, una camera, / tenevo il fiato, ma quello è don Gaetano, / indietro su una poltrona, a bocca aperta, / senza dentiera, russava, avanti / in punta di piedi, una scala, / il camerone da stendere i panni, lenzuoli, / federe, asciugamani, camicie, tovaglie, /

you could get lost here,
isn't that a staircase,
a spiral staircase,
come on now,
carefully,
so you don't slip, what is this smell?
it's like
carbolic acid, a tincture of some sort, and all these beds
in a row, white, where have I ended up? the hospital?
and all this sawdust on the floor, to keep it dry?
right, keep it dry,
can't you see there's already more than an inch of water?
"Quiet Quiet!"
"But sawdust isn't going to do any good,"
"Quiet,
because he's dozed off, just go wherever you need to go,"
"Give it to me straight, is this a place where I'd be better off
                                                    [not being?
"And he's got a strangulated hernia," "I've warned you,
do what you want," and what's that,
what's beyond that glass door?
I felt around, another staircase, a beam, two beams, a door,
ajar, isn't there anyone here? I saw the light under a doorbell,
I rang, "Come in,
come in, should I lay them out for you? "
she was shuffling a deck of cards, "I can't,"
"Just five thousand lire," "It's not the money, I'm in a hurry,"
"Where do you have to be?" "Up higher, where's a
                                                    [staircase?"
"Follow your nose, open that door," "Goodbye,

aquè 'un u s pérd, mo alazò u n'è una schèla?
a luméga, sò, pièn,
da no sguilé, cs'èll ch' l'è st'udòur? cm'e' fóss
acid fènich, tintéura, e tótt chi létt,
in féila, biènch, dò ch'a so vnéu? te bsdèl?
e sté sgadézz ma tèra, pr'asughé?
sè, t'é vòia, a n'avdéi
ch'u i n'è zà piò 'd do dàida? "Ssst! sté zétt!",
"Mo se sgadézz u n s'i fa gnént", "Sté zétt,
ch'u s'è supéi, andé dò ch'i d'andè",
"Dém rèta, quèst l'è un pòst ch' l'è mèi no stèi",
"Mo s'un'ergna struzèda", "Mè a v l'ò détt,
fé vuílt", e alè, ch'a vègga,
csa i èll dlà 'd cla vedrèda? a m'e' sintéva,
un'èlta schèla, un rèm, du rèm, 'na pórta,
la è sno custèda, u n gn'è niseun? ò vést
e' lómm sòtta una bóssla, ò busé, "Avènti,
vní 'vènti, a v faz 'na stàisa?",
la déva dréinta m'un maz 'd chèrti, "A n pòs",
"Zincmella frènch", "U n'è pr'i bócch, ò préssia",
"Duv'iv d'andè?", "D'in èlt, dò ch' l'è una schèla?"
"Drétt me vòst nès, arví cla pórta", "Adio,

qui uno si perde, ma laggiú non è una scala? / a lumaca, su, piano, / da non scivolare, cos'è quest'odore, come fosse / acido fenico, tintura, e tutti quei letti, / in fila, bianchi, dove sono venuto? / nell'ospedale? / e questa segatura per terra, per asciugare? / sí, hai voglia, non vedete / che ce n'è già piú di due dita? "Ssst! state zitto!", / "Ma con la segatura non ci si fa niente", "State zitto, / che si è assopito, andate dove dovete andare", / "Datemi retta, questo è un posto che è meglio non starci", / "Ma con un'ernia strozzata", "Io ve l'ho detto, / fate voi", e lí, che veda, / cosa c'è oltre quella vetrata? me lo sentivo, / un'altra scala, un ramo, due rami, una porta, / è solo accostata, non c'è nessuno? ho visto / il lume sotto una bussola, ho bussato, "Avanti, / venite avanti, vi faccio una stesa?", / mescolava un mazzo di carte, "Non posso", / "Cinquemila lire", "Non è per i soldi, ho fretta", / "Dove dovete andare?", "In alto, dov'è una scala?" / "Dritto al vostro naso, aprite quella porta", "Addio, /

491

and you, you shouldn't stay here waiting, come away,
it's already a morass," "Ah. You don't have to tell me,
this is a house, this is, and when it rains
I have to put bowls all over the place,"
and people are always getting things half-assed backwards,
what good are basins and bowls? can't you hear it down below,
right down here, don't you hear how it sounds like an animal
gasping? no response, fine then, what's the point of talking,
in any case, this must be the final landing,
and the huge door is shut, but there's talking behind it,
a waiter came out, he slipped past me,
they'd finished eating, it was quite a group,
they were squabbling, a cloud of smoke, they didn't even see me,
I made my way to a hallway,
and this door? there's a key inside, let's see,
I could have guessed it, stairs,
and up there, a trapdoor, I grabbed it,
I braced myself against the wall, I hoisted myself up,
and this? it's like walking inside a cloud,
it's filled with tufts of wool, it's Pia's house,
Pia the mattress-maker, and that curl over there
is a railing, at least my vision's still sharp,

mo vò, ènca vò, nu sté spitè, scapé,
u i è zà un pacéugh aquè", "Eh, a l so purtròp,
l'è una chèsa, mè, quèsta, quant e' pióv
a chin mètt dimpartótt dal caldarètti",
e la zénta i capéss sémpra a l'arvérsa,
's'ut caldarètti, mo ta n la sint sòtta,
aquè sòtta, ta n sint cmè un animèli
ch'e' lènsa? gnént, va là, 's'ut zcòrr, piotòst
adès aquè, quèst l'è l'éultum pianètt,
e sté purtòun l'è srèd, però adlà i zcòrr,
l'è scap un camarir, a m so infilé,
i éva finí 'd magnè, mo una tavlèda,
i bacaiéva, un fómm, i n m'à gnénch vést,
ò imbòcch un curidéur,
sta pórta u i è la cèva dréinta, vdémma,
a i ò inzècch ènch' stavólta, un souraschèla,
e alasò u i è un batóss, a m'i so ciap,
pi còuntra e' méur, a m so tiràt sò 'd pais,
e aquè? l'era cmè caminé t'na nóvla,
tótta lèna scarmiéda, l'è la chèsa
dla Pia di mataràz, e alè che rézz
l'è una ringhira, ò un òc ormai, ad sòura

ma voi, anche voi, non state ad aspettare, venite via, / c'è già un paciugo
qui", "Eh lo so purtroppo, / è una casa, io, questa, quando piove, / devo
mettere dappertutto delle bacinelle", / e la gente capisce sempre a rovescio,
/ cosa vuoi bacinelle, ma non la senti sotto, / qui sotto, non senti come un
animale / che ansima? niente, va' là, cosa vuoi parlare, piuttosto / addesso
qui, questo è l'ultimo pianerottolo, / e questo portone è chiuso, però di là
parlano, / è uscito un cameriere, mi sono infilato, / avevano finito di
mangiare, ma un tavolata, / baccagliavano, un fumo, non m'hanno nemmeno
visto, / ho imboccato un corridoio, / questa porta, c'è la chiave dentro, vediamo, ci ho indovinato anche stavolta, un soprascala, / e lassú c'è una bot-
tola, mi ci sono afferrato, / piedi contro il muro, mi sono tirato su di peso,
/ e qui? era come camminare in una nuvola, / tutta lana a bioccoli, è la casa
/ della Pia dei materassi, e lí quel ricciolo / e una ringhiera, ho un occhio
ormai, di sopra /

above it's all horsehair, quiet now, who's moaning?
"Are you hurt?" two of them, "What do you want?"
"Is it Nando?"
"No, please excuse me, I was just passing through,"
"Get the hell out of here," she had covered her face
with her hands, and now where?
stay calm, beyond that net is a door,
with a bolt that's all rusted,
this is a bitch, come on, up and down, up and down,
that's right, budge,
all it needs, come on, up and down, and pull,
that's it, it gave, hurry, come on, unbelievable,
I tripped, I came close to falling, it's pitch dark,
and I'm not finding the switch, here it is, right here,
but this stone feels like tufa, and hanging from it, up high there,
is a rabbit stuffed with straw,
a rubber hose on a nail, bottles, wine flasks, wood, spider webs,
a wine cellar,
or am I delirious? no, there are definitely wine barrels,
my legs are killing me,
stairs and more stairs, I'm going to collapse trying to get to the
[end,
because if the water gets down here,
I'll drown like a rat, how did I get here?
what is happening to me?
damn, why couldn't he have hypnotized me too?

494

l'è tótta créina, zétt, chi ch' s'alaménta?
"A stè mèl?", mo i è in déu, "Csa vut?", "L'è Nando?",
"No, 'i da scusé, a paséva da què",
"Tót de caz!", li la s'era cvért' la faza
sal mèni, e adès dù s val?
'ta bón, adlà 'd cla ràida, l'è una pórta,
s'un carnàz tótt ruznéid, quèst l'è una bés-cia,
dài pò, sò e zò, sò e zò, acsè, da smóval,
u i vó, mo e' vén, sémpra sò e zò e tiré,
ècco, l'è vnéu, andémma dài, 'zidénti!
ò inzampighé, che un èlt pó a casch, l'è un schéur,
e a n tróv e' scròch dla luce, ècco, l'è què,
mo quèst 'l'è tóff, e tachèda sò 'lè
una pèla ad cunéi sla paia dréinta,
una canèla ad gòmma m'un ciód, bòci,
fiasch, lègna, talaràgn, l'è una cantéina,
o ch'a zavèri? no, l'è bòtti, quèlli,
ch'a m so s-cènt bèla al gambi,
schèli e schèli, ò s-ciupè par avní réss,
che s' la s'inféila aquè
l'è la mórta de sòrgh, mo cmè ch'ò fat?
csèll ch'u m suzéd?
porca boia, u n m'avrà mégga indurmént

è tutto crine, zitto, che si lamenta? / "State male?", ma sone in due, "Cosa
vuoi?", "È Nando?" / "No, dovete scusare, passavo di qui", / "Togliti dai
coglioni", lei si era coperta la faccia / con le mani, e adesso dove si va? / sta'
buono, oltre quella rete, è una porta, / con un catenaccio tutto arrugginito,
questo è una bestia, / dai pure, su e giú, su e giú, così, da smuoverlo, / ci
vuole, ma viene, sempre su e giú e tirare, / ecco, è venuto, andiamo, dai,
accidenti! / ho inciampato, che un altro po' cado, è un buio, / e non trovo
l'interruttore, ecco, è qui, / ma questo è tufo, e attaccata su lí / una pelle di
coniglio con la paglia dentro, / una cannella di gomma a un chiodo, bottiglie,
/ fiaschi, legna, ragnatele, è una cantina, / o vaneggio? no, sono botti, quelle,
/ che ho le gambe a pezzi, / scale e scale, sono scoppiato per venire a finire,
/ che se s'infila qui / è la morte del topo, ma come ho fatto? / come mi
succede? / porco boia, non mi avrà mica addormentato / anche a me? no,
ma va' là, che prima /

no, forget it,
first I banged my head, can you feel the lump?
you can just forget about sleep, wait, no, here, there's
nothing, I'm coming up from the plains,
even the houses, the villas, they're steps,
a little boy is coming this way,
whenever you're a nervous wreck,
and not thinking straight, stay calm now,
I just had a good scare, that's the extent of it,
and coming up the stairs, later,
I was all alone, laughing, I mean,
what an imbecile, but enough of that now,
enough, it's passed, I'm way up here,
when you can see down below, or even if not,
even if there's not much to see,
at least you can take a deep breath,
but it doesn't last, feel it, it's so humid
my pants are sticking, every so often a piece of plaster falls,
there it is, look at that mark on the pavement,
down below, there, it's getting bigger, it's here already,
you can't get away from it, you can't escape,
but you can get used to it, plus there's not any choice,
on your haunches and climbing,
even when there's nowhere else to go, when there's nothing
                                                    [left to say,
it seems like you're trapped, then, if you look closely,

ènca mu mè? no, mo va là, che préima
ò batú 'na zuchéda, sint che gnòcch,
èlt che indurmént, spétta, no, ècco, a i so,
gnént, a véngh da la basa,
ènca al chèsi, i palàz, l'è di scaléin,
ch'u i aréiva un burdèl,
mo quant u s'à e' nervòus,
ch'u n s ragòuna, 'ta bón,
a so pas un spaghètt, e sò mal schèli
dop a rideva da par mè, mè déggh
ch'a sarò pò un pataca, mo adès basta,
basta, la è pasa, a so quasò d'in èlt,
quant u s pò guardè ad sòtta, lasa pò,
ènca s'u è póch d'avdài, mo u s téira e' fiè,
sno che la n déura, sint, l'aria la è griva,
i calzéun i s'ataca,
e'casca d'ogni tènt un calzinàz,
l'è li, vèrda cla macia se sulèr,
alè ad sòtta, ch' la s slèrga, la è zà què,
ta n'i scap, ta n t sgavàgn,
mo u s'i fa l'òs, pu u i è póch da capè,
pi te chéul e andè sò,
ènch' quant u n s va piò invéll, ch'u n s pò mai déi,
u t pèr d'ès intraplèd, pu a guardè bén,

ho battuto una testata, senti che bernoccolo, / altro che addormentato,
aspetta, no, ecco, ci sono, / niente, vengo dalla bassa, / anche le case, i pa-
lazzi, sono scalini, / che ci arriva un bambino, / ma quando si ha il nervoso,
/ che non si ragiona, sta' buono, / ho passato uno spaghetto, e su per le scale
/ dopo ridevo da solo, io dico / che sarò pure un salame, ma adesso basta,
/ basta, è passata, sono quassú in alto, / quando si può guardare di sotto, lascia pure, / anche se c'è poco da vedere, ma si tira il fiato, / solo che non
dura, senti, l'aria è pesante, / i calzoni si appicciano, / cade ogni tanto un calcinaccio, / è lei, guarda quella macchia sul pavimento, / lí di sotto, che si al-
larga, è già qui, / non ci scappi, non te la cavi, / ma ci si fa l'osso, poi c'è
poco da scegliere, / piedi nel culo e salire, / anche quando non si va piú da
nessuna parte, che non si può mai dire, / ti pare d'essere intrappolato, poi,
a guardar bene, /

in the back, there's a staircase,
how many times has this happened to me,
and you run up them in a frenzy,
after awhile you're there all over again, here is the wall,
here too, it's all wall, but this time,
you stay there, looking down, but no, it's never going to end,
there could even be a hidden door,
like right now, you've got to pay attention to every little nook
and cranny,
the slightest creaking, matches would really be a help now,
but they're not lighting, the tips are all soggy, wait a second,
let me see, this skinny hanging cord,
wouldn't this be a latch, hey, it opens,
it sure does, it's a tiny staircase, I'm taking off,
I'm yelling, singing, me, even though I'm tone deaf, patience,
no one's making any noise, and there's another staircase over
[there,
didn't I already pass through here already? or not?
places, at any rate,
so many of them are the same, they're all alike,
it's a wild goose-chase,
but banging my head was bad enough,
as long as it's down below, Jesus, did I see right?
beautiful, all spread out like a whore,
I hadn't understood yet, the stone masons
had left it there, it means I can do it,

in fònd u i è una schèla,
quant vólti u m'è suzèst, e t vé sò 'd féuga,
dop un pó ta i si dl'èlt, aquè l'è méur,
ènca què, l'è tótt méur, stavólta mò,
t sté 'lè, a ócc bas, invíci no, mai zéd,
u i putrébb ès 'na mascarèda,
cmè 'dès, bsògna stè 'tènti ènch' m'un ciaplètt,
m'un scòrch, i furminènt, ch'i m farébb bén,
mo i n zènd, al cróccli al s'è spaplèdi, spétta,
fam avdài, sta curdléina
u n sarà una marlètta? ció, la s'éirva
dabón, l'è tótt scaléin, a vagh ch'a vòul,
a rógg, a chènt, ch'a so stunèd, pazinzia,
u n sint niseun, e alà u i è un'èlta schèla,
ch'a i so zà pas da què, o no? i póst ormai,
tanimódi l'è chèsi,
i è tótti cumpàgn, l'è cumè fè e' zéir dl'óca,
mo mè, basta tní bota,
fintènt che li la è sòtta, orca, ò vést bén?
bèla, puzèda alè, cmè una putèna,
u n m'era 'ncòura capitè, i la à lasa
di muradéur, la fa rinséida, quèsta,

in fondo c'è una scala, / quante volte m'è successo, e vai su di furia, / dopo
un po' ci sei di nuovo, qui è muro, / anche qui, è tutto muro, stavolta mo',
/ stai lí, a occhi bassi, invece no, mai cedere, / ci potrebbe essere una porta
mascherata, / come adesso, bisgona fare attenzione anche a un occhiello, /
a uno scrocco, i fiammiferi, che mi servirebbero, / ma non s'acccendono, le
capocchie si sono spappolate, aspetta, / fammi vedere, questa cordicella, /
non sarà un saliscendi? ehi, si apre, / davvero, sono tutti scalini, vado che
volo, / urlo, canto, che sono stonato, pazienza, / non sente nessuno, e là c'è
un'altra scala, / che ci sono già passato di qui, o no? i posti ormai, / tanto
sono case, / sono tutti uguali, è come fare il giro dell'oca, / ma io, a me basta
tener botta, / finché lei è sotto, orca, ho visto bene? / bella, appoggiata lí,
come una puttana, / non m'era ancora capitato, l'hanno lasciata / dei
muratori, fa riuscita, questa, /

it's swaying, and up here at the top, hold tight now,
I climb through the window,
a meeting room, keep going, another staircase, it's marble,
with brass railings, easy street,
then another, they just keep going on and on, and you,
what do you want?
don't you shake all over me, it's complete drenched,
you got me wet,
up until this point the only thing missing was the dog,
go on, go on, get,
you can go to hell, but I'm going to rest,
you've got to catch your breath every once in awhile,
I'm not twenty anymore, all right then, much better,
all I need is five minutes,
just how steep is this? I'm starting now,
it's always like this, if I stop, after awhile,
my head starts spinning like a top,
there's must be some place, somewhere that's dry,
you think you're ever going to get there?
but it's dry, I'm telling you,
dry as a walnut,
with dust like the fluff under the bed,
on those curled-up note cards
on the dresser mirror, and even then,
are you sure the water's not going to come?
I don't know, they're all good questions, who can reply?
but there is one in particular, and that question is this, if we meet,

la dòndla, e quasò in zéima ciapès bén,
a scavèlch la finèstra,
'na sèla, avènti, in'èlta schèla, ad mèrum,
se tinimèn d'utòun, u s va da sgnéur,
pu un'èlta, a n finéss mai, e tè csa vut?
nu scróllti aquè, mòl fràid, u m'à dluvié,
u i amanchéva un chèn, córr, dài, va véa,
va te caséin, che invíci mè a m'arpòuns,
bsògna fè tapa, d'ogni tènt, cumè,
a n'ò méggh' piò vint'an, ècco, a so a pòst,
mè u m basta zéinch minéut,
mo quant'èll ch'a vagh sò? adès a tach,
sémpra acsè, s'a m'aférum, dop pr'un pó,
la testa, un mulinèl, u i sarà pò
da qualche pèrta e' sótt,
ch'a n gn'apa d'arivé? mo sótt dabón,
sótt cmè una néusa,
sla pòrbia ch' la fa i rózzal sòtta e' lèt,
sal cartuléini a rézz
mi véidar dla cardenza, e pu ènca 'lè
sichèur che l'aqua la n'arivarà?
a n'e' so, l'è tótt' dmandi, chi ch' pò 'rspònd?
mo u i n'è óna, mè quèlla, s'a incuntréss,

dondola, e quassú in cima afferrarsi bene, / scavalco la finestra, / una sala,
avanti, un'altra scala, di marmo, / con il corrimano d'ottone, si va da signori,
/ poi un'altra, non finiscono mai, e tu cosa vuoi? / non scrollarti qui, mollo
fradicio, m'ha bagnato tutto, / ci mancava un cane, corri, dai, va' via, / va'
nel casino, che io invece mi riposo, / bisgogna far tappa ogni tanto, / non ho
mica piú vent'anni, ecco, sono a posto, / a me mi bastano cinque minuti, /
ma quant'è che salgo? adesso comincio, / sempre cosí, se mi fermo, dopo
per un po', / la testa, un mulinello, ci sarà pure / da qualche parte l'asciutto,/
che non ci debba arrivare? ma asciutto sul serio, / asciutto come un noce, /
con la polvere chef a la lanugine sotto il letto, / con le cartoline arricciate /
ai vetri della credenza, e poi anche lí, / sicuro che l'acqua non arriverà? / non
lo so, sono tutte domande, chi può rispondere? / ma ce n'è una, io quella, se
incontrassi, /

not him, he doesn't control a thing, with all his fast talk,
he's a pawn, no, it's the ones who are above him,
the ones who really run things,
the ones you could have the talk with,
two words for you: why me?
because when you think about it,
this is a big deal, it's way too big,
I'm here, it seems to me, I was selected at random,
it's a quid pro quo,
which if I were to tell them my name, I'm sure,
they'd be up there looking down at me:
and you, who are you?
that's what I wanted to say to you, who am I?
I'm nothing, I'm, let's be honest,
I'm worth less than the two of clubs,
the otitis makes my ears buzz, I can't see well,
even with these glasses,
which fell off by the way, one of the lenses
is cracked, the one you're talking about
is not me, who knows, maybe it looks like me,
but it's not me, and now you've stopped
now when all I want to do is throw myself on the ground
and stay here as long as I want, I'm not asking much,
and later, if possible, a few stairs down,
in the direction of home, even there, I wouldn't need much,
a game on t.v.,

no léu, ch'u n cmanda gnént, tótt' la su ciacra,
l'è una pedéina, no, quéi ch'i i è sòura,
quéi ch'i cmanda dabón, putèi fè un zcòurs,
do paróli: parchè própia mu mè?
che quant a i péns,
quèst' l'è una roba gròsa, tropa gròsa,
mè què, sgònd mè, a so vnù ciapèd par chès,
l'è un quiproquò,
che s'a i déggh e' mi nóm, a so sichéur,
i starà alè a guardèm: e tu chi sei?
l'è quèll ch'a v vléva déi, chi ch'a so mè?
a n so gnént, mè, zò, a còunt, cmè e' do 'd bastòun,
ch'a patéss ènch' d'otite, pu a i vèggh póch,
e sa sti ucèl ch'i mè casch, ò una lénta
tótta cripèda, quèll ch'a gí vuílt
l'è un èlt, chi sa magari u m s'asarméa,
mo an so mè, e adès farmé,
ch'ò una vòia 'd butém stuglèd ma tèra,
e stè 'lè quant u m pèr, a n dmand 'na masa,
e dop, s'u' s pò, qualche scaléin d'inzò,
vérs chèsa, che ènca 'lè mè u m basta póch,
la partéida ma la televisiòun,

non lui, che non comanda niente, tutta la sua chiacchiera, / è una pedina, no, quelli che gli sono sopra, / quelli che comandano sul serio, potergli fare un discorso, / due parole: perché proprio a me? / che quando ci penso, / questa è una cosa grossa, / troppo grossa, / io qui, secondo me, sono venuto preso per caso, / è un quiproquo, / che se gli dico il mio nome, sono sicuro, / staranno lí a guardarmi: e tu chi sei? / è quello che vi volevo dire, chi sono io? / non sono niente, io, dai, conto come come il due di bastoni, / che pastico anche d'otite, poi ci vedo poco, / e con questi occhiali, che mi sono caduti, ho una lente, / tutta crepata, quello che dite voi /è un altro, chi sa, magari mi somiglia, / ma non sono io, e adesso fermate, / che ho una voglia di buttarmi sdraiato per terra, / e star lí quanto mi pare, non domando molto, / e dopo, se si può, qualche scalino in giú, / verso casa, che anche lí mi basta poco, / la partita alla televisione, /

a little trip every once in awhile, I'd like to see
the Dolomites, I've never been there,
to go out a few nights collecting snails, if it had rained,
because I like the taste of them,
a little bit of this and that, and to keep talking,
by myself, with nothing happening,
but there's no way they understand, they see me all right,
or aren't they looking, where are they? who am I going to tell
that I'm here, that this is all a mistake
which has nothing to do with me.

'na gita d'ogni tènt, a vrébb avdài
al Dolomiti, ch'a n'i so mai stè,
dal nòti andè a luméghi, s' l'à piuvéu,
ch'a m pis, e quèst e quèll, e avènti a zcòrr,
da par mè, e u n suzéd gnént,
ch'i n'apa da capéi, i m'avdirà pò,
o ch'i n guèrda, dò ch'i è? ma chéi ch'a l déggh
che mè què, quèst l'è un sbai, a n gn'éintar gnént!

una gita ogni tanto, vorrei vedere / le Dolomiti, che non ci sono mai stato, / delle notti andare a lumache, se ha piovuto, / che mi piacciono, e questo e quello, e avanti a parlare, / da solo, e non succede niente, / che non debbano capire, mi vedrano pure, / o non guardano? dove sono? a chi lo dico / che io qui, questo è uno sbaglio, non c'entro niente!

SMALL TALK

CIACRI

This is how

This is how, sometimes, when I come home
at night, before putting the key in,
I ring. Ring-ring

                              nobody ever answers

Mo acsè

Mo acsè, dal vólti, quant a tòurn a chèsa,
la sàira, préima d'infilé la cèva,
a sòun, drin, drin,
                    u n'arspòund mai niseun.

Ma cosí. Ma cosí, delle volte, quando torno a casa, / la sera, prima d'infilare
la chiave, / suono, drin, drin, – non risponde mai nessuno.

Sleeping

What a sweet thing it is to sleep.
I've never slept enough.
I haven't. My whole life. When I was a boy, to go to school
I had to get up at six, which was still night,
the bus
came by at six-thirty,
I was drowsy, I never could keep my eyes open.
And when I got older, even worse. For the bakery,
I had to get up every morning at three,
the people setting up on market days
would arrive at two at the piazza
and you could kiss sleep goodbye.
I've never lost that feeling of sleepiness,
even now with the change in my line
of work, I bought The Driver's Bar
on the via Emilia, which was a good business
but you can't make a living from it,
I get myself up at five, the drivers,
but it's not just the drivers,
it's everything, it's a big place, the cafeteria,
two pool tables, which I put my sons in charge of,
but you've got to keep after them,
then in the evening there's always

Durméi

Pu bén durméi, a n'ò mai durmí sà,
mè, te mi mònd, a m'arcórd da burdèl
pr'andè a la scóla, a cnéva stè sò al si,
ch' l'era nòta d'invéran, la curira
la paséva al si e mèz,
un sònn ch'a n gne la féva a tnai vért i ócc,
e pu da grand ancòura pézz, e' fòuran,
a cnéva stè sò al tre tótt al matéini,
i dè 'd marchè la zénta adiritéura
i arivéva al do in piaza, e 's'ut durméi,
e' sònn mè ch'ò mai pérs,
mo enca adès, ch'ò cambiè,
ò tólt e' Bar dl'Autésta sla via Emilia,
ch' l'è un afèri, sè, d'acórd, mo un n s chèmpa,
i camionésta, u m tòcca stè sò al zéinch
la matéina, mo u n'è sno i camionésta,
l'è tótt, e' pòst, l'è grand, tavola calda,
du biglièrd, ch'ò mèss sòtta ènca i mi fiúl,
mo s'a n'i stagh dri mè,
pu la sàira u i è sémpra

Dormire. Che buona cosa dormire, non ho mai dormito abbastanza, / io, nella mia vita, mi ricordo da bambino / per andare a scuola dovevo alzarmi alle sei, / che era notte, d'inverno, la corriera / passava alle sei e mezzo, / un sonno che non ce la facevo a tener aperti gli occhi, / e poi da grande ancora peggio, il forno, / dovevo alzarmi alle tre tutte le mattine, / i giorni di mercato la gente addirittura / arrivavano alle due in piazza, e cosa vuoi dormire, / il sonno che ho mai perso, / ma anche adesso che ho cambiato, / ho preso il Bar dell'Autista sulla via Emilia, / che è stato un affare, sí, d'accordo, ma non si campa, / i camionisti, mi tocca alzarmi alle cinque / la mattina, ma non sono solo i camionisti, / è tutto, il posto è grande, tavola calda, / due bigliardi, che ho messo sotto anche i miei figli, / ma se non ci sto dietro io, / poi la sera ci sono sempre /

511

those two or three tables playing cards,
they're regulars, they drink,
at midnight it's like it's the middle of the day,
and I get to sleep when?
sometimes, sitting behind the bar,
there's no noise, a silence,
just them across the room tapping against the bottles
and for a moment I dream of going to bed,
of sleeping like the dead,
which I can't
you can't do that
there's no way to do it, and boom, just at that moment,
someone's jabbing my shoulder:
"Hey, didn't you hear me? It's about time,"
"You eat, I'll eat later,"
holy shit
what is this madhouse?
who woke me up?
It's wake-up time here.
"What do you want to do now? What have you got?"
"It's three,
don't you need to be going over to Bontadini's?"
"No, I agree with Ettore; he's going,"
let's show a little compassion here, let the righteous get some
                                                    [slumber,
sure, dream on, "These bills, people, are wrong, look,
down at the bottom," "You figure the bill then,"

chi du tri tavuléin ch' zuga a chèrti,
ch' l'è avantéur, i cunsómma,
mo a mezanòta l'è cm'e' fóss mezdè,
e quant a dórum mè?
dal vólti alè disdài dri de bancòun,
u n gn'è niseun, un zétt,
sno déu adlà ch'a sint sbat al bucétti,
e pr'un mumént a insógni d'andè lèt,
'd fè una durméida da óli sènt,
                              ch'a n pòs,
u n s pò, u n gn'è mèzi, a m sint zà bat s'na spala:
"Ció, t n'é sintéi? l'à sunè e' tòcch", "Magné,
mè a véngh a magnè dop", porca putèna,
cs'èll sté caséin? chi è stè ch' l'à mèss la sveglia?
mo aquè l'è tótt' 'na sveglia,
"Csa vut tè 'ncòura? cs'èll ch'u i è?", "L'è al tre,
ta n'é d'andé da Bontadini?", "No,
a so d'acórd sa Ettore, e' va léu",
mo sté un pó bón, lasé durméi la zénta,
sè, t'é vòia, "Sti chéunt, aquè, u n s capéss,
dài, vén ad sòtta", "Mo féi vuìlt i chéunt",

quei due tre tavolini che giocano a carte, / che sono avventori, consumano, / ma a mezzanotte è come fosse mezzogiorno, / e quando dormo io? / delle volte seduto lí dietro il bancone, / non c'è nessuno, un silenzio, / solo due di là che sento picchiare le bocchette, / e per un momento sogno d'andare a letto, / di fare una dormita da olio santo, – che non posso, / non si può, non c'è mezzo, mi sento già battere su una spalla: / "Ehi, non ha sentito? è suonato il tocco", "Mangiate, / io vengo a mangiare dopo", porca puttana, / cos'è 'sto casino? chi è stato che ha messo la sveglia? / ma qui è tutta una sveglia, / "Cosa vuoi tu ancora? cosa c'è?", "Sono le tre, / non devi andare da Bontadini?", "No, / sono d'accordo con Ettore, ci va lui,", / ma state un po' buoni, lasciate dormire la gente, / sí, hai voglia, "Questi conti, qui, non si capisce, / dai, vieni di sotto", "Ma fateli voi i conti", /

"It's better if you watch too," always the same discussion,
if you're not here, if you are not here,
and then
when I'm not here, it goes on the same way, you know it's true,
come on, the world just moves right along even if I'm not
                                        [present here,
then, after you haven't been here a little while,
when it's been awhile since they've seen you
they don't come looking anymore,

Jesus Christ, if only they would forget,
not having to be there for anyone, stretched out on the bed,
pulling up the covers, your thoughts get all muddled,
your eyelids get heavy, you turn out the light,
wait, you don't have to do anything, he does everything,
he takes your hand, he takes you away,
where? you don't want to know, all you want to do is sleep,
a good long stretch,
a sleep for all the sleep you've ever missed,
it's raining outside, the windows are closed,
wake-up time's been given time off,
you took the phone off the hook,
you've bolted the downstairs door,
it's you and sleep-hunger, the room's asleep all the way up to
                                        [the ceiling,

"L'è mèi s' ta i si ènca tè", sémpra sté zcòurs,
s' ta n'i si tè, s' ta n'i tè, che pu
quant a n'i so, i fa tótt, dài, zò, che e' mònd
e' va 'vènti l'istèss ènch' s'a n'i so,
pu dop un pó che ta n'i si, ch'i n t vaid,
i n t zirca gnénca piò,

porca masóla, s'i s zcurdéss, dabón,
no èsi par niseun, stuglèd te lèt,
ta t téir sò al cvérti, i pensír i s'imbròia,
i ócc i t fa la capana, t smórt la luce,
t'aspétt, t n'é da fè gnént, e' fa tótt léu,
u t ciapa par la mèna, u t pórta véa,
dòvv? ta n'e' vu savài, t vu sno durméi,
fè tótt' una tirata,
durméi par tótt e' témp ch' ta n'é durméi,

ad fura e' pióv, al finestri agli è céusi,
la sveglia ormai la è scarga,
t'é stach ènca e' telefan,
la pórta ad sòtta t'i é mèss e' carnàz,
t si tè e e' sònn, la cambra l'è tótt sònn,

"È meglio se ci sei anche tu", sempre questo discorso, / se non ci sei tu, se
non ci sei tu, che poi / quando non ci sono, fanno tutto, dai, su, che il mondo va avanti lo stesso anche se non ci sono, / poi dopo un po' che non ci sei,
che non ti vedono, / non ti cercano neanche piú, // porca masóla, se si
dimenticassero, davvero, / non esserci per nessuno, sdraiato nel letto, / ti tiri
su le coperte, i pensieri s'imbrogliano, / gli occhi ti fanno la capanna, spegni
la luce, / aspetti, non devi far niente, fa tutto lui, / ti prende per mano, ti
porta via, / dove? non lo vuoi sapere, vuoi solo dormire, / far tutta una
tirata, / dormire per tutto il tempo che non hai dormito, // fuori piove, le
finestre sono chiuse, / la sveglia ormai è scarica, / hai staccato anche il telefono, / alla porta di sotto hai messo il catenaccio, / sei tu e il sonno, la camera è tutto sonno /

the hall's asleep, the sitting room, the pull-strings of the
                                    [lights, the water in the
pipes,
the calycanthus in the garden,
the roses, the magnolia,
the post office is sleeping, city hall,
the people in the piazza, birds, horses,
the river Marecchia, the Fabbricone,
the whole world is sleepy,

and you sleep in sheets that need laundering,
they're rumpled, they're scratchy,
you're clutching your pillow, it's soft,
sleeping, mouth closed, so you don't get thirsty,
one foot sticking out from under the covers, to feel the fresh air,
you turn, you rub a knee, is it day?
is it night? it's sleep, it's sleep,
the bed is a ship, the sea is holy oil,
this is lovely, being still and voyaging,
sleeping and going out in the world,
and will I have to wake myself up? yes
like hell I will,
come on, up you go, use your head now, get yourself up,
then what?

fina e' sufétt, l'è sònn e' curidéur,
la sèla, al schèli,
i féil dla luce, l'aqua ti cundótt,
l'è sònn e' calicantus te zardéin,
al rósi, la magnolia,
l'è sònn la Posta, e' palàz de Cuméun,
la zénta in piaza, i gazót, i cavàl,
la Marèccia, e' Fabrécch, l'è sònn e' mònd,

e tè t dórum, si lanzúl ad bughéda,
ch'i è róvd, i ròusga,
se tu cuscéin, ch' ta t'e' tén strètt, l'è mórbi,
durméi, a bòcca céusa, ch'u n t vén sàida,
un pi fura dal cvérti, a sintí e' frèsch,
ta t vólt, ta t grat un znòc, l'è e' dè? l'è nòta?
l'è sònn, l'è sémpra sònn,
e' lèt l'è un bastimént, e' mèr un óli,
che belèzza, stè férum e viazè,
durméi e andè pr'e' mònd,
e a m sarébb da svigé, mè? sè, te fiòch,
dài, zò, mo un pó 'd bón séns, svigés, e pu?

fino al soffitto, è sonno il corridoio, / il salotto, le scale, / i fili della luce, l'acque nelle condutture, / è sonno il calycanthus nel giardino, / le rose, la magnolia, / è sonno la Posta, il palazzo del Comune, / la gente in piazza, gli uccelli, i cavalli, / la Marecchia, il Fabbricone, è sonno il mondo, // e tu dormi, coi lenzuoli di bucato, / che sono ruvidi, pizzicano, / col tuo cuscino, che te lo tieni stretto, è soffice, / dormire, a bocca chiusa, che non ti viene sete, / un piede fuori dalle coperte, a sentire il fresco, / ti volti, ti gratti un ginocchio, è giorno? è notte? / è sonno, è sempre sonno, / il letto è un bastimento, il mare un olio, / che bellezza, star fermo e viaggiare, / dormire e andare per il mondo, / e dovrei svegliarmi, io? sí, col cavolo, / dai, su, ma un po´di buon senso, svegliarsi, e poi?

517

White Flag

for Jeffrey Stovall

Click, against the window, a pebble, every so often. Click,
like it's some kind of game.
Even at night, the telephone calls.
Hello? And the one on the other end is quiet, breathing.
Who are you? Or letters. Letters delivered priority mail,
and inside not even a sheet of paper, an empty envelope.
They're sending me signals, we're here.
They're watching me, they want to wear me out, and their tactic,
they're always near the house, disguised,
chitchatting, strolling,
on market day, just to take an example, three or four of them
in the main piazza, each on his own bench,
I recognize them immediately,
they're big walkers, just like I am,
same thing with the knife-sharpener,
who stops and sets up shop right below me,
it's one of them, does it matter which?
or the masons working at the Credit Union?
two or three of them, I can see from a mile away
but they're not really masons,
so many of them I've stopped counting,

Bandiera biènca

Tic, còuntra la finestra,
un giarúl, d'ogni tènt, tic, cmè par schérz,
ènca ad nòta, pu dal telefonèdi,
a téir sò, pronto? e léu, 'dlà zétt, ch' l'arfièda,
a l sint, chi sit? o dal lèttri, di espréss,
e dréinta gnénca un fòi, 'na bósta svéita,
i m manda di segnèl, a sémm aquè,
i m bèda, i m vó strachè, l'è la su tatica,
i è sémpra tònda chèsa, travistéid,
i ciacàra, i va a spas,
e' dè d' marchè, par déi, u i n'è tri quatar
in piaza granda, ognéun se su banchètt,
ch'a i arcnòss sóbit, l'è ambulènt cmè mè,
e' rudaréin l'istèss,
ch'u s'afèrma a rudè própia aquè sòtta,
l'è 'un 'd lòu, chi vut ch'e' séa?
i muradéur ch'i lavòura te Crèdit,
u i n'è du tréi, ta i vaid dalòungh un méa
ch'u n'è di muradéur,
mo i è ch'a n'i còunt piò,

Bandiera bianca. Tic, contro la finestra, / un sassolino, ogni tanto, tic, come per scherzo, / anche di notte, poi delle telefonate, / tiro su, pronto? e lui di là zitto, che respira, / lo sento, chi sei? o delle lettere, degli espressi, / e dentro neanche un foglio, una busta vuota, / mi mandano dei segnali, siamo qui, / mi badano, mi vogliono stancare, è la loro tattica, / sono sempre attorno casa, travestiti, / chiacchierano, vanno a spasso, / il giorno di mercato, per dire, ce n'è tre quattro / in piazza grande, ognuno col suo banco, / che li riconosco subito, sono ambulanti come me, / l'arrotino lo stesso, / che si ferma ad arrotare proprio qui sotto, / è uno di loro, chi vuoi che sia? / i muratori che lavorano nel Credito, / ce n'è due tre, li vedi lontano un miglio / che non sono muratori, / ma sono tanti che non li conto piú, /

the one who repairs the caning on chairs under the arcade,
the one who fixes umbrellas,
not one gets by me, by now I pick them out,
the bus drivers, both of them,
that small guy who hangs the posters at the movie theater,
then on Sundays, the tourists, all in white,
steady boy, even a child would recognize them,
there are times, if you follow your instinct,
get it all out there in the open, push,
come on, come and get me, what are you waiting for?
the downstairs door, all you need is one good push,
come in, come on in, come upstairs, what are you afraid of?
I'm not armed, I don't even own a pocketknife,
which would be a mistake, however,
that is exactly what they want, for you to scream, for you to
                                                    [lose it,
no, never, with them, it's trouble if you get all worked up
all that is needed is patience
and some chamomile tea,
stay calm, try to think clearly,
it's just that to think straight, I don't understand
the tactics, what are they waiting for?
the whole thing seems like a farce,
all of them wandering around the house every day,

quèll ch' l'impàia al scaràni sòtta i pórtich,
quèll ch'e' cònda agli umbrèli,
u n mu nu n scapa éun, ò un òc ormai,
i autésta, tutt déu dll'Atam,
che znin ch'e' taca sò i cartléun de cino,
pu la dmènga i turésta, vstéid ad biènch,
'ta bón, va là, ch'u i arcnòss un burdèl,
u i è di mumént, s'a déss mént ma l'istéint,
ch'a vrébb arvéi tótt al finestri: forza,
dài, vnéim a tó, cs'èll ch'a sté d'aspitè?
la pórta ad sòtta, e' basta una spatasa,
avènti, antré, vní 'd sòura, cs'iv paéura?
a n so armèd, a n'ò gnénca un temperéin,
ch' sarébb un sbai però,
l'è quèll ch'i vó, lòu, t róggia, ta t sputèna,
no, guai, sa lòu, a fès avní e' nervòus,
aquè u i vó sno pazinzia e capumélla,
bsògna stè chèlum, zarchè d' ragiunè,
sno che ragiòuna pò, mè a n la capéss
sta tatica, cs'èll ch'i sta d'aspitè?
u m pèr adiritéura una cumédia,
lòu tótt e' dè ch'i zéira tònda chèsa,

quello che impaglia le sedie sotto i portici, / quello che ripara gli ombrelli, /
non me ne scappa uno, ho un occhio ormai, / gli autisti, tutt'e due, del-
l'Atam, / quel piccoletto che affigge i cartelloni del cinema, / poi la domenica, i turisti, vestiti di bianco, / sta' buono, va' là, che li riconosce un bambino, / ci sono dei momenti, se dessi retta all'istinto, / che vorrei aprire tutte
le finestre, forza, / dai, venire a prendermi, cosa aspettate? / la porta di sotto,
basta una spinta, / avanti, entrate, venite di sopra, cos'avete paura? / non
sono armato, non ho neanche un temperino, / che sarebbe uno sbaglio però,
/ è quello che vogliono, loro, che urli, che ti sputtani, / no, guai, con loro, a
farsi venire il nervoso, / qui ci vuole solo pazienza e camomilla, / bisogna
star calmi, cercar di ragionare, / solo che ragiona pure, io non la capisco /
questa tattica, cosa stanno ad aspettare? / mi pare addirittura una commedia,
/ loro tutto il giorno intorno a casa, /

I always sit next to these blinds,
they're watching me and I'm watching them,
how much longer is this going to go on?
sometimes I say: what about escaping? Tonight,
in disguise, that's a possibility,
but where do I go?
by escaping you've got to keep escaping,
no, I'll stay home, let them come and get me,
it's just, they're not coming, they're taking their sweet time,
these gravediggers, but I'm in a hurry, let's get this thing over
[and done with,
do whatever you're going to do, but be quick about it,
because there's a thousand of them, it's a thing, even this,
seeing all these people, all this movement
around me, sometimes, if only I weren't aware of it,
but it just makes me start laughing,
and, on the other hand, down below are always so grave,
they come, they go, they window shop,
they pretend to be reading posters,
they ask for the time, what a life, even for them,
a hell of a thing, waiting, it's just
that there's nothing more to do, on top of it I'm bored with it,
enough's enough, where did I put the keys, there they are, on
[the dresser,

mè sémpra què tachèd ma stal persièni,
lòu ch'i m bèda mu mè e mè ma lòu,
quante la à d'andè 'vènti?
dal vólti a déggh: e scapè? adès, stanòta,
travistéid ènca mè, la s'i pò fè,
mo dò ch'a vagh?
pu scapè, dop u t tòcca scapè sémpra,
no, a stagh ma chèsa mea, ch'i m vénga a tó,
sno ch'i n vén, i n'à préssia
sti becamórt, mo ò préssia mè, s-ciantémmla,
fé quèll ch'aví da fè, però sbrighév,
ch'i mélla, l'è una roba, mè, 'nca quèsta,
vdai tótt' sta zénta, tótt sté muvimént
par mè, dal vólti, ch'a sarò incoscient,
mo u m vén da réid,
e lòu invíci ad sòtta, sémpra séri,
i va, i vén, i s'aférma mal vedréini,
i fa féinta da lèz i manifést,
d' dmandè l'òura, che mistír, ènca lòu,
porca putèna, spétta, tanimódi
la bèrca la è ti pèl, pu a m so stóff, basta,
d'òi mèss al cèvi? agli è 'lè, se cumò,

io sempre qui incollato a queste persiane, / loro che badano me e io loro, / quanto deve andare avanti? / delle volte dico: e scappare? adesso, questa notte, / travestito anch'io, ce la si può fare, / ma dove vado? / poi scappare, dopo ti tocca scappare sempre, / no, sto a casa mia, che mi vengano a prendere, / solo che non vengono, non hanno fretta / 'sti beccamorti, ma ho fretta io, finiamola, / fate quel che dovete fare, però sbrigatevi, / che sono mille, è una roba, io, anche questa, / vedere tutta 'sta gente, tutto 'sto movimento / per me, delle volte, che sarò incosciente, / ma mi viene da ridere, / e loro invece, di sotto, sempre seri, / vanno, vengono, si fermano alle vetrine, / fanno finta di leggere i manifesti, / di domandare l'ora, che mestiere, anche loro, / porca puttana, aspetta, tanto, / non c'è più niente da fare, poi mi sono stufato, basta, / dove ho messo le chiavi? sono lí, sul comò, /

I want to get them to laugh, too, a stroll around the block,
maybe two, they're at the door,
you laugh, well isn't this a nice surprise,
I go out, cut past Marchi's shop, take the arcades,
I'm in the piazza, here I am, this undershirt
is the white flag, I didn't know what to attach it to,
then I found this,
my grandfather's cane, you laugh?
with the silver handle,
I surrender, you all win, where are you? Come out,
I give up, but to who? This isn't drawing you forward,
even if it only to make you start to laugh, don't you believe it?
here, I'm emptying my pockets,
a little change, the keys, cigarettes,
a handkerchief, and these are the pocket linings,
what do I have? nothing, I'm laying everything out on the
                                                    [ground,
I'm even taking off my belt, my shoelaces, the tie,
that's it, I'm ready,
if someone wants to come and get me now,
I'm here, so are you coming? or do you not want me to see it?
and not where we're going either?
no big deal, fine, I'm covering my eyes with the handkerchief,

a i ví fè réid ènca ma lóu, un vólt,
du vólt, a so sla pórta,
ridéi, u n'è una bèla improvisèda?
a scap, a tai da Marchi, a imbòcch i pórtich,
a so in piaza, a so què, sta canotira,
l'è una bandira biènca, ch'a n savéva
dò tachèla, pu ò tróv, quèst l'è e' bastòun
de mi nòn, mo ridéi, se mangh d'arzént,
a m'arènd, 'i véint vuílt, dù séiv? vní fura,
a m cunsègn, mo ma chéi? s'a n vu n fé? 'vènti,
ènca s'u v vén da réid, o a n v'afidé?
toh, a m sgòmbar al bascòzi,
un pó 'd bócch spécch, al cèvi, al zigarètti,
e' fazulètt, e quèst' l'è al fódri, 'i vést?
cs'èll ch'éva? gnént, a mètt inquèl ma tèra,
a m chèv ènca la zéngia,
i lazétt, la gravata, ècco, a so pròunt,
se qualcadéun adès u m vó vní tó,
mè a so què, alòura a vnéi? o u n vó ch'a l vègga?
e gnénca dò ch'andémm?
mè, u n'è gnént, a m cruv i ócc se fazulètt,

li voglio fare ridere anche a loro, un giro, / due giri, sono sulla porta, / ridete,
non è una bella improvvisata? / esco, taglio da Marchi, imbocco i portici, /
sono in piazza, sono qui, questa canottiera, / è una bandiera bianca, che non
sapevo / dove attaccarla, poi ho trovato, questo è il bastone / di mio nonno,
ma ridete, col manico d'argento, / mi arrendo, avete vinto voi, dove siete?
venite fuori, / mi consegno, ma a chi? se non vi fate avanti, / anche se vi
viene da ridere, o non vi fidate? / toh, mi vuoto le tasche, / un po' di spiccioli, le chiavi, le sigarette, / il fazzoletto, e queste sono le fodere, avete visto?
/ cosa avevo? niente, metto tutto per terra, / mi tolgo anche la cinghia, / i
lacci, la cravatta, ecco, sono pronto, / se qualcuno adesso mi vuol venire a
prendere, / io sono qui, allora venite? o non vuole che lo veda? / e neanche
dove andiamo? / per me non è niente, mi copro gli occhi col fazzoletto, /

I'm tying it tight behind, there, that's it,
now, I can't see a thing, you can come get me,
are you coming or not? I'm here waiting for you,
I even threw away the flag. But I'm not hearing anything,
no one's making a move,
where are they? What are they doing?
you're in charge now.
how can I explain this to you? it's over, I lost,
but someone has to capture me,
so are you coming?
with this blindfold I can't see anything. Are they coming?
Or not?

a me léigh strètt di dri, ecco, acsè, adès
a n vèggh un azidént, a putí vnéi,
avnéi o no? mè a so què ch'a v'aspétt,
a sbat ènch' la bandira, mo a n sint gnént,
u n s móv niseun,
dò ch'i è? csa fai? adès a cmandé vuílt,
cm'a v l'òi da déi? mè, la è finéida, ò pérs,
mo qualcadéun ch'u m faza prisunír,
alòura insòmma a vnéi?
sa sta bènda a n vèggh gnént, i vén? i n vén?

me lo lego stretto di dietro, ecco, cosí, adesso / non vedo un accidente, potete venire, / venite o no? io sono qui che v'aspetto, / sbatto anche la bandiera,
ma non sento niente, / non si muove nessuno, / dove sono? cosa fanno?
adesso comandate voi, / come ve lo devo dire? io, è finita, ho perso, / ma
qualcuno che mi faccia prigioniero, / allora insomma venite? / con questa
benda non vedo niente, vengono? non vengono?

1948

Twenty-three years old, cute as a button, in love
but her parents wouldn't hear of it,
her father, the screaming,
for weeks on end, a war,
she was even more in love, and the other night
she went to bed early, she closed herself up in the bedroom,
and in the morning she didn't wake up again.
Killing yourself isn't right. You cannot do it, but
this girl, now you tell me
how in the world is God
going to send her to hell?

1948

Vintitrí an, carina, inamurèda,
mo i sóvv i n vléva, e' su bà dal scenèdi,
par dal stmèni, di méis, 'na guèra, li
sémpra piò inamurèda, e l'altresàira
la è 'ndè a lèt prèst, la s'è céusa tla cambra,
e la matéina la n s'è svéggia piò.
Che amazès u n va bén, u n s pò, però
sta burdèla, adès, cm'e' farà e' Signòur
a mandèla a l'inféran?

1948. Ventitre anni, carina, inamorata, / ma i suoi non volevano, suo padre
delle scenate, / per settimane, mesi, una guerra, lei / sempre piú innamorata,
e l'altra sera / è andata a letto presto, si è chiusa in camera, / e la mattina non
s'è svegliata piú. / Che uccidersi non va bene, non si può, però / 'sta bambina, adesso, come farà il Signore / a mandarla all'inferno?

Envious

What Nadia didn't do for me. Some days
I was a wreck. I can't go on,
it's just too huge. And her: it'll pass.
She squeezed my hand. Everything passes.
Even this will pass.
I won't ever forget it. Such patience.
Because I even had times, when I kicked over
chairs, screaming. Then I was sorry.
I had to apologize. And her: just let it out, it's nothing,
it does you good, then you feel better, I'll make you some tea?
And on the street, someone: Nadia.
With a little smile, oh yes, you're in good hands
with Nadia. Those little smiles worse than.
And those who pretend they don't see me,
friends, like hell friends.
And one day Morelli, I wouldn't have expected
it from him, we know each other, sure, but it's not like we're
                                                    [close,
Quinto Morelli, in the piazza,
stopped me: how's it going?
things working a little better? you take it, let them all talk,

Invidiéus

Quèll ch'u n m'à fat la Nadia, ò pas di dè,
a m séra ardótt, a n gne la faz, a géva,
la è tropa gròsa, e li: la pasarà,
la m tnéva strètt 'na mèna, e' pasa tótt,
e' pasarà ènca quèsta,
a n mu n zcurdarò mai, una pazinzia,
parch'éva ènch' di mumént, a déva ad chélz
tal scaràni, di rógg, pu u m dispieséva,
t m'é da scusé, e li: sfógti, u n'è gnént,
u t fa bén, dopo t sté mèi, ch'a t faza un tè?
e par la strèda qualcadéun: la Nadia,
s'un surisín, amo u s fa bén sla Nadia,
che mè ch'i féva féinta da no vdaim,
di améigh, orca ch améigh,
e un dè Morèli, ch'a n mu n l'aspitéva,
a s cnunsémm, sè, mo a n sémm in cunfidenza,
Quinto Morèli, in piaza,
u m'à férum: cum vala?
la n va un pó mei? tén bota, e las' ch'i dégga,

Invidiosi. Quel che non m'ha fatto la Nadia, ho passato dei giorni, / m'ero ridotto, non ce la faccio, dicevo, / è troppo grossa, e lei: passerà, / mi teneva stretta una mano, passa tutto, / passerà anche questa, / non me lo dimenticherò mai, una pazienza, / perché avevo anche dei momenti, davo calci / alla sedie, degli urli, poi mi dispiaceva, / devi scusarmi, e lei: sfogati, non è niente, / ti fa bene, dopo stai meglio, ti faccio un tè? / e per strada qualcuno: la Nadia, / con un sorrisino, e beh, si fa bene con la Nadia, / che io quei sorrisini sono peggio che, / e quelli che facevano finta di non vedermi, / amici, orca che amici, / e un giorno Morelli, che non me l'aspettavo, / ci conosciamo, sí, ma non siamo in confidenza, / Quinto Morelli, in piazza, / mi ha fermato: come va? / non va un po' meglio? tieni botta, e lascia che dicano, /

even about Nadia. I hear them. Don't get angry at them
don't give them
the satisfaction, people, it's only envy, they're corrosive,
and whores
are good.

ènca dla Nadia, i sint, nu t'incapèla,
nu dài sodisfaziòun,
la zénta, l'è sno invéidia, i è catéiv,
e al putèni agli è bóni.

anche della Nadia, li sento, non arrabbiarti, / non dargli soddisfazione, / la
gente, è solo invidia, sono cattivi, / e le puttane sono buone.

The Chairs

We worked together for over than ten years.
For Mansuelli. Then later on I switched.
I'm at CAM now, he always bought the paper every day.
Oh he was good. Intelligent. Exact in his speaking.
Even when he wasn't talking, I picked up on it immediately,
that he was frustrated. He enjoyed business,
buying, selling, selling, buying, he used to say to me:
sometimes it's enough just switching things around,
things can double in value, you've got to be sharp. Looking.
Seeing. And then, that's not enough, you've got to see before
                                    [the others.
And you're going to have debt. I was listened to him.
Debts? aren't you afraid?
Debts are money, what's the difference
if you have money or have to have it?
money comes and goes, it's a circle, do you understand?
and the horses are banknotes. I understood.
And I didn't understand. But he had a knack.
One Saturday afternoon, it seems like the other day, it would
                                    [have been
more than thirty years ago, we went up to the Fossa,
stopped at the Bridge

Al scaràni

Dop mè ò cambiè, adès a so tla Cam,
mo avémm lavurè insén dis an e piò
da Monsuèli, a m'arcórd, ch'e' cumpréva
e' giurnèl tótt i dè, mo l'era brèv,
inteligént, precéis, però, zcurénd,
mo ènch' senza zcòrr, léu u i pieséva
i afèri, cumprè, vènd, vènd, cumprè, u m géva:
dal vólti al robi basta cambièi pòst,
al vèl e' dòppi, bsògna 'vai òc, guardè,
vdai, e pu u n basta,
bsògna vdai préima 'd ch'ilt,
e u i vó i débit, mè a stéva alè a sintéi,
i débit? t'é paéura?
i débit l'è baócch, csa t'arimpórtal
i bócch s' ta i é da dè o s' ta i é d'avài?
i bócch i va e i vén, l'è un zéir, i afèri
l'è una chèursa che ta n si mai rivàt,
u m guardéva e e' ridéva: t'é capéi?
e i cavàl l'è al cambièli, mè a capéva

Le sedie. Dopo io ho cambiato, adesso sono alla Cam, / ma abbiamo lavorato insieme dieci anni e piú, / da Mansuelli, mi ricordo che comprava / il giornale tutti i giorni, ma era bravo, / intelligente, preciso, però, parlando, / ma anche senza parlare, lui, lo vedevi subito, / si sentiva frustrato, a lui gli piacevano / gli affari, comprare, vendere, comprare, mi diceva: / delle volte le cose basta cambiargli posto, / valgono il doppio, / bisogna aver occhio, guardare, / vedere, e poi non basta, / bisogna vedere prima degli altri, / e ci vogliono i debiti, io stavo lí a sentire, / i debiti? hai paura? / i debiti sono soldi, cosa t'importa / i soldi se li devi dare o se li devi avere? / i soldi vanno e vengono, è un giro, gli affari / sono una corsa che non si è mai arrivati, / mi guardava e rideva: hai capito?/ e i cavalli sono le cambiali, io capivo /

here, he said to me, this should be bought up, from Rossi's
property line
all the way to the road, all of it. Now it's just
cabbage, alfalfa, corn, you could get it for nothing,
fifteen hundred, two thousand a meter,
then you wait, in two or three years,
you sell it for a hundred thousand.
A hundred thousand? To who?
To people.
And if people don't buy it?
If they don't buy it it's their loss, because there it'll be.
Afterwards they'll have to pay two hundred thousand.
And to myself I'm saying, this, I'm saying, he just making up
                                                    [numbers,
he's crazy. But, he was right.
In ten years, it all got built up.
Now? a hundred thousand a meter?
No sir, not even close. This guy had a talent for it.
Another time,
a long time ago, he says, There should be a pool here.
A pool? Where? In this town?
There should be.
And now, there's a beautiful pool

e a n capéva, mo léu l'éva e' barnòcal,
un sabat dopmezdè, u m pèr cmè 'dès,
e' sarà stè più 'd trent'an fa, ch'andémmi
sò ma la Fosa, u s'è férum me pòunt,
aquè, u m'à détt, marébb cumprè, da Rossi
fina la strèda, tótt, adès l'è chèval,
spagnèra, furmantòun, la vén sa gnént,
mellazinczént, domélla frénch e' metar,
e pu t sté d'aspité, fra du tri an
ta la arvènd a zentmèlla,
a zentmélla? ma chéi?
ma la zénta, mo se la zénta i n còmpra?
s'i n còmpra pézz par lòu, ch' la staga alè.
dop s'i la vó i t nu n chin dè dusentmélla,
e mè tra 'd mè, quèst, a géva, e' dà i nómar,
l'è mat, invíci l'éva rasòun léu,
in dis an l'è vnú fura una zità,
e adès èlt che zentmélla frènch e' metar,
no, mo léu l'éva e' sbózz, un'èlta vólta,
un pèz fa, dis, aquè u i vó una piscina,
una piscina dòvv? at sté paàis,
la i vó, l'è òura, una bèla piscina,

e non capivo, ma lui aveva il bernoccolo, / un sabato pomeriggio, mi pare
come fosse adesso, / saranno piú di trent'anni fa, che andavamo / su alla
Fossa, s'è fermato al ponte, / qui, m'ha detto, bisognerebbe comprare, da
Rossi / fino alla strada, tutto, adesso sono cavoli, / erba spagna, granoturco,
viene con niente, / millecinquecento duemila lire al metro, / e poi stai ad
aspettare, fra due tre anni / la rivendi a centomila, / a centomila? a chi? /
alla gente, ma se la gente non compra? / se non comprano peggio per loro,
che stia lí, / dopo se la vogliono te ne devono dare duecentomila, / e io tra
di me, questo, dicevo, dà i numeri, / è matto, invece aveva ragione lui, / in
dieci anni è venuta fuori una città, / e adesso altro che centomila al metro,
/ no, ma lui c'era tagliato, un'altra volta, / tempo fa, dice, qui ci vuole una
piscina, /

near downtown, up above, with a nice parking lot.
Or put it just beyond the Big Curve. Always open.
Summer, winter.
Holy Christ and he guesses right on that too.
In Logi's field.
It's always packed.
You get tired of making money,
it's just that with three kids, never mind the pool,
he took a desk job, like me, then two years ago it was almost
a stroke of good fortune when that big mess
at Mansuelli came out, the supposedly installed
new equipment, and then later
they had to cut back, and
to let him go
they gave him a sum, which he never said anything about,
but you knew it had to be seventy or eight million,
and he got out of there a rich man, still young,
he retired at fifty-seven,
with all this money, one fine day it came out,
he'd bought, at first it didn't make any sense,

vérs la Piva, alasò, s'un bèl parchègg,
o ènca dop la Curva, sémpra vérta,
instèda e invéran,
porca putèna, e u i à indiviné 'nca 'lè,
qualch'an dop i glia à fata, te prè 'd Lògi,
ch' l'è sémpra pin ad zénta,
i s stóffa da fè i bócch,
sno che sa tri burdéll, èlt che piscina,
l'à cnú fè l'impieghèd, cmè mè, che pu
du an fa, léu, l'è stè guèsi una furtéuna,
quante da Monsuèli l'è vnú fura
tótt che caséin, sicómm ch'i éva impiantè
di machinèri nóv, e alòura dop
dovevano sfoltire, e par lasè
i i à dè un sbróff, che léu u n'à mai détt gnént,
mo u s'è savéu, stènta utènta migliéun,
léu l'è vnú véa da sgnòur, pu ancòura zòvan,
l'è 'ndè in pensiòun a zinquentasèt an,
e tótt sti bócch, un bèl dè l'è scap fura
ch' l'éva còmpar, te préim u n s'è capéi,
dis, un'ordinaziòun
non andata a buon fine, un camion 'd roba,

una piscina dove? in questo paese, / ci vuole, è ora, una bella piscina, /
verso la Pieve, lassú, con un bel parcheggio, / o anche dopo la Curva, sempre
aperta, / estate e inverno, / porca puttana, e ci ha indovinato anche lí, /
qualche anno dopo gliel'hanno fatta, nel prato di Logi, / che è sempre piena
di gente, / si stufano di fare i soldi, / solo che con tre bambini, altro che
piscina, / ha dovuto fare l'impiegato, come me, che poi / due anni fa, per
lui è stata quasi una fortuna, / quando da Mansuelli è venuto fuori / tutto
quel casino, siccome avevano installato / dei macchinari nuovi, e allora dopo
/ dovevano sfoltire, e per lasciare / gli hanno dato una somma, che lui non
ha mai detto niente, / ma si è saputo, settanta ottanta milioni, / lui è venuto
via da signore, poi ancora giovane, / è andato in pensione a cinquantasette
anni, / e tutti questi soldi, un bel giorno è venuto fuori / che aveva comprato, all'inizio non s'è capito, / dice, un'ordinazione /non andata a buon
fine, un camion di roba, /

from Verona, all these chairs arrived,
there had to have been, who knows, a bankruptcy,
an error, maybe someone had had second thoughts,
at any rate, whoever had ordered them didn't want them
anymore,
and then, even to come back with a full truck,
it's better to sell, he knew this,
someone had told him about them, it was a stroke of luck,
chairs in style, chairs are a big industry in Verona,
like shoes in Murano,
antique-style furniture, but new,
strong, because the antique stuff,
what would you expect,
all the wood's worm-eaten, half-rotten,
and he bought it all, over a hundred chairs,
for a song,
seventy thousand lire each, each of these
they told him would bring, he'd be able to sell them
for two hundred-and-fifty each, easy, at two hundred you be
giving them away,
because they were handmade,
they were worth something, oak, and his idea,
they'd talked about it, he'd go as low, he says, even if I get
a hundred-and-ten,
who's not going to pay you that?

ch' l'avnéva da Veròuna, tótt scaràni,
ch'e' sarà stè, chi lo sa, un falimént,
un sbai, o ènca ch'i i à 'rpéns, insòmma
quèi ch'i gli éva urdinèdi i n li à vlú piò,
e dop, ènch' turné indrí se camion pin,
mèi vènd, léu u l'à savéu,
qualcadéun u gli à détt, l'era una bagia,
sedia in stile, che a Veròuna è un'industria,
cmè a San Mèvar pr'al schèrpi, loro fanno
mobilli in stile antico, però nóv,
rubóst, che invíci al robi antéighi, 's'ut,
tótt lègn tarlèd, mèz fraid,
e léu l'à còmpar tótt, piò 'd zént scaràni,
pr'un s-ciòch ad frósta,
stentamélla frènch l'óna, che lei queste,
i i à détt, il suo prezzo, le può vendere
a duecentocinquantamila lire
come niente, a duecento regalate,
amo parchè agli è lavurèdi a mèni,
hanno un valore, ad róvar, e la su idea,
ch'émm zcòurs, in fònd, dis, mè
s'a ciap ènch' zent zentedismélla frènch,
chi è ch'i n ti dà? quèi ch'i vènd la mobéglia,

che veniva da Verona, tutte sedie, / che sarà stato, chi lo sa, un fallimento, /
uno sbaglio, o anche che ci hanno ripensato, insomma, / quelli che le avevano
ordinate non le hanno volute piú, / e dopo, anche tornare indietro col camion
pieno, / meglio vendere, lui l'ha saputo, / qualcuno glie'ha detto, era una
bazza, / sedie in stile, che a Verona è un'industria, / come a San Mauro per
le scarpe, loro fanno / mobili in stile antico, però nuovi, / robusti, che invece
la roba antica, cosa vuoi, / tutto legno tarlato, mezzo fradicio, / e lui ha comprato tutto, piú di cento sedie, / per uno schiocco di frusta, / settantamila lire
l'una, che lei queste, / gli hanno detto, il suo prezzo, le può vendere, / a
duecentocinquantamila lire / come niente, a duecento regalata, / perché sono
lavorate a mano, / hanno un valore, di rovere, e la sua idea, / che abbiamo
parlato, in fondo, dice, io / se prendo anche cento centodiecimila lire, / chi
è che non te le dà? quelli che vendono i mobili, /

the furniture dealers could mark it up to two-hundred-and fifty,
everyone's happy, it's just that it's difficult,
things, it seems like that to me, the one who's selling the
                                                    [furniture,
he went to see them, he traveled all around,
he was always off somewhere,
Rimini, Cesena,
he went as far as Forlí, Faenza, but those people,
they're old foxes, they talked among themselves
if you ask me, they knew everything, they talked to each other
they were all in on it,
one of them from Bertinoro wanted to buy eight of them,
he promised him sixty thousand each,
he got mad, he did, like it was hot merchandise,
then he tried all along the coast, all those hotels,
they always need chairs, but even there,
the hotel owners, they're lovely chairs,
but the antique style, plus for the young people,
they have a point too,
what would you want with oak chairs at the sea,
in the summer, with that heat,
plus they take up too much room,
they make them to stack, they want stack-ables, of plastic,
which doesn't weigh anything,
then he had to rent half a garage from Gobbi,
which cost money,
and then, after a year, they were piled up inside there,

t li pò mètt a dusentzinquentamélla,
andèmm bén tótt, sno ch' l'è fadéiga, al robi,
e' pèr acsè, mo quéi ch' vènd la mobéglia,
léu u n n'à vést, l'à ziràt, l'è sémpra in zéir,
a Rémin, a Ceséina, l'è rivàt
fina a Furlè, a Faenza, mo l'è zénta,
quèll' l'è quài sguarnèdi, pu i s l'è détt,
sgònd mè, i sa tótt, tra 'd lòu, i è tótt d'acórd,
éun ad Bartnóra u i nu n vléva tó òt,
u i à prumèss sentamélla frènch l'óna,
ch'u s'è incaplè, léu, fóss roba rubéda,
pu l'à próv a maréina, pin d'albérgh,
scaràni u i nu n vó sémpra, mo ènca lè,
i albergadéur, sono sedie bellissime,
però lo stile antico, noi qui è tutto
stile moderno, poi la gioventú,
ch'i à rasòun ènca lòu,
's'ut, dal scaràni ad róvar a maréina,
d'instèda, sa chi chèld, pu al tén trop pòst,
che òz i li fa che ta li amócc, dal pili,
e ad plastica ch'a n pàisa gnént, invíci
pr'al sóvvi léu, l'à cnú fité da Gobi
mèz capanòun, ch' l'è bócch,

le puoi mettere a duecentocinquantamila, / andiamo bene tutti, solo che è
fatica, le cose, / sembra cosí, ma quelli che vendono i mobili, / lui ne ha visti,
ha girato, è sempre in giro, / a Rimini, a Cesena, è arrivato / fino a Forlí, a
Faenza, ma sono gente, / quelli sono vecchie volpi, poi se lo sono detto, /
secondo me, sanno tutto, fra di loro, sono tutti d'accordo, / uno di Bertinoro
gliene voleva comprare otto, / gli ha promesso sessantamila lire l'una, / che
s'è arrabbiato, lui, fosse roba rubata, / poi ha provato al mare, pieno d'alber-
ghi, / sedie ce ne vogliono sempre, ma anche lí, / gli albergatori, sono sedie
bellissime, / però lo stile antico, poi qui è tutto / stile moderno, poi la gioventú, / che hanno ragione anche loro, / cosa vuoi, delle sedie di rovere al
mare, / d'estate, con quei caldi, noi tengono troppo posto, / che oggi le fanno
che le ammucchi, delle pile, / e di plastica che non pesano niente, invece / per
le sue lui ha dovuto affittare da Gobbi / mezzo capannone, che sono soldi,/

they got all messed up, they got ruined,
and at the same time at home
he was always fighting, his wife, his kids,
they were always arguing,
he'd even gone so far as to talk to don Fernando
at the Suffraggio a few months ago,
where better for the antique look?
right from the beginning, there was a misunderstanding,
We'll put on a little plaque on each chair, don Fernando said,
what plaque? The Calisesi Family. He thought it was a gift,
an offering,
what? how? these chairs, are for sale,
and the priest throws out is arms, oh, I'm so sorry,
I'm so terribly sorry, but buying now,
it's not something we need. Then he went to Savignano
where they were building a multiplex,
but that came to nothing,
it folded right away. The chairs? Please.
They want armchairs now,
if there aren't armchairs
no one is going to go,
but he had such initiative,
he knew exactly what to do,
it's just that, at that moment, right then
it was a little, that he,
he was traveling around the countryside,

l'è piò d'un an, pu a stè mucèdi alè
al patéss, al s'arvéina, e intènt ma chèsa
l'è sémpra un ragnadézz, la mòi, i fiúl,
che ragnè ormai, mo léu l'è 'ndè 'nca a zcòrr
qualch' màis fa te Sufraz sa don Fernando,
mèi ch' nè 'lè e' stile antico, che te préim
però i n s'è intéis,
poi su ogni sedia, e' géva don Fernando,
metiamo la targhetta, che targhetta?
Famiglia Calisesi, léu u s cridéva
ch' fóss un reghèl, 'n'ofèrta, come? cosa?
mo queste sedie, io, sono da vendere,
e cl'èlt l'à slèrgh al brazi, oh, mi scusi,
mi scusi tanto, mo comprare adesso
non sono in caso, pu l'è stè a Savgnèn,
ch'i è dri ch'i fa una multisala, mo,
gnént, i l'à férum sóbit, al scaràni?
par carità, i vó al pultròuni adès,
s'u n gn'è al pultròuni, e' cino u n vén niseun,
no, mo l'à iniziatéiva, u s dà da fè,
sno che, e' sarà e' mumént, adiritéura
l'è un pó, léu, ch'e' zéira ènca la campagna,

è piú di un anno, poi a stare ammucchiate lí / patiscono, si rovinano, e
intanto in casa / è sempre un litigio, la moglie, i figli, / che litigare ormai, ma
lui è andato anche a parlare / qualche mese fa al Suffragio con don Fernando, / meglio di lí lo stile antico, che in un primo tempo, / però non si sono
intesi, / poi su ogni sedia, diceva don Fernando, / mettiamo la targhetta, che
targhetta? / Famiglia Calisesi, lui credeva / che fosse un regalo, un'offerta,
come? cosa? / ma queste sedie, io, sono da vendere, / e l'altro ha allargato
le braccia, oh, mi scusi, / mi scusi tanto, ma comprare adesso, / non sono in
caso, noi è stato a Savignano, / che stanno facendo una multisala, ma, / niente, l'hanno fermato subito, le sedie? / per carità, ci vogliono le poltrone
adesso, / se non ci sono le poltrone, al cinema non ci viene nessuno, / no,
ma ha iniziativa, si dà da fare, / solo che, sarà il momento, addirittura, / è un
po', lui, che gira anche la campagna, /

because farm people have money saved,
but with farm people it's hard, the wife likes them but he
wants to trade with some grapes, grapes?
what are you talking about?
you could make wine, but he didn't have the equipment,
he'd never made wine,
I sometimes say: what was he thinking,
going off and setting up an operation, I don't know,
it made no sense to me,
it's that business doesn't always go like it's supposed to go,
even the ones who are best at it sometimes get into a bind,
then what can you do? I think about it all the time,
that he needed to do something that no one
was expecting, I had an idea that something might,
but I kept it to myself,
I thought about it again, and I was more convinced,
except that he was still focused on selling,
and he didn't see that things were,
because more than a hundred chairs,
is a lot, and people, I heard them, now you could see,
that he was slacking off, that he was always sitting around,
they laughed, people need to have something to do,
he, and I know this for a fact, he must just be crazy,
we're at the end of February now, in three or four weeks,
it'll be the feast of St. Joseph, burning everything,
making a bonfire,
in the middle of the fairgrounds,

che i cuntadéin i è pin 'd baócch, però
si cuntadéin la è gnara, éun, la su mòi
a li pieséva, e léu u i vléva dè dl'óvva,
dl'óvva? cumè? a putí fè de véin,
mo u n'è trezèd, léu, u n l'à mai fat e' véin,
che mè dal vólti a déggh: csa i èll suzèst?
andès a mètt t'n'impràisa, mè a n'e so,
che sa mè e' féva di ragiunamént,
l'è che i afèri, la n va sèmpra drétta,
ènca i piò brèv, dal vólti la va tórta,
e adès cs'èll ch'e' pò fe? ch'a i péns spèss, léu
l'avrébb da fè una roba ch'u n s la aspétta
niseun, mè a la ò un'idea, mo a m tratèngh,
pu a i arpéns, e a so sémpra piò cunvéint,
sno che léu l'è fiséd ancòura a vènd,
e u n vaid che al robi,
parchè piò 'd zént scaràni agli è una masa,
e la zénta, mè a i sint, t'avdiré adès
ch'u s'arpòunsa, e' starà sémpra disdài,
i réid, la zénta, l'à da fè qualquèl,
léu, e mè a l so, l'à da fè una matéria,
a sémm la féin 'd febrèr,
tre quatar stmèni e pu l'è San Jusèf,

che i contadini sono pieni di soldi, però, / coi contadini à dura, uno, a sua
moglie / le piacevano, e lui gli voleva dare dell'uva, / dell'uva? come sarebbe?
dice, potete fare il vino, / ma non è attrezzato, lui, non l'ha mai fatto il vino,
/ che io delle volte dico: cosa gli è successo? / andarsi a mettere in un'impresa, io non so, / che con me faceva dei ragionamenti, / è che gli affari, non va
sempre dritta, / anche i piú bravi, delle volte va storta, / e adesso cosa può
fare? che ci penso spesso, lui / dovrebbe fare una cosa che non se l'aspetta
/ nessuno, io ce l'ho un'idea, ma mi trattengo, / poi ci ripenso, e sono sempre
piú convinto, / solo che lui è fissato ancora a vendere, / e non vede che le
cose, / perché piú di cento sedie sono tante, / e la gente, io li sento, vedrai
adesso / che si riposa, starà sempre seduto, / ridono, la gente, deve far qualcosa, / lui, e io lo so, deve fare una matería, / siamo alla fine di febbraio, / tre
quattro settimane ed è San Giuseppe, /

547

more than a hundred chairs, a little gasoline and that's it,
it's got to be the biggest bonfire
there's ever been, it was like watching a big up-yours,
he did it out of spite, you can all just wait at the edge of hell
fucking freezing over, this
is how I get even, I'm the one laughing now, a big wind it up
and screw-you-all,
the bigger you screw up, the more people respect you,
it seemed to me that seeing him there, there they are, all upset,
they're looking at the fire, they can't understand it,
but it's worth millions, yes, millions, they're mine,
so you burn them, then what? they'll never ever forget it,
then they'll say: Calisesi's chairs,
and you, the name remains, you get it?
it's like I'll never die,
the way one speaks of Baracócc's walnuts
and Elpidio's riddles, the name remains,
they'll remember the flames
that blazed higher than the Rocca,
the dry wood that was crackling, the legs, the supports,
all the straight backs you could ever want, plus
they don't make anymore either, gone the way as those women
with those hand-knit hand-warmers
that go all the way up the arm,

bruséli tótti, fè una fugaréina,
te mèz de canfiré,
piò 'd zént scaràni, un pó 'd benzina e via,
l'à d'avnéi la piò granda fugaréina
ch'u s séa mai vést, e i pataca a guardè,
fèl par dispèt, andé tótt te caséin,
ò pérs, a i 'i vú góst, quèst l'è l'ariéut,
a réid mè 'dès, freghèsni 'd tótt, la zénta
piò t la fé gròsa e piò i t pórta rispèt,
u m pèr d'avdaii, i sta lè, scumbuiéd,
i guèrda e' fugh, i n'aréiva a capéi,
mo l'è migliéun, sè, l'è migliéun, l'è i méi,
a i bréus, e alòura? i n s'e' zcurdarà piò,
dop i girà: al scaràni ad Calisàis,
e tè, e' tu nóm l'arvènza, t'é capéi?
l'è cmè ta n muréss mai,
parchè u s dí pò: agli anéusi ad Baracócch,
i paraghéun ad Pidio, lasci un nome,
i s'arcurdarà al fiambi
ch'agli arivéva piò d'in èlt dla Roca,
lègn sècch, un s-ciuptadézz, gambi, cavéi,
spaliri ch'al vuléva, pu una roba
ch' la n s fa piò adès, cal dòni

bruciarle tutte, fare una focarina, / in mezzo al campo della fiera, / piú di cento
sedie, un po' di benzina e via, / deve venire la piú grande focarina / che si sia mai
vista, e i coglioni a guardare, / farlo per dispetto, andate tutti nel casino, / ho
perso, ci avete gusto, questa è la rivincita, / rido io adesso, fregarsene di tutti, la
gente, / piú la fai grossa piú ti portano rispetto, / mi par di vederli, stanno lí,
scombuiati, / guardano il fuoco, non arrivano a capire, / ma sono milioni, sí,
sono milioni, sono i miei, / li brucio, e allora? non se lo dimenticheranno piú, /
poi diranno: le sedie di Calisesi, / e tu, il tuo nome rimane, hai capito? / è come
se non morissi mai, / perché si dice pure: le noci di Baracócch, / i paragoni di
Elpidio, lasci un nome, / si ricorderanno le fiamme / che arrivavano piú in alto
della Rocca, / un legno asciutto, che scoppiettava, gambe, traverse, / spalliere che
volavano, poi una cosa / che non si fa piú, quelle donne /

how many arms, a mountain-worth of chair arms
for all those hand warmers, and I'm sure that he,
because you didn't think about this part
but to tell them about it,
if they tell them about it,
because things,
he understands them in a flash, he's not a mean man,
he knows what time it is,
he's been there,
I know him well,
he's never put anyone down,
to be completely in charge, for one night
heating up Santarcangelo, everybody there,
driving them crazy,
their mouths hanging open, afraid even,
being king, burning the world,
no one else will ever do it, never, you do it,
Jesus if he were still here, someone should do it, someone
needs to tell them this, but I don't dare.

si scaldéin ch'agli avnéva par la brèsa,
quanta brèsa stavólta, una muntagna,
da rimpéi méll scaldéin,
e a so sichéur che léu, parchè u n'i pensa,
mo a déie, s'a i e' géssmi, parchè al robi
léu u li capéss al volo, mo poi lui
non è un uomo meschino, l'à un argòi,
u i starébb, mè al cnòss bén,
u n s'è mai fat mètt sòtta da niseun,
cmandè léu pr'una nòta,
arscaldè Santarcanzal, tótt quant i è,
fèi dvantè mat, /
a bòcca vérta, ènca un pó spavantèd,
ès e' rè, brusé e' mònd,
ch'u n'e' farà niseun, mai, ta l fé tè,
orca léu s'u i starébb, mo u i vrébb, u i vó
qualcadéun ch'u i e' dégga, mè a n m'aréisgh.

con gli scaldini che venivano per la brace, / quanta brace questa volta, una montagna, / da riempire mille scaldini, / e sono sicuro che lui, perché non ci pensa, / ma a dirglielo, se glielo dicessimo, perché le cose / lui le capisce al volo, ma poi lui / non è un uomo meschino, ha un orgoglio, / ci starebbe, lo conosco bene, / non s'è mai fatto metter sotto da nessuno, / comandare, lui, per una notte, / riscaldare Santarcangelo, tutti quanti sono, / farli diventare matti, / a bocca aperta, anche un po' spaventatati, / essere il re, bruciare il mondo, / che non lo farà nessuno, mai, lo fai tu, / orca lui se ci starebbe, ma ci vorebbe, ci vuole / qualcuno che glielo dica, io non m'arrischio.

551

Peek-a-boo

Here's a game I don't understand.
I feel my eyes getting covered
with hands from behind: peek-a-boo, who is it?
What's this all about? come on, we're not kids anymore,
Riccardo, you're still full of shit. No?
you're not Riccardo? Tonino? no?
all right then. Loris? what the hell then?
who is it? who is it. I turn around.
where'd that jerk go? there's nobody.

Cucú

L'è un schérz ch'a n'e' capéss, a m sint srè, a m sint srè i ócc
sal mèni da di dri: cucú, chi è?
e quèst csa vól? dài, ch'a n sémm piò burdéll,
Ricardo, tè t'é sémpra voia, no?
ta n si Ricardo? t si Tonino, no?
a i so, t si Loris, no? porca putèna,
chi èll? chi sit? a m vólt,
mo dò ch' l'è 'ndè st' pataca? u n gn'è niseun.

Cucú. È uno scherzo che non capisco, mi sento chiudere gli occhi / con le mani da dietro: cucú, chi è? / e questo cosa vuole? dai, che non siamo piú bambini, / Ricardo, tu hai sempre voglia, no? / non sei Ricardo? sei Tonino, no? / ci sono, sei Loris, no? porca puttana, / chi è? chi sei? mi volto, / ma dov'è andato 'sto coglione? non c'è nessuno.

Small Talk

I had bad dreams all night, all these snakes,
how did you make this coffee? look at this, spills,
every time it's like this, with you
you've got to have someone
there with you every second, is it possible
you're never going to learn at this point, you're old,
and don't walk on it, we need a rag here,
leave it alone, I'll do it, with my bones aching,
listen, do you hear it, it's eight already, I'm going out to do
                                        [some shopping.

My goodness, I feel it too, the sirocco,
my bones are aching, – Clara, is it true
that your brother has bought,
that he wants to go stay at Poggio?
has he gone crazy?
what's he going to do up at Poggio?
I wouldn't go up there either, up on that cliff,
and his wife, she's your cousin, or what?
does she want to go up there?
well that's a different story then,
if she likes it up there, it's for the grandmother's sake?
his mother, I know, she's up there,

Ciacri

Ò insugné mèl stanòta, dal gran béssi,
mo cmè t fé a fè e' cafè? vè ach pisarèla,
l'è tótt' al vólti acsè, ma tè u t vó óna
ch' la t vénga dri dò t pas, mo èl dóbbi, zò,
ta n'apa da imparè, ch' t si bèla vèc,
e nu caméini sòura, aquè u i vó e' straz,
lasa 'lè, ch'a faz mè, ch'ò un mèl tagli òsi,
sint, l'è zà agli òt, a vagh a fè un pó 'd spàisa,

orca che curinaza a l so ènca mè
ch'u m dól agli òsi,
                    Clara, ció, dabón
che, e' tu fradèl l'à còumpar,
ch'e' vó 'ndè stè me Pózz? mo l'è dvént mat?
csa val a fè me Pózz?
che mè a n'i starébb gnénca sa che grèpp?
e la su mòi, la tu cugnèda, cs'èll?
la è vlú 'ndè li? alòura l'è un èlt zcòurs,
ció, s'u i pis alasò, l'è par la nòna?
la mama ad léu, a l so, la sta 'lasò,

Chiacchiere. Ho sognato male stanotte, tante di quelle bisce, / ma come fai a fare il caffè? ve' che pisciarella, / è tutte le volte cosí, a te ti ci vuole una / che ti venga dietro dove vai, ma è possibile / tu non abbia a imparare, / che ti venga dietro dove vai, ma è possibile / tu non abbia a imparare, che sei ormai vecchio, / e non camminarci sopra, qui ci vuole uno straccio, / lascia lí, faccio io, che ho un male nelle ossa, / senti, sono già le otto, vado a fare un po' di spesa, // orca che scirocco, lo so anch'io / che mi dolgono le ossa, – Clara, ma è vero / che tuo fratello ha comprato, / che vuol andare a stare al Poggio? ma è diventato matto? / cosa va a fare al Poggio? / che io non ci starei neanche su quel greppo, / e sua moglie, tua cognata, cosa? / è voluta andare lei? allora è un altro discorso, / se le piace lassú, è per la nonna? / la mamma di lui, lo so, sta lassú, /

I understand completely, with three boys, the grandmother,
now that's something you can count on, why wouldn't it be?
but certainly, even for them, it's still a big change,
but they're young, then, yes, it's true,
you do feel good up there,
even at Poggio,
up there, the air's better,
I was up at Nazario's,
he showed it to you too?
yes, well goodbye too, we'll get together, Caterina,
where are you going?
you're in such a hurry, to the hospital, who do you have in
                                              [the hospital?

Gianni? you're related, a little distant,
you're children of cousins, or no? how is he?
which I think, in my opinion *that* is a sickness,
he, it's been two years, since Yole died,
there was a big change, he's not himself anymore,
he's never in the shop,
he's always at the café, sweets, it's gluttony,
shots, which with that, he was a heavy man to start with,
he's going to kill himself like that,
but you're saying what' I'm saying, it's her,
it's his wife, Franca, who was at fault,
she, with Gianni, she never understood him he's

ò capí tótt, sa tri burdéll, la nòna
l'è un bèl apòz, cumè,
zért ch'ènca lòu però l'è un cambiament,
mo i è zóvan, pu, sè, zò, ch'u s sta bén
ènca mé Pózz, d'in èlt, aria piò féina,
a m férum da Nazario,
mo ènca tè fat avdài, a s'incuntrémm
sémpra par chès,
                          Caterina, dú vét?
t'é una préssia, te bsdèl? chéi t'é te bsdèl?
Giani? ch'a si parént, un pó a la lònga,
a si fiúl ad cuséin, o no? cum stal?
che mè, sgònd mè, quèll l'è una malatéa,
léu, l'è du an, da quant ch' l'è mórt' la Jole,
l'à fat un cambiamént, u n'è piò léu,
tla butàiga u n gn'è mai,
l'è sémpra te cafè, pasti, luvéri,
biciaréin, che acsè, zà ch' l'è 'nca un òm griv,
acsè e' vó déi mazès,
amo tè t déi quèll ch'a déggh mè, l'è li,
l'è la su mòi, la Franca, ch' la à sbaiè,
li ma Giani la n l'à mai capéi, léu

ho capito tutto, con tre bambini, la nonna / è un bell'appoggio, come no, /
certo che anche loro però è un cambiamento, / ma sono giovani, poi, sí, dai,
che si sta bene / anche al Poggio, / in alto, aria piú fina, / mi fermo da Nazario, / ma anche tu fatti vedere, c'incontriamo, / sempre per caso, – Caterina, dove vai? / hai una fretta, all'ospedale? chi hai all'ospedale? / Gianni? che
siete parenti, un po' alla lontana, / siete figli di cugini, o no? come sta? / che
io, secondo me, quella è una malattia, / lui, sono due anni, da quando è
morta la Jole, / ha fatto un cambiamento, non è piú lui, / in negozio non c'è
mai, / è sempre al caffè, paste, golosità, / bicchierini, che cosí, già che è
anche un uomo pesante, / cosí vuol dire ammazzarsi, / ma tu dici quel che
dico io, è lei, / è sua moglie, la Franca, che ha sbagliato, / lei a Gianni non
l'ha mai capito, lui /

557

a little prickly, yes, nothing's ever right
but he's not mean, you have to know how to take him,
you can't always be contradicting him,
you can't always argue,
then afterwards, little by little,
a Yole emerges,
which even there, then, Franca was wrong,
all the scenes,
I understand, yes, letting off steam, but certain things,
you can't go around town saying,
that he hadn't even moved out, yes,
he did that for the boy, yes, but however in any case
they're together, you, now, stay another second,
how can I say it, to stop trying,
if you shout it's worse, then they're pointing fingers at you,
but Franca, certain things, she never had to deal with,
no, you're right, it's all just talk, all this, it wears you out,
you do the best you can, from the outside, we all look good
but when you're there, and you see your husband,
I'm here now, I'll see you Caterina.

do you have any that's fresh, Nazario? sausage?
three good long pieces, no, make it four, and a little of the
                                                    [crackling,

l'è un pó sgustòus, sè, u n'i va mai bén gnént,
mo u n'è catéiv, bsògna savàil ciapè,
t n'i pò dè sémpra còuntra,
ta n pò sémpra ragnè, dop, dài e dài,
e' vén fura un Jole,
ch'ènca 'lè, zò, la Franca la à sbaiè,
tótt chi spatéran,
ò capéi, sè, sfughès, mo zérti robi
ta n li pò 'ndè dí in piaza,
ch'u n'era gnénca scap da chèsa, sè,
u l'à fat pr'e' burdèl, mo però intént
a sté insén, e tè 'lòura sta un pó bóna,
cm'òi da déi? nu l ziménta,
se t rógg l'è pézz, dop u la ciapa ad péunta,
mo la Franca zért' robi la n gn'aréiva,
no, t'é rasòun, l'è zchéurs, quést, l'è fadéiga,
bsògna pruvè, da 'd fura a sémm brèv tótt,
mo quant t si 'lè, che t vaid e' tu maréid,
mè a so rivàta, a s'avdémm, Caterina,

te la é frèsca, Nazario, la sunzézza?
tri budéll, no, fa quatar,

è un po' spigoloso, sí, non gli va mai bene niente, / ma non è cattivo, bisogna
saperlo prendere, / non puoi dargli sempre contro, / non puoi sempre litigare, dopo, dai e dai, / viene fuori una Jole, / che anche lí, poi, la Franca ha
sbagliato, / tutte quelle scene, / ho capito, sí, sfogarsi, ma certe cose / non
le puoi andare a dire in piazza, / che non era neanche uscito di casa, sí, / l'ha
fatto per il bambino, ma però intanto / siete insieme, e tu allora, sta' un po'
buona, / come devo dire, non cimentarlo, se urli è peggio, dopo la prende di
punta, / ma la Franca, certe cose, non ci arriva, / no, hai ragione, sono
discorsi, questi, è fatica, / bisogna provare, da fuori siamo bravi tutti, / ma
quando sei lí, che vedi tuo marito, io sono arivata, ci vediamo, Caterina, //
ce l'hai fresca, Nazario, la salciccia? / tre budelli, no, fa' quattro, /

which Paolo likes,
yesterday you gave me a piece of meat you couldn't eat,
I used it to make broth, I'm telling you it was tough,
you know it too, come on, don't put me on,
what's steer meat got to do with it?
the steer meat was good, I didn't tell you?
but the meat, Paolo got mad,
he likes it tender, he, how can I explain it to you?
what do you mean he's spoiled? are you pulling my leg?
And you, what about you?

Bina, and where have you been that I haven't seen you in a
[century?

oh, a trip? where? how nice, and me,
mine won't budge, but now I'd like to, I'd like,
every once in awhile
to take a trip, see some things but him, sure,
and now where are you going?
I've got to go to Elda's
instead to get some spinach,
do you have some greens too?
a half kilo, which is even too much, there, that's good,
where did you leave Nino? he's in bed?
with a fever? the flu? oh well, it's going around,

e un pó 'd grasúl, che ma Pèval i i pis,
ir ta m'é dè una chèrna ch' la n s magnéva,
ò capéi da fè e' bród, mo l'era stòppa,
ch' ta l sé 'nca tè, zò, nu fa la cumédia,
csa i éintral e' castrè?

e' castrè l'era bón, a t'ò détt gnént?
mo la chèrna, Pèval u s'è incaplè,
u la vó tèndra léu, cm'a t l'òi da déi?
cumè, viziéd, ta m tó 'nca in zéir?
                                        e tè?
Bina, mo dò t si stè ch' l'è un témp ch'a n t vèggh,
ah, t'é viazè? duvò? pu bén, che mè,
quèll che là u n s móv e gnénca,
che invíci u m pisarébb, mè, d'ogni tènt,
andè in zèir, vdai dal robi, mo léu sè,
e adès du vét? mè invíci ò da pasè
da l'Elda a tó i spinàz,
                            u i è 'nca al rósli?
mèz chéll, ch'agli è 'nca tropi, ècco, acsè, basta,
dò, ch' ta l'é mèss ma Nino? l'è te lèt?
sla févra? un'influenza? amo la è fura,

e un po' di ciccioli, che a Paolo gli piacciono, / ieri m'hai dato una carne che
non si mangiava, / ho capito da fare il brodo, ma era stoppa, / che lo sai
anche tu, dai, non fare la commedia, / cosa c'entra il castrato? / il castrato
era buono, t'ho detto niente? / ma la carne, Paolo s'è arrabbiato, / la vuol
tenera, lui, come te lo devo dire? / come, viziato, mi prendi anche in giro? –
e tu? / Bina, ma dove sei stata che è un secolo che non ti vedo, / ah, hai
viaggiato, dove? che bello, e io, / quello là non si muove neanche, / che
invece mi piacerebbe, a me, ogni tanto, / andare in giro, vedere delle cose,
ma lui sí, / e adesso dove vai? io invece devo passare / dalla Elda a prendere
gli spinaci, – ci sono anche le rosole? / mezzo chilo, che sono anche troppe,
ecco, cosí, basta, / dove l'hai messo Nino? è a letto? / con la febbre?
un'influenza? e beh, è fuori, /

561

Flavia's sick in bed too, she's got a bad cold,
and she smokes on top of it,
which I'm always telling her, I do, smoking's not good for you,
it's poison, sure, try talking to her, what time is it?
it's ten? really, I'll see you – oh there's Dolores, wait,
Dolores, I've got one thing to ask you,
are you in a hurry, it'll take just a second,
you knew Missiroli well, didn't you?
because last night we were arguing,
he says, he's so stubborn,
he says that he came from Verucchio,
which I don't know where
he gets these things, he was from Bellaria, wasn't he?
see, see there, that I'm right, I was sure of it,
I remember, your mother, worked twenty years in his shop,
but Paolo when he digs his heels in, I know, it's late,
we're all in a hurry, say hello to your mother for me,
which I'm always saying I'm going to stop by and visit,
then I put it off, put it off, days go by,

la è te lèt ènch, la Flavia, la à un mamòun,
li pu la fómma ènca,
ch' a i è déggh sémpra, mè, u t fa mèl fumé,
l'è un vlén, sè, mo va a zcòrr sa li, che or'èll?
l'è al dis, dabón? ch'a n n'ò mélla da fè,
Elda, a s'vdémm,
                oh, la Dolores, spétta,
Dolores, ò una roba da dmandèt,
t'é prèssia? l'è un minéut,
tè ta l'é cnunsú bén Misirúl, no?
che irisàira émm ragnè, se mi maréid,
léu dis, mo l'è un tistòun,
dis ch' l'avnéva da Vrócc, che mè a n'e' so
'ddò ch'u li téira fura zèrti robi,
l'era 'd Belaria, o no?
vitt, ch'ò rasòun? mo mè a séra sichéura,
a m'arcórd, la tu mà
la à lavurè vint'an tla su butàiga,
mo Pèval quant e' péunta, a l so, l'è tèrd,
émm préssia tótt, saléutmi la tu mà,
che mè a déggh sémpra ch'a vi vní a truvèla,
pu a la armand, a la armand, e' pasa i dè,

è a letto anche la Flavia, ha una costipazione, / lei poi fuma anche, / che
glielo dico sempre, io, ti fa male fumare, / è un veleno, sì, ma va' a parlare
con lei, che ora è? / sono le dieci, davvero? che ne ho mille da fare, / Elda,
ci vediamo, – oh la Dolores, aspetta, / Dolores, ho una cosa da chiederti, /
hai fretta? è un minuto, / tu l'hai conosciuto bene Missiroli, no? / che ieri
sera abbiamo litigato, con mio marito, / lui dice, ma è un testone, / dice che
veniva da Verucchio, che io non so / da dove tira fuori certe cose, / era di
Bellaria, o no? / vedi, che ho ragione? ma io ero sicura, / mi ricordo, tua
madre / ha lavorato vent'anni nel suo negozio, / ma Paolo quando s'impunta, lo so, è tardi, / abbiamo fretta tutti, salutami tua mamma, / che dico
sempre che voglio venire a trovarla, / poi rimando, rimando, passano i giorni, /

but sooner or later I'm coming, –
here's Giorgio,
you'll be glad about this, I saw your Milena
in her uniform, oh my gosh
she rides a motorbike too? she drives?
you understand I wouldn't even know how to steer a
[wheelbarrow,
but wasn't she a teacher, your daughter?
ah, she didn't like school, to make a career of it, today
there aren't any obstacles anymore, today a woman,
don't you see them? they do everything, even the military,
everything's handed to them on a platter, well what can you
[do about it?
say hello to Graziella for me, –
and now, here, so I don't forget
some coarse salt, sugar, oil, a bar of soap, the other one's
just a sliver at this point,
a packet of talcum powder,
here, fizz tablets, which I forgot all about,
and I want to get some honey too, I'm a little hoarse,
which if you dissolve it in some hot milk,
and then I should go and see Lucia
who lives so far down there it's the end of the earth, wait now,

mo préima o dop a véngh,

                      e quèst l'è Giorgio,
t saré cuntént? ò vést la tu Milena
in divéisa, ció, la fa una fighéura,
la va 'nca se mutòur? la guéida li?
t'é capéi, mè a n guéid gnénca la carióla,
però, la n'era mèstra la tu fióla?
ah, u n'i pieséva da fè scóla, e alòura,
ch' la farà ènca carira, òz u n gn'è pió
nisun impediment, òz una dòna,
ta n li vaid? al fa tótt, ènca e' suldè,
la va par lòu, Giorgio, u n gn'è gnént da fè,
saléutmi la Graziella,

                      e adès aquè
ch'a n mu n zcórda, e' sèl gròs, e' zóccar, l'óli,
'na savunètta, ch'u i n'è ormai 'na scaia,
'na bósta ad boratalco,
ècco, l'Idrolitina, ch'a m zcurdéva,
e a ví tó 'nca de mél, ò un pó 'd rampàzna,
che se lat chèld e' s-ciòi,
e pu avrébb da pasè da la Lucia,
ch' la sta alazò a l'inféran, spétta, mo

ma prima o poi vengo, – e questo è Giorgio, / sarai contento, ho visto la tua Milena / in divisa, accidenti, fa una figura, / va anche in motocicletta? guida lei? / hai capito, io non guido neanche la carriola, / però, non era maestra, tua figlia? / ah, non le piaceva far scuola, e allora, / che farà anche carriera, oggi non c'è piú / nessun impedimento, oggi una donna, / non le vedi? fanno tutto, anche il militare, / va per loro, Giorgio, non c'è niente da fare, / salutami la Graziella, – e adesso qui / che non mi dimentichi, il sale grosso, lo zucchero, l'olio, / una saponetta, che ce n'è ormai una scaglia, / una busta di borotalco, / ecco, l'Idrolitina, che mi dimenticavo, / e voglio prendere anche del miele, ho un po' di raucedine, / che col latte caldo scioglie, / e poi dovrei passare dalle Lucia, / che sta laggiú all'inferno, aspetta, ma / non è lei, la Lucia, quella là? // che stavo per venir giú da te, e allora /

isn't that Lucia, the one over there?

I was just about do go down to see you, and so
have you finished the skirt? no? I knew it,
you promised, promised me, wasn't there enough material?
really? it was such a pretty pattern,
and now nothing can be done with it,
goodness, you're right, a flounce, either blue
or a dark brown, we'll go together to Miro's,
how about now? can you go right now?
tomorrow then, Lucia, see you tomorrow,

bread, no, there's yesterday's
which we throw away and people are dying of hunger,
it's a crime, I'm ashamed, I am, but him, sure,
if he doesn't have fresh bread, all right, fine,
a roll, for that pain-in-the-neck, bread's good,
even the next day bread's good, why wouldn't it be,
the flavor comes out more,

have you gotten yourself ready?
it'll be winter by the time you're ready,
so where did Missiroli come from,
last night you just about bit my head off,
from Bellaria, Dolores told me,

u n'è li, la Lucia, quèlla che là?

ch'a stéva pr'avnì zò da tè, e alòura
cla sutèna t la é fata? no? a l savéva,
tè t prumètt, tè t prumètt, u n gn'è sà stofa?
dabón? ch' l'è una piò bèla fantaséa,
e alòura u n'i vén gnént?
orca, zà, t'é rasòun, 'na bèlza, bló
o un maròun schéur, andémm insén da Miro,
ènca adès, ta n pò, 'dès?
admatéina, Lucia, a s'avdémm 'dmatéina,

e e' pèn, gnént, u i è quèll d'ir,
ch'a n butémm véa, e u i è chi ch' mór ad fèma,
l'è delétt, a m vargògn, mè, mo léu, sè,
s'u n'à e' pèn frèsch, va bén, zò, una rusètta
ma che nuiòus, ch' l'è bón ènca e' dè dop
e' pèn, cumè, pu e' fa 'nca piò rinséida,

t'é parcè tè? admèn e' fa la nàiva,
alòura addò ch' l'avnéva Misirúl?
che irisàira ta m'é magnè la faza,
da Belaria, la m l'à détt la Dolores,

quella sottana l'hai fatta? no? lo sapevo, / tu prometti, prometti, non c'è
abbastanza stoffa? / davvero? che è una cosí bella fantasia, / e allora non ci
viene niente? / orca, già, hai ragione, una balza, blu / o un marrone scuro,
andiamo insieme da Miro, / anche adesso, non puoi adesso? / domattina,
Lucia, ci vediamo domattina, // il pane, niente, c'è quello di ieri, / che ne
buttiamo via, e c'è chi muore di fame, / è un delitto, mi vergogno, io, ma lui,
sì, / se non ha il pane fresco, va bene, dai una rosetta / per quel noioso, che
è buono anche il giorno dopo / il pane, come no, e poi fa anche piú riuscita,
// hai apparecchiato tu? domani fa la neve, / allora da dove veniva Missiroli?
/ che ieri sera mi hai mangiato la faccia, / da Bellaria, me l'ha detto la Dolores, /

but then everyone knows it, it's only you that didn't know,
and you just had to be right, when you dig in,
you're truly unpleasant, –
I ran into Giorgio uptown,
no, Giorgio Magalotti, who with that daughter,
it seemed like, she did very well, she was the best
in school, who knows how far she could have gone?
and now she's a meter maid, nice, huh?
she studied, she studied,
to be handing out parking tickets, and she looks so bad
in that uniform, a girl, come on now,
get off it, a traffic officer,
then that cap with the visor, it's all shoved up inside there,
the only nice feature she had was her hair, – what should we eat?
there's still a few drops of broth, which with the stale bread,
I'll make some zuppa di pane,
and two pieces of sausage,
which who says zuppa di pane isn't good? listen,
I complained to Nazario, oh this broth,
turned out especially good, just look at those beautiful little tear
                                              [drops floating,
one piece of sausage, it's too much for me, and here I'll give you
a couple of pieces of crackling, but don't eat it all,

mo pu i la sa tótt, sno tè ta n'e' savévi,
e t vlévi avài rasòun, quant ta t'i mètt,
t si piò intipatich,
                          ò incòuntar Giorgio in piaza,
no, Giorgio ad Magalòt, che sa cla fióla,
e' pareva che, brèva, la piò brèva
tla scóla, chi sa dò ch' la arivarà,
e adès la fa la guèrdia, bèla roba,
la à studié, la à studié,
par fè al contravenziòun, ch' la sta piò mèl
sa cla divéisa, una ragaza, zò,
mo va là, a fè la guèrdia,
pu che brètt sla visira, tótt calchèd,
ch' la à sno i cavéll ad bèl,
                          cs'èll ch'a magnémm?
u i è 'ncóura un gòzzal 'd bród, sa sté pèn déur
a faz una stuvèda,
e du budéll 'd sunzézza,
ch' la è sémpra bóna la stuvèda, sint,
ò ragnè sa Nazario, mo sté bród
l'è specièl, vè che stèli,
un budèl, l'è ènca trop, mè, e quést che què
l'è du grasúl, però nu magni tótt,

ma poi lo sanno tutti, solo tu non lo sapevi, / e volevi aver ragione, quando ti
ci metti, / sei veramente antipatico, – ho incontrato Giorgio in piazza, / no,
Giorgio Magalotti, che con quella figlia, / pareva che, brava, la piú brava, a
scuola, chi sa dove arriverà, / e adesso fa il vigile, bella roba, / ha studiato, ha
studiato / per fare le contravvenzioni, che sta cosí male / con quella divisa,
una ragazza, dai, / ma va' là, a fare il vigile, / poi quel berretto con la visiera,
tutto calcato, / che di bello ha solo i capelli, – cosa mangiamo? / c'è ancora un
goccio di brodo, con questo pane raffermo / faccio la zuppa di pane, / e due
budelli di salciccia, / che è sempre buona la zuppa di pane, senti, / ho prote-
stato con Nazario, ma questo brodo / è speciale, ve' che stelle, / un budello,
è anche troppo per me, e questi qui / sono due ciccioli, però non mangiarli
tutti, / ti fanno male, tutti, lasciane un po' per stasera, /

it doesn't sit well, all of it, leave a little for tonight,
that's enough, come on, then afterwards you won't digest it,
I'm not going to get it for you anymore, I swear it, I'm not
                                      [going to buy it again,
because when you feel bad it's unbearable,
do you want a pear? no, it'll clean you out,
I'll peel it for you, a slice,
just taste this, it's butter, –
are you going out now?
you won't miss out on anything, you don't even seem
yourself anymore,
with that television set you're like a clock,
it makes me jumpy, switching it around, aren't you tired of it?
when it's that time, he turns it on,
there could be an earthquake, but he'd still turn it on,
I myself, I'd throw it out the window,
I would, that remote control,
just sit there and listen to it, it's all chatter, come on now,
it's a waste of breath listening, (it's all a waste of time), always
the same stuff,
and you can't say a word, *they* should be the ones shutting up,
shouldn't they?
those jerks, they've just got to talk, well let them,
come on, you're, with that television,
always glued to it, go on and go uptown,
go to the cafe, go take a walk, doesn't she ever shut up?
it's them that should be quiet, enough, come on now,
watch all you want, I'm going over there to iron,
yes, what am I ironing? here, just look at all this stuff,
which these were brand new, these pants, what am I
supposed to do?

i t fa mèl, tótt, lasni un pó par stasàira,
basta, zò, che dop ta n'i digeréss,
a n t'i tóggh piò, a zéur, a n t'i tóggh piò,
che quant t sté mèl u n s chèmpa,
t l vó una pàira? no? ch' la t lèva dréinta,
a t la sbózz mè, una fètta,
sint che roba, un butír,

u t'è scap l'òura?

va là che ta n pérd gnént, tè ta n t vaid mégga,
sa cla televisiòun t si cmè un arlózz,
che ta m fé vní un nervòus, cambia, ta n t stóff?
léu quant l'è cl'òura e' zénd,
e' pò vnì e' taremòt, mo léu e' zénd,
ch'a te butarébb vèa da la finestra,
mè, che telecomando,
par stè sintéi, ch' l'è tótti ciacri, zò,
i n chèva, un ragn da un béus, sémpra al stèss' robi,
e u n s pò di gnént, bsògna stè zétt, cumè,
l'à da zcòrr chi pataca, lasa andè,
va là, t fé un schiv sa cla televisiòun,
sémpra tachèd alè, mo va un pó in piaza,
va te cafè, va a fè una pasegèda,
a n stagh mai zétta?

/ basta, su, che dopo non li digerisci, / non te li prendo piú, lo giuro, non te
li prendo piú, / che quando stai male non si campa, / la vuoi una pera? no?
che ti lava dentro, / te la sbuccio io, una fetta, / senti che roba, un burro, –
t'è scappata l'ora? / va' là che non perdi niente, tu non ti vedi mica, / con
quella televisione sei come un orologio, / che mi fai venire un nervoso,
cambia, non ti stufi? / lui quand'è quell'ora accende, / può venire il terremoto, ma lui accende, / che te lo butterei via dalla fineestra, / io, quel telecomando, / per stare a sentire, che sono tutte chiacchiere, dai, / non cavano
un ragno dal buco, sempre le stesse cose, / e non si può dir niente, bisogna
star zitti, come no, / devono parlare quei coglioni, lascia andare, / va' là, fai
uno schifo con quella televisione, / sempre attaccato lí, ma vai in piazza, /
vai al caffè, vai a fare una passeggiata, / non sta mai zitta?

holes you could put a hand through,
you've got to be kidding, here
these should be thrown away, it's always like this, he,
if he has a certain thing, you can't tear it away from him,
this suit coat too, look, what's the use of mending it,
this one's shot, the elbows, never mind worn out,
you can see the lining, he falls in love, he does,
with a jacket, always that one, always that one,
he's worn it down to a rag, which then people,
look at how she sends him out, he's making me look bad,
which people too,
if they would just mind their own business,
no, this one's gone, I'm throwing it away,
you could put on some of that velour,
which would even work better,
but he's got so many, he's got more clothes than I do,

well let's just keep at it, just look at this mountain of stuff,
I never have had a big love for ironing,
I like knitting better, for me, knitting,
I made him a pullover, last year, which he was proud of,
he showed it off,

l'è lòu ch'i n sta mai zétt, basta, va là,
guèrda quèll t vu, mè a vagh adlà a stiré,

sè, cs'èll ch'a stéir, aquè, vèrda che roba,
ch'i era nóv, sti calzétt, mo cmè ch'u s fa?
di béus ch'u i pasa un braz, aquè t'é vòia,
quést i è da buté véa, sémpra acsè, léu,
se una roba la i pis u n la smètt piò,
ènca sta sèrga, vè, 's'ut rinacè,
quèsta la è 'ndèda, i gómat, èlt che sléis,
u s vaid la fódra, u s'inamoura, léu,
t'na sèrga, sémpra quèlla, sémpra quèlla,
l'ardéus un straz, e dop, t si mat, la zénta,
vè cmè ch' la l manda, u m fa fè dal fighéuri,
ch'ènca la zénta, s'i badéss par lòu,
no, quèsta, via, a glia bótt tla mundèzza,
u s mitrà quèlla 'd vléut, ch'e' sta ènca mèi,
mo u n n'à tènti, l'à piò vistí ch' nè mè,
e avènti pò, vè che muntagna ad roba,
che stiré a n'ò mai vú 'na gran pasiòun,
u m pis piò i férr, mè, lavurè si férr,
a i ò fat un maiòun, an, ch'u, s stiméva,

sono loro che non stanno mai zitti, basta, va' là, / guarda quel che vuoi, io
vado di là a stirare, // sí, cosa stiro, qui guarda che roba, / che erano nuove,
'ste calze, ma come si fa? / dei buchi che ci passa un braccio, qui hai voglia,
/ queste sono da buttar via, sempre cosí, lui, / se una cosa gli piace non se
la toglie piú, / anche questa giacca, ve', cosa vuoi rammendare, / questa è
andata, i gomiti, altro che lisi, / si vede la fodera, s'innamora, lui, / d'una
giacca, sempre quella, sempre quella, / la riduce un cencio, che dopo la gente, / ve' come lo manda, mi fa fare delle figure, / che anche la gente, se
badassero ai fatti loro, / no, questa, via, gliela butto nell'immondizia, / si
metterà quella di velluto, che sta anche meglio, / ma ne ha tante, ha piú
vestiti di me, // e avanti pure, ve' che montagna di roba, / che a stirare non
ho mai avuto un gran passione, / mi piacciono piú i ferri, a me, lavorare ai
ferri, / gli ho fatto un maglione, l'anno scorso, che si vantava, /

and now outside, with the watering,
which if I don't keep on top of things, he,
Emma, come look at my garden? do you like it, come on in,
you're taking a walk, I'll come and open it, you can take home
three or four tomatoes, which in a salad,
if you use them tonight, tell me, – I'll put them
in this bag, no, it's not too much, can't you see
how many there are? who's going to eat them all?
and it's not that I haven't fed him any, I, sometimes,
in the afternoon, a tomato with bread,
for a snack, I don't even wash it, with a little salt,
and so tell me, which you're near
Giordana, I heard some talk, you too, I was talking to,
it might have been Dora, it might have been Marina,
which they really should, it's better to say nothing,
but come on, one day, I saw her crying to Giordana,
"I have two sisters who. . ." she was ashamed,
and now it comes out, which I just couldn't believe, you either,
and well, she always did what was expected,
you couldn't have said a bad word, never, her mother
used to brag, are you crazy, her Giordana,
then out of the blue, *that's* what I'm saying,
there's so many of these kinds of messes these days,
how did she end up
pregnant? and with who? she's not saying a word,

un péunt ad vàird,

                    e adès fura a daquè,
che s'a n'i stagh dri mè mal robi, léu,
Emma, t guèrd e' mi órt? u t pis? vén dréinta,
fa e' zéir, a t véngh arvéi, ta t pórt a chèsa
tri quatar pumidór, che in insalèda,
s' ta i fé stasàira, ta m giré,

                            a i mitémm
at sté sachèt, no, ch'i n'è trópp, ta n vaid
quant u i n'è? chi è ch'i i magna?
e a n gn'ò mégga dè gnént, mè u i è dal vólti,
e' dopmezdè, un pumidór se pèn,
pr'imbrènda, a n'e' lèv gnénca, s'un pó 'd sèl,
e alòura déim, che tè ta i sté tachéda
ma la Giordana, mè ò sintéi dal ciacri,
ènca tè? ch'a so 'rvènza,
fóss stè la Dora, fóss stè la Marina,
che lòu dabón, l'è mèi stè zétt, va là,
un dè a la ò vésta piànz ma la Giordana:
"Ò do surèli che", la s vargugnéva,
e adès e' scapa fura,
che mè a n'aréiv a cràidi, gnénca tè?

un punto di verde, – e adesso fuori a innaffiare,/ che se non ci sto dietro io
alle cose, lui, / Emma, guardi il mio orto? ti piace? vieni dentro, / fa' il giro,
ti vengo ad aprire, ti porti a casa / tre quattro pomodori, che in insalata, / se
li fai stasera, mi dirai – li mettiamo / in questo sacchetto, no, che non sono
troppi, non vedi / quanti ce ne sono? chi li mangia? / e non gli ho mica dato
niente, io, delle volte, / il pomeriggio, un pomodoro col pane, / per merenda, non lo lavo neanche, con un po' di sale, / e allora dimmi, che tu di casa
le stai vicino, / alla Giordana, ho sentito delle chiacchiere, / anche tu? sono
rimasta, / fosse stata la Dora, fosse stata la Marina, / che loro davvero, è
meglio star zitti, va' là, / un giorno l'ho vista piangere alla Giordana: / "Ho
due sorelle che", si vergognava, / e adesso viene fuori, / che io non arrivo
a crederci, neanche tu? /

they say she's not talking, that's what they're saying, that's what
                                                    [it seems like,
you've heard it too? with Walter Lucchi,
which I don't know, I, even her, with a married man,
who's intelligent, so intelligent that,
he's got brains, he doesn't use them? and they say that Elsa
already knows everything, it's been two or three days
that no one's seen Walter, he's away, even there, suiting himself,
two families ruined,

so, you're going to make a salad tonight,
does it give you the runs?
it kills him, but you can eat whatever you want to,
they have such a perfume, smell it,
no, I'm going to make scrambled eggs,
with spinach, it's six, I'm going in now to get things started,
thank you for what? for two or three tomatoes?

amo, cumè, la è sémpra stè a e' su pòst,
u n s'è putéu dí gnént, mai, la su mà
la s stiméva, t si mat, la su Giordana,
e tótt t'un bot, mo l'è quèll ch'a déggh mè,
u i è tènt ad chi pastrócc òz, cmè ch'u s fa
'rvanzè in cinta? e sa chéi? li la n dí gnént,
dis ch' la n dí gnént, mo u i è chi ch' déi, e' pèr,
ta l'è sintí, 'nca, tè? sa Walter Lucchi,
ch'a n'e' so, mè, ènca li, s'un òm spusèd,
ch' la è inteligenta, inteligenta ad chè?
t'é e' zarvèl, ta n'e' dróv? e dis che l'Elsa
la sa zà tótt, Walter l'è du tri dè,
ch'u n s vaid, l'è fura, ènca 'lè 'dès cundèla,
do famèi arvinédi,

mo tè stasàira ta t fé un'insalèda,
t'é tólt e' squaquaròun? l'è la su mórta,
mo pu ta i pò magnè sa quèll ch'u t pèr,
i à un parfómm, sint che roba,
mè invíci a faz agli óvi sfritulédi
si spinàz, l'è al si, a i vagh a mètt sò 'dès,
mo grezia ad chè, par du tri pumidór?

e beh, è sempre stata al suo posto, / non s'è potuto dir niente, mai sua madre
/ si vantava, sei matto, la sua Giordana, / e tutt'a un tratto, ma è quello che
dico io, / ci sono tanti di quei pastrocchi oggi, come si fa / a rimanere incin-
ta? e con chi? lei non dice niente, / dice che non parla, ma c'è chi dice, pare,
/ l'hai sentito anche tu? con Walter Lucchi, / che non lo so, io, anche lei, con
un uomo sposato, / che è intelligente, / intelligente che? / hai il cervello, non
lo adoperi? e dice che l'Elsa / sa già tutto, Walter sono due tre giorni / che
non si vede, è fuori, anche lí adesso accomodarla, / due famiglie rovinate, //
ma tu stasera ti fai un'insalata, / hai preso lo squacquarone? è la sua morte,
/ ma poi li puoi mangiare con quello che ti pare, / hanno un profumo, senti
che roba, / io invece faccio le uova al tegame / con gli spinaci, sono le sei,
li vado a mettere su adesso, / ma grazie di che? per due tre pomodori? /

577

it's been awhile since we've talked,
I'll see you and say hello to Mariola for me,
I'd love to have a sister like her too,
she can make anything, and the next time, remember,
when you come by here, there's figs, look at now many there are,
in two or three weeks they'll be ripe,

what do you mean it's early, it's ringing seven-thirty,
when do you want to eat? come on now, hurry up, it's getting
                                                              [cold,
is it too bland? put in some salt, you
like it salty, which isn't good for you,
it's not me saying it, it's the doctors saying it,
too much salt is bad for you,
you've always got to complain about something, you,
now eat those eggs, and be quiet a second

tonight I'd like to see some television
for a change, *A Thousand Dreams* is on,
they say someone is going to win ten million
if they call you on the phone, yes, I understand,
but even if they called, you wouldn't pick it up,

u i n'è ch'a n'i stémm dri,
a s'avdémm, e saléutmi la Mariula,
una surèla acsè la m vrébb mu mè,
la à al mèni d'ór, e st'èlta vólta, arcórdti,
quant t pas da què, u i è i féigh, vè quant u n n'à,
fra dis quéngg dè i è fat,

cumè, l'è prèst, l'è al sèt e mèz sunèdi,
quant t vu magnè? zò, sbréigti, ch'al s'agiàza,
agli è s-ciavéidi? e mètti e' sèl, ma tè
u t pis salèd, ch'u n va mégga tènt bén,
a n so sno mè ch'à l déggh, u l dí i dutéur,
troppo sale fa male,
bsògna magnè s-ciavéid,
ch' l'è pu s-ciavéid par tè, par mè e' va bén,
t'è sémpra da sbruntlè-tè,
mo magna cal do óvi, e sta un pó zétt,

che invíci mè stasàira a la ví vdai
un pó 'd televisiòun, u i è Millesogni,
dis ch'u s véinz dis migliéun
s'i t cèma me telefan, sè, ò capéi,
mo tè 'nca s'i ciaméss, tè ta n'arspònd,

ce n'è che non ci stiamo dietro, / ci vediamo, e salutami la Mariola, / una
sorella cosí mi ci vorebbe a me, / ha le mani d'oro, e 'st'altra volta, ricordati,
/ quando passi di qui, ci sono i fichi, ve' quanti ne ha, / fra dieci quindici
giorno sono maturi, // come, è presto, sono le sette e mezzo suonate, /
quando vuoi mangiare? dai, sbrigati, che si freddano, / sono insipide? e met-
tici il sale, a te / ti piace salato, che non va mica tanto bene, / non sono io
che lo dico, lo dicono i dottori, / troppo sale fa male, / bisogna mangiare
insipido, / che poi è insipido per te, per me va bene, / hai sempre da
brontolare, tu, / ma mangia quelle due uova, e sta' un po' zitto, // che invece
io stasera la voglio vedere / un po' di televisione, c'è Millesogni, / dice che
si vincono dieci milioni / se ti chiamano al telefono, sí, ho capito, / ma anche
se chiamassero, tu non rispondi, /

579

you never answer, it pains me,
here, here we are, they're starting, this one here,
there's all possible ways, the way she talks,
you can't understand anything, she mumbles,
and this one, he's even worse,
he's always sneering, and people like him?
people don't understand anything, and now,
what are they doing? I say that,
what are they racking their brains about?
you do certain things,
they win all this money, and you, you numskull, every year
you're just not content until you pay, 'till you're on the up-

                                       [and-up,

for the television fee, which then they give us,
look what they're giving them,
look at all that stuff, they're advancing, no, no, that's enough,
I'm tired of it, come on now, what time is it?
nine-thirty? really, it's already nine-thirty?
Well, you know what I have to say to you? I'm going to bed.

ta n'arspònd mai, u m tòcca córr mu mè,
ècco, a i sémm, i ravéa, quèsta che què
la i i è ad tótt i brudétt, la zcòrr t'un módi,
u n s capéss gnént, la pzézza, e st'èlt ancòura,
ch' l'è piò ghignòus, e ma la zénta, e adès,
mo cs'èll ch'i fa? mè a déggh-che,
cs'èll ch'i va a strulghè mai, mo fé dal robi,
ch'i ciapa tènt 'd chi bócch, e tè, salàm,
tótt i an, tè ta n sté bén s' ta n vé a paghè
l'abonament, ch'i s dà, vè quèll ch'i s dà,
vè che roba, e i va 'vènti, no, no, basta,
a m so zà stóffa, mo va là, che or'èll?
l'è al nóv e mèz? dabón, zà al nóv e mèz?
ció, ta l sé cs'èll ch'a t déggh? a vagh a lèt.

non rispondi mai, mi tocca correre a me, / ecco, ci siamo, cominciamo,
questa qui, / c'è in tutte le salse, parla in un modo, / non si capisce niente,
farfuglia, e quest'altro, ancora, / che è cosí ghignoso, e alla gente gli piace, /
non capiscono mica niente la gente, e adesso / che cosa fanno? io dico che,
/ cosa vanno mai a strologare, ma fate delle cose, / che prendono tanti di
quei soldi, e tu, salame, / tutti gli anni, tu non stai bene se non vai a pagare,
/ l'abbonamento, che ci danno, ve' quel che ci danno, / ve' che roba e vanno
avanti, no, no, basta, / mi sono già stufata, ma va' là, che ore sono? / le nove
e mezzo? davvero? già le nove e mezzo? / beh, lo sai cosa ti dico? vado a
letto.

Now

I can do whatever I want now at night.
Keeping the light on until one. Until two.
And nobody complains.
Pull all the covers over onto my side.
No one grumbles. On the highway in the car
I can do a hundred and forty kilometers,
a hundred and fifty, faster,
whereas before if I went above a hundred and ten.
I can go to the movies every so often,
but also I just enjoy staying at home.
With my work, I'm running around all day long,
I'm tired, no, there are some evenings
where I'd like to go get a pizza, go down to Rimini,
but by myself, I don't think so, where eating is concerned,
even spending the money, it's a thing, which, every time,
how much should I spend? because I'm a glutton, I am, and
                                                    [money,
pasta, soup, it's never enough, and now
I can eat as much as I want to,
now nobody's saying anything anymore, no commentary.
What am I doing here, what's this? tears?

Adès

A pòs fè quèll ch'u m pèr adès, la nòta
tní zais' la luce fina un'òura, al do,
e niseun ch' ragna,
tiré al cvérti tótti da la mi pèrta,
e nisun ch' sbròuntla, sl'autostrèda in machina
ai zentquarènta, ai zentzinquènta e piò,
che préima s'a paséva i zentedís,
e' cino d'ogni tènt,
mo l'è un pó ch'u m pis ènch' da stè ma chèsa,
e' mi lavòur, e' dè a so sémpra in zéir,
dop a so strach, ècco, no, u i è dal sàiri
ch'a vrébb andé a magné 'na pizza a Rémin,
mo da par mè, 'ta bón, a zcòrr, 'd magnè,
ènch' la fòurma, una roba, tótt' al vólti,
mo quant t n mètt? ch'a so lòvv, mè, la fòurma,
da sótt o in bród, la n basta mai, e adès
a n pòs mètt quant' a vói,
adès u n dí piò gnént niseun, adès
mo cs'èll ch'a faz, a piànz?

Adesso. Posso fare quello che mi pare adesso, la notte / tenere accesa la luce fino all'una, alle due, / e nessuno che protesta, / tirare le coperte tutte dalla mia parte, / e nessuno brontola, sull'autostrada in macchina / ai centoquaranta, ai centocinquanta e piú, / che prima se superavo i centodieci, / al cinema ogni tanto, / ma è un po' che mi piace anche stare in casa, / il mio lavoro, il giorno sono sempre in giro, / dopo sono stanco, ecco, no, ci sono delle sere, / che vorrei andare a magiare, / anche il grana, una roba, tutte le volte, / ma quanto ne metti? che sono goloso, io, il grana, / pastasciutta o minestra, non basta mai, e adesso / ne posso mettere fin che voglio, / adesso non dice piú niente nessuno, adesso / ma cosa faccio, piango?

The Watch

But I have found the way, I move my watch ahead,
fifteen minutes, a half hour, even as much as an hour,
which had I figured it out earlier, from then on,
but the important thing is I figured it out, it's been at least a
[year,
and now it's a whole new ballgame, before, hear me out,
everything was always last minute,
I was always running, swearing, fits of anger,
but now, well, it's been good while, how long?
That I've been keeping it ahead? I tried, an hour-and-a-half,
which what I said about was: it won't be too much?
No, it's never too much,
in the big scheme of things, when you think about it, what's
an hour-and-a-half? nothing, it's not even the hours
that matter, what matters
is something else, it's a matter that comes before the hours,
because time, of course it doesn't do it intentionally,
but it seems like it's making fun of you,
there are minutes that are endless, and days,
when evening rolls around,
you haven't accomplished a thing, and a whole day's gone by,
it's like they've gotten you all turned around,
if it weren't for the fact I have this watch,

L'arlózz

Mo ò tròv e' módi, a mètt l'arlózz avènti,
d'un quèrt, d'una mèz'òura, ènca d'una'òura,
ch' s'a i arivéva préima, e alòura pu,
mo insòmma a i so rivàt, l'è bèla un an,
e adès l'è un èlt. campè, préima, 'ta bón,
tótt' al robi se bréus,
chéursi, nervòus, biastéimi, incapladéuri,
adès invíci, amo l'è un pó, quant'èll?
ch'a l téngh avènti, ò próv, d'un'òura e mèz,
ch'a géva: u n sarà trop? no, u n'è mai trop,
de rest un'òura e mèz, s' ta i péns, cs'èll ch' l'è?
gnént, mo u n'è gnénca agli òuri ch' còunta, e' zcòurs,
l'è un èlt, l'è un zcòurs ch'e' vén préima dagli òuri,
parchè e' témp, che magari u n'e' fa pòsta,
mo e' pèr ch'u t tógga in zèir, u i è di minéut
ch'i n finéss mai, e di dè, ch'e' vén sàira,
ta n'é fat gnént, e l'è pas 'na zurnèda,
l'è cm'i t'éss imbruiè,
s'u n'i fóss ch' t'é l'arlózz,

L'orologio. Ma ho trovato il modo, metto l'orologio avanti, / d'un quarto, d'una mezz'ora, anche d'un'ora, / che se ci arrivavo prima, e allora poi, / ma insomma ci sono arrivato, è ormai un anno, / e adesso è un altro campare, prima sta' buono, / tutte le cose all'ultimo momento, / corse, nervoso, bestemmie, arrabbiature, / adesso invece, e beh, è un po', quant'è? / che lo tengo avanti, ho provato, d'un'ora e mezzo, / che dicevo: non sarà troppo? no, non è mai troppo, / del resto un'ora e mezzo, se ci pensi, cos'è? / niente, ma non sono neanche le ore che contano, il discorso / è un altro, è un discorso che viene prima delle ore, / perché il tempo, che magari non lo fa apposta, / ma pare che ti prenda in giro, ci sono dei minuti / che non finiscono mai, e dei giorni, che viene sera, / non hai fatto niente, ed è passata una giornata, / è come t'avessero imbrogliato, / se non fosse che hai l'orologio, /

585

which seems like nothing, tick-tick-tick
but they can't trip it up,
it says, tick-tick or tick-tock, but time never stops,
and who wants to stop it?
I'm not crazy here,
the watch marks them off,
because when you get right down to it
the only peculiar talent time has is for that particular job,
it passes and that's it,
it can't do anything else, even when
you're stirring your coffee,
even when you're mailing a letter,
it's still time that's passing,
and if it doesn't it's worse, what would you do then?
sit there
with the spoon still in your cup?
or the envelope in your hand?
then another thing, which you don't think about, time,
it's always the two of you, even on the interstate in a car,
it seems like you're alone, you're driving like a demon,
but you're not alone, it's you and him,
who's getting there first,
and it's always all tangled together, the faster you go,
the faster it goes,
you're a child on the merry-go-round
who never catches up to the horse in front,
but with a watch it's an altogether different discussion,

ch'e' pèr gnént, tic tic, mo léu i n l'imbròia,
dis, tic tic o tic tac, e' témp t n'e' férum,
e chi è ch'i l vó farmè? a n so mégga mat,
l'arlózz u i tó al miséuri, parchè in fònd
e' témp l'è bón da fè sno che mistír,
e' pasa e basta,
u n fa èlt, ènca quant se cuciaréin
t dé dréinta me cafè,
ènch' quant t'impòst 'na lèttra,
l'è sémpra témp ch'e' pasa,
e s'u n pasa l'è pézz, csa fét? t sté 'lè
sémpra férum se cuciaréin tla taza?
o sla bòsta tal mèni?
pu un'èlta roba, ch'u n s'i pensa, e' témp,
t si sémpra in déu, ènch' sl'autostrèda in machina,
ch'u t pèr d'ès da par tè, t vé cmè e' spavént,
invíci a si tè e léu, chi aréiva préima,
e l'è sémpra un imbròi,
piò t córr tè, piò e' córr léu,
t si cmè un burdèl sla giostra
ch'u n gn'aréiva mai me cavàl davènti,
mo sl'arlózz l'è un èlt zcòurs,

che pare niente, tic tic, ma a lui non l'imbrogliano, / dice, tic tic o tic tac, il
tempo non lo fermi, / e chi lo vuol fermare? / non sono mica matto, /
l'orologio gli prende le misure, perché in fondo / il tempo è capace di fare
solo quel mestiere, / passa e basta, / non fa altro, anche quando col cucchiaino / mescoli il caffè, / anche quando imbuchi una lettera, / è sempre
tempo che passa, / e se non passa è peggio, cosa fai? stai lí / sempre fermo
col cucchiaino nella tazza? / o con la busta in mano? / poi un'altra cosa, che
non ci si pensa, il tempo, / sei sempre in due, anche sull'autostrada in macchina, / che ti pare d'essere solo, vai come lo spaveto, / invece siete tu e lui,
chi arriva prima, / ed è sempre un imbroglio, / piú corri tu, piú corre lui, /
sei come un bambino sulla giostra / che non raggiunge mai il cavallo davanti,
/ ma con l'orologio è un altro discorso, /

because time, sure, it's always there passing,
but it doesn't have a lot of smarts,
it can't even count,
it doesn't know how to, it, what's a minute,
an hour, even noon, if the bell tower doesn't sound it,
it's all the same to him, evening, morning,
Christmas, Easter, it passes, it just plows on ahead,
Stop, Idiot, I'm not saying it for my own sake,
it's for your own good,
look at the world a little,
oh sure, it's like trying to insult a jackal by calling it a whore,
you can't reason with time, you can't have a discussion,
you never know how to understand it,
but luckily there's the watch, with a watch,
you can put it up to your ear, you hear it ticking,
this is a different kind of sounding,
this thing knows how to keep track,
nothing gets by it,
not even a minute or a second gets by,
the watch has no time for small talk,
time is in its hands, it's in charge, and you,
if you can come to some kind of agreement with it,
if you put it ahead,
you can run ahead too, you can run faster than time,
you sit down, and you wait for it,

parchè e' témp, sè, l'è sémpra dri ch'e' pasa,
mo u n'à méggh' 'na gran testa,
u n'è gnénch' bón 'd cuntè,
u n'e' sa, léu, quèll ch' l'è un minéut, un'òura,
ènch' mezdè, s'u n gn'e' sòuna e' Campanòun,
par léu l'è tótt cumpagn, sàira, matéina,
Nadèl, Pasqua, léu e' pasa, e' va drétt,
férmat, pataca, a n déggh par mè, par tè,
guèrda un pó e' mònd,
sè, l'è cmè déi putèna ma la vòulpa,
u n s ragiòuna se témp, ta n pó fè un zcòurs,
ta n sé mai cmè ciapèl,
mo par furtéuna u i è l'arlózz sl'arlózz,
ta t'e' mètt m'un'urèccia, t sint ch'e'bat,
quèst' l'è un'èlta sunèda,
o chéunt quèst u i sa fè, u n'i scapa gnént,
quèst u n'i scapa gnénca un minéut sgònd,
l'arlózz e' vó póch' ciacri,
l'è tal su mèni e' témp, u l gvérna, e tè
s' ta t mètt d'acórd sa léu, s' ta l mètt avènti,
t córr avènti ènca tè, t córr pió ch' nè e' témp,
ta t mètt disdài, t l'aspétt,

perché il tempo, sí, è sempre lí che passa, / ma non ha mica una gran testa, / non è neanche capace di contare, / non lo sa, lui, cos'è un minuto, un'ora, / anche mezzogiorno, se non glielo suona il Campanone, / per lui è tutto uguale, sera, mattina, / Natale, Pasqua, lui passa, va dritto, / fermati, coglione, non lo dico per me, per te, / guarda un po' il mondo, / sí, è come dire puttana alla volpe, / non si ragiona col tempo, non puoi fare un discorso, / non sai mai come prenderlo, / ma per fortuna c'è l'orologio, con l'orologio, / te lo metti a un orecchio, senti che batte, / questa è un'altra suonata, / i conti questo li sa fare, non gli scappa niente, / a questo non gli scappa neanche un minuto secondo, / l'orologio vuol poche chiacchiere, / è nelle sue mani il tempo, lo governa, e tu, / se ti metti d'accordo con lui, se lo metti avanti, / corri avanti anche tu, corri piú del tempo, / ti siedi, lo aspetti, /

you feel it arriving, it's like saying, na-na-na-na-na,
because it's never going to catch up with you, you're always ahead,
it cannot catch up to you, it's like the paradox of Columbus's egg,
but I, everything's all different now,
I'm telling you the honest-to-God truth,
now I do everything with serenity, no rushing,
it's never late,
but it's not only this, it's not just the things that have to get done,
material things, I, it's that,
putting it like this might seem like, but it's not a joke,
or putting it better, it's a joke that you're playing on time,
because for time a watch is like
looking at itself in a mirror,
but if you've put the watch ahead,
it's like those mirrors that distort the face,
time passes, and that fellow?
he doesn't stop for one minute, he never can recover himself,
maybe he's having some fun,
who knows, maybe instead he gets ticked off,
and you're there laughing under the mustache,
what hour have the two of us fabricated?
this time you tripped up yourself.

ta l sint ch' l'aréiva, ta i fé maramao,
che pu u n t'aréiva mai, t si sémpra avènti,
u n t pò rivé, ch' l'è l'uovo di Colombo,
mo mè, l'è cambiè e' mònd, a l géva pò,
a faz tótt se mi còmad, senza préssia,
u n'è mai tèrd,
ch' pu u n'è sno quèst, u n'è al robi da fè,
al robi materièli, mè, l'è ènca,
che a déil acsè magari, mo u n'è un schérz,
o par dí mèi, l'è un schérz ch' ta i fé me témp,
parchè l'arlózz pr'e' témp
l'è cmè guardès te spèc,
mo se l'arlózz tè ta l'é mèss avènti,
l'è cmè chi spécc ch'i t fa la faza tórta,
e' témp e' pasa, e quèll?
u n s'aferma un minéut, però u n s'artróva,
magari u s divertéss,
chi sa, magari invíci u s'incapèla,
e tè t réid sòtta i bafi, che òura émm fat?
t l'è imbruié tè stavólta?

lo senti che arriva, gli fai maramao, / che poi non ti arriva mai, sei sempre avanti,
/ non ti può arrivare, che è l'uovo di Colombo, / ma io, è cambiato il mondo, lo
dicevo pure, / faccio tutto con comodo, senza fretta, / non è mai tardi, / che poi
non è solo questo, non sono le cose da fare, / le cose materiali, io, è anche, / che
a dirlo cosí magari, ma non è uno scherzo, / o per dir meglio, è uno scherzo che
fai al tempo, / perché l'orologio per il tempo / è come guardarsi allo specchio, /
ma se l'orologio tu l'hai messo avanti, / è come quegli specchi che ti fanno la faccia
storta, / il tempo passa, e quello? / non si ferma un minuto, ma non si ritrova, /
magari si diverte, / chi sa, magari invece s'arrabbia, / e tu ridi sotto i baffi, che ora
abbiamo fatto? / l'hai imbrogliato tu stavolta.

Hygiene

I understand, sure, hygiene, these days,
if you're not paying attention,
with all these sicknesses, you think I'm not aware?
I'm not saying not to bathe, are you crazy?
you don't want to wash? I'm just saying not to go overboard,
because there's clean, that's fine, but not clean and shiny,
it's just that people now, bath foams, bath salts,
a bar of soap's not good enough,
no, instead, sometimes, by washing too much,
some things even get lost, the other day,
there was one lady, I didn't know her,
even if you tell me her name, she's not from here,
she's from Rimini, we had met each other by chance,
two months ago, then we met again,
again by chance, we exchanged a few words, we laughed,
but it's not like now, I'm wanting, I'm just telling you,
to give you an idea, it was a Tuesday afternoon,
at her house, her husband was away,
she started to unzip me, she was wearing a dressing gown,

L'igiene

Ò capéi, sè, l'igiene, òz, s' ta n sté, 'ténti,
sa tótt' stal malatéi, t vu ch'a n'e' sapa?
mo mè a n déggh mégga d' no lavès, t si mat?
ta n t vu lavè? a déggh? sno d' no esagerè,
parchè puléid, va bén, no smerigléid,
sno che la zénta, bagnoschiuma, sèl,
u n'i basta gnénch' piò la savunètta,
che invíci mè, dal vólti, lavès trop,
e' va pérs ènch' dal robi, l'altredè,
sa óna, ta n la cnòss,
ènca s'a ta n la cnòss,
ènca s'a t déggh e' nóm, la n'è d'aquè,
óna ad Rémin, a s sémm cnunséu par sbai,
du méis fa, dop a s sémm incòuntr'ancòura,
sémpra par sbai, dal paróli, émm ridéu,
mo u n'è mè adès ch'a vòia, a t la racòunt,
par dèt 'n'dea, l'è stè mèrt dopmezdè,
ad chèsa sóvva, e' maréid l'era fura,
la m'è vnú 'vréi, la aveva una vestaglia,

L'igiene. Ho capito, sí, l'igiene, oggi, se non stai attento, / con tutte queste malattie, vuoi che non lo sappia? / ma io non dico mica di non lavarsi, sei matto? / non ti vuoi lavare? dico solo di non esagerare, / perché puliti, va bene, no smerigliati, / solo che la gente, bagnoschiuma, sali, / non gli basta neanche piú la saponetta, / che invece io, delle volte, lavarsi troppo, / vanno perdute anche delle cose, l'altro giorno, / con una, non la conosci, / anche se ti dico il nome, non è di qui, / una di Rimini, ci siamo conosciuiti per sbaglio, / due mesi fa, dopo ci siamo incontrati ancora, / sempre per sbaglio, delle parole, abbiamo riso, / ma non è che io adesso voglia, te la racconto / per darti un'idea, è stato martedí pomeriggio, / in casa sua, il marito era fuori, / mi è venuta ad aprire, aveva una vestaglia, /

we'd been drinking, we'd danced, then we went to bed,
she climbed on top of me, quiet now,
and today is Thursday
and I still smell her, do you
understand?

émm bivéu, émm balè, pu dop te lèt
la m'è vnú sòura, ssst! aquè a cmand mè,
e òz l'è la zóbia,
e mè a la sint ancòura, t'è capéi?

abbiamo bevuto, abbiamo ballato, poi dopo a letto / mi è venuto sopra, ssst!
qui comando io, / e oggi è giovedí, / e io la sento ancora, hai capito?

Interstate

Work is work, there are those times
when work is hard, sure, but even
with these rough spots, to be working and working
steady, contracts, benefits, all of it, which my kids,
kids, in a manner of speaking,
in April the oldest will be twenty-four,
and he's still out of work,
he went to school, but school
doesn't mean a thing anymore, today
with a diploma you can wipe your ass,
which if it weren't for me, with two years
of middle school, but if it weren't for this old man,
who for more than thirty years
it's been me carrying the load,
nobody can take my place, plus right here, right now,
you better believe it, you could really get hurt,
we're insured, yes, up until now
nothing terrible has happened, let's hope not,
and keep going on, but we have a machine
like an enormous grater, except it's round, it spins with
incredible power,
and it grates, and the earth is sliced away
like butter, the ground is clay, tufa, sand,

La superstrèda

E' lavòur l'è lavòur, u i è di mumént
ch' la è déura, sè, mo insòmma
sa sti cièr 'd léuna lavurè e in regola,
librètt, marchètti, tótt, che i mi burdéll,
burdéll par módi 'd déi, e' grand st'avréil
u n n'à vintquàtar, e l'è ancòura a spas,
ch' l'à studié, mo studié u n vó dí piò gnént,
una vólta un diploma,
òz se diploma ta t puléss e' chéul,
ch' s'a n'i fóss mé, mè ò sno la sgònda media,
mo s'u n'i fóss sté vèc,
l'è piò 'd trent'an, mè, ch'a téir la carióla,
e niseun u m dà e' cambi, pu aquè 'dès,
t'è vòia, aquè u i è da fès mèl se séri,
ch'a sémm asicuréd, mo brótti robi
finòura u n n'è suzèst, sperémma bén,
e andémm avènti, amo avémm una machina,
l'è una specie 'd gratéusa, però tònda,
ch' la zéira, s'una fórza,
e la grata e la tèra la vén véa,
cmè un butír, tèra, sabia, gràida, tóff,

La superstrada. Il lavoro è lavoro, ci sono dei momenti / che è dura, sí, ma insomma / con questi chiari di luna lavorare e in regola, / libretto, marchette, tutto, che i miei ragazzi, / ragazzi per modo di dire, il grande ad aprile / ne ha ventiquattro, ed è ancora a spasso, / che ha studiato, ma studiare non vuol dire piú niente, / una volta un diploma, / oggi col diploma ti pulisci il culo, / che se non ci fossi io, io ho solo la seconda media, / ma se non ci fosse questo vecchio, / è piú di trent'anni, io, che tiro la carriola, / e nessuno mi dà il cambio, poi, qui addesso, / hai voglia, qui c'è da farsi male sul serio, / che siamo assicurati, ma brutte cose / finora non ne sono successe, speriamo bene, / e andiamo avanti, ma abbiamo una macchina, / è una specie di grattugia, però rotonda, / che gira, con una forza, / e gratta e la terra viene via /come burro, terra, sabbia, argilla, tufo, /

there's no rock, rock if you hit it, won't grate,
you need dynamite,
huge blasts, like an earthquake,
upward and onward in this line of work,
it's going to be an interstate, in four hours you can be in Rome,
you can cut off thirty kilometers,
underground, of course, as the crow flies,
there'll be an opening right here,
you wait and see, you better believe
there's going to be a floodgate with all the money flowing,
trips, businessmen, tourism,
can you imagine summer alone? flocking to the coast
do you know how many people there'll be?
there'll be so many people that
all they'll all be shoving each other out of the way,
they've studied the situation, you bet they've done studies,
they've been at it
a hell of a long time,
maps, blueprints,
calculations, debates,
and then they finally started, started
we've been excavating for two years,
twenty-seven months, and we've come a long way,

it's just that, yes, we're happy about it, but they could have,
the ones in charge could have, said something,
to let them know,

bast' ch'u n séa gènga,
la gènga, s' ta t'i imbàt, u n gn'è gratéusa,
u i vó la dinamite,
dal carichi ch'e' pèr e' taremòt,
e sémpra avènti, mo l'è un lavòur, quèst,
e' vén 'na superstrèda,
in quatr'òuri t si a Roma,
ta t sparàgn, a dí póch, trenta chilometri,
amo cumè, sòtta tèra u s va drétt,
è vén un sbòcch aquè, 'ta bón, va là,
u i sarà un muvimént, un zéir, 'd baócch,
viaz, afèri, turéisum,
ta t fighéur, sno d'instèda, a vní maréina,
la zénta ch'u i sarà? i farà al spatasi,
mo i la à studié, t'é vòia, i i è 'ndè dri
tènt ad che témp, diségn, piènti, progétt,
chéunt, discusiòun, e pu i à tach, émm tach,
l'è du an ch'a sbusémm,
l'è vintsèt méis, e a n n'avémm fat dla strèda,

sno che, sè, a sémm cuntént, mo s'u s putéss,
ch'i géss qualquèl quéi ch' cmanda, da savài,

purché non sia roccia, / la roccia, se ti c'imbatti, non c'è grattugia, / ci vuole la dinamite, / delle cariche che pare il terremoto, / e sempre avanti, ma è un lavoro, questo, / viene una superstrada, / in quattro ore sei a Roma, / ti risparmi, a dir poco, trenta chilometri, / e beh, sotto terra si va dritto, / viene uno sbocco, qui, sta' buono, va' là, / ci sarà un movimento, un giro di soldi, / viaggi, affari, turismo, / t'immagini, solo d'estate, a venire al mare, / la gente che ci sarà? faranno a spintoni, / ma l'hanno studiata, hai voglia, ci sono andati dietro / tanto di quel tempo, disegni, pianti, progetti, / conti, discussioni, e poi hanno cominciato, abbiamo cominciato, / sono due anni che buchiamo, / sono ventisette mesi, e ne abbiamo fatta di strada, // solo che, sí, siamo contenti, ma se si potesse, / che dicessero qualcosa quelli che comandano, da sapere, /

I've been on the job since day one, but if I had said,
I don't know how much farther we can go on this,
even my pals, we don't talk much,
with us, there's always a clash,
he starts yelling at you,
then you end up not understanding anyway,
and then someone, on his own,
it could even be the kind of work,
underground, you never see the sun,
all these huge lights, it's always daytime here,
it could even be all this electricity
in the air, and I'm already the nervous type,
at any rate, it's when work had stopped,
at noon, I'm there eating, and I think,
I start asking myself about things, I start making
comparisons,
I try to answer them,
but then I come up with new questions,
hey, I don't know, well, it's always the same story,
they must know, but these people never say anything,
every once in awhile I try, I do, with Calzolari,
I give it a try, an offhand remark, a comment,
he's from Ferrara, Calzolari, like the engineer,
some come from Bologna, from Parma, Reggio Emilia, but
                                              [Calzolari,

mè a s què da e' préim dè, mo s'éss da déi,
a n'e' so mégga quant a sémm avènti,
e ènca i mi cumpagn, ch'a zcurémm póch
però tra 'd néun, u i è sémpra un scatramàz,
u t tòcca rógg, pu u n s capéss gnént l'istèss,
e dop éun, da par sè,
e' sarà 'nca e' lavòur,
sòtta tèra, che e' sòul ta n'e' vaid mai,
u i è di gran fèr, aquè, l'è sémpra e' dè,
e' sarà ènch tótt' st'eletricità
ch'u i è tl'aria, zà che mè a so un tip nervòus,
insòmma, mè, l'è un pó, quant l'è tótt férum,
a mezdè, ch'a so 'lè ch'a magn, e a péns,
a m dmand dal robi, a faz di paraghéun,
a zirch d'arspònd, u m vén, dagli èlti dmandi,
a n'e' so, boh,
           ch' l'è pu sémpra che zcòurs,
marébb savài, mo quést i n dí mai gnént,
d'ogni tènt a próv, mè, sa Calzolari,
a l zimént, 'na batéuda, 'na paróla,
l'è 'd Frèra, Calzolari, cmè l'inznír,
mo u i n'è 'd Bulògna, ad Pèrma,

io sono qui dal primo giorno, ma se dovessi dire, / non lo so mica quanto siamo avanti, / e anche i miei compagni, che parliamo poco, / però, tra di noi, c'è sempre un fracasso, / ti tocca urlare, poi non capisci niente lo stesso, / e dopo uno, da solo, / sarà anche il lavoro, / sotto terra, che il sole non lo vedi mai, / ci sono dei gran fari, qui, è sempre giorno, / sarà anche tutta quest'elettricità / che c'è nell'aria, già che io sono un tipo nervoso, / insomma, io, è un po', quando è tutto fermo, / a mezzogiorno, che sono lí che mangio, e penso, / mi domando delle cose, faccio dei paragoni, / cerco di rispondere, mi vengono delle altre domande, / non lo so, boh, – che è poi sempre quel discorso, / bisognerebbe sapere, ma questi non dicono mai niente, / ogni tanto provo, io, con Calzolari, / lo cimento, una battuta, una parola, / è di Ferrara, Calzolari, come l'ingegnere, / ma ce n'è di Bologna, di Parma, /

he's here every day, he's the assistant,
and so I, I did say it, when I saw,
seeing him go by, to an engineer, everything all right?
fine, and you? me too, everything's fine,
well how am I supposed to answer him?
but I'm not at all put at ease
it seems like he's just saying that to keep me happy,
which then, everything's fine means everything
and means nothing at all,
wouldn't it be better to have a little talk?
because even whoever is working,
someone who gets paid more, they don't understand
that if the other person is sufficiently satisfied, I don't
want to be privy to things that I don't need to know,
but it's not right either to be working in the dark,
you get an impulse to say: how do things stand?
where are we on this thing?
because if we were to talk a little
among ourselves, really,
one says it's like this, the other says it's like that,
you discuss things, you think things through,
even if there are times
where we look at each other in silence, sometimes
a look is all it takes, there's no need to talk,
because here, that's how it is,
we all have the same thought, but we don't say a thing,
and as long as we're quiet,
Calzolari's right, everything's fine,

then I don't know, even us,
sometimes I say, being here underground all the time,

602

ad Regemiglia, però Calzolari,
léu l'è què tótt i dè, l'è l'asistént,
e alòura mè, a déggh pò, quant a so 'lè,
ch'a l vèggh pasè, geometra, cm'andémmi?
tutto bene, e tu? anch'io, tutto bene,
amo csa i pòsi arspònd? mo a n so tranquéll,
u m pèr ch'u l dégga cmè par cuntantèm,
che pu ènca tutto bene, e' vó dí tótt
e u n vó dí gnént, u n sarébb mèi fè un zcòurs?
parchè 'nca chi ch' lavòura,
éun e' rènd ènca ad piò, i n la capéss mégga,
s' ta i dé sodisfaziòun, che pu mè a n vói
savài dal robi ch'a n li ò da savài,
però cma s fal, ènch' lavurè a la ziga,
u t vén d'istéint da déi: cmè ch'a sémm méss?
dò ch'a sémm aquè sòtta?
ch' s'a zcuréssmi un pó 'd piò tra 'd néun, dabón,
éun e' déi, cl'èlt l'arbàt,
u s dischéut, u s ragiòuna,

ènch s'u i è di mumént
ch'a s guardémm tótt da zétt, basta un'ucèda

di Reggio Emilia, però Calzolari, / lui è qui tutti i giorni, è l'assistente, / e
allora io, dico pure, quando sono lí, / che lo vedo passare, geometra, come
andiamo? / tutto bene, e tu? anch'io, tutto bene, / e beh, cosa posso rispondergli? ma non sono tranquillo, / mi pare che me lo dica per accontentarmi,
/ che poi anche tutto bene, vuol dire tutto / e non vuol dire niente, non
sarebbe meglio fare un discorso? / perché anche chi lavora, / uno rende
anche di piú, non lo capiscono mica, / se gli dai soddisfazione, che poi io
non voglio / sapere delle cose che non devo sapere, / però, come si fa, /
anche lavorare alla cieca, / ti viene d'istinto da dire: come siamo messi? /
dove siamo qui sotto? / che se parlassimo un po' di piú tra di noi, davvero,
/ uno dice, l'altro ribatte, / si discute, si ragiona, // anche se ci sono dei
momenti / che ci guardiamo tutti in silenzio, basta un'occhiata /

it's been two years, and two years is not one day,
we're way too keyed up, we should have already gotten there,
but instead it's taking its own sweet time,
we're chewing up a mountain here,
there's got to be something of a timetable,
they should keep to it,
it's a battlefield, this is,
but then, that's enough, the ones in charge,
it's in their interest too, isn't it? to get it done soon,
so what do you expect, there's not much to discuss,
until we get there we've got to keep going,

but even this is a discussion, I understand, yes,
their interests, the ones in charge,
but even they need to know how they're positioned,
and to see if they can't do better? and they can't say it? but
here, I, it's not clear,
there's silence, it's the silence I don't like,

dal vólti, u n gn'è bsògn d' zcòrr,
parchè què tanimódi
avèmm tótt che pensír, però a n gémm gnént,
e fintènt ch'a stémm zétt
l'à rasòun Calzolari, tutto bene,
che pu a n'e' so, ènca néun,
dal vólti a déggh, a stè sémpra aquè sòtta,
l'è du an, u n'è un dè.
émm tropa smègna, a vréssmi ès zà rivàt,
che invíci u i vó e' su témp,
a sémm dri ch'a s magnémm una muntagna,
e u i vó 'nca un pó d'argòi, bsògna tní bota,
l'è un chémp 'd bataia, quèst,
mo pu, andémma, quéi ch' cmanda,
l'è ènca e' su interès, no? da fè prèst,
e alòura, 's'ut, u i è póch da dischéut,
fintènt ch'a n sémm rivàt bsògna 'ndè 'vènti,

che però 'nch' quèst l'è un zcòurs, ò capéi, sè,
e' su interès, quéi ch' cmanda,
mo ènca lòu bsògna vdai cm'i è vnú ciapèd,
s'i n pò fè mèi? e i n'e' pò déi? insòmma
aquè, mè, la n'è cièra,

delle volte, non c'è bisogno di parlare, / perché qui, tanto, / abbiamo tutti
quel pensiero, però non diciamo niente, / e finché stiamo zitti / ha ragione
Calzolari, tutto bene, // che poi non so, anche noi, / delle volte dico, a stare
sempre qui sotto, / sono due anni, non è un giorno, / abbiamo troppa smania, voremmo essere già arrivati, / che invece ci vuole il suo tempo, / ci stiamo mangiando una montagna, / e ci vuole anche un po' d'orgoglio, bisogna
tener botta, / è un campo di battaglia, questo, / ma poi, andiamo, quelli che
comandano, / è anche il loro interesse, no? di far presto, / e allora, cosa
vuoi, c'è poco da discutere, / finché non siamo arrivati bisogna andare
avanti, // che però anche questo è un discorso, ho capito, sí, / il loro interesse, quelli che comandano, / ma anche loro bisogna vedere come si sono
trovati, / se non possono far meglio? e non possono dirlo? insomma / qui,
io, non è chiara, /

do they have something to hide?
which we're not supposed to know about? not saying anything
is worse,
I'm not an educated man,
for me two and two makes four,
you can't milk anymore out of it,
but
there are some things
that do not require massive studies, you listen to them,
we're not right here, we're not going the right way,
even if nobody says anything, we all feel it,
and Calzolari knows it, it's a farce, he knows it too, someone
made a mistake,
there was a mistake made, a huge mistake,
and the farther along we go the bigger it gets,
those of us here, at first I used comparisons,
it's like being on a train, that's going straight through, where's
it going?
you don't see a station, you can't get off,
and what can you do? what do you do?
you've got to keep going

and we've gotten pretty far along
if it were only a matter of that, there are a lot of us,
here even at night,
because going home is a trek, and when you get off work
you've been tired a long time already,
which at first, oh my God, always underground,

u i è un zétt, l'è sté zétt, mè, ch'u, n mu n pis,
i à qualquèl da masè?
ch'a n l'avémm da savài?
mo a no dí gnént l'è pézz, mè a n'ò studié,
par mè do e do e' fa quatar,
piò in là d'alè a n'aréiv, mo u i è dal robi
ch'u n'i vó di gran stéudi, ta li sint,
aquè a n'i sémm, a n'andémm pr'e' vérs gióst,
ènch' s'u n dí gnént niseun, a l sintémm tótt,
e Calzolari u l sa, e' fa la cumédia,
mo u l sa ènca léu, qualcadéun l'à sbaiè.
u i è stè un sbai, un sbai gròs,
e piò ch'andémm avènti e piò u s'ingròsa,
néun aquè, préima a géva i paraghéun,
l'è cm'ès s'un treno, ch'e' va drétt, dú val?
u n s vaid una staziòun, u n s pò smuntè,
e csa put fé? csa fét? t chin andè 'vènti,

ch'a sémm avènti un pèz, pr'e' còunt, u i è tint
ch'i arvènza aquè 'nch' la nòta,
parchè 'ndè chèsa ormai l'è un viàz, quant t smòunt,
zà che t si strach,
che mè te préim, ció, sémpra sòtta, tèra,

c'è un silenzio, è questo silenzio che a me non mi piace, / hanno qualcosa da
nascondere? / che non dobbiamo saperlo? ma non dire niente è peggio, io
non ho studiato, / per me due e due fanno quattro, / piú in là di lí non arrivo, ma ci sono delle cose / che non ci vogliono dei grandi studi, le senti, /
qui non ci siamo, non andiamo per il verso giusto, / anche se non dice niente
nessuno, lo sentiamo tutti, / e Calzolari lo sa, fa la commedia, / ma lo sa
anche lui, qualcuno ha sbagliato, / c'è stato uno sbaglio, uno sbaglio grosso,/
e piú andiamo avanti piú s'ingrossa, / noi qui, prima dicevo i paragoni, / è
come essere su un treno, che va dritto, dove va? / non si vede una stazione,
non si può scendere, / e cosa puoi fare? cosa fai? devi andare avanti, // che
siamo avanti molto, se è per questo, ci sono tanti / che rimangono qui anche
la notte, / perché andare a casa ormai è un viaggio, quando smonti, / già che
sei stanco, / che io dapprincipio, beh, sempre sotto terra, /

I resisted, then they convinced me,
I haven't budge for twenty days,
for Ghécc it's been more than twenty months
since he's seen his,
no, but it's alright here, plus we're all together,
because when you go home, we do go home
every so often, you arrive, sure, say your hellos, stay at home,
you go out, see people, meet someone,
talk, but people don't understand,
they want to talk, but because they don't know how things are,
and talk-talk-talk,
shut up about it please, because, the thing is, I'm made
in a certain way, here I complain, I criticize,
I say whatever I want to say, but if someone contradicts me,
I get mad, what do you expect, you have a problem?
you have to keep it to yourself,
you can't go shooting your mouth off
about matters, what do you know? you don't know anything,
here people work, you don't make small talk, you punch
                                                    [through,
you reinforce,
you put up cement reinforced with those rods
that look like the lengths of sausage,
this, boys and girls, is going to be a tunnel
that can withstand anything

and then there are those moments, which if your aren't
inside,
you can't understand, you can't understand from the outside,

a séra un pó gristòus, pu a m so cunvéint,
l'è vint dè ch'a n mu n móv,
e' Ghécc l'è piò 'd du méis ch'u n vaid i sóvv,
no, mo u s sta bén aquè, pu a sémm tra 'd néun,
parchè 'nca quant u s tòurna, ch'a turnémm
d'ogni tènt, sè, t'aréiv, t saléut, t sté 'lè,
t scap, la zénta, t'incòuntar qualcadéun,
t fé do ciacri, mo u s fa fadéiga a intèndsi,
i vó zcòrr, ch'i n sa 'l robi, e quèst e quèll,
mo stè zitéin, parchè mè pu a so fat
t'un zèrt módi, mè què a sbròuntal, a crétich,
a dèggh tótt quèll ch'u m pèr, mo s'u l dí un èlt,
a m'incapèl, csa vut tè? cs'ét d'avài?
bsògna èsi dréinta, ta n pò zcòrr purséa,
tal robi, csa sét tè, che ta n sé gnént?
aquè u s lavòura, u n s ciacra, u s fòura, u s'èrma,
dal gitèdi ad cimént
sa di tundéin cmè di budéll 'd sunzézza,
quèsta, burdéll, e' vén 'na galeréa
ch' la n'à paéura 'd gnént,

e pu u i è di mumént, s' ta n'i si dréinta,
da fura u n s pò capéi,

ero un po' restio, poi mi sono convinto, / sono venti giorni che non mi
muovo, / il Ghécc è piú di due mesi che non vede i suoi, / no, ma si sta bene
qui, poi siamo tra di noi, / perché anche quando si torna, che torniamo /
ogni tanto, sí, arrivi, saluti, stai lí, / esci, la gente, incontri qualcuno, / fai due
chiacchiere, ma si fa fatica a intendersi, / volgiono parlare, che non sanno
le cose, e questo e quello, / ma statevene zitti, perché io poi sono fatto / in
un certo modo, io qui brontolo, critico, / dico tutto quello che mi pare, ma
se lo dice un altro, / m'arrabbio, cosa vuoi tu? devi avere qualcosa? / bisogna
esserci dentro, non puoi parlare a vanvere, / nelle cose, cosa sai tu, che non
sai niente? / qui si lavora, non si chiacchiera, si buca, si arma, / delle gettate
di cemento / con dei tondini come budelli di salciccia, / questa, ragazzi,
viene una galleria / che non ha paura di niente, / / e poi ci sono dei momenti, se non ci sei dentro, / da fuori non si può capire, /

when you hear the whistle, stop everything! stop!
we all stop, silence!
and stand still, do you hear something over there?
from the others who are supposed to meet us coming from
the other direction,
sometimes it seems like, really, what's happened?
a thump? are they banging? is it them?
we bang, too, then we're quiet, then again,
no one's answering from the other side, let's wait,
let's wait a little longer, nothing, you can't hear anything,
we were wrong, that's it, the whistle, and you start up again,

us from this direction and them from the other,
will we ever see each other?
weeks pass, months,
and always onward, we keep our heads lowered,
we have an inner strength, which I don't know,
is it courage? is it fear? try to figure that one out,
it's spite, too,
the more desperate we are, the farther we've gone ahead,
ahead where? the engineer knows,
who in any case isn't around much anymore,
he comes, makes the rounds,

quant t sint fis-cé, fermate tutto, alt!
ch'a s farmémm tótt, silenzio!
e a stémm alé, s'u s sint qualquèl adlà,
ad quéi ch'i à d'arivé da cl'èlta pèrta,
u i è dal vólti ch'e' pèr, dabón, cs'èll stè?
'na bota? i bat? i è lòu?
a batémm ènca néun, pu zétt, pu ancòura,
da dlà u n'arspònd, niseun, spétta, però,
a stémm alè un èlt pó, gnént, u n s sint gnént,
a s sémm sbaiè, ècco, i fés-cia, u s'artàca,

néun adquà, lòu adlà, a s'avdirémm mai?
e' pasa al stmèmi, i méis,
e sémpra avènti, a i démm a testa basa,
émm una fórza dréinta, ch'a n'e' so,
l'è curàg? l'è paéura? va a capéi,
l'è ènca cativéria,
piò ch'a sémm sprèd e piò ch'andémm avènti,

avènti dòvv? u l sa l'inznír, ch ormai
u s vaid piò póch però,
l'aréiva, e' zéira un pó d'in quà e d'in là,

quando senti fischiare, fermate tutto, alt! / che ci fermiamo tutti, silenzio! /
e stiamo lí, se si sente qualcosa di là, / di quelli che devono arrivare dall'altra
parte, / c'è delle volte che pare, davvero, cos'è stato? / una botta? battono?
sono loro? / battiamo anche noi, poi zitti, poi ancora, / da di là non risponde
nessuno, aspetta, però, / stiamo lí un altro po', niente, non si sente niente, /
ci siamo sbagliati, ecco, fischiano, si riprende, // noi di qua, loro di là, ci
vedremo mai? / passano le settimane, i mesi, / e sempre avanti, ci diamo a
testa bassa, / abbiamo una forza dentro, che non so, / è corraggio? è paura?
va' a capire, / è anche cattiveria, / piú siamo disperati e piú andiamo avanti,
// avanti dove? lo sa l'ingegnere, che ormai / si vede piú poco però, / arriva,
gira un po' in qua e in là, /

611

he looks like he's aged, he wipes his glasses,
his hands tremble,
Calzolari leads him through, says a few things to him,
he nods his head, yes, and a few minutes later
he waves, he's gone, he doesn't ever say anything,
and so, what can he say?
he's the one who made the mistake, right? he's in charge,
which he, who knows, maybe he's still hoping,
let's wait, let's see,

well they'll still be seeing each other, right here,
really, which we believed when we signed on,
maybe there's a vein, yes, all rock, there was rock
and more rock, it never ends,
but we stuck with them,
you better believe we stuck with them, a month and a half,
almost two months, then one day, way up top
there were some shouts: land!
it's land! we're on land!
these are moments,
who's ever going to be able to pay you for that?
you shout too,
you start laughing, you start to cry,
and the grater keeps churning, it's all noise,
you hug the guys, joy, sweating,

e' pèr cmè ch'u s séa 'nvcè, u s puléss i ucèl,
u i trema al mèni,
Calzolari u i fa strèda, u i dí dal robi,
léu e' fa 'd sè sla testa e dop un pó
e' saléuta e e' va véa, u n dí mai gnént,
amo cs'èll ch'e' pò déi?
l'è stè léu ch' l'à sbaiè, no? e' cmanda léu,
che léu, chi sa, magari e' spera ancòura,
spitémma, vdémma,

ch'u s nu n vaid sémpra aquè,
'ta bón, quant'émm incòuntar, ch'a s cridémmi
ch' fóss 'na véina, sè, l'era tótta gènga,
gènga e pu gènga, la n finéva piò,
mo a i sémm stè dri, t'é vòia, un mais e mèz,
guèsi du méis, pu alasò in zéima un dè
di rógg: tèra! l'è tèra! a sémm tla tèra!
ch' l'è di mumént, chi è ch'i t'i pèga? t rógg
ènca tè, u t vén da réid, u t vén da piànz,
e la gratéusa ch' la s'invéa, un malàn,
ta t'abràz si cumpàgn, ligar, sudéd,

pare come invecchiato, si pulisce gli occhiali, / gli tremano le mani, /
Calzolari gli fa strada, li dice delle cose, / lui fa sí con la testa e dopo un po'
/ saluta e va via, non dice mai niente, / e beh, cosa può dire? / è lui che ha
sbagliato, no? comanda lui, / che lui, chi sa, magari spera ancora, / aspettiamo, vediamo, // che se ne vedono, sempre, / qui, sta' buono,
quando'abbiamo incocciato, che credevamo / fosse una vena, sí, era tutta
roccia, / roccia e poi roccia, non finiva piú, / ma ci siamo stati dietro, hai
voglia, un mese e mezzo, / quasi due mesi, poi lassú in cima un giorno /
degli urli: terra! è terra! siamo nella terra! / che sono momenti, chi è che te
li paga? urli / anche tu, ti viene da ridere, ti viene da piangere, / e la grattugia
che si avvia, un baccano, / ti abbracci coi compagni, allegri, sudati, /

you don't think of anything else, listen to it scraping, listen,
even if it doesn't go anywhere,
even if it doesn't get there, which then, who knows,
what do we know? not knowing anything,
everything can happen,
and so we go forward, always, forward and that's it.

ta n péns ma gnént, sint cmè ch' la grata, sint,
ènch s'u n s va invéll,
ènch' s'u n s'aréiva mai, che pu, chi sa,
cs'èll ch'a savémm?
no savài gnént, e' pò suzéd inquèl,
e alòura avènti, sémpra, avènti e basta.

non pensi a niente, senti come gratta, senti, / anche se non si va da nessuna
parte, / anche se non s'arriva mai, che poi, chi sa, / cosa sappiamo? / a non
sapere niente, può succedere tutto, / e allora avanti, sempre, avanti e basta.

On the Train

We were friends, well almost friends,
we'd gone to school together
in Rimini, she was studying to become a teacher,
not together really, I was in general studies,
and then in Bologna at the university,
going back and forth on the train,
we'd run into each other all the time,
we'd talk, we'd lend each other books,
she lent me a detective novel with a strange title,
With You, the best detective novel I'd ever read,
then we'd talk about movies,
she liked Kramer versus Kramer,
I did too, but I really liked
The Big Chill, "Go and see it,"
and then she told me, "It was wonderful, you were right,"
"Well, the Americans are good, have you seen
Blade Runner? That one is truly a masterpiece,"
that's what I mean, those kinds of conversations,
and that night we were coming back
from Bologna, we'd left at eight, it was already dark,
we'd found an empty compartment,
right in the middle, "In Ravenna, on Sunday,

In treno

A sérmi améigh, insòmma guèsi amèigh,
avémmi studié insén
a Rémin, li la féva al magistrèli,
no própia insén, mè a féva l'Institéut,
e pu a Bulògna, a l'università,
sò a zò se treno, a s'incuntrémmi spèss,
a ciacarémmi, a s'impristémmi i léibar,
la m'à imprèst un zal ch' l'éva un tétal strèn,
Con te, mo bél, e' piò bèl zal ch'ò lèt,
pu a zcurémmi di film
li u i era pieséu Kramer contro Kramer,
ènca mu mè, mo mè u m'era pieséu
'na masa Il grande freddo, "Val a vdai",
e dop la m'à détt: "Bèl, t'évi rasòun",
"Amo i americhèn i è brèv, t'é vést
Blade Runner? quèll dabón l'è un cheplavòur",
ècco, di zchèurs acsè,
e cla saèira partí agli òt, l'era zà nòta,
avémmi tróv un scompartiment svéit,
própia te mèz, "Dmènga a Ravènna u i è

In treno. Eravamo amici, insomma quasi amici, / avevamo studiato insieme/
a Rimini, lei faceva le magistrali, / non proprio insieme, io facevo l'Istituto,
/ e poi a Bologna all'università, / su e giú in treno, c'incontravamo spesso,
/ chiacchieravamo, ci prestavamo i libri, / m'ha prestato un giallo che aveva
un titolo strano, / Con te, ma bello, il piú bel giallo che ho letto", / poi
parlavamo di film, / a lei era piaciuto Kramer contro Kramer, / anche a me,
ma a me era piaciuto / molto Il grande freddo, "Vallo a vedere", / e dopo
mi ha detto: "Bello, avevi ragione", / "E beh, gli americani sono bravi, hai
visto Blade Runner? quello davvero è un capolavoro", / ecco, dei discorsi
cosí, / e quella sera tornavamo da Bologna, / eravamo partiti alle otto, era
già notte, / avevamo trovato uno scompartimento vuoto, / proprio al centro,
"Domenica a Ravenna c'è

Vasco Rossi's performing, do you know him? He's a little wild,"
"You're going to go see him?" "and you?"
and right at that moment, boom, the lights go out,
you couldn't see anything anymore,
I asked her: "Are you afraid?" and she said: "and you?"
we laughed softly, we were quiet for awhile,
then I'm not even sure how it happened,
it was her perfume too,
faint, but it just went right into me,
I reached for her with a hand, an arm, the shoulder,
gently, without squeezing, her hair, what thick hair,
then all around her neck, then I kissed her, and she
and she kissed me back, and there we were,
we didn't know what to say,
then I kissed her eyes, they were gentle, almost sweet,
still not saying a word, then another kiss, a long one,
we were quiet, the way I see it,
it was all even wondrous, we hadn't expected
to fall in love all of a sudden that Wednesday evening,
in the dark, in a train, just outside Forlimpopoli.

Vasco Rossi, ta l cnòss? éun un pó mat",
"Ta l vé a sintéi?", "E tè?"
e at che mumént, tac, l'è vnú mènch la luce,
u n s'avdéva piò gnént,
a i ò dmand: "T'é paéura?", e li: "E tè?",
émm ridéu pièn, a sémm stè sétt un pó,
pu a n'e' so gnénca mè cmè ch' l'è suzèst,
l'è stè e' su parfómm,
stil, mo u m'antréva dréinta,
a la ò zirca s'na mèna, e' braz, la spala,
pièn, senza strènz, i cavéll, quant cavéll,
pu tònda e' còl, pu a l'ò basèda, e li
la m'à basè ènca li, e a stémmi alè,
a n savémmi quèll déi,
pu a i ò basè i ócc, téndar, guèsi déulz,
sémpra senza dí gnént, pu un èlt bès, lòngh,
a stémmi zétt, sgònd mè,
ènch' da la maravèia, a n s l'aspitémmi
d'inamurès ad bot che mircal sàira,
te schéur, in treno, un pó préima 'd Frampùl.

Vasco Rossi, lo conosci? uno un po' matto", / "Lo vai a sentire?", "E tu?"
/ e in quel momento, tac, è mancata la luce, / non si vedeva piú niente, / le
ho chiesto: "Hai paura?" e lei: "E tu?" / abbaiamo riso piano, siamo stati zitti
un po', / poi non so neach'io com'è successo, / è stato anche il suo profumo,
/ sottile, ma mi entrava dentro, / l'ho cercata con una mano, un braccio, la
spalla, / piano, senza stringere, i capelli, / quanti capelli, / poi intorno al
collo, poi l'ho baciata, e lei / m'ha baciato anche lei, e stavamo lí, / non
sapevamo cosa dire, / poi le ho baciato gli occhi, teneri, quasi dolci, / sempre
senza dir niente, poi un altro bacio, lungo, / stavamo zitti, secondo me, /
anche dalla meraviglia, non ce l'aspettavamo / d'innamorarci di colpo quel
mercoledí sera, / al buio, in treno, un po' prima di Forlimpopoli.

The Cricket

Just listen to that cricket singing away,
he's really going at it with gusto,
how could he possibly
have gotten up here,
he must be in that flower pot
that had the dahlias,
all right I'll leave it dark, it'll work better with a flashlight,
I can't open the balcony door,
he's here somewhere, what are you afraid of,
I'm not going to do anything to you, go ahead, chirp,
with all these weeds
you can't see a blasted thing,
nothing, where's the hand shovel, now I'm digging,
wait a second, you want him to think you're going to bury
                                        [him, come out,
what's he gone and done with himself? he wants to
antagonize me,
I'm getting the water now, jump up, you little idiot,
jump up, do you want to drown?
or am I the idiot here?
he at least
has escaped into the pot with the roses,
over there in the wild grass, enough now,
I'm worn out, plus, I kind of, hearing him sing,
then too, a cricket at night can be some company.

E' gréll

Sint cm'e' chènta che gréll,
u i dà s'una pasiòun, mo cm'avràl fat
a rivé 'quasò in zéima?
l'à da ès te vès grand, dò ch'u i era al dagli,
senza zènd, mèi sla pila,
ècco, e' sta zétt, a n pòs arví la bóssla,
léu l'è què, 's'ét paéura? a n t faz gnént, chènta,
l'é che sa tótta st'èrba ch' l'è vnú sò
u n s vaid un azidént,
gnént, u i vó la palètta, adès a vangh,
spétta un èlt pó, ta t vu fè spléi? vén fura,
dò ch'u s'è instècch? tè ta m vu fè rabiè,
e mè a dróv l'aqua, sèlta, quaiòun, dài,
sèlta, ta t vu fughè?
o e' quaiòun a so mè? che léu magari
l'è zà te vès dal rósi,
o alè tla sparigina, no, gnént, basta,
a m so stóff, che pu mè, sintéil cantè,
un gréll ad nòta u m fa 'nca cumpagnéa.

Il grillo. Senti come canta quel grillo, / ci dà con una passione, ma come avrà fatto / ad arrivare quassú in cima? dev'essere nel vaso grande, dove c'erano le dalie, / senza accendere, meglio con la pila, / ecco, sta zitto, non posso aprire la porta del terrazzo, / lui è qui, / cos'hai paura? non ti faccio niente, canta, / è che con tutta quest'erba che è venuta su / non si vede un accidente, / niente, ci vuole la paletta, adesso vango, / aspetta un altro po', ti vuoi far seppellire? vieni fuori, / dove s'è cacciato? mi vuoi fare arrabbiare / e io adopero l'acqua, salta, coglione, dai, / salta, vuoi affogare? / o il coglione sono io? che lui magari / è già nel vaso delle rose, / o lí nell'asparigina, no, niente, basta, / mi sono stufato, poi io, a sentirlo cantare, / un grillo di notte mi fa anche compagnia.

Fat

Stocky-fat and with those stubby arms,
he was laughable, Fridays at the market
from four in the morning, loading, unloading,
what an appetite, at noon, bellows: Even in my sleep
I see macaroni—then seven or eight months with illness
there was a big change, even his eyes, it was like they weren't
                                    [black anymore,
he looked at you and said nothing
he walked along the Passeggio
even thinner, at the end, in death, in his bed,
he looked, if you could have seen him, like a professor.

Gras

Gras imbraghèd e sa cal brazi chéurti,
e' féva réid, e' vèndar se marchè,
dal quatar dla matéina, carga, scarga,
una fèma, a mezdè, di rógg: "A vèggh
tótt macaréun!",
         pu in sèt òt méis, se mèl,
l'à fat un cambiamént, u s'è sughé,
di labar stil, ènch'i ócc, cm'i fóss piò nir,
u t guardéva da zétt,
l'andéva da par léu sò me Pasègg,
sempra piò féin, tl'éultum, da mórt, te lèt,
ch'u s fóss vést, e' pareva un profesòur.

Grasso. Grasso inquartato e con quelle braccia corte, / faceva ridere, il venerdí al mercato, / dallo quattro della mattina, carica, scarica, / una fama, a mezzogiorno, degli urli: "Vedo / tutti maccheroni", – poi in sette otto mesi, col male, – ha fatto un cambiamento, si è asciugato, / delle labbra sottili, anche gli occhi, come fossero piú neri, / ti guardava in silenzio / andava da solo per il Passeggio / sempre piú fine, in ultimo, da morto, nel letto, / si fosse visto, sembrava un professore.

What's it Like?

What does she want?
I could be her father, she was just a delicate flower,
she was dancing around me, people were muttering
under their breath, my brother: "Be careful,"
even for her parents, but she's chasing me, I,
but then later on, even I don't believe it,
does she like me? is she after money? it's not clear,
then that day I lost my temper: "You are a psycho!"
And *you* run off, you're always running off. Are you afraid?"
and there I was, I wasn't expecting it,
in a teasing tone, "Do I scare you?"
well, she is an oddball, she's different, she's way out there,
about everything, is she joking or what? try to figure it out,
is she being serious? for her it's always a game,

it's just that ever since that day it's a game with two players,
                                                [sometimes
in Rimini, in Cesena, on the street,
she starts laughing, for no apparent reason, and we both laugh,
like two idiots, someone turns around,
and she sticks out her tongue,

Cmè ch' l'è?

Cs'èll ch' la vó quèsta?
ch'a pòs ès e' su bà, mo l'era un fiòur,
la m ziréva datònda, qualcadéun,
mézz zcéurs tra i dint, e' mi fradèl: "Sta 'ténti",
ènca pr'i sóvv, mo mè, la m zirca li,
ch' pu ènca mè a n m'afidéva,
a i pis mè? u i pis i bócch? la n'era cièra,
dop, un dè a m so incaplè: "Tè t si balènga!"
"E tè t scap, tè t scap sémpra, t'é paéura?"
che mè a so 'rvènz alè, a n mu n l'aspitéva,
s'un'aria da tó in zéir, "A t faz paéura?"
amo l'è un tip, la è balènga, cumè,
tótt' al robi, la scherza? va a capéi,
la dí se séri? li, l'è sémpra un zugh,

sno che e' zugh da che dè l'è in déu, dal vólti
a Rémin, a Ceséina, par la strèda,
u i vén da réid, acsè, e a ridémm tutt déu
cmè du pataca, qualcadéun u s vólta,
e li la i fa la lèngua,

Come'è? / Cosa vuole questa? / che posso essere suo padre, ma era un fiore,
/ mi girava attorno, qualcuno, / mezzi discorsi tra i denti, mio fratello: "Stai
attento", / anche per i suoi, ma io, mi cerca lei, / che poi anch'io non mi
fidavo, / le piaccio io? le piacciono i soldi? non era chiara, / poi quel giorno
mi sono arrabbiato: "Tu sei balenga!" / "E tu scappi, tu scappi sempre, hai
paura?" // che sono rimasto lí, non me l'aspettavo, / con un'aria da prendere
in giro, "Ti faccio paura?" / eh, ma è un tipo, è balenga, altroché, / in tutte
le cose, scherza? vai a capire, / fa sul serio? per lei è sempre un gioco, //
solo che il gioco da quel giorno è in due, delle volte / a Rimini, a Cesena, per
la strada, / le viene da ridere, cosí, e ridiamo tutt'e due / come due sciocchi,
qualcuno si volta, / e lei gli fa la lingua, /

in bed, she'll be there with her eyes closed, shut tight,
for a long time,
then she'll open them: "You're still here? wonderful."
she starts snuggling down low,
then she comes up slowly, slowly, like an animal,
at certain times, in the silence, she'll suddenly ask:
"What are you thinking about now?
Don't think about it, tell me,"
she comes out with things that I,
things that are just absurd: "We were born at the wrong time,
yet we found each other anyway,
what if I'd been born in London,
how would we have found each other then,
I don't even speak English?"
she's loopy, really, in Riccione the other day:
"There are moments that it seems to me
like it's just the two of us
in the whole wide world, don't laugh," "I'm not laughing."
"Me and you, it seems like it's not much, but it's everything,"
I looked at her,
"It's too much, it can't last,"
and we keep going,
it's been over a year now, I have fun,
I like it this way, I like her,
but for her it's a whole different thing,
for awhile now, every so often, she says to me:
"Let's run away?" "And where would we go?" "To a place

te lèt la sta si ócc céus, férma, pr'un pèz,
pu la i éirva: "T si sémpra què? pu bén!",
la s mètt tótta argugléda alazò in fònd,
pu la vén sò pièn pièn, cmè un animèli,
di mumént ch'a stémm zétt la m dmanda ad bot:
"Cs'èll che t pensévi adès? nu pénsi, déime",
la scapa fura ènch' sa di schéurs che mè,
dal robi strambalèdi: "Émm sbaiè a nas,
mo a s sémm tróv, pensa s'a naséva a Lòndra,
cmè ch'a fémmi a truvès,
ch' ta n sé gnénca l'inglàis?",
la è un pó mata, dabón, l'altredè a Rzéun:
"U i è di mumént, mè, ch'u m pèr che te mònd
a i sémma sno nun déu, nu réid", "A n réid",
"Mè e tè, e' pèr gnént, l'è tótt", a la guardéva,
"L'è trop, la n pò duré",
                                    e andémm avènti,
ormai l'è piò d'un an, a m divertéss,
u m pis, la m pis, mo li, l'è un'èlta roba,
adès l'è un pó che d'ogni tènt la m déi:
"Scapémma véa?", "E dò ch'andémm"?, "T'un pòst

a letto sta con gli occhi chiusi, ferma, per un bel po', / poi li apre: "Sei sempre
qui? che bello!", / si mette accoccolata laggiú in fondo, / poi viene su piano
piano, come un animale, / in certi momenti di silenzio mi domanda di colpo:
/ "Cosa pensavi adesso? non pensarci, dimmelo", / viene fuori anche con
certi discorsi che io, / delle cose strampalate: "Abbiamo sbagliato a nascere,
/ ma ci siamo trovati, pensa se nascevo a Londra, / come facevamo a trovarci,
/ che non sai neanche l'inglese?" / è un po' matta, davvero, l'altro giorno a
Riccione: // Ci sono dei momenti, io che mi pare che nel mondo / ci siamo
solo noi due, non ridere," "Non rido", / "Io e te, pare niente, ma è tutto", la
guardavo / "È troppo, non può durare", – e andiamo avanti, / ormai è piú
d'un anno, mi diverto, / mi piace questa storia, mi piace lei, ma lei, è un'altra
cosa, / adesso è un po' che ogni tanto mi dice: / "Scappiamo via?", "E dove
andiamo?", "In un posto /

that's far, far away, where no one knows us," it truly
scares me, she's lost her mind.

I, on the other hand, am forty-four years old,
my head's screwed on straight.
I think straight, it works for me, I've had my ladies.
I like them, but always just like it is now,
even this one, I'm being totally honest here, I like her, but
she's not the only one, and for her there's only me,
and I, sometimes I think about it, I'd like,
there I've said it, to try, what's it like?
what does it feel like inside?
that you're you and not you,
that it's just her in the world, that it's just enough seeing her,
that you're fine, that you're not fine,
that you scream, that you bang your head against the wall,
that you're always giving all of them
something to laugh about,
but you'll never change with anyone,
isn't it ever going to happen for me? not even one time?
to be out of your mind, to not understand anything anymore?

dalòngh, ch'u n s cnòss niseun", la m fa paéura
dabón, la à pérs la testa,

invíci mè l'è quarentaquatr'an
ch'ò la testa sal spali,
ch'a ragiòun, ch' la m va bén, ò vú al mi dòni,
al m'è pieséudi, mo sémpra cmè 'dès,
ènca quèsta, a déggh pò, la m pis, però
u n gn'è sno li, li invíci a i so sno mè,
e mè, dal vólti a i péns, u m pisarébb,
ècco, pruvè, cmè ch' l'è? cs'èll ch'u s sint dréinta?
ch' t si tè e ta n si piò tè.
ch'u i è sno li te mònd, ch'u t basta vdàila,
che t sté bén, che t sté mèl,
che t rógg, che t sbat la testa còuntra i méur,
ch' ta t fé réid dri,
mo che ta n farébb cambi sa niseun,
ch'u n m'apa da suzéd? ènch' sno una vólta?
da dvantè mat, da no capí piò gnént?

lontano, dove non ci conosce nessuno", mi fa paura / sul serio, ha perso la
testa, // invece io sono quarantaquattro anni / che ho la testa sulle spalle, /
che ragiono, che mi va bene, ho avuto le mie donne, / mi sono piaciute, ma
sempre come adesso, / anche questa, dico pure, mi piace però / non c'è solo
lei, lei invece ci sono solo io, / e io, delle volte ci penso, mi piacerebbe, /
ecco, provare, com'è? cosa si sente dentro? / che sei tu e non sei piú tu, /
che c'è solo lei nel mondo, che ti basta vederla, / che stai bene, che stai male,
/ che urli, che sbatti la testa contro il muro, / che ti fai ridere dietro, / ma
non faresti cambio con nessuno, / che non mi debba succedere? anche solo
una volta? / di diventare matto, di non capire piú niente?

Bad Luck

What can you do, bad luck,
first my son, then my mother, now me,
I'm almost ashamed to say
how much of it has happened to me,
no, I'd better keep it to myself,
besides no one can help me,
plus people, when it accumulates to too much,
laugh.

Sgraziéd

Gnént, a so stè sgraziéd,
préima, e' mi fiúl, pu la mi mà, 'dès mè,
quant u m n'è mai suzèst',
a m vargògn guèsi a déili,
no, mèi stè zétt,
tanimódi niseun u m pò iuté,
pu la zénta, quant agli è tropi, i réid.

Sfortunato. Niente, sono stato sfortunato, / prima mio figlio, poi mia madre, adesso io, / quante me ne sono mai successe, / mi vergogno quasi a dirle, / no, meglio star zitto, / tanto nessuno mi può aituare, / poi la gente, quando sono troppe, ridono.

Candles

And I'd convinced myself, I must be wrong.
But then the way he laid it out: *"This* is a war," he said.
"Which is far and near, no one knows
how it's going to end, because there are interests
out there, everywhere in the world,
and we're the ones put in the worst position,
we do not have natural resources,
gas petroleum coal, we've got none of it,
we are entirely dependent
on foreign countries. When they get a cold
we get pneumonia.
Which I, even without a war,
all this stuff that comes from far away,
that travels in pipes for hundreds, no thousands,
of kilometers, you don't think about it, but
if you do think about it, even now,
as we're here talking, it's out there flowing,
it's always flowing through,
it's traveling across nations, crossing rivers, forest, deserts,
it crosses oceans,
in these pipes, the world's full of tubes at this point,

Al candàili

E mè a l so stè a sintéi, avrò sbaiè,
però e' su zcòurs, "Quèst' l'è una guèra", e' géva,
"ch' la è dalòngh e davséin, e non si sa
cumè ch' la andrà a finéi, perchè ci sono
degli interessi, lí, di tutto il mondo,
a néun a sémm quèi ch'i è mèss pézz, a n'émm,
noi non abbiamo le materie prime,
gas, petrólio, carbòun, a n'avémm gnént,
noi dipendiamo tutto
dall'estero, quante ch'ilt i à e' fardòur,
néun émm la palmonite,
che mè, 'nca senza guèra,
tótt' sta roba ch' la aréiva da dalòngh,
ch' la córr ti téub par zantnèra, par mièra
ad chilometri, parchè u n s'i pensa, mo
se ta i péns, ènca adès
ch'a zcurémm, li la córr, li la córr sémpra,
la traversa al naziòun, la pasa i fiómm,
al forèsti, i desért, la pasa i mèr,
ad sti téub, l'è pin 'd téub e' mònd ormai,

Le candele. E io mi son fatto convincere, avrò sbagliato, / però il suo discorso, "Questa è una guerra", diceva / "che è lontana e vicina, e non si sa / come andrà a finire, perché ci sono / degli interessi, lí, di tutto il mondo, / e noi siamo quelli che son messi peggio, / noi non abbiamo le materie prime, / gas, petrolio, carbone, non abbiamo niente, / noi dipendiamo tutto / dall'estero, quando gli altri hanno il raffreddore, / noi abbiamo la polmonite, / che io, anche senza guerra, / tutta 'sta roba che arriva da lontano, / che corre nei tubi per centinaia, per migliaia / di chilometri, perché non ci si pensa, ma / se ci pensi, anche adesso che parliamo, lei corre, lei corre sempre, / attraversa le nazioni, passa i fiumi, / le foreste, i deserti, passa i mari, / in questi tubi, è pieno di tubi il mondo ormai, /

and if the people working underground one day lose it
and turn off the spigot, even if they don't shut it off,
a single bomb would be enough, everything would go up in
                                                  [smoke,
and what are we going to do then
this winter to stay warm? and then at night,
there won't be any light, we won't be able to see,
because even for light you need petroleum,
we'll go around groping, smacking into the walls,
and I, you do what you want, but I've already bought
two or three cases of candles." "You bought what?"
"Candles, why not? at least you'd be able to see,
you want to be in the dark? Faiantéin's got some left,
but if you're not quick about it."
"You're not really telling me this?"
"What do you mean *really*, just wait, just wait a little longer,
don't you see what's happening
on television every night?
"I see." "Well?" And especially with his being, he, Cecarelli,
he was an office worker at the Credit Union,
because in the banks,
they've got their antennae up, they're able to take the pulse
of the situation, and I, you know, given all this,
what else could I have done? I bought some too,
three or four cases,
which just about pulled my arms out of the sockets,

e se quéi chi 'lazò un dè u i ciapa e' mat
e i céud e' rubinètt, mo ènca s'i n céud,
basta una bòmba, e' sèlta pr'aria inquèl,
e néun dop cmè ch'a fémm
st'invéran a 'rscaldès? mo pu la nòta
l'avnirà mènch la luce, a n s'avdirémm,
parchè 'nca par la luce u i vó e' petróli,
andrémm a tast, a sbatarémm ti méur,
e mè, tè fa quèll t vu, mè a m so zà còmpar
do tre casi ad candàili", "Cs'èll t'é còmpar?"
"Al candàili, cumè, emènch d'avdài,
t vu stè te schéur? che i Faiantéin i n n'à,
però s' ta n t sbréigh", "No, mo dabón tè t déi?"
"Cumè dabón, sta d'aspitè un èlt pó,
mo ta n vaid tótt' al sàiri
ma la televisiòun quèll ch'e' suzéd?"
"A vèggh", "E alòura?", pu léu, Cecarèli,
l'era impieghèd te Crèdit, che tal bènchi
i à agli antènni, loro sentono il polso
della situazione, e mè, ció, 'lè,
cs'évi da fè? ò còmpar ènca mè,
tre quatar casi, ch'a m so s-cent al brazi,

e se quelli laggiú un giorno gli prende il matto / e chiudono il rubinetto, ma anche se non chiudono, / basta una bomba, salta in aria tutto, / e noi dopo come facciamo, / 'st'inverno a riscaldarci? ma poi la notte / mancherà la luce, non ci vedremo, / perché anche per la luce ci vuole il petrolio, / andremo tentoni, sbatteremo contro i muri, / e io, tu fai quello che vuoi, io mi sono già comprato / due tre casse di candele", "Cos'hai comprato?", / "Le candele, come no, almeno per vedere, / vuoi stare al buio? che i Faiantéin ne hanno, / però se non ti sbrighi", "No, ma davvero tu dici?" / "Come davvero, sta' ad aspettare un altro po', / ma non vedi tutte le sere / alle televisione quel che succede?" / "Vedo", "E allora?", poi lui, Ceccarelli, / era impiegato al Credito, che nelle banche / hanno le antenne, loro sentono il polso, / della situazione, e io, sai, lí, / cosa dovevo fare? ho comprato anch'io, / tre quattro casse, che mi sono rotto le braccia, /

what's heavy is the wax,
but I wanted to remain calm, we're all tangled up in this mess,
we're all bound up in this, and in winter, the nights never end,
if the weather turns bad, you're going to need some candles,

it's out there though where things get settled,
settled in a manner of speaking, because there's always
a particular hatred, a particular division, but war,
well, there hasn't been anymore gunfire, it's all been
in the hands of diplomacy,
which works, works like cats and dogs
getting along, and in the meantime years pass,
more than twenty have gone by, let's get this straight, better
that a few candles go unused, rather than having a war,
plus nothing's really lost, they're all still
right in their cases, in the closet under the stairs,
it's not like you have to feed them,
in fact, every once in awhile, I light one, that's how it started,
on a whim, two or three months ago, I was looking
for something under the staircase,
one of the cases was open, I pulled out
a candle from the box, new, white,
I held it in my hands, I told myself: *this*

quèll ch'e' paisa la zira,
mo a vléva stè tranquéll, s sémm, in bal,
balémma, al nòti a n finéss mai d'invéran,
s' la bótta mèl, u i nu n vrà dal candàili,

che alazò invíci al robi pu al s'è còndi,
còndi par módi 'd déi, perché c'è un odio
sempre, una divisione, mo la guèra,
insòmma, u n s'è sparè piò, e adesso è tutto
nelle mani della diplomazia,
che lavora, mo l'è cmè mètt d'acórd
c' chèn e e' gat, e intént e' pasa i an,
u n n'è pas véint e piò, intendéssum, mèi
ch' vaga pérs dal candàili, ch' nè la guèra,
che pu u n'è 'ndè pérs gnènt, agli è 'lè tótti
ancòura tal su casi, te sottoschèla,
a n magna mégga, ènzi, l'è un pó, mè, acsè,
par chès, l'è stè du tri méis fa, a zarchéva
te sottoschèla qualquèl,
'na casa la era vérta, ò tirat fura
da un pachètt sta candàila, nova, biènca,
e la tnéva tal mèni, a géva: quèsta

quel che pesa la cera, / ma volevo star tranquillo, siamo in ballo, / balliamo,
le notti non finiscono mai d'inverno, / se butta male, ce ne vorranno di
candele, // che laggiú invece le cose poi si sono aggiustate, / aggiustate per
modo di dire, perché c'è un odio / sempre, una divisione, ma la guerra, /
insomma, non s'è sparato piú, e adesso è tutto / nelle mani della diplomazia,
/ che lavora, ma è come mettere d'accordo / il cane e il gatto, e intanto passano gli anni, / ne sono passati venti e piú, intendiamoci, meglio / che vadano perse delle candele, piuttosto che la guerra, / che poi non è andato perso
niente, sono tutte / ancora nelle loro casse, nel sottoscala, / non mangiano
mica, anzi è un po', io, che / ogni tanto ne accendo una, ho cominciato, cosí,
/ per caso, è stato due tre mesi fa, cercavo / nel sottoscala qualcosa, / una
cassa era aperta, ho tirato fuori / da un pacchetto 'sta candela, nuova, bianca,
/ la tenevo in mano, dicevo: questa /

it is for the purpose of being lit,
well, if you don't, what good are they?
candles are for lighting, but for who?
and this, too, is a very good question,
at any rate,
I had some of those stumpy white matches in my pocket,
and I lit it without any specific notions,
and there I was standing with this lit candle,
now where do I put it? I know, on top
of the corner cupboard. I went up into the kitchen,
I got a good-sized plate, a large one,
I stuck it into some melted wax so it wouldn't fall,
I was making it up as I went along,
nearby was the calendar,
January seventeenth, the feast day of Sant'Antonio,
patron saint of animals,
which made me remember my mother:
"Whoever loves animals
loves his fellow man,"
and that makes all the sense in the world,
this candle is for Sant'Antonio, even if I don't go to church

but then seeing it there lit, which seems like nothing,
a candle, which is what?

la è sno da zènd,
amo se no cs'èll ta t nu n fé? al candàili
agli è fati da zènd, però ma chéi?
ch'ènca questa l'era una bèla dmanda,
e insòmma, tla bascòza éva i ziréin,
e a la ò zaisa, mo senza un'intenziòun,
e a stéva alè sa sta candàila zaisa,
adès dò ch'a la mètt? ècco, aquè sòura,
se tracantòun, a so 'ndè tlla cuséina,
ò tólt un bèl piat, grand,
ò fat culè un pó 'd zira, acsè la n s móv,
mo l'è stè tótt par chès, alè tachèd
u i era e' calendèri,
òz che dè ch' l'è? e' disèt ad znèr, la festa
'd Sant'Antóni dal bés-ci,
che la mi mà a m'arcórd: "Chi ch'e'e vó bén
mal bés-ci e' vó bén ènca mi cris-cèn",
e alè l'è vnú 'd su pi,
ènch' s'a n vagh a la mèssa, sta candàila
la è par Sant'Antóni,

mo pu a guardèla zaisa, ch'e' pèr gnént
'na candàila, cs'èll ch' l'è?

è solo da accendere, / e beh, se no cosa te ne fai? le candele / sono da accendere, però a chi? / che anche questa era una bella domanda, / e insomma, in
tasca avevo i cerini, / e l'ho accesa, ma senza un'intenzione, / e stavo lí con
questa candela accesa, / adesso dove la metto? ecco, qui sopra, / sul canto-
nale, sono andato in cucina, / ho preso un bel piatto, grande, / ho fatto
colare un po' di cera, cosí non si muove, / ma è stato tutto per caso, lí vicino
/ c'era il calendario, / oggi che giorno è? il diciassette gennaio, la festa /
Sant'Antonio delle bestie, / che mia madre mi ricordo: "Chi vuol bene / alle
bestie vuol bene anche ai crisitiani", / e lí è venuto naturale, / anche se non
vado a messa, questa candela / è per Sant'Antonio, // ma poi a guardarla
accesa, che pare niente / una candela, che cos'è? /

a little bit of wax and a wick,
but that flame, which was going upwards, going up higher,
okay, it might even seem like an exaggeration,
but it seemed to me that it was a living creature,
that it was something alive, how can I explain it,
what's true is that it dies, that you see it at the end,
the dripping, the melting, the wick, the black,
it can't stand on its own two feet anymore, the flame
blinks, a little smoke and that's all she wrote,
and when it's really night, I put it out myself,
what can I tell you, in the dark,
that phantom dancing around, all those shadows,
I like light at night, on the other hand during the day
not everyday, it would be annoying,
plus too often, it loses something,
whenever it comes into my head, a morning,
an afternoon, whenever I get the urge,
a candle, for myself, I make a circle around it, I look at it,
and another one for Sant'Antonio, also, because,
one never knows.

un pó 'd zira e un stupéin,
però cla fiàmba,
ch' la va d'in èlt, ch' la n sta mai férma, mè,
magari, e' sarà un'esageraziòun,
insòmma, u m pèr ch'e' séa 'na creatéura,
è qualcosa di vivo, cm'òi da déi?
tènt'è vèrra ch' la mór, ta la vaid tl'éultum,
un culadézz, squaièda, e' stupéin, nir,
u n gne la fa piò a stè d'impí, la fiamba
la sbat i ócc, un pó 'd fómm, e bonanòta,
e s' l'è nòta dabón, a la smórt mè,
's'ut ch'a t dégga, te schéur
che fantèsma che bala, tótt' cagli òmbri,
la nòta u m pis la luce, mè, e' dè invíci,
no tótt i dè, se no e' dvénta un impègn,
pu trop spèss u gn'è góst,
quant u m vén in ament, una matéina,
un dopmezdè, quant u m vén vòia, a zènd,
'na candàila, par mè, a zéir, a la guèrd,
e ènca par Sant'Antóni, ció, u n s sa mai.

un po' di cera e uno stoppino, / però quella fiamma / che va in alto, che non
sta mai ferma, io, / magari sarà un'esagerazione, / insomma, mi pare che sia
una creatura, / è qualcosa di vivo, come devo dire? / tant'è vero che muore,
la vedi alla fine, / un colaticcio, squagliata, lo stoppino, nero, / non ce la fa
piú a stare in piedi, la fiamma / sbatte gli occhi, un po' di fumo, e buonanotte, / e se è notte davvero, la spengo io, / cosa vuoi che ti dica, nel buio
/ quel fantasma che balla, tutte quelle ombre, / la notte mi piace la luce, a
me, il giorno invece, / non tutti i giorni, se no diventa un impegno, / poi
troppo spesso non c'è gusto, / una mattina, quando mi viene in mente, / un
pomeriggio, quando mi vién voglia, accendo, / una candela, per me, giro, la
guardo, / e anche per Sant'Antonio, beh, non si sa mai.

The Jacket

No, but dying your hair, you shouldn't be surprised,
lots do it, it's nothing, if someone doesn't like white hair,
he can dye it, you can always tell from a distance,
no big deal, all right fine, but even with his jackets,
yellows, reds, flowered, but if he likes them that way,
then in summer, that kind of jacket, tight,
how do you wear them? how do you stand them?
when to button it you've got to suck in your gut,
he thinks that's the way to go, because it's better than,
I don't know, these are the things that get tiresome,
but even I will say it and I'll say it again:
he's past seventy-seven,
he's aged well, but she's thirty-eight.

La sèrga

No, mo tènzsi i cavéll, 's'sut, i l fa in tint,
u n'è gnént, s'u n'i pis i cavéll biènch
éun u s'i tènz, ch ta i vaid da dalòngh,
fighéurt, mo insòmma, e 'nca al caméisa, ròssi,
zali, si fiéur, ció, s'a gli pis acsè,
pu d'instèda, no mè, l'è al sèrghi, strètti,
cma fét, ch' ta n'i sté dréinta, e butunèdi,
u n'è la tu miséura, ta n t la sint?
ch'e' chin stè tótt tiràt, da tnai e' fiè,
léu u s craid, acsè, che invíci e' sarébb mèi,
però a n'e'e so, l'è robi ch' l'è faidéiga,
ènca mè a déggh a déggh,
parchè léu l'à sentasèt'an sunèd,
ch'u i pórta bén, mo li la n n'à trentòt.

La giacca. No, ma tingersi i capelli, cosa vuoi, lo fanno in tanti, / non è niente, se non gli piacciono i capelli bianchi / uno se li tinge, che li vedi da lontano, / figurarsi, ma insomma, e anche le camicie, rosse, / gialle, a fiori, beh, se gli piacciono cosí, / poi d'estate, no, io, sone le giacche, strette, / come fai, che non ci stai dentro, e abbottonate, / non è la tua misura, non te la senti? / che deve stare tutto tirato, da tenere il fiato, / lui crede, cosí, che invece sarebbe meglio, / però non so, sono cose che è fatica, / anch'io dico dico, / perché lui ha sessantasette anni suonati, / che li porta bene, ma lei ne ha trentotto.

Summer and Winter

In the summer, heat, sweat, mosquitoes,
no, for me, I like winter, those gorgeous days
with sun, frigid air,
iced-over puddles,
trees with no leaves, where every so often,
amidst branches, you see a nest.

Instèda e invéran

D'instèda chèld, un sudadézz, zanzèri,
no, u m pis l'invéran, mè, cal bèl' zurnèdi,
se sòul, 'n'aria ch' la taia,
al piscòlli gelèdi,
e i èlbaar senza fòi, ch d'ogni tènt
tra 'l rèmi u s vaid un néid.

Estate e inverno. D'estate caldo, un sudaticcio, zanzare, / no, mi piace l'inverno a me, quelle belle giornate / col sole, un'aria che taglia, / le pozzanghere
ghiacciate, / e gli alberi senza foglie, che ogni tanto / tra i rami si vede un
nido.

The House

He says, why are you staying here, in that tenement, sell it,
buy a condominium, they can take care of it in no time,
but I was born here, in this house, yes, I understand,
it's big, well, and at one time there were a thousand of us,
now it's just me,
and a person gets used to his own house,
plus I have my vegetable garden,
which I don't keep up, I don't have time,
but there's that almond-tree,
and that plum,
they're unique, from Queen Claudia,
and they want me to sell, they, they want to send me to live
in a condominium, me in a condominium,
it's like living on a bus,
everybody sandwiched together,
those walls where you hear everything,
you, he says, always by yourself,
in that rundown house, what do you mean, alone?
they all talk just to hear themselves talk, people,
alone in your own house, you're the boss,
in my house, I'm in charge, I do whatever I want,
nobody's busting my balls, all right?

La chèsa

Dis, mo csa stét alè, at che svariòun, vènd,
t còmpar t'un condominio, i fa prèst, lòu,
mo a i so nèd, mè, ad sta chèsa, sè, ò capéi,
la è granda, ció, una vólta a sérmi mélla,
adès a i so sno mè,
e éun abituèd ad chèsa sóvva,
pu mè a i ènca e' zcvért,
ch'a n'i stagh dri, a n'ò témp, mo u i è cl'amandal,
e che suséin, ch'a n s tróva piò al suséini,
agli è specièli, dla Regina Claudia,
e i m vó fè vènd, lòu, i m vó fè 'ndè stè
t'un condominio, che mè e' condominio,
u m pèr ch'u s staga cumè sla curira,
tótt atachèd, e i méur ch'u s sint inquèl,
parchè ènca tè, dis, sémpra da par tè,
ad che casòun, csa vól déi da par tè?
i zcòrr par zcòrr, la zénta,
da par sè ad chèsa sóvva éun l'è e' padròun,
ad chèsa mea a cmand mè, a faz quèll ch'u m pèr,
u n mu n ròmp i quaiéun niseun, va bén?

La casa. Dice, ma cosa stai lí, in quel casermone, vendi, / compri in un
condominio, fanno presto loro, / ma ci sono nato, io, in questa casa, sí, ho
capito, / è grande, e beh, una volta eravamo mille, / adesso ci sono solo io,
/ e uno abituato a casa sua, / poi io ho anche l'orto, / che non ci sto dietro,
non ho tempo, ma c'è quel mandorlo, / e quel susino, che non si trovano piú
le susine, / sono speciali, della Regina Claudia, / e mi vogliono far vendere,
loro, mi vogliono far andare a stare / in un condominio, che io il condominio, / mi pare che ci si stia come sulla corriera, / tutti pigiati, e i muri
che si sente ogni cosa, / perché anche tu, dice, sempre da solo / in quel
casone, cosa vuol dire da solo? / parlano per parlare, la gente, / dal solo in
casa propria uno è il padrone, / a casa mia comando io, faccio quello che mi
pare, / non mi rompe i coglioni nessuno, va bene? /

and if it's big, a little patience, that's all,
better big than small, I've closed up
four rooms, I never go in them, during the winter
I only heat the room where I sleep, the kitchen
the bathroom, that's it,
and then alone? I'm never alone,
yesterday, for example, I dropped the water pitcher,
holy shit, what a crash, pieces everywhere,
and it seems like there were a lot of us living here,
really, sometimes, when it's left running,
the faucet, you're in another room,
hearing the water running and it sounds like talking,
then there's the dresser drawers that creak,
then the worms that are gnawing away at the chest,
there are even times when I open the wardrobe,
nothing moving, a silence, jackets, coats,
all hanging there, it can give the impression,
then you put yourself inside with them, you feel them behind you,
a quick brush, and that's it,
they're ours, they're part of this house, because things,
it seems like they're things, but they're like people,

e s' la è granda, pazinzia,
mèi granda ca nè znina, quatar cambri
agli ò céusi, a n'i vagh mai, d'invéran
a 'rschèld sno dò ch'a dórum, la cuséina,
e' bagn, e basta,
ch' pu da par sè, ta n si mai da par tè,
ir par déi, u m'è casch la bucalètta,
porca boia, un malàn, cózz dimpartótt,
e u m'è pèrs cmè ch'a fóssmi in tint, dabón,
mo ènca quant l'arvènza vért, dal vólti,
e' rubinètt dla scafa, tè t si dlà,
e t sint l'aqua ch' la córr, ch'e' pèr ch' la zcòrra,
pu u i è e' cumò ch'e' scrécca,
i tèral ch'i lavòura te cassòun.
ècco, magari, sè, u i è 'nch' di mumént,
quante t'éiruv l'armèri,
ch'u n s móv un féil, un zétt, sèrghi, capótt
tótt impichéd alè, e' pò fè impresiòun,
pu ta ti mètt, ta i sint madòs, 'na bota
sla scupètta, e la è fata,
i è di nóst, i è dla chèsa, parchè al robi,
e' pèr acsè, mo agli è cumè i cris-cèn,

e se è grande, pazienza, / meglio grande che piccola, quattro camere / le ho chiuse, non ci vado mai, d'inverno / riscaldo solo dove dormo, / la cucina, / il bagno, e basta, / che poi da solo, non sei mai da solo, / ieri, per dire, m'è caduta la caraffa, / porco boia, un fracasso, cocci dappertutto, / e m'è sembrato che fossimo in tanti, davvero, / ma anche quando rimane aperto, delle volte, / il rubinetto del lavandino, tu sei di là / e senti l'acqua che corre, che pare stia chiacchierando, / poi c'è il comò che scricchiola, / i tarli che lavorano nel cassone, / ecco, magari, sí, ci sono anche dei momenti, / quando apri l'armadio, / che non si muove un filo, un silenzio, giacche, cappotti, / tutti impiccati lí, può fare impressione, / poi te li metti, li senti addosso, un colpo / di spazzola, ed è fatta, / sono dei nostri, sono di casa, perché le cose,/ pare cosí, ma sono come i cristiani, /

you feel affectionate towards them, they become related to you,
there are people who refuse to eat
if they don't have their own spoon,
someone else will only have coffee in a certain cup,
another only drinks from glasses with handles,
but it doesn't even have to be as big as that, in the evening, I,
sometimes, I'm ready to go to bed,
I stand and I look in the mirror, I twist my mouth around,
make faces with my teeth, my tongue, I squint,
who is this fool? both of us laugh.

ta t'i afeziòun, al dvénta di parént,
u i è quèll ch'u n magna s'u n'à e' su cucèr,
cl'èlt e' tó e' cafè sémpra tla su taza,
un èlt e' bai sno te bicír se mangh,
mo pu e' basta ènca mènch, la sàira mè,
dal vólti, a so 'lè ch'a stagh pr'andè lèt,
a m férm e a m guérd e spèc, a stórz la bòcca,
a faz i dint, al lèngui, a scrécch un òc,
mo chi èll st' pataca? e a ridémm tutt déu.

ti ci affezioni, diventano dei parenti, / c'è quello che non mangia se non ha il suo cucchiaio, / l'altro prende sempre il caffè nella sua tazza, / un altro beve solo nel bicchiere col manico, / ma poi basta anche meno, la sera io, / delle volte, sono lí che sto per andare a letto, / mi fermo e mi guardo allo specchio, torco la bocca, / faccio i denti, le lingue, strizzo un occhio, / ma chi è sto' coglione? e ridiamo tutt'e due.

Dreams (1)

At night, one dream following right after another,
every night, it's a movie theater,
no really, when I fall asleep, it's like I've paid for a ticket,
the stuff that happens to me, I run, I fly, places I've never seen,
they chase me, terrible fears, my heart rate goes up,
women, who are stunning, cities where I get lost,
colors, living people, dead people, combinations of things that
make me sometimes say, still in the dream, this
I really want to tell, then in the morning,
I wake up, I think, I think, and I can't recall what.

I insógni (1)

La nòta, mè, un insógni taca cl'èlt,
tótt' al nòti, l'è un cino, mo dabón,
mè quant a m'indurmént,
l'è cm'a féss e' biglètt, quèll ch'u m suzéd,
a córr, a vòul, di póst ch'a n gn'ò mai vést,
i m dà dri, dal paéri, u m bat e' cór,
dal dòni, bèli, dal zità ch'a m pérd,
di culéur, zénta véiva, zénta mórta,
mo dal cumbinazióun ad robi che
dal vólti a déggh, sémpra tl'insógni, quèsta
a la ví racuntè, pu la matéina
a m svégg, a péns, a péns, e a n m'arcórd gnént.

I sogni (1). La notte, io, un sogno via l'altro, / tutte le notti, è un cinema, ma davvero, / io quando m'addormento, / è come se facessi il biglietto, quello che mi succede, / corro, volo, dei posti che non ho mai visto, / m'inseguono, delle paure, mi batte il cuore, / delle donne, belle, delle città che mi perdo, / dei colori, gente viva, gente morta, / ma delle combinazioni di cose che / delle volte dico, sempre nel sogno, questa / la voglio raccontare, poi la mattina, / mi sveglio, penso, penso, e non mi ricordo niente.

Dreams (2)

Me too, what I dream every night,
and telling them,
because I remember them, oh Lord yes, I remember them,
don't I remember them,
and not one of him,
not once, I never dream of him, what's that supposed to mean?
I have moments where I feel like it's my fault,
it must be my fault, my fault,
even if you don't control your dreams, they just happen,
but why doesn't he come? that would be enough, once,
from way deep down I ask to dream of him every once in awhile,
what is a dream? a dream, that's all, because it's been hard,
I would never have thought something like this,
we were always together,
both of us crazyloco
this past August, laughing,
at Baiòca's, that evening,
dancing, like a couple of kids,
we were dancing and we were laughing, and now nothing more.

I insógni (2)

Enca mè, quèll ch'a insógni tótt al nòti,
che a racuntèi,
parchè a m'i arcórd, mè, orca s'a m'i arcórd,
e léu mai una vólta,
mai, a n l'insógni mai, cs'èll ch'e' vrà déi?
ò di mumént ch'u m pèr ch' séa còulpa méa,
ènch' se i insógni ta n'i cmand, i vén,
mo parchè léu u n vén? ch'u m bastarébb,
in fònd mè a dmand da insugnél d'ogni tènt,
cs'èll ch' l'è un insógni? parchè la è stè gròsa,
a n mu n cridéva mè una roba acsè,
ch'a sérmi sémpra insén,
mat tutt déu, a m'arcórd, st'agòst, e' réid,
da Baiòca, cla sàira,
a balè, ch'a parémmi du raghézz,
a balémmi e a ridémmi, e adès piò gnént.

I sogni (2). Anch'io, quel che sogno tutte le notti, / che a raccontarli, / perché me li ricordo, io, orca se me li ricordo, / e lui mai una volta, / mai, non lo sogno mai, cosa vorrà dire? / ho dei momenti che mi pare sia colpa mia, / anche se i sogni non li comandi, / vengono, / ma perché lui non viene? che mi basterebbe, / in fondo io chiedo di sognarlo ogni tanto, / cos'è un sogno? perché è stata grossa, / non credevo io una cosa così, / che eravamo sempre insieme, / matti tutt'e due, mi ricordo quest'agosto, il ridere, / da Baiòca, quella sera, / a ballare, che sembravamo due ragazzi, / ballavamo e ridevamo, e adesso più niente.

Dreams (3)

Certainly, dreams, are stuff that never lasts, anywhere,
what are you left with later?
they're soap bubbles, but sometimes,
like the other night, that was a dream,
we were embracing, where? Where's here?
it was dark, "Where are we?" and she said: "Be still,
be still, don't say anything," and we stayed just like that,
in an embrace,
without saying anything, still tighter, it was her and me,
so that when I woke up, I was trembling,
and I stayed awake awhile, and I was fine.

I insógni (3)

Zért, i insógni, l'è roba ch' la n sta invéll,
cs'èll ch'u t'arvènza dop?
l'è dal bòlli 'd savòun, però dal vólti,
cmè l'altrenòta, quèll l'è stè un insógni,
a sérmi brazèd, dòvv? "Aquè dò ch' l'è?"
l'era un schéur, "Dò ch'a sémm?" e li: "Sta zétt,
zétt, nu dí gnént," sémpra piò strétt, mè e li,
ch'a m so svégg, a treméva,
e a so stè svégg un pèz, e a stéva bén.

I sogni (3). Certo, i sogni, è roba che non sta da nessuna parte, / cosa ti resta dopo? / sono bolle di sapone, però delle volte, / come l'altra notte, quello è stato un sogno, / eravamo abbracciati, dove? "Qui dove'è?" / era un buio, "Dove siamo", e lei, "Sta' zitto, / zitto, non dire niente", e stavamo cosí, abbracciati, / senza dir niente, sempre piú stretti, io e lei, / che mi sono svegliato, tremavo, / e sono rimasto sveglio parecchio, e stavo bene.

The Room

Sure I have moments, like now,
two pillows under my head, a sip of orange juice,
I've come down with a fever, but I can't rest,
then every so often, here on my side, in part it's because,
what's this? that's what it is, I'm fine now, but if I start
thinking about it, it happens,
it starts slowly, then it grows, a pain, it grows,
if I don't take small swallows, for a while I manage,
but because of the phlegm, I have such coughing fits,
that I choke, then I need to calm myself down again,
flat on my back, it's just that with this mattress protector,
                                       I've made a trench,
I'm trapped in a big bag, and my back, as a kid,
I fell from a motor bike, the lumbar vertebrae,
it's like I'm being gnawed on by dogs,
I'm clutching at the headboard,
I stick a pillow under the sacrum,
which helps, that's better, and if I could just
fall asleep, doze off, five minutes,
but it's starting all over again,
my skin, tight as a drum,
is there swelling? it's nothing,

La cambra

Sè, ò di mumént, cmè 'dès,
sa du cuscéin di dri, un gòzz d'aranciata,
u m'è calè la févra, mo a n m'arpòuns,
pu d'ogni tènt, aquè da chènt, l'è un pó,
csa i èll aquè? ècco, a i sémm, s'a i péns la è fata,
e' taca pièn, pu e' crèss, un mèl,
ch' s'a n mu n mètt ad panzètta, e pr'un pó a chèmp,
mo ò un bulilròun, u m vén dal boti 'd tòsa
ch'a m'afógh, a m chin arvultè d'arnóv,
stuglèd, sno che la ràida, ò fat la fosa,
e a stè insachèd, la schéina, da burdlàz
a so casch se mutòur, i anéll tra i lómb,
l'è cmè ch'u m déss ad mórs di chèn rabièd,
a m ciap ma la tistira
e a a m'inféil un cuscéin sòtta e' cudròun,
ècco, la va un pó mèi, e s'arivéss,
a indurmantèm, un parlózz, zéinch minéut,
però aquè a faz l'archètt,
la pèla, sint, la m téira cmè un tambéur,
o a so gòunfi? gnént, a m mètt ad curtèl,

La camera. Sí, ho dei momenti, come adesso, / con due cusini di dietro, un goccio d'aranciata, / mi è calata la febbre, ma non mi riposo, / poi ogni tanto, qui di fianco, è un po', / cosa c'è qui? ecco, ci siamo, se ci penso è fatta, / comincia piano, poi cresce, cresce, un male, / che se non mi metto bocconi, e per un po' campo, / ma con tutto 'sto catarro, mi vengono dei colpi di tosse / che soffoco, devo girarmi di nuovo, / supino, solo che la rete, ho fatto la fossa, / e a stare insaccato, la schiena, da ragazzo, / sono caduto col motorino, le vertebre tra i lombi, / è come se mi mordessero dei cani arrabbiati, / mi afferro alla testiera / e m'infilo un cuscino sotto l'osso sacro, / ecco, va un po' meglio, e se riuscissi / ad addormentarmi, un sonnellino, cinque minuti, / però qui faccio l'arco, / la pelle, senti, mi tira come un tamburo, / o sono gonfio? niente, mi metto di fianco, /

I'll just roll to my side,
towards the window, slowly though, because my head is
spinning, what can I do, no appetite, I'm not eating,
I'm weak,
and now what's going on? this leg, I can't feel it anymore,
it's numb,
if I had fallen asleep, why should I expect that,
I never sleep anyway,
it's that I'm lying on it, the blood isn't flowing as it should,
feel it, it's like a piece of meat,
slowly, in the direction of the wall, then it'll be on top,
and put some packs on it, see how it's coming back, and now
the other leg's twitching, stop, the foot,
is cramping, the toes, feel it
constricting, it's shooting up, like it's a piece of wire
all the way to the calf, I want to scream
it needs a good yank,
one two three, harder, come on now, I don't have the guts,
one two, I just can't do it, Jesus H. Christ, stay calm,
it went back in place by itself, who knows, maybe I moved
into the right position, what did I do in my lifetime
to deserve this sentence, I don't make things up
so they'll send me home, I know, it's still early,
I understand the whole set up,
just a second of breathing easier,
because insofar as this goes,

vérs la finestra, adèsi, che la testa,
e' zéira inquèl, amo a n'ò ptéita a n magn,
l'è tótta debolèzza,
e adès mo cs'èll, sta gamba, a n la sint piò,
u m'à ciap al furméighi,
ch'avrò durméi, 's'ut ch'apa mai durméi,
l'è che stèi sòura, dop e' sangh u n córr,
sint, l'è un parsótt,
pièn, vérs e' méur, ch' la vénga sòura, acsè,
e dèi dal pachi, vitt, ch' la arvén, e intènt
cl'èlta gamba, dvanè, no férma! e' pi,
u m s'incavala un nérv, al dàidi, sint,
al s'incrécca, e' vén sò, l'è cmè una spranga,
fina e' pulpàz, da rógg, u i vó un tiròun,
éun, déu, tréi, forza, dài, a n'ò e' curàg,
éun, déu, a n gne la faz, orca, 'ta bón,
l'è 'ndè pòst, da par léu, chi sa, a m so mòs
pr'e' su vérs, mo cs'òi, fat mè te mi mònd
d'ès cundanèd, che mè a n pretènd dal robi,
ch'i m manda a chèsa, a l so, l'è 'ncòura prèst,
a so tótt, mo ch'u s pòsa tiré e' fiè,
parchè ènca da sta pèrta,

verso la finestra, adagio, che la testa, / gira tutto, e beh, non ho appetito, non
mangio, / è tutta debolezza, / e adesso, ma cos'è? 'sta gamba, non la sento
piú, / mi s'è intorpidita, / che avrò dormito, cosa vuoi che abbia mai dormito,
/ è che starci sopra, dopo il sangue non corre, / senti, è un prosciuotto, /
piano, verso il muro, che venga sopra, cosí, / e darci delle pacche, vedi che
rinviene, e intanto / con l'altra gamba andare di qua e di là, no ferma! il piede,
/ mi si accavalla un nervo, le dita, senti, / si contraggono, viene su, è come fil
di ferro, / fino al polpaccio, da urlare, ci vuole uno strattone, / uno, due, tre,
forza, dai, non ho il coraggio, / uno, due, non ce la faccio, orca, sta' buono,
/ è andato a posto, da solo, chi sa, mi sono mosso / nel verso giusto, ma cosa
ho fatto io nella mia vita / da essere condannato, che non pretendo delle cose,
/ che mi mandino a casa, lo so, è ancora presto, / so tutto, ma che si possa
tirare il fiato, / perché anche da questa parte, /

I'm fairly robust, the heart's bearing all the weight,
I already get short of breath and if I don't get myself up
pretty soon,
all I do is roll over and over, there's not a moment of peace,
I can't do this anymore,
then those pills, my face is flushed,
it's burning up, everywhere,
I'm starting to sweat, I'm dripping, a pool is forming,
pajamas, sheets, soaked,
if I move I get cold,
I'm my own cold front, I don't know
if I'm going to get out of this one
the thoughts are coming at me in their usual tangle
and when they come, look out,
it's a real party,
insanity stuff, alone in a room, I boasted:
I said: I am the boss here, I turn on lights, I extinguish them,
I keep windows open, I do whatever I want,
you bet, instead, it's a prison,
the call button, I've been holding on to it
since this afternoon, glued to it,
I'm trying to yell, but I have no voice,
I'm throwing things against the door,
the spoon, the fork, whatever I can find,

a so un pó griv, mè, e' pais l'è tótt se cór,
ò zà un afàn, s'a n faz prèst a vultèm,
l'è tótt un ruglamént, aquè, u n gn'è pèsa,
a n nu n pòs piò,
pu cal pastéini, u m vén di chèld tla faza,
l'è come un fugh, dimpartótt,
a tach a sudé, a còul, a faz e' lègh,
e' pigiama, i lanzúl, tótt attachèd,
e s'a m móv a ciap frèdd,
a m faz vént da par mè, che aquè a n'e' so
s'a m la sgavagnarò, u m vén 'd chi pinsír,
di avilimént,
che quant a so rivàt, 'ta bón, 'na festa,
t si mat, 'na cambra da par mè, a m stiméva,
a géva: aquè a so un sgnòur, a zènd, a smórt,
a téngh vért' la finestra, a faz cm'u m pèr,
invíci, mo va là, l'è un'imparsòun,
e' campanèl, l'è da òz dopmezdè,
a so sémpra tachèd ma sta pirètta,
a próv ènca ad ciamè, mo a so runchèd,
a téir còuntra la pórta
e' cucèr, la furzéina, quèll ch'a tróv,

sono un po' robusto, io, il peso è tutto sul cuore,/ ho già un affanno, se non faccio presto a voltarmi, / è tutto un rotolare, qui, non c'è pace, / non ne posso piú, / poi quelle pastiglie, mi viene un calore in faccia, / è come un fuoco, dappertutto, / comincio a sudare, colo, faccio il lago, / il pigiama, i lenzuoli, tutti appiccicati, / e se mi muovo prendo freddo, / mi faccio vento da solo, che qui non so, / se me la caverò mi vengono di quei pensieri, / un avvilimento, / che quando sono arrivato, sta' buono, una festa, / roba da matti, una camera da solo, mi vantavo, / dicevo: qui sono un signore, accendo, spengo, / tengo aperta la finestra, faccio come mi pare, / invece, ma va' là, è una prigione, / il campanello, è da oggi pomeriggio, / sono sempre attaccato a questa peretta, / provo anche a chiamare, ma sono rauco, / tiro contro la porta / il cucchiaio, la forchetta, quello che trovo, /

except I don't have enough strength, I can't throw that far,
and the others, in the other rooms are ringing, all of them,
lovely isn't it, listen, it's a real orchestra, the nurses,
back and forth, commotion in the hallway,
and me here, like I don't exist, hours pass,
in my opinion, it's the bell itself that's not working, it's broken,
how am I going to let them know
I have a call button that doesn't call? what can I sound?
just so they can tell us, well, bad luck,
the call switch is under the same bad spell,
I've been pressing it all night long, I call, I protest, no one shows.

mo a n'ò fórza, a n gn'aréiv,
e ch'ilt, dagli èlti cambri, i sòuna, tótt,
pu bén, sin, l'è u orchestra, i infermír,
avènti, indrí, un dafè te curidéur,
e mè què, cm'a n'i fóss, e' pasa agli òuri,
sgònd mè, l'è e' campanèl ch'u n dà, u s'è guàst,
e cmè ch'a faz adès a fèi savài
ch'ò e' campanèl ch'u n sòuna? cs'èll ch'a sòun?
fórza 'd dèi, vè, e' sarà pò una disdètta,
u s'è inciudè ènca e' scòch, l'è tótt' la nòta
ch'a zach, a cèm, a ragn, u n vén niseun.

ma non ho forza, non ci arrivo, / e gli algri, dalle altre camere, suonano, tutti, /
che bello, senti, è un'orchestra, gli infermieri, / avanti, indietro, un daffare nel
corridoio, / e io qui, come non ci fossi, passano le ore, / secondo me, è il campanello che non risponde, s'è guastato, / e come faccio adesso a fargli sapere /
che ho il campanello che non suona? cosa suono? / a forza di darci, ve', sarà pure
una disdetta, / s'è incantato anche il pulsante, è tutta la notte / che schiaccio,
chiamo, protesto, non viene nessuno.

At This Point

This year, it's been something else, even this season alone,
in one winter, how many, well, well so, who was cut down and
                                                    [harvested?
Vanóla, Biondi, Buzz, holy Christ,
Culumbòun's sweet Ida, then all those others I'm forgetting,
what's his name, Sack– Lucky, it hit like that,
wait, Fonso Muschín, which when I think about them,
all that's missing is me, then that'll be everyone.

Ormai

St'an, mo l'è stè una roba, ènch' la stasòun,
l'è 'ndè un'invérna, insòmma, ció, i à mdéu,
Vanóla, Biondi, e' Ciócch, porca masóla,
la Ida 'd Culumbòun, pu quéi ch'a m zcórd,
cós, Malètt, Bigi, l'è st' un tirasègn,
spétta, Fonso 'd Muschín, che quant a i péns,
a i amènch sno mè ormai, pu i è mórt tótt.

Ormai. Quest'anno, ma è stata una roba, anche la stagione, / è andato un inverno,
insomma, hanno mietuto, / Vanóla, Biondi, il Ciócch, porca masóla, / la Ida di
Culumbòun, poi quelli che mi dimentico, / coso, Malètt, Bigi, è stato un tirassegno, / aspetta, Alfonso di Muschín, che quando ci penso, / manco solo io
ormai, poi sono morti tutti.

War

No, the bureaucracy's got nothing to do with it,
it's them, they have it in for me,
I'm in their big, black book, and I know why,
it happened the year before last, in summer, at Fasúl's,
we were sitting outside, talking,
they wanted to tear down the schools, they wanted to build them
down at the Mulini, are you kidding, come off it,
it just came out of my mouth,
what did I say? that up at the top there should be a broom
a clean sweep, that's what I said, something to that effect,
and they, go figure, knew about it the next day,
they have so many spies, and from that day I was singled out,
there hasn't been one day that's gone by,
laws, regulations, it's enough to drive you crazy,
it's been more than two years now, but I work,
you better believe I work,
a thousand years could pass,
they wouldn't forgive me, for this, it's a bill
that I signed for, and I have to pay it,
but they don't know me, all their arrogance, piss on them then,

Guèra

No, la burocrazéa la n gn'éintra gnént,
l'è lòu, i la à sa mè,
a so te léibar nir e a so e' parchè,
l'è stè l'altr'an, d'instèda, da Fasúl
disdài 'd fura, a zcurémmi,
ch'i vó buté zò al scóli, i li vó fè
alazò mi Muléin, 'ta bón, va là,
l'è robi che, e mè 'lè u m'è scap da déi,
cm'òi détt? ad sòura u i vrébb una garnèda
e fè pulire, ècco, una roba acsè,
e lòu, t si mat, i l'à savú e' dè dop,
i à tènt' 'd cal spéi, e d'alòura a so sgnèd,
i n mu nu n pasa óna,
lèzi, regolamént, da dvantè mat,
ch' l'è piò 'd du an ormai, mo lòu, t'é vòia,
e' pò pasè méll'an,
i n pardòuna, quèst', mè, l'è una cambièla
ch'a i ò firmé, e a la chin paghè, però
i n mu n cnòss lòu mu mè,
tótt' la su prepotenza, mè a i péss sòura,

Guerra. No, la burocrazia non c'entra niente, / sono loro, ce l'hanno con me, / sono nel libro nero, e so perché, / è stato l'altr'anno, d'estate, da Fasúl, / seduti fuori, parlavamo, / che vogliono buttar giú le scuole, vogliono farle / laggiú ai Mulini, sta' buono, va' là, / sono cose che, e io lí m'è scappato detto, / come ho detto? di sopra ci vorebbe una scopa / e fare pulizia, ecco, una cosa cosí, / e loro, figuararsi, l'hanno saputo il giorno dopo, / hanno tante di quelle spie, e da allora sono segnato, / non me ne passano una, / leggi, regolamenti, da diventare matto, / che sono piú di due anni ormai, ma loro, / hai voglia, / possono passare mille anni, / non perdonano, questa, io, è un cambiale, / che gli ho firmato, e la devo pagare, però / non mi conoscono loro a me, / tutta la loro prepotenza, io ci piscio sopra, /

and I'm not just saying it either, I piss, I do, in the evening,
when they don't see me,
even sometimes in the afternoon, just be careful,
in the winter, with that cold, certainly, it's easier,
people don't go out much,
in the summer on the other hand they're out and about until late,
but in the summer, it's more satisfying,
in August, under the big passageway,
the assessor, Mr. Public Property
walks right through there, I call him Public Property,
I hold it until I'm ready to burst, and when I let loose,
I piss like a horse, a stench, you can't even inhale, you can
imagine,
underneath the Vault, in August,
then if the wind's coming from the southwest,
it's that I refuse to stop, I learned from them,
I won't forgive,
and I won't go home, it's target practice, because
there are some who piss wherever they feel like it,
they take a piss and that's it,
in the corners, along the wall behind the old people's home,
against the gas pump
at the Shell station that's been closed for years,
wherever it's always been pissed on,
but my case is completely different,
it's war, I piss under the Arch, I piss

a n déggh par déi, a péss, dabón, la sàira,
quant i n mu n vaid,
mo ènca e' dopmezdè, basta stè 'ténti,
d'invéran, sa chi frédd, zért, u s fa mèi,
la zénta i scapa póch,
d'instèda invíci i sta in zéir fina tèrd,
però d'instèda u i è piò sodisfaziòun,
d'agòst, sòtta e' Vultòun, che da lè e' pasa
l'asesòur de Demanio, a t'e' dagh mè,
e' Demanio, parchè a la téngh ch'a s-ciòp
e quant a i dagh la mòla
l'è dal pisédi da caval, 'na pózza
ch'u n s'arfièda, t si mat,
alè sòtta, d'agòst, pu s' l'è garbéin,
l'è ch'a n m'aférum, ò imparè da lòu,
non perdono, a n pardòun,
e a n vagh purséa, l'è un tirasègn, parchè
u i n'è ch'i péssa in zéir, mo i péssa e basta,
ti cantéun, te méur di dri di Ricóvar,
còuntra la pòumpa de distributòur
dla Shell ch' l'è di an ch' l'è céus,
insòmma dò ch'u s'è sémpra pisé,
invíci mè, l'è tótt'un'èlta roba,
l'è una guèra, a péss sòtta l'Èrch, a péss

non dico per dire, piscio, davvero, la sera, quando non mi vedono, / ma anche
il pomeriggio, basta stare attenti, / d'inverno, con quei freddi, certo, si fa
meglio, / la gente esce poco, / d'estate invece stanno in giro fino a tardi, /
però d'estate c'è piú soddisfazione, / d'agosto, sotto il Voltone, che da lí tengo
da scoppiare / e quando mi libero / sono delle pisciate da cavallo, una puzza
/ che non si respira, te l'immagini, / lí sotto, d'agosto, poi se è libeccio, / è
che non mi fermo, ho imperato da loro, / non perdono, / e non vado a caso
è un tirassegno, perché / ce n'è che pisciano in giro, ma pisciano e basta, /
negli angoli, nel muro di dietro del Ricovero, / contro la pompa del distribu-
tore / della Shell che è chiuso da anni, / insomma dove s'è sempre pisciato,
/ invece io, è tutt'un'altra cosa, / è una guerra, piscio sotto l'Arco, piscio /

671

from up above, down on the steps of town hall,
it runs down, I piss against the glass door
of the Tourism Office, on the columns of the Credit Union,
I piss on the band shell, there are nights,
I wake up and I rush out, I don't ever use the toilet,
I get up, go to the piazza, I step up
on the fountain and I piss inside,
and the next morning I walk by,
like nothing happened, I look, nice gush, and I laugh,
that's how you piss.

da d'in èlt zò mal schèli de Cuméun,
ch' la va ch' la córr, a péss còuntra la bóssla
dla Pro Loco, tal culònni de Crèdit,
a péss se pèlch dla banda, u i è dal nòti,
a m svégg ch' la m scapa, mo a n vagh méggh' te cès,
a stagh sò, aréiv in piaza, a m mètt d'impí
sla funtèna e a i péss dréinta,
e la matéina dop a pas d'alè,
cmè gnént, a guèrd, un piò bèl zèt, e a réid,
pisé vuílt acsè.

dall'alto giú per le scale del Comune, / che va corre, piscio contro la porta
a vetri / della Pro Loco, nelle colonne del Credito, / piscio sul palco della
banda, ci sono delle notti, / mi sveglio che mi scappa, ma non vado mica al
cesso, / mi alzo, arrivo in piazza, mi metto in piedi / sulla fontana e ci piscio
dentro, / e la mattina dopo passo di lí, / come niente, guardo, che bel getto,
e rido, / pisciate voi cosí.

Who's There?

What would it, come on now, what would it cost him
to give her permission,
a phone call every once in awhile,
not right away, that might even be too much of a shock,
they're barely dead, no, let some time pass,
a few months, years even, two years, then one day,
ring. ring. who's there? who's talking? this voice,
it's her, it's her voice, you, it's you?
really? it's really you?
you sound a little far away, talk closer,
there, that's better, it's like, it's like you were right here,
your voice, how long has it been since I've heard it?
it hasn't changed one bit, I *rre*-cognized you
as soon as you said hello, am I frightened?
no, frightened of what? because of my stuttering?
you know all about that,
that's what happens whenever I get nervous,
but it's already passed, what?
if I'm pleased?
it's just I wasn't expecting it, I was in the middle of
making coffee, I ran get to the phone,
what are you talking about, the coffee, what does that matter,

Chi parla

Cs'èll ch'e' sarébb, zò, cs'èll ch'u i gustarébb
dèi e' permèss,
una telefonèda d'ogni tènt,
no sóbit, ch'e' purtébb ènch' fè impresiòun,
'pena mórt, no, lasè, pasè de témp,
di méis, ènch' di an, un an, du an, pu un dè
drin drin, pronto, chi parla? mo sta vòusa,
l'è li, l'è su vòusa, t si, t si tè?
dabón? t si própia tè?
a t sint un pó dalòngh, zcòrr piò tachèda,
ècco, acsè, l'è cmè, l'è cmè t fóss aquè,
la tu vòusa, quant'èll ch'a n la sintéva,
la n'è cambièda gnént, a t'ò 'rcccnuséu
apena ò sintí pronto, spavantèd?
no, spavantèd ad chè? parchè a tartài?
ta l sé pò, me u m fa 'csè quant ò e' nervòus,
mo u m'è zà pas, cumè, s'a so cuntént,
sno ch'a n mu n l'aspitéva, a séra dri
ch'a m féva un gòzz, 'd cafè, ò fat 'na chéursa,
mo che zchéurs t fé, e' cafè, csa m'arimpórtal

Chi parla? Cosa sarebbe, su, cosa gli costerebbe, / dargli il permesso, / una telefonata ogni tanto, / non subito, che potrebbe anche far impressione, / appena morti, no, lasciar passare del tempo, / dei mesi, anche degli anni, due anni, poi un giorno, / drin drin, pronto, chi parla? ma questa voce, / è lei, è la sua voce, sei, sei tu? / davvero? sei proprio tu? / ti sento un po' lontana, parla piú vicino, / ecco, cosí, è come, è come fossi qui, / la tua voce, quant'è che non la sentivo, / non è cambiata per niente, ti ho rrriconosciuta / appena hai detto pronto, spaventato? / no spaventato di che? perché tartaglio? / lo sai pure, mi fa cosí quando sono nervoso, / ma mi è già passato, come, se sono contento, / solo che non me l'aspettavo, stavo / faccendomi un goccio di caffè, ha fatto una corsa, / ma che discorsi fai, il caffè, cosa m'importa /

the coffee, if it gets cold I'll make some more,
yes, I'm gasping a little, but it's nothing, it's just
with the telephone up here in the sitting room,
you've always got to run, to tell you the truth, it is
inconvenient,
going up the stairs, it's enough to kill you sometimes,
because then there are those who don't let it ring,
just a couple of times, and that's it,
and you go to pick up, hello?
no one's there,
which just infuriates me, just hold on a second,
let it ring, if I'm in the garden I can't even hear it,
we've got to put in another phone jack, we must have said it
a thousand times, remember? then we didn't do anything,
you? how are you at fault?
it's me who was always
putting things off, but I'll call them tomorrow,
or if not, I'll go to Rimini, it's better to go
in person, another jack, in the kitchen
and another phone,
because with just one,
then it's the same as before, you're downstairs, they call
upstairs,
you're upstairs, they call downstairs, you need two,
no, tomorrow, first thing, I'll go to Rimini,
I need to drop by the motor club anyway,
and that's enough about the coffee, don't you ever change?

676

de cafè, s'u agiàza, a m l'arfarò,
sè, a lèns un pó, no, mo un n'è gnént, l'è che
e' telefan aquè 'd sòura tla sèla,
t chin sémpra córr, a l gémmi pò, l'è scòmad,
sò mal schèli dal vólti u i è d'amazès,
parchè pu u i è 'nca 'd quéi ch'i sòuna póch,
do tre sunèdi e via, tè t córr, t córr,
e quant t téir sò, pronto? u n gn'è piò niseun,
ch'a m'incapèl, mè, mo spité un mumént,
fé sunè, s'a so tl'órt a n sint e gnénca,
bsògna mètt 'n'èlta pràisa, a l'avrémm détt
méll vólti, ta t'arcórd? pu a n'émm fat gnént,
tè? cs'èll ta i éintrar tè? a so mè che al robi
agli armànd sémpra, mo admatéina a i cèm,
o se no a vagh a Rémin, che ad persòuna
l'è mèi, un'èlta pràisa, tla cuséina,
e 'nca un èlt aparècc, parchè éun sno, dop
l'è cmè préima, t si 'd sòtta, i cèma ad sòura,
t si 'd sòura, i cèma ad sòtta, u i nu n vó déu,
no, admèn, e' préim lavòur, a vagh a Rémin,
ch'ò ènch' da pasè ma l'Aci,
e dàila se cafè, ta n cambi mai?

del caffè, se si fredda, me lo refarò, / sí, ansimo un po', no, ma non è niente,
è che/ il telefono qui di sopra nel salotto, / devi sempre correre, lo dicevamo
pure, è scomodo, / su per le scale delle volte c'è da ammazzarsi, / perché
poi ci sono anche quelli che fanno suonare poco, / due tre squilli e via, tu
corri corri, / e quando tiri su, pronto? non c'è piú nessuno, / che m'arrabbio,
io, ma aspettate un momento, / fate suonare, se sono nell'orto non sento
nemmeno, / bisogna mettere un'altra presa, l'avremo detto / mille volte, ti
ricordi? poi non abbiamo fatto niente, / tu? cosa c'entri tu? sono io che le
cose / le rimando sempre, ma domattina li chiamo, / o se no vado a Rimini,
che di persona / è meglio, un'altra presa, in cucina, / e anche un altro
apparecchio, perché uno solo, dopo / è come prima, sei di sotto, chiamano
di sopra, / sei di sopra, chiamano di sotto, ce ne vogliono due, / no, domani,
il primo lavoro, vado a Rimini, / che devo anche passare all'Aci, / e dagliela
col caffè, non cambi mai? /

you're always thinking of others,
you should think about yourself,
see, there, see how we've already started to bicker,
over crazy stuff,
and now this whistling, I'm not hearing you clearly,
do you hear me?
what? it's a signal? what do you mean three minutes?
you only had three minutes? but even for you, tell me,
tell me right away, I just went along like normal didn't I?
if you don't say anything, no one knows, what?
yes, I believe you, that you're sorry too,
but you need to be on top of these things, tell me these things,
the next time, when is it? no one knows? don't they tell you?
no one knows? fine, patience then, if they don't say,
see now, we've gone and lost time
on the phone, and then you too
going on about the coffee, they'll disconnect
in a little while? it's better if we say goodbye now,
then keep talking, and when they disconnect, hello?
there, see, I've already said goodbye to you, and the next time,
we'll know about it, we'll do a better job, hello? where are you?
hello? they've disconnected, my God, they're zealots,
right to the exact minute, just keep it open,
for a couple more words, what could happen?
and then the first time, why do they have to be there

678

tè t péns sémpra ma ch'ilt, pensa ma tè,
vè, a tachémm za a ragnè, roba da mat,
e adès sté fés-ci, a t sint mèl, tè ta m sint?
cs'èll? l'è un segnèl? cumè tri minéut, t'évi
sno tri minéut? però ènca tè, mo déime,
déime sóbit, a m regoléva, no?
s' ta n mu n dí gnént, éun n'e' sa, cma s fal?
sè, mo a t craid, ch'u t dispís ènca ma tè,
però sta 'ténti alòura, déimli al robi,
st'èlta vólta quant'èll? u n s sa? i n t'e' déi?
non si sa, ció, pazinzia, s'i n'e déi,
mo vèrda 'lè, a sémm andè pérd e' témp
sal pràisi de telefan, pu ènca tè
sa che cafè t la é fata lònga, i staca
tra un pó? l'è mèi ch'a s salutémma adès,
pu andémm avènti, e quant i staca, pronto?
ècco, alòura a t saléut, e st'èlta vólta,
ch'a l savémm, a fémm mèi, pronto? du sit?
pronto? i a stach, orca, cmè ch'i è zelènt,
i sta me minéut sgònd, mo lasé córr,
par do paróli 'd piò, cs'èll ch' pò suzéd?
e pu la préima vólta 's'ut stè 'lè

tu pensi sempre agli altri, pensa a te,/ ve', cominciamo già a litigare, roba da matti,
/ e adesso questo fischio ti sento male, tu mi senti? / cosa? è un segnale? come
tre minuti? avrei / solo tre minuti? però, anche tu, ma dimmelo, / dimmelo
subito, mi regolavo, no? / se non mi dici niente, uno non lo sa, come si fa? / sí,
ma ti credo, che ti dispiace anche a te, / però stai attenta allora, dimmele le cose,
/ 'st'altra volta quand'è? non si sa? non te lo dicono? / non si sa, be', pazienza,
se non lo dicono, / ma guarda lí, siamo andati a perdere il tempo, / con le prese
del telefono, poi anche tu / con quel caffè l'hai fatta lunga, staccano / fra un po'?
è meglio che ci salutiamo adesso, / poi andiamo avanti, e quando staccano, pronto? / ecco, allora ti saluto, e quest'altra volta, / che lo sappiamo, facciamo meglio,
pronto? dove sei? / pronto? hanno staccato, orca, come sono zelanti, / stanno
al minuto secondo, ma lasciate correre, / per due parole in piú, cosa può succedere? / e poi la prima volta cosa volete star lí /

with a gun to your head, it's that they've got, who knows,
they've got their orders too, it's hard though,
three minutes? come on now,
what can you do with three minutes? what can you say?
nothing would be better,
at least then you don't get all churned up,
which isn't true, no, I'm just saying, because
yes, I was upset, but for just a second,
when she said: hello, as if she didn't dare say it,
hello, hello, it's me, with a voice which,
because it seems like nothing, the voice,
but when you hear it,
her voice, it's her, it's her there, completely,

there, now I'm complaining, I'm grumbling,
but when it comes down to it,
I shouldn't have expected that much, Morandi,
on the contrary, said to me, his brother, Loriano,
it's been four years now, and not a word, he doesn't call,
but I, with this system, which on top of it all
they cut off your conversation, I'm not at all convinced,
Bianca, with Ruggero, never mentioned
the three minutes, we've discussed this many times,
she should have told me,

se s-ciòp puntéd, l'è ch'ènca lòu, chi sa,
ènca lòu i avrà di éurdin, l'è fadéiga,
però, zò, tri minéut,
csa fét in tri minéut? csa déit? mèi gnént,
emench' ta n t guast e' sangh,
ch'u n'è vèrra, no, a déggh acsè, parchè,
sè a so arvènz mèl, però l'è stè un mumént,
quant la à détt: pronto, cmè ch' la n s'arisghéss,
pronto, pronto, a so mè, s'na vòusa che,
parchè e' pèr gnént, la vòusa,
mo quant t la sint,
la su vòusa, l'è li, la è 'lè, l'è tótt,

che mè a sbròuntal, a m'alamént, mo in fònd
a n'ò cnú gnènca spité tènt, Murand
invíci u m géva, e' su fradèl, Loriano,
l'è pas bèla quatr'an, e u n s sint, u n cèma,
però mè, sté sistema, ch' te piú bèl
i t taia e' zcòurs, a n so mégga cunvéint,
la Bianca sa Rugero i tri minéut
la n m'i a mai luminè, émm zcòurs tènt' vólti,
la m l'avrébb détt,

col fucile puntato, è che anche loro, chi sa, / anche loro avranno degli ordini,
è fatica, / però, dai tre minuti, / cosa fai in tre minuti? cosa dici? meglio
niente, / almeno non ti guasti il sangue, / che non è vero, no, dico cosí,
perché, / sí, sono rimasto male, però è stato un momento, / quando ha
detto: pronto, come se non s'arrischiasse, / pronto, pronto, sono io, con una
voce che, / perché pare niente, la voce, / ma quando la senti, / la sua voce,
è lei, è lí, è tutto, // che io brontolo, mi lamento, ma in fondo, non ho neanche dovuto aspettare tanto, Morandi, / invece mi diceva, suo fratello, Loriano, / sono ormai passati quattro anni, e non si sente, non chiama, / però io,
questo sistema, che sul piú bello / ti tagliano il discorso, non sono mica
convinto, / la Bianca con Ruggero i tre minuti / non me li ha mai nominati,
abbiamo parlato tante volte, / me l'avrebbe detto, /

maybe, who knows, it could be that they decided,
the first time, to keep it to themselves, because
even with an emotion that's too strong,
in fact it did so happen that afterwards
someone got sick,
at any rate, there must be a reason, there has to be one,
if not, how, do you explain it? you can't,
they can't, even Morandi,
he's not telling everything, Sirio,
because with these kind of things
you've got to be aware, he'd had an argument
with Loriano, I mean a blow up,
and then afterwards, that Sunday,
going fishing at the reservoir, he slips?
he suddenly has an attack?
they found him face down, mouth open,
the day after in a pool of water, and now Sirio,
who doesn't say anything, but still, he'd like it,
if Loriano would call him, to make peace,
you can't, come on, be so full of rage even after he's dead,
Sirio's right, about this, you're two brothers, what's the point
of being right? but after all, it's all just talk,
we don't know a thing, we, how things were left,
what do we know about where Loriano let matters stand?
and then what about Irma?

forse, chi sa, e' pò ès ch'i apa decéis,
la préima vólta, da tnais strétt, parchè
anche una comozione troppo forte,
magari l'è suzèst che qualcadéun
dop l'è stè mèl, insòmma
u i sarà una rasòun, la i à da ès,
se no, cumè, i fa al diferenzi? u n s pò,
non possono, ch'ènca Murand però,
u n la dí tótta, Sirio, parchè al robi
bsògna savàili, sa Loriano léu
l'éva ragnè, mo fórt, e dop cla dmènga,
pr'andè a pischè l'è stè, tl'Éus, l'à sguilé?
u i è vnú mèl? i l'à tróv a bòcca 'd sòtta
e' dè dop t'na razèra, e Sirio adès,
ch'u n dí gnént, però insòmma, léu e' vrébb
se Loriano u l ciaméss, da fè la pèsa,
ta n pò, zò, stè instizéid ènca dop mórt,
l'à rasòun Sirio, aquè, a si du fradéll,
's'ut tnai e' mórs, che però l'è tótt zchéurs,
a n savémm gnént néun cm'agli è mèssi al robi,
cs'èll ch'a savémm néun cmè ch' l'è mèss Loriano?
e l'Irma alòura?

forse, chi sa, può essere che abbiano deciso, / la prima volta, di tenersi stretti, perché / anche una commozione troppo forte, / magari è successo che qualcuno / dopo è stato male, insomma / ci sarà una ragione, ci deve essere, / se no, come, fanno le differenze? non si può, / non possono, che anche Morandi però, non la dice tutta, Sirio, perché le cose bisogna saperle, con Loriano lui / aveva litigato, ma forte, e dopo, quella domenica, / per andare a pescare è stato, nell'Uso, è scivolato? / gli è venuto un malore? l'hanno trovato bocconi / il giorno dopo in uno specchio d'acqua, e Sirio adesso, / che non dice niente, però insomma, lui vorrebbe, / se Loriano lo chiamasse, per far la pace, / non puoi, su, stare in collera anche dopo morto, / ha ragione Sirio, qui, siete due fratellli, / cosa vuoi tenere il morso, che però sono tutti discorsi, / non sappiamo niente, noi, come sono messe le cose, / cosa sappiamo noi com'è messo Loriano? / e l'Irma allora? /

683

six years she's been waiting, and no one calls,
and she didn't even have an argument, they should put things
right,
Irma and her father, listen to this one,
they made an ugly mess of it,
no, you can't say a word about it, you have to take what comes,
Decio, his son, called him two years ago,
ten years later, he died in eighty-six,
and he's so happy, are you kidding, now, folks,
I can wait another ten years,
it was such a thing that, when I heard about it,
it's better not to talk about it, I'm shaking, look,
just thinking about it,
oh well, you've just got to keep trying, Vittorina's,
it's already been four years, no, five, that her Debora,
now there too, that's another terrible thing,
a girl seventeen years old, and she,
it's been awhile that she doesn't go out anymore,
always there inside,
she's waiting, she says, what if she calls and I'm out?
then afterwards when will she call me back again?
and then can she call me again? and her husband,
Manilo, he does all the shopping now,
I see him, with all those sacks, we say hello, he shakes his head,
a mother is always a mother,

li l'è si an ch' la aspetta, e nisun cèma,
e la n'à méggh' ragnè, sè, i s vléva un bén
l'Irma e e' su bà, 'ta bón, i féva schiv,
no, u n s pò dí gnént, bsógna tó quèll ch'e' vén,
Decio, e' su fiúl, u l'à ciamè du an fa,
dis an dop, l'era mórt dl'utentasí,
e léu cuntént, t si mat, adès, burdéll,
a pòs stè d'aspitè dagli èlt dis an,
l'è stè una roba, quant a l'ò sintéi,
l'è mèi no zcòrr, a trém, vè, sno a pensèi,
amo bsògna pruvè, la Vitorina,
l'è zà quatr'an, no, zéinch, ch la su Debora,
ènca quèlla l'è stè una bèla sgèzia,
una burdèla ad disèt an, e li
l'è un pó ch' la n scapa pió, la è sémpra alè
ch' la aspétta, dis, s' la m cèma ch'a so fura?
dop, quant la m pò 'rciamè?
e pu la m pò 'rciamè? e e' su maréid,
Manglio, l'è léu adès ch' va a fè la spàisa,
a l vèggh, sa chi sachétt,
a s salutémm, e' scrólla un pó la testa,
la mama l'è la mama, l'è fadéiga,

lei sono sei anni che aspetta, e nessuno chiama, / e non ha mica litigato, si volevano un bene / l'Irma e suo padre, sta' buono, facevano schifo, / no, non si può dir niente, bisogna prendere quel che viene, Decio, suo figlio lo ha chiamato due anni fa, / dieci anni dopo, era morto nell'ottantasei, / e lui contento, sei matto, adesso, ragazzi, / posso aspettare altri dieci anni, / è stata una cosa, quando l'ho sentito, / è meglio non parlarne, tremo, ve', solo a pensarci, / e be', bisogna provare, la Vittorina, / sono già quattro anni, no, cinque, che la sua Debora, / anche quella à stata una bella disgrazia, / una bambina diciasette anni, e lei /è un po' che non esce piú, è sempre lí, / che aspetta, dice, se mi chiama che sono fuori? / dopo, quando mi può richiamare? / e poi mi può richiamare? e suo marito, / Manlio, è lui adesso che va a fare la spesa, / lo vedo, con quei sacchetti, / ci salutiamo, scuote un po' la testa, / la mamma è la mamma, è fatica, //

but you've just got to be grateful,
you've always got to be grateful,
they're giving you a gift,
you know, it's not just a dream,
it's them, you hear them, it gives you goose bumps,
it's just that sometimes, I don't understand it myself,
things come out that you can't understand,
Nardo, for example, in the piazza yesterday,
says that before Christmas his sister-in-law,
Angela, called him, he's been separated for a long time now,
he even got scared, you're Angela? which Angela? what?
he couldn't take it all in, then she set things straight,
he was listening a minute, but you call
your sister now, too, call her right away,
because she's definitely waiting, you know
Olga, we see less often, there, I'm saying it,
these messed-up situations, how they happen
I don't know, no one knows, we're always there,
we don't know a thing, that Angela wanted
to talk specifically with him, with Nardo,
sisters-in-law sometimes,
who knows, there could even have been feelings,

però bsògna dí grèzia, ènch' s' l'è fadéiga,
bsògna sémpra dí grèzia, i t fa un reghèl,
amo cumè, u n'è mégga un insógni,
l'è lòu, ta i sint, ch'u t vén la chèrna pléina,
sno che dal vólti, a n'e' so gnénca mè,
e' vén fura dal robi, ch'u n s capéss,
Nardo, par déi, a l'ò vést ir in piaza,
dis che préima 'd Nadèl u l'à ciamè
la us cugnèda, l'Angela, che léu
l'è separèd da mò, l'à vú ènch' paéura,
t si l'Angela? che Angela? cumè?
u n gn'à vú góst par gnént, pu u l'à 'rmidiéda,
u la è stè sintí un pó, però adès cèma
ènca la tu surèla, cèmla sóbit,
che li sichéur la aspétta, mè, ta la sé,
sl'Olga a s'avdémm piò póch, ècco, mè a déggh,
questi disguidi, cmè ch'i pò suzéd?
non lo so, non si sa, a sémm sémpra alè.
a n savémm gnént, che l'Angela magari
la vléva zcòrr própia sa léu, sa nardo,
al cugnèdi dal vólti,
chi sa, u i putrébb ès stè 'nch' un sentiment,

però bisogna dire grazie, anche se è fatica, / bisogna sempre dire grazie, ti
fanno un regalo, / e be', non è mica un sogno, / sono loro, li senti, ti viene
la pelle d'oca, / solo che delle volte, non so neanch'io, / vengono fuori delle
cose, che non si capisce, / Nardo, per dire, l'ho visto ieri in piazza, / dice che
prima di Natale l'ha chiamato / la sua cognata, l'Angela, che lui / è separato
da tanto, ha avuto anche paura, / sei l'Angela? che Angela? come? / non gli
è piaciuto per niente, poi l'ha rimediata, / è stato ad ascoltarla un po', però
adessso chiama / anche tua sorella, chiamala subito, / che lei di sicuro aspetta, io, lo sai, con l'Olga, ci vediamo piú poco, ecco, io dico, / questi disguidi,
come possono succedere? / non lo so, no si sa, siamo sempre lí, / non sappiamo niente, che l'Angela magari / volveva parlare proprio con lui, con
Nardo, / le cognate delle volte, / chi sa, ci potrebbe essere state anche un
sentimento, /

which she hid from him, and then afterwards, now,
but even this is just an explanation,
what I'm doing here, she needs to find out, perhaps,
in that case,

at any rate, for Nardo it's five minutes,
five minutes of confusion,
whereas Tina,
quiet down now, you know, Tina Quadarléin
who, she still won't talk about it, now that was something,
talk about a mix-up,
everything all messed up, come on now, which I,
there's no logical way to follow it, because,
if these phone calls are supposed to be
a consolation,
where you hear one of your loved ones,
with Dario, it was just the opposite,
he just lit into her, her husband,
said things, called her names, screamed, a scene,
she was a wreck afterwards, Tina, and still is now,
if you could see her, he was a kid,
Dario, we all knew him,
Dario, he was the schoolteacher,
but even him, for God's sake,
may he be up there resting in heavenly peace,
but, you know, he should understand,
she was a girl when he died,

che lei lo nascondeva, e dop, adès,
ch'ènca quèst però l'è un ragiunamént
ch'a l faz mè què, li, bsògna vdai, alà,

insòmma, Nardo l'à pas zéinch minéut,
mo a paragòun, la Tina,
sta zétt, va là, la Tina 'd Quadarléin,
ch' la n nu n vó zcòrr, li, mo l'è stè una roba,
èlt che disguéid,
tótt' 'na roba a l'arvérsa, zò, che mè,
lí non c'è un filo logico, parchè
se stal telefonèdi agli à da ès
una consolaziòun,
che tu senti un tuo caro, Dario invíci
u i à magnè la faza, e' su maréid,
robi, numàz, di rógg, una piazèda,
ch' la è stè mèl dop la Tina, e 'ncòura adès,
s' t la vaid, ch' l'era un ragaz,
Dario, a l'émm cnunsú tótt, pu l'era mèstar,
però ènca léu, par carità, che séa
te mèz de paradéis,
però insòmma ènca léu l'à da capéi,
li l'era una burdèla quant l'è mórt,

che lei lo nascondeva, e dopo, adesso, / che anche questo però è un ragio-
namento / che faccio io qui, lei bisogna vedere, là, // insomma, Nardo ha
passato cinque minuti, / ma al confronto, la Tina, / taci, va' là, la Tina di
Quadarléin, / che non ne vuol parlare, lei, ma è stata una cosa, / altro che
disguido, / tutt'una cosa all rovescia, dai, che io, / lí non c'è un filo logico,
perché / se queste telefonate devono essere / una consolazione, / che tu
senti un tuo caro, Dario invece / le ha mangiato la faccia, suo marito, /
cose, nomacci, degli urli, una scenata, / che è stata male, dopo, la Tina, e
ancora adesso, / se la vedi, che era un ragazzo, / Dario, l'abbiamo conosciuto tutti, poi era maestro, / però anche lui, per carità, che sia / nel mezzo
del paradiso, / però insomma anche lui deve capire, / lei era una bambina
quand'è morto, /

she tried to make peace for him, the flowers, that tomb
was a garden, but later,
blood is thicker than water, time passes,
and how long is it now that she's had her "friend,"
a guy from Savignano, she's got rights too,
and he can't, he can't, if it is him, because people,
it's been awhile that these rumors have been going around,
which I find difficult to believe, I do, but,
they're saying it's all a big joke
by a couple of kids having fun,
that's all it is, just for something different to do,
which I say: how could it be, aren't you thinking straight?
what kind of joke? those are just reckless things,
to hurt people, that Tina
still doesn't know about, no one's said anything about them,
they don't have the courage to,
but someone should tell her, I'd like to see you,
she could just go downhill all over again,
but she's got to be told about it though, because she's,
for her at this point Dario's, while he, poor soul,
he understood, not another word from him,
no, these are low-lifes, it's just cruelty,

ch' la i vléva un bén, i fiéur, l'era un zardéin
cla tòmba, però dop,
il sangue non è acqua, e' pasa e' témp,
e adès quant'èll che si è fatta un compagno,
éun ad Savgnèn, ènca li la à dirétt,
e u n pò, léu,
                    s' l'è stè léu, parchè la zénta,
l'è un pó ch'u i è in zéir dal ciacri,
ch'a faz fadéiga a cràida, mè, però,
ció, i l déi, dis ch' l'è stè un schérz, di squaiunèd,
acsè, par fè una roba originèla,
che mè a déggh: mo cma s fal, a n'i pensé?
che schérz èll? quèll l'è robi da incosciént,
da fè stè mèl la zénta, che la Tina
la n'e' sa 'ncòura, i n gn'à détt gnént niseun,
i n s'è risghé.
amo a t ví vdai, la pò stè mèl d'arnóv,
che però bsògna déie, parchè li,
par li adès Dario, invíci léu, puréin,
léu l'à capéi, lui non s'è fatto vivo,
no, l'è di delinquént, l'è cativéria,

che gli voleva un bene, i fiori, era un giardino / quella tomba, però dopo, /
il sangue non è acqua, passa il tempo, / e adesso quant'è che si è fatta un
campagno, / uno di Savignano, anche lei ha diritto, / e non può, lui, – se è
stato lui, perché la gente, / è un po' che ci sono in giro delle chiacchiere, /
che faccio fatica a crederci, io, però, / be', lo dicono, dice che è stato uno
scherzo, dei buontemponi, / cosí, per fare una cosa originale, / che io dico:
ma come si fa, non ci pensate? / che scherzo è? / quelle sono cose da inco-
scienti, / da far star male la gente, che la Tina / non lo sa ancora, non le ha
detto niente nessuno, / non si sono arrischiati, / e be', ti voglio vedere, può
star male di nuovo, / che però bisogna dirglielo, perché lei, / per lei adesso
Dario, invece lui, poverino, / lui ha capito, lui non s'è fatto vivo, / no, sono
dei delinquenti, è cattiveria, //

who only make people suffer, then
there are those who say it's all one big joke,
who laugh, oh I have a premonition, a dead person talking,
playing the critic, and if someone doesn't have a telephone?
they've all got phones, today, come on now,
they even carry it around with them, you see them talking,
on the street, on the train, everywhere,
but the first sign of trouble if you don't have one
is that they make you go and get one, so you can talk to them,
they say they tried calling
and leaving a message, and no answering machine,
then later, you're out of your mind,
you see how it's all lies?

all of it, but you better forget about the lies, because
who isn't thinking straight, this is what I have to say,
they are not calls like the others,
that it's some other kind of thing, there's no way of talking,
they've got this idea that it's no big deal afterwards,
but they call and then what?
where does that put us? there's been nothing and they call,
this is what makes everything come undone,
they don't know what to say,
where do they connect?

l'è ch'i n fa sno patéi la zénta, dop
u i è quéi ch'i déi ch' l'è tótt' una cumédia,
ch'i réid, quarantasèt, morto che parla,
ch'i fa 'l crétichi, e s'éun u n'à e' telefan?
ch'i l'à tótt e' telefan, òz, andémma,
i s'e' pórta ènca dri, ta i vaid ch'i zcòrr
par la strèda, se treno, dimpartótt
mo pu a la préima sgrèzia, se ta n l'è,
ta t'e' fé métt, l'è che va a zcòrr sa lòu,
dis ch'i à 'nca próv una telefonèda
da registréla e u n'è vnú fura gnént,
alòura dop, t si mat, vitt ch' l'è buséi?
ch' l'è tótt buséi? mo che buséi, l'è vuílt
ch'a n ragiuné, quèst e' vó própia déi
ch'u n'è telefonèdi cmè cagli èlti,
ch' l'è un'èlta roba, mo u n gn'è módi 'd zcòrr,
lòu i à cl'idea, che non c'è niente dopo,
mo i telefona, e alòura?
cm'a la mitémmi? u n gn'è gnént e i telefona,
questo gli smonta tutto, i n sa quèll déi,
dò ch'i s'ataca?

è che non fanno solo patire la gente, dopo / ci sono quelli che dicono che è
tutta una commedia, / che ridono, quarantasette, morto che parla, / che
fanno le critche, e se uno non ha il telefono? / che ce l'hanno tutti il telefono,
oggi, andiamo, / se lo portano anche dietro, li vedi che parlano / per strada,
in treno, dappertutto, / ma poi alla prima disgrazia, se non ce l'hai, / te lo fai
mettere, è che vai a parlare con loro, / dice che hanno anche provato una
telefonata / a registrarla e non è venuto fuori niente, / allora dopo, sei matto,
vedi che sono bugie? / che sono tutte bugie? ma che bugie, siete voi / che
non ragionate, questo vuol proprio dire / che non sono telefonate come le
altre, / che è un'altra cosa, ma non c'è modo di parlare, / loro hanno quel-
l'idea, che non c'è niente dopo, / ma telefonano, e allora? / come la mettiamo? non c'è niente e telefonano, / questo gli smonta tutto, non sanno cosa
dire, / dove s'attaccano? //

693

if it weren't that people,
Mara di Bòt has been going around awhile saying,
that Fabio Tassinari calls her,
that he's called her more than once,
which makes no sense at all, now those, yes, those are all lies,
she never meant a thing to him,
Fabio never even looked at her, then there she is saying it,
come off it, come on now,
can't you just see her, with that sagging butt of hers?
Mara has always been jealous
of Giovanna, which Fabio, with Giovanna,
now them yes, they were in love, both of them,
they never wanted to get married, but they were together,
and Giovanna, she's waiting too,
and Fabio, what do you expect,
no word from him, but it's still too soon,
it hasn't even been two years, and anyway Mara,

there's not just Mara,
Rosetta says that her son calls her once a month,
come on, it can't be true,
but given that Libera is saying
that this year her mother,
and we're still in July here,
he had already called her four times,
what I say is, is this a competition?
is this some kind of tournament?
they've called me more than you?

s'u n'i fóss che la zénta,
la Mara ad Bòt l'è un pó ch' la va dí 'n zéir
ch'u i telefona Fabio Tassinari,
ch'u i à telefonè piò d'una vólta,
ch' la n sta invéll, quèlli, sè, l'è tótt' buséi,
che ad li ma Fabio un gn'à impurtè mai gnént,
u n la à mai guèrsa, pu la è 'lè, zò, andémma,
ta n la vaid? s' che cul bas, l'è che la Mara
la è stè sémpra invidiòusa dla Giovanna,
che Fabio sla Giovanna,
lòu sè che i era inamurèd, tutt déu,
i n s'è mai vlú spusè, mo i stéva insén,
e la Giovanna, ènca li adès la aspétta,
Fabio, ció, u n s fa sintéi, ch' l'è 'ncòura prèst
però, u n'è pas du an, e intènt la Mara,
l'è ch'u n gn'è sno la Mara,
la Rosetta, e' su fiúl dis ch'u i telefona
tótt i méis, ch'u n'è vèrra, zò, u n pò ès,
mo sicómm che la Libera la déi
che st'an la su mà, e a sémm ancòura ad lói,
la i à telefonè zà quatar vólti,
che mè a déggh, l'è una gara? un campionèd?
mè i m telefona piò ca nè ma tè?

se non fosse che la gente, / la Mara di Bòt è un po' che va a dire in giro / che
le telefona Fabio Tassinari, / che le ha telefonato piú di una volta, / che non
sta in piedi, quelle, sí, sono tutte bugie, / che di lei a Fabio non gli è im-por-
tato mai niente, / non l'ha mai guardata, poi à lí, dai, andiamo, / non la vedi?
con quel culo basso, è che la Mara / è sempre stata invidiosa della Gio-vanna,
/ che Fabio con la Giovanna, / loro sí che erano innamorati, tutt'e due, / non
si sono mai voluti sposare, ma stavano insieme, / e la Giovanna, anche lei
adesso aspetta, / e Fabio, cosa vuoi, non si fa sentire, che è ancora presto /
però, non sono passati due anni, e intanto la Mara, // è che non c'è solo la
Mara, / la Rosetta, suo figlio dice che le telefona / tutti i mesi, che non è vero,
dai, non può essere, / ma siccome la Libera dice, / che quest'anno sua madre,
e siamo ancora in luglio, / le ha telefonato già quattro volte, / che io dico, è
una gara? un campionato? / a me mi telefonano piú che a te, /

sure it's possible, I don't know, they're things,
that it's best to keep quiet about these things,
they're private things, instead,
it's who can tell the most lies, to impress people,
or could it even be it's those people
who nobody ever calls,
the phone doesn't ring, and they let loose this way,

but the thing is, with with lies,
you've got to consider how it's intended, sometimes
a lie's necessary, Gigi Magnani, found himself in a situation,
he couldn't have done anymore than he did,
look at his wife, every day crying,
over her brother, she was like a mother,
to Gianpiero, and she was the one
who sent him to Rimini that morning,
no big deal, to buy herbs, to make tea,
which, for her, helped her feel good,
and you can't find them here,
and in Celle, it was raining,
he was going straight, a Mercedes came
from the other direction, it hit him head on, he died instantly,
and then, she says, it's my fault, I killed him,

mo èl dóbbi, mè a n'e' so, l'è robi, quèlli,
che bsògna sno stè zétt,
sono cose private, invíci, sè,
l'è chi ch' dí piò buséi, par fè fighéura,
o magari ènch' l'è zénta
ch'u n'i cèma niseun,
e' telefan u n sòuna e i s sfóga acsè,

che pu al buséi,
éun, bsògn vdai cm'e' vén ciapèd, dal vólti
una buséa la i vó, Gigín Magnèni,
lui s'è trovato
ch'u n putéva fè mèi, t vaid la tu mòi
che tótt e' dè la piànz
par che fradèl, parchè li ma Giampiero
la i éva fat da mà, e l'è stè li
che cla matéina la l'à mand a Rémin,
mo gnént, a tó dagli érbi, una tisana,
che ma li la i fa bén, e aquè la n s tróva,
e mal Zéli, e' piuvéva,
léu l'è 'ndè drétt, l'avnéva una Mercedes
da dlà, la l'à fat sècch, l'è mórt se còulp,
e dop, l'è còulpa méa, a l'ò mazè mè,

ma è possibile, io non lo so, sono cose, quelle, / che bisogna solo star zitti, /
sono cose private, invece, sí, / fanno a chi dice piú bugie, / per far figura, /
o magari anche è gente / che non li chiama nessuno, / il telefono non suona
e si sfogano cosí, // che poi le bugie, uno, bisogna vedere come viene preso,
delle volte / una bugie ci vuole, Gigi Magnani, / lui s'è trovato / che non
poteva far meglio, vedi tua moglie / che tutto il giorno piange / per quel
fratello, perché lei a Giampiero / gli aveva fatto da mamma, ed è stata lei /
che quella mattina l'ha mandato a Rimini, / ma niente, a comprare delle erbe,
una tisana, / che a lei fa le fa bene, e qui non si trova, / e alle Celle, pioveva,
/ lui è andato dritto, veniva una Mercedes / dall'altra parte, l'ha fatto secco,
è morto sul colpo, / e dopo è colpa mia, l'ho ucciso io, /

she couldn't get any peace, and Gigi, with such patience,
he supported her, it was a horrible thing, horrible things
happen to everyone, you can't be shaking your fist at the sky,
you pray, you have masses said, beyond that?
you want to follow them there?
silent and crying, she was shattered, and him,
well, he thought and thought,
he found a guy, a young fellow, not from here,
a guy from San Bartolo, sharp, intelligent,
he instructed him how to do it, they had practice runs,
and one day this young fellow calls, hello, I'm Gianpiero,
you're not to blame at all, you, it was me,
it was my mistake, I wasn't looking, it's my fault,
but she understood immediately, it's not you,
you're not Gianpiero, and she was just stricken,
it was just mortifying for her,
because of what happened afterwards,
because Gianpiero really did call,
and nothing, she didn't, she didn't even listen to him,
enough with this farce, leave me alone,
which Gigi was outside, when he came back in,
he saw her, what's happened? tell your friend
to stop, I can't take it anymore, what friend?

la n'éva pèsa, e Gigín 'na pazinzia,
u i stéva dri, l'è stè una sgrèzia, al sgrèzi
al vén ma tótt, ta n pò dè un pógn te zil,
t pràigh, ta i fé dí dal mèssi, piò d'acsè?
ta i vu 'ndè dri ènca tè? li zétta e piànz,
la s'era ardótta, e léu, ció, pensa pensa,
l'à tróv éun, un burdlàz, no éun d'aquè,
éun ad San Bèrtal, svégg, inteligént,
u i à insgné tótt, i à fat al próvi, e un dè,
st' burdlàz l'à ciamè, pronto, a so Giampiero,
ta n n'é nisuna cóulpa, tè, l'è mè
ch'ò sbaiè, ch'a n'ò guèrs, l'è cóulpa méa,
mo li la à capí sóbit, ta n si tè,
ta n si Giampiero, e la la à ciapa mèl,
par li l'è stè una mortificaziòun,
mo quèll ch' l'è suzèst dop,
parchè Giampiero l'à ciamè dabón,
e li gnént, la n l'è gnénca stè a sintéi,
basta sa sta cumédia, lasém stè,
che Gigín l'era fura, quant l'è tòuran,
u la à vésta, cs'èll stè? dí me tu améigh
ch'e' lasa andè, ch'a n nu n pòs piò, che améigh?

non aveva pace, e Gigi una pazienza, / le stava dietro, è stata una disgrazia,
le disgrazie / vengono a tutti, non puoi dare un pugno nel cielo, / preghi, gli
fai dire delle messe, piú di cosí? / ci vuoi andare dietro anche tu? lei zitta e
piangere, / s'era ridotta, e lui, be', pensa pensa, / ha trovato uno, un giovane,
no uno di qui, / uno di San Bartolo, sveglio, intelligente, / gli ha insegnato
tutto, hanno fatto le prove, e un giorno / 'sto giovane ha chiamato, pronto,
sono Giampiero, / non ne hai nessuna colpa, tu, sono io, / che ho sbagliato,
che non ho guardato, è colpa mia, / ma lei ha capito subito, non sei tu, / non
sei Giampiero, e l'ha presa male, / per lei è stata una mortificazione, / ma
quello che è successo dopo, / perché Giampiero ha chiamato davvero, / e
lei niente, non l'è stato neanche a sentire, / basta con questa commedia,
lasciatemi stare, / che Gigi era fuori, quando è rientrato, / l'ha vista, cos'è
successo? di' al tuo amico / che la smetta, che non ne posso piú, che amico?/

your friend who called, what are you saying?
it was the one time, it was that one time,
and that's it, so that first time it was him,
the second Gianpiero, and I didn't even let him talk,
who knows what he might have said, my sister went crazy
and now I'm going out of my mind too,
it was just a desperate situation,
and well, there are things, those things, like telling lies,
even if the intention is good, you think hard about it,
you ponder, then you lie just the same,

which I, however, I'm thinking about something else,
that even, with all these big mix-ups,
with all this nattering on and on,
there's no respect, and here, it's got to end,
because those people might even get tired of it,
then afterwards, if they have their say, I don't know,
there's not much you can do about it,
this one, was something,
it started out one way and then it ended up,
which you can't, do you understand?
there's no accountability sometimes,
you can't even say that they're wrong, the ones who say
it's all a big farce, in my opinion,
those people are even showing too much restraint,

e' tu améigh ch'e' telefona, csa déit?
l'è stè una vólta sno, l'è stè cla vólta,
e basta, alòura préima l'era léu,
l'era Giampiero, e mè a n l'ò gnénch' fat zcòrr,
chi sa quèll ch' l'avrà détt, la è dvénta mata
la mia surèla, che mè què a dvént mata
dabón, insòmma una disperaziòun,
amo l'è robi, quèlli, cmè t fé t sbai,
ènch' s' l'intenziòun la è bóna,
ta i péns bén, ta t cunséi, pu t sbai l'istèss,

che però mè a péns ènch' un'èlta roba,
tótt sti zavài, tótt sté ciacaradézz,
u n gn'è rispèt, e aquè, mè, e' va a finéi,
parchè i s pò 'nca stufé quéi che là, e dop,
s'i dí basta, a n'e' so,
amo, u i vó póch, era una cosa, questa,
nata in un modo e dopo è diventata,
che non si può, ta n vaid?
non c'è nessuna serietà, dal vólti
ta n'i pò gnénch' dè tórt ma quéi ch'i déi
ch' l'è tótt' una cumédia, mè, sgònd mè,
i à 'nca tropa pazinzia quéi che là,

il tuo amico che telefona, cosa dici? / è stato una volta sola, è stato quella
volta, / e basta, allora prima era lui, / era Giampiero, e io non l'ho neanche
lasciato parlare, / chi sa quel che avrà detto, è diventata matta / mia sorella,
che io qui divento matta / davvero, insomma un disperazione, / e be', sono
cose, quelle, come fai sbagli, / anche se l'intenzione è buona, / ci pensi bene,
ti consigli, poi sbagli lo stesso, // che però io penso un anche un'altra cosa,
/ tutti questi pasticci, tutto questo chiacchiericcio, / non c'è rispetto, e qui,
io va a finire, / perché si possono anche stufare quelli là, e dopo, / se dicono
basta, non lo so, / e be', ci vuol poco, era una cosa, questa, / nata in un modo e dopo è diventata, / che non si può, non vedi? / non c'è nessuna serietà,
delle volte / non puoi neanche dar torto a quelli che dicono / che è tutta una
commedia, secondo me, / hanno anche troppa pazienza quelli là, /

if one day, he's all worked up,
they don't need to ask your permission,
they just cut you off, that's it, go ahead,
wait and see what happens,
call the phone company,
                    which if they really cut you off,
that telephone call,
about the receiver, the coffee, I just tossed it out,
I just said it to encourage her, to reassure her,
she'd asked me if I was angry,
which was a moment at the beginning, and then
I said it just like that, what came into my head,
I tried, you know, to be natural, I said,
to myself: next time she calls,
which there is no the-next-time, forget about it,
they cut it off, I'm sure of it,
and then, even if there is,
the more I think of it, the worse I feel,
because I want her to talk, I don't know a thing,
I don't, about her,
she needs to talk, and I need to be quiet, listening,
but instead, no, I've got to be the one talking to her,
please forgive me, I'll say to her,
but I can't wait, you don't know
how many things I still have left to say to you,

se un dè u i vén e' nervòus,
i n t'à méggh' da dmandè e' permèss ma tè,
i céud e basta, dop sta d'aspitè,
cèma la Sip,
            che se dabón i céud,
mè, cla telefonèda, quant a i péns,
pràisi, cafè, a la ò bótta véa, però
l'è stè ènch' par fèi curag, par rinfranchèla,
la m'éva dmand s'a séra spavantèd,
ch' l'è stè un mumént, dabón, te préim, e alòura
ò détt, acsè, quèll ch'u m'è vnú in amént,
ò zarchè, zò, d'ès naturèl, a géva
dréinta ad mè: st'èlta vólta, quant la cèma,
ch' la n gn'è piò st'èlta vólta, mo va là,
i céud, a so sichéur,
e pu ènca s' la i sarà,
piò a i péns e piò a stagh mèl, parchè 'nca mè
a ví ch' la zcòrra li, a n so gnént, mè, ad li,
la à da zcòrr, e mè zétt, a stè sintéi,
e invíci no, préima a i ò da zcòrr mè,
t m'é da scusé, a i girò,
mo a n pòs stè d'aspitè, tè ta n'e sé
quanti mai robi ch'u m'è 'rvènz da déit,

se un giorno gli viene il nervoso, / non devono mica chiedere il permesso a
te, / chiudono e basta, dopo aspetta pure, / chiama la Sip, – che se davvero
chiuduono, / io, quella telefonata, quando ci penso, / prese, caffè, l'ho buttata via, però / è stato anche per farle coraggio, per rinfrancarla, / m'aveva
chiesto se ero spaventato, / che è stato un momento, davvero, all'inizio, e
allora / ho detto, cosí, quello che m'è venuto in mente, / ho cercato, dai,
d'essere naturale, dicevo / dentro di me: quest'altra volta, quando chiama, /
che non c'è piú quest'altra volta, ma va' là, / chiudono, sono sicuro, / e poi
anche se ci sarà, / piú ci penso piú sto male, perché anch'io, / voglio che
parli lei, non so niente, io, di lei, / deve parlare, e io zitto, ad ascoltarla, / e
invece no, prima ho da parlarle io, / devi scusarmi, le dirò, / ma non posso
aspettare, tu non sai / quante cose mai mi sono rimaste da dirti, /

and I ask myself about them sometimes, at night,
which when I wake up and reach out an arm,
why didn't I tell you them then,
I don't know, well, you always figure it out afterwards,
what times they were,
we were together almost thirty-nine years,
we went places, we ate well,
we ate poorly, in Verona I bought you
the coral necklace, it's still there,
in the top drawer, the night we went to the movies,
you liked Paul Newman,
we laughed, we quarreled, we made up,
we made love, do you remember what you told me
when we made love, no, I won't say it, I won't,
but do you remember? there, you see, I got lost,
I need to tell you so many things like this, but instead
I get lost in small talk, you used say that to me too,
you're a chatterbox, you never keep quiet, which then,
all the things I could have told you, but what did I do?
and now I think of all the times, I talked,
I talked, I talked, and told you nothing.

a m'e' dmand da par mè dal vólti, ad nòta,
ch'a m svégg e a slòngh un braz,
parchè a n t li ò détti alòura?
a n'e' so, boh, u s'i aréiva sémpra dop,
che de témp u i n'è stè,
a sémm stè insén guési trentanóv an,
a sémm andè ti póst, émm magnè bén,
èmm magnè mèl, a Veròuna a t'ò còmpar
la culèna 'd curài, la è 'ncòura alè
te préim casètt, la sàira andémmi e' cino,
u t pieséva Paul Newman,
émm ridéu, émm ragnè, émm fat la pèsa,
émm fat l'amòur, ta t'arcórd cs'èll ta m gévi
quant a fémmi l'amòur? no, a n'e' déggh, no,
mo ta t'arcórd? ècco, vitt, ècco, a m pérd,
ch'a t'ò da déi tènt ad cal robi, invíci
a m pérd tal ciacri, t m'e' gévi ènca tè:
t si un ciacaròun, ta n sté mai zétt, che alòura
quèll ch'a t putéva déi, mo cmé ch'ò fat?
e adès a i péns dal vólti,
ò zcòurs, ò zcòurs, ò zcòurs, e a n t'ò détt gnént.

e me lo domando da solo delle volte, di notte, / che mi sveglio e allungo un
braccio, / perché non te le ho dette allora? non lo so, boh, ci si arriva sempre
dopo, / che tempo ce n'è stato, / siamo stati insieme quasi trentanove anni,
/ siamo andati nei posti, abbiamo mangiato bene, / abbiamo mangiato male,
a Verona ti ho comprato / la collana di corallo, è ancora lí / nel primo cassetto, la sera andavamo al cinema, / ti piaceva Paul Newman, / abbiamo
fatto l'amore, ti ricordi quello che mi dicevi? / quando facevamo l'amore?
no, non lo dico, no, / ma ti ricordi? / ecco, vedi, ecco, mi perdo, / che ti
devo dire tante di quelle cose, invece / mi perdo in chiacchiere, me lo dicevi
anche tu: / sei un chiacchierone, non stai mai zitto, che allora / quel che ti
potevo dire, ma come ho fatto? / e adesso ci penso delle volte, / ho parlato,
ho parlato, ho parlato, e non t'ho detto niente.

ACKNOWLEDGMENTS

I would like to thank the editors and staff members of the journals in which translations of the poems have been published: *Agni, American Poet, Arts & Letters, Beacons, Diner, Hunger Mountain, Italian Poetry in Translation, Journal of Italian Translation, Margie: The American Journal of Poetry, Metamorphoses, Poetry, Poetry Daily, Seneca Review,* and *Two Lines.*

I am grateful to Daniele Benati and Walter Valeri for long-running conversations and for generous comments and suggestions. Thank you to Kate Dalton-Hoffman for proofreading. And to her mother, editor and wit, Mary Dalton-Hoffman, who taught her how to write clear, beautiful sentences. I would like to also thank my mother-in-law, Virginia Stovall, who helped watch over my sons while I was in Rome, thinking about dialect. I would like to thank Davide Argnani, Marisa Turci, Franco Guarnieri, and Manuela Ricci of the Casa Marino Moretti for their generous support in bringing about this tri-lingual edition of the poems of Raffaello Baldini. Thank you to Luigi Fontanella and Gradiva Publications for supporting this project. Thank you also to Donna Severino who designed this book.

I am grateful to the American Academy of Poets and to the American Academy in Rome. I want to thank the kind and excellent members of the staff who made it possible to complete work on *Small Talk* in such a beautiful, quiet place, surrounded by the hum of background talk. I would especially like to thank Alfredo de Palchi and to express my gratitude for the The Raiziss /de Palchi Translation Award. I'm grateful to Geoffrey Brock, Eamon Grennan, and Stephen Sartarelli, the translators who awarded the prize.

These translations are dedicated to Rebecca J. West, professor of Italian at the University of Chicago.

706

About the Author and Translator

Raffaello Baldini (1924-2005) was born in 1924 in San-tarcangelo di Romagna and lived in Milan from 1955 until his death on March 29, 2005. His collections of poetry, all written in the Romagnolo dialect, include *È solitèri* (1976), *La nàiva* (1982) *Furistír* (1988); *Ad nòta* (1995), *La nàiva, Furistír, Ciacri* (2000) and *Intercity* (2003). The collection, *Furistír*, was awarded the 1988 Viareggio Prize, the first time the prize was awarded to a work written in dialect. Baldini wrote three theatrical mono-logues: *Carta canta, Zitti tutti!* and *In fondo a destra* (1998).

Adria Bernardi is the author two novels, *Openwork* and *The Day Laid on the Altar,* a collection of short stories, *In the Gathering Woods,* and an oral history, *Houses with Names: The Italian Immi-grants of Highwood, Illinois.* She has translated, from the Italian, the work of Tonino Guerra and Gianni Celati.